A HANDBOOK
on
THE BOOK OF JOSHUA

The Handbooks in the **UBS Handbook Series** are in-depth commentaries providing valuable exegetical, historical, cultural, and linguistic information on the books of the Bible. They are prepared primarily to assist practicing Bible translators as they carry out the important task of putting God's Word into the many languages spoken in the world today. The text is discussed verse by verse and is accompanied by running text in at least one modern English translation.

Over the years church leaders and Bible readers have found the UBS Handbooks to be useful for their own study of the Scriptures. Many of the issues Bible translators must address when trying to communicate the Bible's message to modern readers are the ones Bible students must address when approaching the Bible text as part of their own private study and devotions.

The Handbooks will continue to be prepared primarily for translators, but we are confident that they will be useful to a wider audience, helping all who use them to gain a better understanding of the Bible message.

UBS Helps for Translators

Handbooks:

A Handbook on . . .

Leviticus
The Book of Joshua
The Book of Ruth
The Book of Job
The Book of Psalms
Lamentations
The Book of Amos
The Books of Obadiah and Micah
The Book of Jonah
The Books of Nahum, Habakkuk,
  and Zephaniah
The Gospel of Matthew
The Gospel of Mark
The Gospel of Luke
The Gospel of John
The Acts of the Apostles

Paul's Letter to the Romans
Paul's First Letter to the Corinthi-
  ans
Paul's Letter to the Galatians
Paul's Letter to the Ephesians
Paul's Letter to the Philippians
Paul's Letters to the Colossians
  and to Philemon
Paul's Letters to the Thessalonians
The Letter to the Hebrews
The First Letter from Peter
The Letter from Jude and the
  Second Letter from Peter
The Letters of John
The Revelation to John

Guides:

A Translator's Guide to . . .

Selections from the First Five
  Books of the Old Testament
Selected Psalms
the Gospel of Mark
the Gospel of Luke
Paul's Second Letter to the Corin-
  thians

Paul's Letters to Timothy and to
  Titus
the Letters to James, Peter, and
  Jude
the Revelation to John

Technical Helps:

Old Testament Quotations in the
  New Testament
Short Bible Reference System
New Testament Index
The Theory and Practice of Trans-
  lation
Bible Index

Fauna and Flora of the Bible
Marginal Notes for the Old Testa-
  ment
Marginal Notes for the New Testa-
  ment
The Practice of Translating

A HANDBOOK ON

The Book of Joshua

by Robert G. Bratcher
and Barclay M. Newman

UBS Handbook Series

United Bible Societies
New York

Books in the series of **Helps for Translators** may be ordered from a national Bible Society, or from either of the following centers:

United Bible Societies
European Production Fund
W-7000 Stuttgart 80
Postfach 81 03 40
Germany

United Bible Societies
1865 Broadway
New York, New York 10023
U.S.A.

L.C. Cataloging in Publication Data

Bratcher, Robert G.
    [Translator's handbook on the book of Joshua]
    A handbook on the book of Joshua / by Robert G. Bratcher and Barclay M. Newman.
        p. cm. — (UBS handbook series) (UBS helps for translators)
    Originally published: A translator's handbook on the book of Joshua. London : New York : United Bible Societies. c1983.
    Includes bibliographical references and index.
    ISBN 0-8267-0109-4 : $8.95
    1. Bible O.T. Joshua—Translating.   2. Bible. O.T. Joshua—Commentaries. I. Newman, Barclay Moon, 1931- .
II. Title. III. Title: Book of Joshua. IV. Series. V. Series: UBS helps for translators.
[BS1295.5.B73 1992]
222'.2077—dc20   92-20510
                                    CIP

ABS-1992-300-2,200-CM-4-102710

Contents

040701

Preface

A *Translator's Handbook on the Book of Joshua* is a continuation of the series of Handbooks in the United Bible Societies' Helps for Translators series. No change in the format and development of recent Handbooks has been introduced. Special attention has been given to the structure of the discourse so that the translator will be able to understand the movement and the logical progression of the sections of this book and how they contribute to the message of the whole.

The Today's English Version (TEV) and Revised Standard Version (RSV) translations are shown at the beginning of each section. TEV is then reproduced again at the beginning of the discussion of each verse. When TEV is quoted in the discussion, the words are underlined, while quotation marks are used when other translations are quoted.

As is true for both Handbooks and Guides in the series, this volume concentrates on exegetical matters that are of prime importance for translators, and it attempts to indicate possible solutions for translational and linguistic problems that may occur. Translators' Guides provide important information in a relatively condensed form, using a format that makes it possible to retrieve the information easily. Handbooks such as this volume are biblical commentaries that deal with the full range of information important to translators. However, the authors do not attempt to provide the kind of help not directly related to translating, which other scholars and theologians may be seeking, since much of that information is available elsewhere. A limited Bibliography is included for the benefit of those who are interested in further study. Details of interest to translators with advanced training in textual studies and exegesis are included in the Notes that follow the text of the Handbook.

A Glossary is provided that explains technical terms according to their usage in this volume. An Index gives the location by page number of some of the important words and subjects discussed in the Handbook, especially as help is provided the translator in rendering these concepts into the receptor language.

Abbreviations Used in This Volume

Translating the Book of Joshua

The Purpose of a Translator's Handbook

A Translator's Handbook is a small reference volume that provides specific information and instruction for the understanding, interpretation, and translation of a biblical book. In each Handbook there are four areas that receive special attention: (1) Text. Before any book of the Bible may be translated, prior decisions must be made concerning what words are judged to belong to the original text. (2) Exegesis. After the words of the text are decided upon, the next step is to determine as precisely as possible the meaning that these words held for the writer. (3) Structure and Thematic Development. In order to translate a book accurately and adequately, the translator must understand how the author has developed its major themes. (4) Application of Translation Principles. Since each language is different from all other languages, the translator must be constantly aware of both the possibilities and limitations involved in the application of translation principles.

Many problems of text, exegesis, and structure will receive a more detailed discussion in commentaries, Bible dictionaries, books on special subjects, and scholarly journals. Translators who have such resources available and who have the training to employ them are certainly encouraged to do so. But many translators will not have these resources readily available in a moment of need, while still others will lack either the time or the training required to take full advantage of them. In the Handbook the translator will discover a summary discussion of textual, exegetical, and structural problems, together with a brief evaluation of various ways that biblical scholars have resolved these problems. Suggestions will also be offered for the proper application of valid translation principles in specific contexts, a feature not found in other sources. In this way each Handbook should serve as a tool that will enable the translator to resolve problems in the most satisfactory way possible and in a minimum amount of time.

How to Use the Joshua Handbook

The initial step in the translation of any biblical book is to develop an understanding of its content, structure, and overall purpose. Therefore this Handbook includes discussions of the following items: (1) Religious Outlook of the Book of Joshua, (2) Survey of the Contents, (3) A Note on Two Special Translation Problems in Joshua, and (4) Outline. The translator is advised to read the first three discussions, and then to follow with a careful reading of the book of Joshua itself in light of the outline.

The next step is to make a detailed analysis of the first section of the book. The Handbook clearly identifies each section of the book by keeping to the section headings of TEV. For the translator's convenience each section heading is followed by a presentation of TEV and RSV in parallel columns, so that a comparison may be made of the two translations. RSV will generally provide a formal translation of the Hebrew text, whereas TEV attempts a more dynamic restructuring into contemporary English. For the most part, the interpretation represented in the two translations is the same, only the form is different. The first in a series of related sections will always contain a statement of how each of these sections fits into the total framework of that part of the book. This is so that the translator will constantly be reminded how each section is related to the immediate and overall context of the book while dealing with the details of translation.

A third step in the translation process is to undertake a detailed study of the text, verse by verse. In the Handbook the biblical verse is printed immediately preceding the discussion of it. This makes each verse easy to find, which is especially important at a later stage when it may be necessary to refer back to a particular verse. TEV has been chosen for this purpose, because it is a constant reminder that each language requires a fresh restructuring of its own. The detailed study of the verse will involve an appraisal of its textual, exegetical, and translational problems. The Handbook will serve as guide for this study, and then it will follow with one or more suggested patterns for restructuring. When a verse is fully translated, it should be reviewed to be sure that all its parts fit together in a way that is natural. This same procedure should be followed for every verse.

Translation involves more than the satisfactory analysis and restructuring of individual verses and sentences. So the Handbook encourages translators to take note of the way in which sentence follows sentence and paragraph joins paragraph. When a section is completed it is good policy to read it aloud to someone else in order to get the reactions of one who must depend upon the hearing of the text without seeing it. Finally, when the entire book is completed, it should be read through in its entirety so as to guarantee a consistency of style and level of language. Needless to say, a thorough exegetical check should also be made of the book upon its completion. The Handbook will also provide the information necessary for those persons who have the responsibility of checking the translated text for accuracy.

Religious Outlook

Each book in the Bible was written with certain religious goals in mind, and the book of Joshua is no exception. This is in part what makes these books sacred literature. Definite religious themes have in fact determined not only the content and structure of Joshua but also its place in the Hebrew Old Testament. We shall first consider the religious significance of the place which it occupies in the Hebrew Old Testament.

It may be argued that the book of Joshua was placed immediately following the "Books of Moses" primarily for logical and chronological reasons. No doubt this was in some respects a determining factor, for

the book of Joshua does indeed describe the continuation of events put
into motion in these earlier books. However, its oneness with the content of the first five books of the Old Testament is more theological
than chronological. That is, the author's primary concern is to reveal
how the Lord kept his promise to give the land of Canaan to the descendants of the patriarchs (see Gen 13.14-17; 15.7,18; 17.8; 26.3-4).

The book of Joshua also forms a theological bridge to the period
of the judges and of the kings. It thereby draws a sharp contrast between the idealized period under Moses and Joshua, when the people of
Israel were faithful to God, and the evil times which followed, when
the people were not firm in their commitment. Joshua is the first book
in the section of the Hebrew Bible known as "the former prophets"
(Joshua—2 Kings), and it unfurls a prophetic interpretation of history.
It sees history as determined by the response which God's people make
to him. Obedience guarantees them the possession of the land, whereas
disobedience deprives them of this possession and ultimately drives
them into exile. 2 Kings, the last of "the former prophets," closes
with the account of the fall of Jerusalem, the destruction of the Temple, and the deportation of the people to Babylonia. Thus the author of
this section closes with a message of warning for his readers: remain
faithful to the Lord, as did Joshua and the people of his generation;
otherwise there is always the danger of losing the land, as it happened
during the time of the kings.

The basic religious thrust of the book of Joshua is the affirmation
of the Lord's absolute sovereignty in the life of Israel. The conquest
of their enemies was accomplished solely by the Lord's power. It was he
who made the walls of Jericho crumble, and later caused the sun to stand
still so that Israel's victory over the Amorites would be absolute. The
assigning of the cities and the territories to the various tribes is in
itself an act of God's grace, and even the lists of towns and of terri-
torial boundaries take on a theological significance. The same Lord who
gave the land to Israel now determines the relationship of the tribes
to one another and to their Lord.

This double act of salvation, which consists of victory over Israel's enemies and of creating an organized society, is best summarized
in the Lord's own words:

"But I gave you victory over them all. As you advanced, I
threw them into panic in order to drive out the two Amorite
kings. Your swords and bows had nothing to do with it. I
gave you a land that you had never worked and cities that
you had not built. Now you are living there and eating
grapes from vines that you did not plant, and olives from
trees that you did not plant" (24.11b-13, TEV).

Survey of the Contents

The book of Joshua divides naturally into two parts of approximately equal length. The first twelve chapters narrate the conquest of
Canaan, while the last twelve chapters are concerned primarily with
the division of the land.

Chapters 1—5 provide the setting for the conquest, which is then described in chapters 6—11. Chapter 12 is a summary chapter, providing a list of the kings defeated by Moses (verses 1-6) and by Joshua (verses 7-24). The theme for the entire book is summarized in 1.1-9: After the death of Moses, the Lord calls Joshua to be his successor. He commands him to prepare the people of Israel to cross the Jordan River and capture the land that he had promised them. The borders of their future territory are defined, and the Lord promises to be with Joshua, as he was with Moses, thus guaranteeing success in the campaign. But in order to receive what the Lord has promised, the people of Israel must rely absolutely upon him and obey the whole Law that his servant Moses gave them. They must be sure that it is always read in their worship. It must be studied day and night, and everything written in it must be obeyed. Only then will they be prosperous and successful.

In 1.10-18 Joshua commands the people of Israel to ready themselves for the crossing of the Jordan. In particular he reminds the tribes of Reuben and Gad and the half tribe of Manasseh, who have already settled on the eastern shore of the Jordan, that their men are obligated to help in the campaign.

Before the invasion of Canaan, spies are sent out to explore the territory near the city of Jericho, which is the first stronghold to be attacked. The spies return with a favorable report: "We are sure that the LORD has given us the whole country. All the people there are terrified of us" (2.24, TEV). The crossing of the Jordan and the piling up of memorial stones to commemorate the event, together with the fear that came upon the Amorite kings when they heard of the crossing, are recounted in 3.1—5.1. Before the holy war begins, the men who had not been circumcised during the wilderness journeys are circumcised at Gilgal (5.2-12). The events preliminary to the actual attack on the Canaanites are concluded with the rather unusual account of the appearance of "the commander of the Lord's army" to Joshua (5.13-15).

The conquest proper is actually accomplished in three stages. The Israelites first establish a strong foothold in the central hill country by capturing the cities of Jericho (6.1-27) and Ai (8.1-29) and by establishing an alliance with the people of Gibeon (9.1-27). Following the victories over Jericho and Ai, the Israelites erect an altar to the Lord on Mount Ebal, where Joshua reads to the people "the whole Law, including the blessings and the curses, just as they are written in the book of the Law."

The second phase of the campaign takes place in the south (10.1-43). It is initiated by the defeat of the five Amorite kings, who had come to attack the people of Gibeon (10.1-27). Then Joshua attacks and captures a number of cities in that region, including Makkedah (10.28), Libnah (10.29-30), Lachish (10.31-33), Eglon (10.34-35), Hebron (10.36-37) and Debir (10.38-39). In summary, "Joshua's campaign took him from Kadesh Barnea in the south to Gaza near the coast, including all the territory of Goshen, and as far north as Gibeon" (10.41, TEV). In the translation of this chapter, as in other chapters where geographical place-names are mentioned, it will be necessary to make constant reference to the map on page 7. An attempt has been made within the body of the commentary to picture the geographical relationships between the various places mentioned.

[4]

The final phase of the conquest takes place in Galilee (11.1-15). Joshua and his army gain much territory and conquer many cities, although only the city of Hazor is actually destroyed (11.11). The last part of the chapter (11.16-23) is a summary of Joshua's victories throughout the land, including his destruction of the race of giants called Anakim (21.22). After the military campaigns are concluded, "the people rested from war" (23b).

The major topic of the last half of the book is the division of the land among the tribes of Israel (13.1—21.45). The territories which belong to the tribes east of the Jordan are first described (13.1-33); then the same procedure is followed for the tribal territories west of the Jordan (14.1—19.51). The cities of refuge are designated (20.1-9), as are the cities of the Levites (21.1-45). With words of encouragement from Joshua, the eastern tribes return to their territory (22.1-34). The book concludes with Joshua's farewell address (23.1-16), accompanied by the renewal of the covenant at Shechem (24.1-33).

A Note on Two Special Translation Problems in Joshua

Each book of the Bible presents its own unique translation problems, and in this regard Joshua is no exception. Two problems in particular stand out: (1) The existence of what some scholars call "seams," that is, dividing lines that can be drawn between portions of a narrative or discourse that do not appear to fit smoothly together as a continuous or coordinated discourse. Some scholars therefore believe that a writer or final editor has brought together information from more than one source and has "sewn" it, or joined it together, into one discourse. (2) The mention of geographical places which cannot be located with precision. Both of these problems occur in various passages throughout the book and will be dealt with individually wherever they are found. But these matters deserve a more general treatment as well.

The second of these problems does not cause the same intensity of concern for translators that the first one does. Translators have no difficulty in realizing that the writer of an ancient document and his original readers knew of places that for some reason or another have either disappeared or lost their identity in the course of time. Moreover, in most instances it is possible to determine with relative certainty the general geographical area that the writer had in mind, especially in passages where numerous geographical items are mentioned together.

But some people may respond negatively to the suggestion that the writer may have used several sources of information, or that he may have served as an editor in combining such sources. Very likely we will never know exactly how this book was written. In any case, suggestions of this sort should not be a cause for alarm, for they do not deny or compromise the belief in the divine inspiration of these documents. Rather, they are a recognition of the fact that the Hebrew text, as we have it, has certain features that pose a problem which the translator must recognize and solve in order to represent faithfully in the receptor language the meaning of the Hebrew text.

[5]

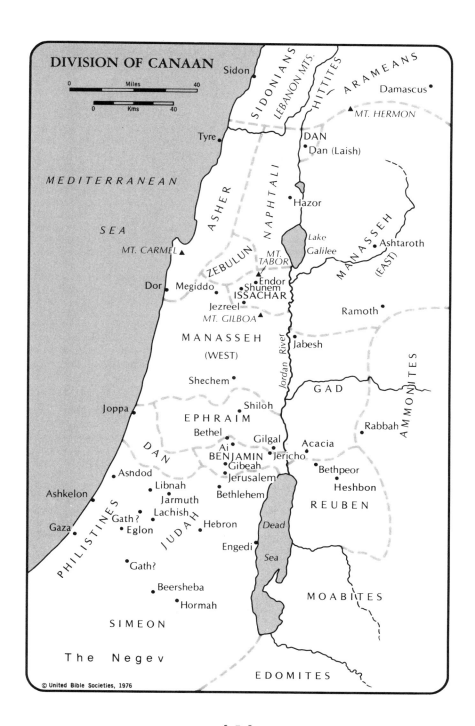

DIVISION OF CANAAN

0 — Miles — 40
0 — Kms — 40

SIDONIANS
LEBANON MTS.
HITTITES
ARAMEANS

Sidon

Damascus

MT. HERMON

Tyre

DAN
Dan (Laish)

MEDITERRANEAN

ASHER

NAPHTALI

Hazor

SEA

Lake Galilee

MANASSEH (EAST)

Ashtaroth

MT. CARMEL

ZEBULUN

MT. TABOR

Dor
Megiddo

Endor
Shunem
ISSACHAR

Jezreel
MT. GILBOA

Ramoth

MANASSEH
(WEST)

Jordan River

Jabesh

AMMONITES

Shechem

Joppa

Shiloh

GAD

EPHRAIM
Bethel

DAN

Ai
BENJAMIN
Gibeah

Gilgal
Jericho

Acacia

Rabbah

Ashdod

Jerusalem

Bethpeor
Heshbon

Ashkelon

Libnah
Jarmuth
Lachish

Bethlehem

REUBEN

Gaza

Gath?
Eglon

JUDAH

Hebron

Dead

PHILISTINES

Gath?

Engedi

Sea

Beersheba
Hormah

MOABITES

SIMEON

The Negev

EDOMITES

© United Bible Societies, 1976

[7]

Chapter 1

God Commands Joshua to
Conquer Canaan

1 After the death of the
LORD's servant Moses, the LORD
spoke to Moses' helper, Joshua
son of Nun. 2 He said, "My servant Moses is dead. Get ready now,
you and all the people of Israel,
and cross the Jordan River into
the land that I am giving them.
3 As I told Moses, I have given
you and all my people the entire
land that you will be marching
over. 4 Your borders will reach
from the desert in the south to
the Lebanon Mountains in the north;
from the great Euphrates River in
the east, through the Hittite country, to the Mediterranean Sea in
the west. 5 Joshua, no one will be
able to defeat you as long as you
live. I will be with you as I was
with Moses. I will always be with
you; I will never abandon you.
6 Be determined and confident, for
you will be the leader of these
people as they occupy this land
which I promised their ancestors.
7 Just be determined, be confident;
and make sure that you obey the
whole Law that my servant Moses
gave you. Do not neglect any part
of it and you will succeed wherever
you go. 8 Be sure that the book of
the Law is always read in your worship. Study it day and night, and
make sure that you obey everything
written in it. Then you will be
prosperous and successful. 9 Remember that I have commanded you to
be determined and confident! Do

1 After the death of Moses the
servant of the LORD, the LORD said
to Joshua the son of Nun, Moses'
minister, 2 "Moses my servant is
dead; now therefore arise, go over
this Jordan, you and all this people, into the land which I am giving to them, to the people of
Israel. 3 Every place that the
sole of your foot will tread upon
I have given to you, as I promised
to Moses. 4 From the wilderness
and this Lebanon as far as the
great river, the river Euphrates,
all the land of the Hittites to
the Great Sea toward the going
down of the sun shall be your territory. 5 No man shall be able to
stand before you all the days of
your life; as I was with Moses,
so I will be with you; I will not
fail you or forsake you. 6 Be strong
and of good courage; for you shall
cause this people to inherit the
land which I swore to their fathers
to give them. 7 Only be strong and
very courageous, being careful to
do according to all the law which
Moses my servant commanded you;
turn not from it to the right hand
or to the left, that you may have
good success wherever you go. 8 This
book of the law shall not depart
out of your mouth, but you shall
meditate on it day and night, that
you may be careful to do according
to all that is written in it; for
then you shall make your way prosperous, and then you shall have

not be afraid or discouraged, for
I, the LORD your God, am with you
wherever you go."

good success. 9 Have I not commanded you? Be strong and of good
courage; be not frightened, neither
be dismayed; for the LORD your God
is with you wherever you go."

The first part of the book of Joshua (1.1—12.24) narrates the
conquest of Canaan, that is, the land west of the Jordan River. The
first chapter is an introduction to the narrative, and it divides into
three parts: (1) Joshua is ordered to cross the Jordan and occupy the
land (1.1-9); (2) preparations are made to cross (1.10-11); and (3) the
two and one-half tribes east of the Jordan promise to help (1.12-18).

The Hebrew personal name for the God of Israel is written with
the consonants YHWH, usually spelled "Yahweh" when vowels are added
today. However, to avoid pronouncing the sacred name, the Jews, when
reading aloud, regularly pronounced the word Adonay, which means "the
Lord." TEV, RSV, and other modern translations use the term "LORD,"
written in capital letters, to represent YHWH, while "Lord" then translates Adonay when it appears in the text. This Handbook will simply use
"Lord" in its discussions, but will use "LORD" when required for accurate quotations of translations, or to indicate in a suggested translation where "LORD" would properly represent YHWH. Translators will
have to determine what is the best term in the receptor language for
the personal name of God, whether an equivalent of "Yahweh," "LORD,"
or "Lord."

In the section heading it may be better to replace God Commands
with "The LORD commands," since throughout 1.1-9, and indeed throughout the entire book, "the LORD" is used more frequently than "God" when
reference is made to Israel's God. It is, of course, not obligatory that
the references in section headings be determined by names used in the
text, but as a general rule this is a good guideline. Since Joshua
will not conquer Canaan alone, one may want to translate "The LORD
commands Joshua to lead his people (or, the people of Israel) into (or,
to conquer) the land (or, the people) of Canaan."

The scene opens in the territory of Moab, east of the Jordan, across
from Jericho, where the people of Israel are camped (see Num 33.48-50;
36.13). Moses has died and his helper Joshua is now in charge. The Lord
tells Joshua to lead the people across the Jordan into Canaan. He says
that he will keep the promises he made to their ancestors and give his
people the whole land. But his promise to be with Joshua has a condition; Joshua must study the Law and obey all its commands, and in this
way he will be assured of the Lord's help in all that he undertakes.

1.1   After the death of the LORD's servant Moses,
           the LORD spoke to Moses' helper, Joshua son of Nun.

The book opens in the Hebrew as a continuation of the narrative
in Deuteronomy 34: "And it was...and the Lord spoke to Joshua...say-
ing." The death of Moses is reported in Deuteronomy 34.1-8; after
leading the people for 40 years, he dies at age 120 without being permitted to enter the promised land. His successor is his helper, Joshua

son of Nun.[1] The Hebrew word translated helper means "servant" (RSV);
New American Bible (NAB) "aide"; New English Bible (NEB) "assistant";
Soggin "minister." Moses himself is the Lord's servant, a title used
more often of him than of anyone else (applied also to Joshua in 24.29).

After the death of...Moses may be translated "After Moses had
died." In many languages it will be difficult, if not impossible, to
include in one statement both bits of information: (1) "After Moses
died" and (2) "Moses was the LORD's servant." And some translations
have even omitted from this verse the information that Moses was the
Lord's servant. However, this information is in the Hebrew, and it does
need to be included somewhere in the translation, though not necessarily
at this place (see comments at verse 2). In order to include all of the
information in a manner that is natural, one may need to translate this
verse as two sentences: "Moses had served the LORD, and Joshua son of
Nun had been Moses' helper. After Moses died, the LORD spoke to Joshua."
Or, "As long as Moses lived he served the LORD, and Joshua son of Nun
helped him. When Moses died, the LORD told Joshua what to do."

1.2   He said, "My servant Moses is dead. Get ready now,
            you and all the people of Israel, and cross the
            Jordan River into the land that I am giving them.

It should be noted that here in verse 2 the Lord specifically refers to Moses as My servant Moses. The omission of the explicit identification of Moses as the LORD's servant in verse 1 may therefore be
justified, if that information is included in verse 2. In fact, the
repetition the LORD's servant (verse 1)...My servant (verse 2) may be
stylistically unsatifactory in some languages. If My servant is retained in verse 2, it may be helpful to translate "Moses served me
while he lived, but he is dead now."

Get ready translates a verb usually rendered "Arise" (Revised
Standard Version [RSV]); it occurs very often as a sort of auxiliary,
expressing a sense of urgency or immediacy: "Go on and cross." In such
cases it does not imply that the subject has been sitting or lying
down.

In Hebrew the two imperatives Get ready...and cross are directed
first of all to Joshua, and the structure you and all the people of
Israel represents a typical Hebrew structure in which the primary subject is mentioned first, then followed by the secondary subject or
subjects who also participate in the same action. Since Joshua is the
first subject addressed, it is possible to assume that he is to lead
the others across the Jordan River. Indeed, the entire context presupposes that Joshua is now assuming the role of leadership that Moses
once held, and that the manner in which he will prove his leadership
is in the leading of the people of Israel across the Jordan. Therefore
it is legitimate to translate "You (singular) must now enter the land
that I will give you. Lead all the people of Israel across the Jordan!"
This restructuring is also more natural in English, and it avoids a
Hebraism such as one finds in Today's English Version (TEV).

The Jordan River translates "this Jordan" (RSV), which does not
mean that there is another Jordan somewhere else; it simply indicates
the river, on whose east bank the people are camped.

[11]

That I am giving to them is literally "that I am giving to them, the sons of Israel." The phrase "the sons of Israel" is redundant and is omitted by the Greek Old Testament. Moreover, the use of them may imply that Joshua is excluded from the promise. For languages which have a plural form of the pronoun "you," the shift may be made from them to "you" (plural). This will leave no doubt that Joshua is included in the promise. One may also translate "you my people" or "you, the people of Israel." The Hebrew of verse 3 is in fact "you" (plural), and the introduction of the second person pronoun in the present verse can give a consistency in the use of personal pronouns, which is an important feature of many languages. In many languages it is not natural to make changes in the persons of verbs that one frequently finds in the Hebrew Old Testament, and translators must be constantly alert to the distinctions between Hebrew and their own language.

1.3   As I told Moses, I have given you and all my people
         the entire land that you will be marching over.

As I told Moses: see Deuteronomy 11.24-25. The Hebrew verb translated told can mean "promise" or "speak to." As I told Moses...my people may be translated, "I promised Moses that I would give my people."
    In verse 3 the Lord speaks directly to the people; in verse 2 he had spoken to Joshua, and the "you" is singular; in verse 3 "you" is plural. The Lord is speaking to all the people (through Joshua, of course); so TEV translates you and all my people.
    The phrase you and all my people may cause problems similar to the pronoun them of the previous verse. That is, the conjunction and may suggest to the reader that the person referred to by you is excluded from the group all my people. This problem may be resolved by translating "you my people"; no reader will assume thereby that Joshua is excluded from the people. This will balance out nicely if at the end of verse 2 the text has been translated to read either "you my people" or "you, the people of Israel."
    The phrase the entire land that you will be marching over translates the Hebrew "every place on which the sole of your (plural) foot steps." For some readers, marching over might imply an orderly band of soldiers or some other highly organized group. The reference, of course, is to the entire group of Israelites, and one may translate "walk on" or "set foot on."

1.4   Your borders will reach from the desert in the south
         to the Lebanon Mountains in the north; from the great
         Euphrates River in the east, through the Hittite
         country to the Mediterranean Sea in the west.

Your borders: Your is plural, referring to the people of Israel and not just to Joshua.
    The Hebrew text seems to define the territory as follows: "from the wilderness and this Lebanon and to the great river, the Euphrates River, all the land of the Hittites and to the great sea at the going

down of the sun will be your borders." TEV takes this to indicate the
four limits of the territory: south, "the wilderness," traditionally
called the Negev, and referring to the dry country extending from Beersheba to the desert of Sinai and the Gulf of Aqaba; north, the Lebanon
Mountains; east, the Euphrates River; and west, the Mediterranean Sea.
In Hebrew "this Lebanon" is puzzling; most translations have simply
"the Lebanon." The name does not refer to the country known today as
Lebanon but to the Lebanon Mountains. The Hebrew of verse 4 is literally "From the wilderness (desert)...shall be your border." TEV inverts
the Hebrew order and translates Your borders will reach from.... But the
result is a sentence which is both lengthy and difficult, and it will
help the reader if the sentence is restructured. For example, "I will
give you (plural) all the land from the desert in the south to the
Lebanon Mountains in the north. Your borders (or, The borders of your
land) will reach from the great Euphrates River in the east. It will
include the Hittite country as far as the Mediterranean Sea in the
west." A restructuring of this type will have at least two advantages:
(1) It will break verse 4 into two less difficult sentences, and (2) it
will tie verse 3 ("I promised Moses that I would give") more closely
with verse 4 ("I will give").

"All the land of the Hittites" (RSV) is omitted in the Greek Old
Testament and is thought by some scholars to be a later addition to
the text (see Bible de Jérusalem [BJ]); it denotes the northern part
of Syria, which had been part of the Hittite empire. See the similar
description of the promised land in Deuteronomy 11.24, which does not
include the phrase "all the land of the Hittites." It seems best to
follow the Hebrew text here. Only during the time of David and Solomon
did the Israelites actually occupy much of this land.

1.5   Joshua, no one will be able to defeat you as long
            as you live. I will be with you as I was with Moses.
            I will always be with you; I will never abandon you.

Now the Lord speaks directly to Joshua again, promising him victory in all his undertakings. TEV introduces Joshua as a noun of address, to indicate that he is the one to whom the Lord is now speaking.
For languages which possess both singular and plural forms of "you,"
the shift will be obvious without specific mention of the name. In such
instances one may translate "No enemy will be able to stand against you
(singular)."

Will (not) be able to defeat translates the verb "hold one's
ground, oppose, withstand."

In Hebrew you (in all of its occurrences in the verse) is singular
and refers to Joshua. The Greek Old Testament translators rendered the
first occurrence as a plural form, thereby referring it to the people
of Israel. However, the focus throughout the verse is upon Joshua as
he assumes the role of leadership from Moses, and in languages where
distinctions exist, a singular form should be used in translation.

The Lord promises to help Joshua as he did Moses, and tells him
he will not forsake or abandon him. The Hebrew uses two synonymous
verbs, "to fail, let go," and "to abandon, forsake"; TEV uses two

expressions, negative and positive: I will always be with you; I will never abandon you. In some languages it may be more effective not to have the repetition of verbs. That is, one may use either "I will always be with you" or "I will never abandon you," but not both. This is especially true in cultures where the accumulation of synonymns tends to weaken rather than to strengthen an affirmation.

1.6   Be determined and confident, for you will be the leader of these people as they occupy this land which I promised their ancestors.

Verse 6 opens with a command expressed in Hebrew by two synonymous verbs: "be strong and be courageous" (also verses 7,9,18). These are translated in a variety of ways: NEB "be strong, be resolute"; Jerusalem Bible (JB) "be strong and stand firm"; An American Translation (AT), Traduction Oecuménique de la Bible (TOB) "Be strong and brave"; Moffatt (Mft) "Be strong, be brave."
You will be the leader of these people as they occupy this land translates "you will cause this people to inherit the land." The Hebrew verb translated "to inherit" expresses the basic idea that the land is a gift from the Lord to his people; they "inherit" it from him. After all is said and done, the land of Canaan will be theirs not because of their strength or prowess in battle but because the Lord gives it to them. TEV avoids the use of the traditional "inherit" (RSV), since for English readers this would imply that someone has died, and in the context it would be the Lord! One may restructure as two coordinate clauses: "You will lead these people, and together you will occupy this land."
I promised translates the verb "to vow, to swear," that is, to make a solemn pledge which is strengthened by an oath; it validates the promise and makes it permanently binding. The reader may be helped if this verse is arranged somewhat chronologically. For example, "I promised this land to the ancestors of this people. So be determined and confident and lead the people to occupy the land."

1.7   Just be determined, be confident; and make sure that you obey the whole Law that my servant Moses gave you. Do not neglect any part of it and you will succeed wherever you go.

Verse 7 begins with a repetition, "Only be strong and very courageous." The Greek Old Testament omits "very," probably because it does not appear in the parallel at verse 6.
The command is now followed by the equally strong command, make sure that you obey the whole Law that my servant Moses gave you. The Greek Old Testament omits the whole Law and has only "obey what my servant Moses commanded you." It is suspected that the whole Law is a later addition to the Hebrew text (see Bright, Soggin), particularly since in the following, "do not depart from it," the pronoun "it" in Hebrew is masculine, not feminine as it should be if referring to the Hebrew feminine word for "law." But the phrase is in the Hebrew text

[14]

and should be represented in translation. Its omission by the Greek Old
Testament was perhaps an attempt to ease the problem of the Hebrew text.
This "whole Law" probably refers to part, if not all, of the book of
Deuteronomy (see verse 8 "this book of the Law").

In Hebrew make sure that you obey the whole Law is literally "to
obey to do according to the whole Law." The structure "to obey to do"
reflects the fondness of Hebrew for the use of parallel expressions.
Actually both verbs, "obey" and "do," carry the same force in Hebrew,
and the combination of the two verbs serves to make the command more
emphatic. This is the basis for TEV make sure that you obey; one may
also translate "see to it that you obey," or merely "obey," if the use
of a single verb in the receptor language is more emphatic than the use
of two verbs. The Hebrew structure "according to the whole Law" has the
function of identifying "the whole Law" as the object of the two verbs.
One may translate "everything that is taught in my (that is, the LORD's)
Law" or "everything that my Law teaches you to do."

The imperative obey the whole Law may be rendered either "faithfully obey the (or, my) Law" or "completely obey my Law" by shifting
the modifier "whole" from the noun "Law" to the verb "obey."

If Joshua faithfully follows everything the Law requires, he will
succeed in all he undertakes. Do not neglect any part of it (literally
"do not turn from it to the right or to the left") is a way of saying
not to deviate, but to remain faithful in following what is required.
Wherever you go refers not simply to movement or travel as such but to
all of one's activities; so JB "in all you do." Succeed translates a
verb meaning "to prosper, be successful"; the clause may be rendered,
"then you will succeed in everything that you undertake."

In Hebrew the second person singular in verses 7-9 seems to have
Joshua as the one to whom the Lord is talking; it very well may be,
however, that the Lord is really speaking to Israel (so Bright). The
demands and promises are addressed to Israel as a whole and not just to
Joshua personally. But most translations apparently utilize the singular form, and this would seem to be the best course to follow.

1.8   Be sure that the book of the Law is always read in
       your worship. Study it day and night, and make sure
       that you obey everything written in it. Then you
       will be prosperous and successful.

Be sure that the book of the Law is always read in your worship
takes the Hebrew "This book of the Law is not to depart from your
mouth" to refer to the use of the Scriptures in public worship and
proclamation, and not just in private reading. If the command is believed to be addressed to Joshua alone, then one may translate "Read
the book of the Law to the people every time they worship"; if it is
understood to be addressed to the people, "Be sure that someone reads
the book of the Law to you every time you worship." It must be made
clear that "the book of the Law" of this verse refers to the "whole
Law" of verse 7.

The command to "meditate on it day and night" (RSV) recalls the
language of Psalm 1.2. The same Hebrew verb (literally "mutter, read

in a low voice") is used here; it means to study (TEV), "pore over"
(Mft); "keep it in mind" (NEB).

At the end of verse 8 two synonymous verbs are used: "cause to
prosper" and "be successful" (as in verse 7); TEV you will be prosperous and successful; NEB "you will prosper and be successful in all that
you do." The combination prosperous and successful reflects the Hebrew
practice of placing together two modifiers in what appears to be a
coordinate relationship. However, the use of "and" in such structures
is deceptive, for a coordinate relationship is not really intended. In
reality one adjective is meant to qualify the other. For example,
"wicked and sinful" would mean "very wicked (sinful)." So then, prosperous and successful may be understood to have the meaning "very prosperous" or "very successful."

1.9   Remember that I have commanded you to be determined
        and confident! Do not be afraid or discouraged, for
        I, the LORD your God, am with you wherever you go."

The promise to Joshua is repeated by the use of a negative rhetorical question, "Have I not commanded you?" (RSV). TEV has transformed
the difficult rhetorical question into a positive statement: Remember
that I have commanded you. One may also render "Do not forget that..."
or "I tell you once again: Be brave and strong!"

The two verbs of verse 6 ("be strong and be brave") are now followed by two synonymns denoting fear: "tremble" (the Hebrew verb used
only here in the book) and "be afraid." TEV represents these verbs by
the adjectives afraid and discouraged. One may also translate "Do not
tremble with fear" or "Do not let fear conquer you." Idiomatic expressions may also be available in some languages.

I, the LORD your God: it should be noticed that in Hebrew the
phrase is simply "the LORD your God." Since God is the speaker, TEV
has used the more natural style of first person. The possessive pronoun "your" is singular, but the language seems more appropriate if
Israel is being addressed, not just Joshua.

Wherever you go is the same phrase used at the end of verse 7.

The parts of this verse lend themselves to different arrangements,
depending upon what is the most natural order in the receptor language.
For example, "Remember that I am the LORD your God, and I have commanded
you to be determined and confident! So do not be afraid or discouraged,
for I am with you wherever you go." Or, "Remember that I the LORD your
God have commanded you to be determined and confident! I will be with
you wherever you go, so do not be afraid or discouraged."

TEV	1.10-18	RSV

Joshua Gives Orders to
    the People

10 Then Joshua ordered the leaders to 11 go through the camp	10 Then Joshua commanded the officers of the people, 11 "Pass

and say to the people, "Get some food ready, because in three days you are going to cross the Jordan River to occupy the land that the LORD your God is giving you."

12 Joshua said to the tribes of Reuben and Gad and to half the tribe of Manasseh, 13 "Remember how the LORD's servant Moses told you that the LORD your God would give you this land on the east side of the Jordan as your home. 14 Your wives, your children, and your livestock will stay here, but your soldiers, armed for battle, will cross over ahead of their fellow Israelites in order to help them 15 until they have occupied the land west of the Jordan that the LORD your God has given them. When he has given safety to all the tribes of Israel, then you may come back and settle here in your own land east of the Jordan, which Moses, the LORD's servant, gave to you."

16 They answered Joshua, "We will do everything you have told us and will go anywhere you send us. 17 We will obey you, just as we always obeyed Moses, and may the LORD your God be with you as he was with Moses! 18 Whoever questions your authority or disobeys any of your orders will be put to death. Be determined and confident!"

through the camp, and command the people, 'Prepare your provisions; for within three days you are to pass over this Jordan, to go in to take possession of the land which the LORD your God gives you to possess.'"

12 And to the Reubenites, the Gadites, and the half-tribe of Manasseh Joshua said, 13 "Remember the word which Moses the servant of the LORD commanded you, saying, 'The LORD your God is providing you a place of rest, and will give you this land.' 14 Your wives, your little ones, and your cattle shall remain in the land which Moses gave you beyond the Jordan; but all the men of valor among you shall pass over armed before your brethren and shall help them, 15 until the LORD gives rest to your brethren as well as to you, and they also take possession of the land which the LORD your God is giving them; then you shall return to the land of your possession, and shall possess it, the land which Moses the servant of the LORD gave you beyond the Jordan toward the sunrise." 16 And they answered Joshua, "All that you have commanded us we will do, and wherever you send us we will go. 17 Just as we obeyed Moses in all things, so we will obey you; only may the LORD your God be with you, as he was with Moses! 18 Whoever rebels against your commandment and disobeys your words, whatever you command him, shall be put to death. Only be strong and of good courage."

Joshua Gives Orders to the People may be translated, "Joshua commands the people to get ready to conquer Canaan" or "...to get ready to enter the land of Canaan." On the basis of verses 12-18, which comprise the larger part of this section, one may want to alter the focus of the section heading. For example, "The eastern tribes promise to help (conquer the land of Canaan)" or "The tribes that settled east of the Jordan promise to help the other tribes conquer the land of Canaan."

<u>1.10-11</u>   Then Joshua ordered the leaders to 11 go through the camp and say to the people, "Get some food ready, because in three days you are going to cross the Jordan River to occupy the land that the LORD your God is giving you."

<u>Joshua ordered the leaders to go through the camp</u> and tell the people to prepare to march. It is not certain what was the precise nature of these "officers of the people" (RSV). In 23.2 and 24.1 they appear with three other groups of leaders; probably the basic idea is that of military officers. In Exodus 5.6,10,14,15,19 the word is used of the Hebrew "foremen" of the people in their slave work. TEV has deleted "of the people" on the grounds that this information is clearly implicit. However, the manner in which <u>the leaders</u> appears in the TEV text assumes that these are persons already known to the readers (old information), whereas for the readers of the translation the reference is to persons not previously mentioned in the text (new information). Moreover, this is the first verse in a new section. It will help therefore if <u>the leaders</u> are described as either "the leaders of the people of Israel" or "the leaders of the tribes of Israel." It is true that the precise function of these leaders is unknown, but it is also just as clear from the text that they were tribal representatives responsible for conveying Joshua's orders to their respective tribes.

The people must "prepare their provisions" (see RSV) for the march; there won't be time to do it as they advance. The command <u>Get some food ready</u>, as the first of Joshua's instructions to the people, may be a problem. That is, the reader's first inclination may be to take this as a command intended for the present situation, with the meaning "Get some food ready to eat now." The difficulty can be lessened in part by translating "Get some food ready for our journey into the land." However, an even better solution is to rearrange the parts of the sentence. For example, "In three days you are going to cross the Jordan River to occupy the land that the LORD your God is giving you. So get enough food ready for the march." This arrangement will immediately make clear why the people are being ordered to get their food ready.

<u>In three days</u> means what a native speaker of English understands by "the day after tomorrow," not "three days from now." <u>In three days</u> may be rendered idiomatically as "after the sun has gone down twice" or as "two days from now."

A further problem relates to <u>you...your God...giving you</u>. These second person pronouns can imply that Joshua will not be among those who are going to cross the Jordan River to occupy the land, and that he will not receive any of it as a gift from the Lord. To avoid this misunderstanding, a translational shift may be made to the first person inclusive: "we (including the speaker and those addressed)...our God...us."

The verb translated <u>occupy</u> means "to possess, to take as one's own." The Hebrew is repetitive, "to possess the land which the LORD your God is giving you to possess it."

<u>1.12</u>   Joshua said to the tribes of Reuben and Gad and
          to half the tribe of Manasseh,

Verses 12-18 narrate how Joshua secured the help of the two and
one-half tribes that settled on the east side of the Jordan. Numbers
32.1-42, Deuteronomy 3.12-22, and Joshua 13.8-13 narrate how Moses assigned to the tribes of Reuben and Gad and to half the tribe of Manasseh
land on the east side of the Jordan River (the other half of the tribe
of Manasseh settled on the west side). So before Joshua directs the people across the Jordan to the west bank he asks these two and one-half
tribes to promise to help their fellow Israelites invade the land on
the west side and possess it, after which they may return to their territories on the east side of the river (see 22.1-9). They promptly promise to do so and pledge their allegiance to Joshua.
     In some languages it may be more natural in verse 12 to follow the
order of the Hebrew text so as to have Joshua's address to the people
immediately follow the verb "said": "To the tribes of Reuben and Gad
and to the half tribe of Manasseh, Joshua said...." Or, "Then Joshua
gave some special instructions to the tribes of Reuben and Gad and to
the half tribe of Manasseh. He said...."

<u>1.13</u>   "Remember how the LORD's servant Moses told you that
          the LORD your God would give you this land on the
          east side of the Jordan as your home.

<u>Remember</u> serves as an "attention getter" for the words which fol-
low; it is not to imply that the people had forgotten. In some languages
this emphasis may be more effectively conveyed by rendering it as a separate sentence: "Remember! The LORD's servant Moses told you...." Or the
force of the word may be translated, "You know that...." In other languages a better impact may be conveyed without specific mention of the
verb "remember," as for example, "Moses, the servant of the LORD, promised you:...." It may be more natural to use direct discourse: "Remember that the LORD's servant Moses told you, 'The LORD your God will
give you this land on the east side of the Jordan as your home.'"
     In verse 13 TEV, for clarity, includes <u>on the east side of the
Jordan</u>, which in Hebrew comes in verse 14 (RSV "the land...beyond the
Jordan"). In biblical language "beyond the Jordan" is the east side,
the point of reference being the land of Israel on the west side of the
river. A literal rendering of "the land...beyond the Jordan" (RSV) is
misleading, for when these words are spoken the people of Israel are
still on the east side of the Jordan; a literal translation would imply
that "the other side" is the western side. Many languages have idiomatic
expressions for the points on the compass, and consideration should be
given to the appropriateness of using these in translation. It is possible even to translate without reference to the points on the compass,
for example, "the land on this side of the Jordan." It will have to be
clear in the reader's mind, however, that the people of Israel were
east of the Jordan at the time Joshua addressed them.
     <u>As your home</u> (RSV "is providing you a place of rest") translates
the causative form of the Hebrew verb meaning "to settle down, to

[19]

rest." The idea is that of a place where they will live in security
and peace; NEB "will grant you security here"; NAB "will permit you
to settle." Some languages have very specific terminology to denote
"home" or "homeland" as it relates to a tribe or nation; for example,
"land and water" or "village and yard."

1.14   Your wives, your children, and your livestock will
            stay here, but your soldiers, armed for battle,
            will cross over ahead of their fellow Israelites
            in order to help them

Their wives, children, and livestock will remain on the east side,
while the men themselves, armed for battle, will take the lead in crossing over to the west side ahead of their fellow Israelites.
Soldiers translates a phrase "men of valor among you" (RSV), "all
the warriors among you" (NEB, NAB), "all of you who are fighting men"
(JB). They were not permanent military men, as the modern term means,
but men of twenty years of age or older who were fit for battle, equivalent to a modern militia. They were "citizen soldiers," not professional
warriors. Since the Hebrew word "soldiers" does not refer specifically
to military men, one might render "able-bodied men" or "men fit for battle." The clause may then be translated, "But all of your men who are
fit for battle must take their weapons and cross over...."
Armed for battle translates the participle of a verb related to
the word "five," and may designate a battle formation of five groups;
one in the lead, one in the rear, one in the middle, and one on each
side. Since these men would not have their families and animals with
them, they would go first. Although armed for battle does originally
come from the word "five," it is not necessary (and is probably impossible) to reproduce this root meaning in translation. In fact, it is
quite likely that even for the author of the book the term no longer
held this specific meaning. Soldiers, armed for battle may be rendered
"battle-ready men" or "able-bodied men."

1.15   until they have occupied the land west of the Jordan
            that the LORD your God has given them. When he has
            given safety to all the tribes of Israel, then you
            may come back and settle here in your own land east
            of the Jordan, which Moses, the LORD's servant, gave
            to you."

Verse 15 in Hebrew is quite wordy, and TEV has tried to reduce
the number of words without loss of meaning. It is possible, however,
to do even better. Since it is clear in the readers' mind that Joshua
is now addressing the tribes east of the Jordan (verse 12), it may not
be necessary to mention explicitly west of the Jordan. The last part
of verse 14 and the first part of verse 15 may then be rendered, "in
order to help them 15 occupy the land that the LORD your God is giving
them." As previously noted, it may be necessary to say "the LORD our
God" in place of "the LORD your God."

Joshua foresees the time when all resistance is crushed and all the tribes of Israel are safe in their territories. The emphasis throughout is on the LORD's power: he will give the western tribes safety (as in verse 13), as he has to the eastern tribes; he is giving them the land. Has given safety to all the tribes of Israel may be rendered "has given all the tribes of Israel a place where they can live in safety." The Hebrew verb rendered given safety to in TEV does not always include the idea of "safety" but may mean "to give a place to live" or "to give a home to." After the land on the west side is occupied, then the two and one-half tribes can return to their own territories on the east side (literally "beyond the Jordan toward the rising of the sun").

Although the Hebrew text once again qualifies Moses as the LORD's servant, the repetition of this phrase may be unnatural and unnecessary in some languages. One may delete it and render "which Moses gave to you."

1.16   They answered Joshua, "We will do everything you
            have told us and will go anywhere you send us.

Verse 16 reports how the men of Reuben, Gad, and East Manasseh promptly agreed to Joshua's demand. They may need to be identified as "The tribes of Reuben and Gad and the half tribe of Manasseh," since the last mention of them was in verse 12.

It may be helpful to change the order of the command and responses in the clauses We will do everything you have told us and will go everywhere you send us. For example, "You have given us commands, and we will obey them all, and when you command us to go somewhere, we will go there." Or, since the initial response immediately follows Joshua's speech, it may be necessary to reorder only the second in the series: "We will do all the things that you have told us to do, and when you send us somewhere, we will go there." In these two proposed restructurings, it should be noted that the subject "we" is repeated before the second verb of which it is the subject; this is because in TEV We will do is a closely bound unit, whereas We will do...and will go has the subject We at some distance from the second verb will go.

1.17   We will obey you, just as we always obeyed Moses,
            and may the LORD your God be with you as he was
            with Moses!

The eastern tribes promise to obey Joshua as they had obeyed Moses, and they also express the wish that the Lord will be with Joshua as he was with Moses. But this is more than a pious wish; it is also a way of saying that any man who aspires to lead and command the people of God must demonstrate that he has the Lord's approval. Moses had many proofs of God's authority, and Joshua must have them also. So Bright: "The tribesmen thus promise to obey Joshua, but only if he shows himself to be the man designated of God."

[21]

For the first two clauses of this verse it may be better to follow the order of the Hebrew, since it is arranged in proper chronological sequence. For example, "We always obeyed Moses, and we will always obey you." Or, "We always did what Moses told us to do, and we will always do what you tell us to do." Or, "Moses told us what to do, and we always obeyed him; when you tell us what to do, we will always obey you."

The last half of the verse may be rendered, "and we ask the LORD our God to be with you" or "...to stand beside you...."

1.18   Whoever questions your authority or disobeys any of your orders will be put to death. Be determined and confident!"

The response of the tribes to Joshua ends with the refrain "Be strong and courageous!"

Questions your authority translates what is literally "rebels against your mouth" (the word "mouth" here standing for "order," synonymous with the following "word"). The phrase may be translated "opposes you." Or, it is possible to take the two verb phrases questions your authority and disobeys any of your orders as a Hebrew parallelism, and therefore synonymous in meaning. One may then translate "refuses to obey any of your commands (or, orders)."

For some readers it will also be advantageous to change the passive will be put to death to an active form, "we will put to death anyone who...." Or, "If anyone refuses to obey any of your commands, we will put him to death."

Chapter 2

Joshua Sends Spies into Jericho

1 Then Joshua sent two spies from the camp at Acacia with orders to go and secretly explore the land of Canaan, especially the city of Jericho. When they came to the city, they went to spend the night in the house of a prostitute named Rahab. 2 The king of Jericho heard that some Israelites had come that night to spy out the country, 3 so he sent word to Rahab: "The men in your house have come to spy out the whole country! Bring them out!"
4-6 "Some men did come to my house," she answered, "but I don't know where they were from. They left at sundown before the city gate was closed. I didn't find out where they were going, but if you start after them quickly, you can catch them." (Now Rahab had taken the two spies up on the roof and hidden them under some stalks of flax that she had put there.) 7 The king's men left the city, and then the gate was shut. They went looking for the Israelite spies as far as the place where the road crosses the Jordan.

1 And Joshua the son of Nun sent two men secretly from Shittim as spies, saying, "Go, view the land, especially Jericho." And they went, and came into the house of a harlot whose name was Rahab, and lodged there. 2 And it was told the king of Jericho, "Behold, certain men of Israel have come here tonight to search out the land." 3 Then the king of Jericho sent to Rahab, saying, "Bring forth the men that have come to you, who entered your house; for they have come to search out all the land." 4 But the woman had taken the two men and hidden them; and she said, "True, men came to me, but I did not know where they came from; 5 and when the gate was to be closed, at dark, the men went out; where the men went I do not know; pursue them quickly, for you will overtake them." 6 But she had brought them up to the roof, and hid them with the stalks of flax which she had laid in order on the roof. 7 So the men pursued after them on the way to the Jordan as far as the fords; and as soon as the pursuers had gone out, the gate was shut.

The real focus in the section entitled <u>Joshua Sends Spies into Jericho</u> is upon the interaction between the <u>Israelite spies and Rahab</u>. One may therefore say "A Canaanite woman helps the Israelite spies" or "A woman in the city of Jericho helps the Israelite spies." If the TEV form is maintained, it may be necessary to mark Jericho as "the city (town) of Jericho."

[23]

This event falls naturally into three parts: (1) the two spies
enter Jericho and are hidden by Rahab (verses 1-7); (2) Rahab gets them
to promise to spare her and her family in the coming conquest of the
city (verses 8-14); and (3) the spies return safely to camp (verses
15-24).

2.1   Then Joshua sent two spies from the camp at
             Acacia with orders to go and secretly explore the
             land of Canaan, especially the city of Jericho.
             When they came to the city, they went to spend
             the night in the house of a prostitute named Rahab.

In the phrase sent two spies, the word spies may convey to some
readers a highly specialized and technical meaning. To avoid this complication, one may render "secretly sent two men." This may be an excellent solution if it is certain that the readers will understand
secretly to apply only to the people of Canaan and not to the people
of Israel as well. In order not to be misunderstood, one may translate
"Then Joshua sent two men from the camp at Acacia to go and secretly
explore the land of Canaan." Or, if direct discourse is more appropriate, "While the people of Israel were camped at Acacia, Joshua told
two of the men, 'Go and secretly explore the land of Canaan....'"
    The Israelite camp was at Acacia northeast of the Dead Sea, oppo-
site Jericho (see Num 25.1; 33.49). The Hebrew name "Shittim" (RSV)
means "the acacias," a flowering tree (see *Fauna and Flora of the Bible,*
pages 87-88). For English speakers the noun "Shittim" sounds like a
vulgar word and should be avoided. This is also a principle that should
be followed in any language; in the translation or transliteration of
terms, any vulgar-sounding words or word combinations should be avoided.
    Explore the land of Canaan may be rendered, "to find out all they
(you) can about the land of Canaan" or "to find out what the land of
Canaan is like."
    Jericho, the most important city in the region, was west of the
Jordan. The Hebrew text "to go and look at the land and Jericho" is
rather strange; RSV, TEV both translate "especially Jericho"; JB "the
country at Jericho"; TOB, BJ "the land of Jericho." NEB (without any
textual note) translates "...with orders to reconnoitre the country.
The two men came to Jericho" (which represents neither the Hebrew nor
the Greek Old Testament).
    A prostitute: commentators make the point that the two Israelites
would have a good chance of going unnoticed in a house of prostitution.
Her home was built into the city wall (see verse 15). Josephus (*Antiq-
uities* V.i.2) speaks of Rahab as an innkeeper, not a harlot. (She may
have been both.) If the translation is intended for young readers, no
harm will be done to the text if a prostitute is represented by "a
woman." The last sentence of this verse may be rendered in a chronological sequence: "When they came to the city, they went to the house
...in order to spend the night."

2.2-3   The king of Jericho heard that some Israelites had
        come that night to spy out the country, 3 so he sent
        word to Rahab: "The men in your house have come to
        spy out the whole country! Bring them out!"

   The news of the arrival of the Israelite spies reached the king
of Jericho. It is possible to render The king of Jericho heard...that
night as "That same evening the king of Jericho heard...." The Hebrew
word translated king is used in the general sense of ruler; Jericho
was a city-state, an autonomous city. So the king sent word to Rahab
to turn the spies over to him. In verse 3 the Hebrew text does not refer explicitly to the king's messengers (or officers, or soldiers) who
took the message to Rahab; it is in verse 5 that the text makes clear
the presence of the royal messengers, who heed Rahab's advice and set
out to capture the Israelite spies (verse 7). On the basis of verses
5 and 7, sent word to Rahab may be translated "sent some men (or messengers, or soldiers) to say to Rahab."
   Since it is quite possible that more than two men were in Rahab's
house, The men in your house have come to spy out may be rendered either
"There are two men in your house who have come to spy out" or "Two of
the men in your house have come to spy out."
   Bring them out may imply accompaniment, and so the command may be
translated "Send them out (to us)!"

2.4-6   "Some men did come to my house," she answered,
        "but I don't know where they were from. They left
        at sundown before the city gate was closed. I didn't
        find out where they were going, but if you start
        after them quickly, you can catch them." (Now Rahab
        had taken the two spies up on the roof and hidden
        them under some stalks of flax that she had put
        there.)

   TEV has restructured these verses in order to put them in a logical
and chronological sequence, and thus make the narrative easier for the
reader to understand. RSV follows the order of the Hebrew text: verse
4a, narrative—Rahab hides the Israelite spies; verses 4b-5, Rahab's
answer to the king's messengers; verse 6, narrative—a more detailed
description of how the two spies were hidden.
   Rahab is able to save the Israelite spies by lying to the king's
messengers. Apparently the king's men set out from Jericho in pursuit
of the spies just before dark (RSV, verse 7b), that is, before the city
gate was closed for the night; there is a slight difficulty, since in
verse 5 Rahab states that the two spies had left just before the gate
was closed.
   In verse 4 "and hidden them" (RSV) translates a text which in Hebrew seems to mean "and hidden him" (the singular, not the plural pronominal suffix); so NEB has a textual footnote, but none of the other
translations has one. The United Bible Societies' (UBS) committee on
the Hebrew Old Testament Text Project (HOTTP) takes the Hebrew to mean
"the woman (in fact) took the (two) men, but she hid it," that is, she

kept it a secret. It seems better to change the text to say "and she hid them"; certainly the Hebrew seems to mean "and hid him" (see Gray; Soggin refers to Gesenius-Kautzsch, *Hebrew Grammar*, §60.d, page 161). The Greek Old Testament has "and hid them," an obvious attempt to make the account harmonize.

Verse 6 (see RSV) describes how Rahab had hidden the spies; the implication seems to be that the king's men searched the house (including the roof) and so believed her story; it is difficult to believe that they would simply have accepted her explanation without seeing for themselves if she was telling the truth.

Perhaps from a purely logical point of view, one might assume that the king's men would have searched the house before pursuing after the spies. But this is not a necessary conclusion, especially if the men had no reason to suspect that Rahab was lying to them. Moreover, for the telling of the story the author evidently felt that immediate pursuit produced a more dramatic effect. In any case the Hebrew text does not provide grounds enough on which to conclude that the king's men made a search of the house.

By placing verses 4-6 together TEV sought to produce a text which is easier to understand; compare, for example, the RSV. But the result is the creation of a parenthetical statement at the end of the paragraph which speaks of an event that happened prior to the events described in the first part of the paragraph. The net result will be that the average reader will face a double difficulty, both a parenthetical statement and a flashback, that is, a reference to an event which had occurred earlier. The problem may be somewhat eased, however, if the information contained in the parenthetical statement is placed first in the paragraph. This is legitimate, for the Hebrew text does not make it clear whether Rahab hid the two spies before the king's men came for them or immediately after the arrival of the king's men. TEV apparently assumes that the action was prior to their arrival, though there is a slight bit of ambiguity about the TEV text. If one assumes that she hid the men as soon as the messengers came from the king, an alternative restructuring is possible: "4-6 Rahab went up on the roof and hid the two men under some stalks of flax that she had put there. Then she said to the men who had been sent by the king, 'Two men did come to my house....'"

For many readers there will be no problem regarding the closing of the city gate at sundown; for others it may be necessary to include a note indicating that this was done each night for protection. Before the city gate was closed may be rendered "before it was time to close the city gate." But since the city gate was normally closed at sundown, it is also possible to render "They left right at sundown, just before the men of the city closed the city gate."

I didn't find out may be rendered "I don't know."

Where they were going is the equivalent of "in which direction they went."

Flax is a plant from whose stem a fiber was made, to be used for weaving into linen cloth (see *Fauna and Flora of the Bible*, pages 119-120). The stalks had been laid out on the flat roof to dry out, and this may indicate that it was springtime (see 3.14-15).

<u>2.7</u>   The king's men left the city, and then the gate was
shut. They went looking for the Israelite spies as
far as the. place where the road crosses the Jordan.

The <u>king's men</u> left Jericho and went east toward the Jordan, and
there they gave up the search. On the assumption that the messengers
left immediately in pursuit of the spies, it is allowable to include
the adverb "immediately" and to follow the order of the Hebrew text
more closely by placing in final position the information about the
closing of the gate: "The guards immediately took up pursuit and went
as far as the place where the road crosses the Jordan River." Also, on
the assumption that the gate was closed following the departure of the
spies and had to be opened a second time for the pursuers to get out,
one may render "The city gate was again closed behind them."

TEV   <u>2.8-14</u>   RSV

8 Before the spies settled down for the night, Rahab went up on the roof 9 and said to them, "I know that the LORD has given you this land. Everyone in the country is terrified of you. 10 We have heard how the LORD dried up the Red Sea in front of you when you were leaving Egypt. We have also heard how you killed Sihon and Og, the two Amorite kings east of the Jordan. 11 We were afraid as soon as we heard about it; we have all lost our courage because of you. The LORD your God is God in heaven above and here on earth. 12 Now swear by him that you will treat my family as kindly as I have treated you, and give me some sign that I can trust you. 13 Promise me that you will save my father and mother, my brothers and sisters, and all their families! Don't let us be killed!"

14 The men said to her, "May God take our lives if we don't do as we say!*a* If you do not tell anyone what we have been doing, we promise you that when the LORD gives us this land, we will treat you well."

*a*May God...say; *or* We will protect you if you protect us.

8 Before they lay down, she came up to them on the roof, 9 and said to the men, "I know that the LORD has given you the land, and that the fear of you has fallen upon us, and that all the inhabitants of the land melt away before you. 10 For we have heard how the LORD dried up the water of the Red Sea before you when you came out of Egypt, and what you did to the two kings of the Amorites that were beyond the Jordan, to Sihon and Og, whom you utterly destroyed. 11 And as soon as we heard it, our hearts melted, and there was no courage left in any man, because of you; for the LORD your God is he who is God in heaven above and on earth beneath. 12 Now then, swear to me by the LORD that as I have dealt kindly with you, you also will deal kindly with my father's house, and give me a sure sign, 13 and save alive my father and mother, my brothers and sisters, and all who belong to them, and deliver our lives from death." 14 And the men said to her, "Our life for yours! If you do not tell this business of ours, then we will deal kindly and faithfully with you when the LORD gives us the land."

[27]

Since chapter 2 is a rather lengthy section, it may be to the reader's advantage to introduce a new section heading for verses 8-14, and perhaps again for verses 15-24. A section heading here may be "The agreement between Rahab and the Israelites" or "Rahab makes an agreement with the Israelites" or "...with the (two) Israelite spies."

Verses 8-14 narrate the way in which Rahab and the two spies came to an agreement. It may well be that this took place before the arrival of the king's men, and so explains her lying to them about the Israelite spies. She knew who the spies were; she had heard how the Lord had worked miracles for the Israelites in their departure from Egypt, and knew how they had defeated their enemies on the east side of the Jordan. So she decided to help them on condition that the Israelites spare the lives of all her family in the inevitable fall of the city to the Israelites. The two spies agreed to her demands.

Rahab tells the two spies that she knows Jericho will be captured by the Israelites; their fame has preceded them, and the inhabitants of Jericho realize that the Lord, the God of Israel, is invincible. She sounds practically like an Israelite as she confesses the Lord's majesty and might (especially verse 11).

2.8   Before the spies settled down for the night, Rahab went up on the roof

Before the spies settled down for the night may be translated "Before the spies got ready for bed that night." It may even be helpful to identify the spies as "the two Israelite spies" or "the two Israelite men."

Rahab went up on the roof may need to be rendered "Rahab went back up on the roof" or "Rahab went up on the roof again." The phrase on the roof may need to be rendered "on the roof where they were" or "on the roof where she had hidden them." The roof was flat and provided a good place to hide.

2.9   and said to them, "I know that the LORD has given you this land. Everyone in the country is terrified of you.

Is terrified of you translates the Hebrew noun phrase "the fear of you (has fallen upon us)" (see RSV). The next clause, "and that all the inhabitants of the land melt before you" (see RSV), is simply another way of saying "they are terrified." NEB, like TEV, combines the two. The two clauses may also be translated, "All of its people tremble before you; because of fear they are like lame people."

2.10   We have heard how the LORD dried up the Red Sea in front of you when you were leaving Egypt. We have also heard how you killed Sihon and Og, the two Amorite kings east of the Jordan.

Reports had reached the people of Jericho about the Israelites' departure from Egypt; according to the biblical chronology this had taken place some forty years earlier. The Red Sea is an unsatisfactory translation of the Hebrew phrase, which means "Sea of Reeds." The Greek Old Testament translated "Red Sea," and the Greek New Testament follows this translation. Most scholars believe the actual body of water crossed by the Israelites was a marsh or lake somewhere between the northern end of the Gulf of Suez and the Mediterranean Sea (see footnote at TEV Exo 13.18). What is today called the Red Sea lies south of the Gulf of Suez, which is close to 300 kilometers long; and from Rameses, the point of departure of the Israelites (Num 33.3-5), to the northern end of the Gulf of Suez is about 115 kilometers. Neither the Gulf of Suez nor the Red Sea is likely to have been the body of water crossed by the Israelites. BJ, JB, TOB, New Jewish Version (NJV), Luther, Zürcher Bibel (Zür) all translate "Sea of Reeds."

In front of you when you were leaving Egypt may need to be translated "so you could cross it when you were leaving Egypt."

For the defeat of Sihon and Og, in the territory east of the Jordan, see Numbers 21.21-35. Killed in this verse translates a Hebrew verb which means "dedicate or devote to God"; anything thus "dedicated to God" had to be completely destroyed (see further in 6.17). The focus here and in many contexts is upon the end result, that is, either the killing of people or the total destruction of property. In other contexts it may be helpful to give a footnote indicating the root meaning of the word, but here the focus is upon the act of killing.

2.11   We were afraid as soon as we heard about it; we have
       all lost our courage because of you. The LORD your
       God is God in heaven above and here on earth.

We were afraid translates the Hebrew "our hearts melted"; the synonymous we have all lost our courage translates "and everyone's spirit no longer rose up." In place of employing two nonfigurative statements (We were afraid and we have all lost our courage), it may be more effective to use a figurative expression, as the Hebrew text does. Languages abound with their own expressions of fear, and it may be natural to use two such figures, as with the Hebrew. On the other hand, it may be that the intensity of the fear is actually strengthened by the use of a single statement, whether figurative or nonfigurative. It is possible also to combine a nonfigure with a figure: "We were so frightened that our bones knocked."

The last sentence may be rendered, "The LORD your God rules in heaven above and also here on earth." Or, it may be necessary to preface the statement with a comment such as "We know that the LORD your God rules...."

2.12   Now swear by him that you will treat my family as
       kindly as I have treated you, and give me some sign
       that I can trust you.

[29]

The Hebrew particle translated Now is used to strengthen the urgency of Rahab's request; it is not a temporal marker.

By him is literally "by the LORD" (RSV), but since the Lord has last been referred to by name at the end of the previous verse, it is more natural in English to follow with a pronominal reference as TEV has done.

Now swear by him may be rendered "Now make me a (solemn) promise in the name of your God."

Rahab gets the spies to promise that she and her family will be spared when the Israelites destroy Jericho. In verse 12 treat...kindly (RSV "deal kindly") translates the verb "do," followed by a word which more often means "goodness, love, loyalty"; it is a word particularly appropriate in the context of an agreement, a pact, a covenant, and it characterizes the spirit of faithfulness and loyalty with which each party of the covenant will follow its stipulations.

It may be helpful to rearrange this verse in a somewhat chronological order, such as "I have shown kindness to you. Now swear by the LORD your God that you will treat my family with the same kindness."

My family translates the Hebrew phrase "the house of my father." The next verse defines the extent of Rahab's "family"; in translation one should be careful not to use a term which might include merely the immediate family, since the extended family is obviously intended.

And give me some sign that I can trust you translates a passage which is lacking in the Septuagint; some commentators believe it is not original, but it is in the Hebrew text. The red cord in verse 18 is the sign (or signal).

2.13   Promise me that you will save my father and mother,
            my brothers and sisters, and all their families!
            Don't let us be killed!"

The request of the previous verse is repeated and includes all the immediate members of Rahab's family (father, mother, brothers, sisters) and their families. Verses 12-13 may be combined by relating the sign to the content of the promise in verse 13: "I beg you, swear to me by him that you will treat my family as I have treated you. Prove your faithfulness to me in this way: Let my parents and my brothers and sisters and their families live. Save us from death!"

2.14   The men said to her, "May God take our lives
            if we don't do as we say!ᵃ If you do not tell anyone
            what we have been doing, we promise you that when the
            LORD gives us this land, we will treat you well."

            ᵃMay God...say; or We will protect you if you protect
            us.

The answer the Israelites give to Rahab's request is difficult to understand. In Hebrew it is literally "Our lives for yours (plural) to death." As Soggin says, this is "a self-cursing formula which guarantees the promise that they make." So TEV has <u>May God take our lives if we</u> <u>don't do as we say!</u> But the alternative <u>translation in the footnote</u> is also possible, though less likely. The clause <u>if we don't do as we say</u> may also be phrased, "if anything happens to one of you." To avoid two consecutive "if" clauses, the second may be rendered, "But you must not tell anyone that we were here." The next clause may then be rendered, "Then when the LORD gives us this land, we will keep our promise to treat you and your family well."

The only condition they impose is that Rahab keep strict silence about their activities. <u>We will treat you well</u> translates the verb "we will do" followed by two Hebrew words which may be translated "loyalty and constancy" (or, "faithfulness"). NEB has "we will deal honestly and faithfully by you"; AT "we will deal kindly and honestly with you."

TEV   <u>2.15-24</u>   RSV

15 Rahab lived in a house built into the city wall, so she let the men down from the window by a rope. 16 "Go into the hill country," she said, "or the king's men will find you. Hide there for three days until they come back. After that, you can go on your way."

17 The men said to her, "We will keep the promise that you have made us give. 18 This is what you must do. When we invade your land, tie this red cord to the window you let us down from. Get your father and mother, your brothers, and all your father's family together in your house. 19 If anyone goes out of the house, his death will be his own fault, and we will not be responsible; but if anyone in the house with you is harmed, then we will be responsible. 20 However, if you tell anyone what we have been doing, then we will not have to keep our promise which you have made us give you." 21 She agreed and sent them away. When they had gone, she tied the red cord to the window.

22 The spies went into the hills and hid. The king's men looked for them all over the countryside for three days, but they did not find them, so they

15 Then she let them down by a rope through the window, for her house was built into the city wall, so that she dwelt in the wall. 16 And she said to them, "Go into the hills, lest the pursuers meet you; and hide yourselves there three days, until the pursuers have returned; then afterward you may go your way." 17 The men said to her, "We will be guiltless with respect to this oath of yours which you have made us swear. 18 Behold, when we come into the land, you shall bind this scarlet cord in the window through which you let us down; and you shall gather into your house your father and mother, your brothers, and all your father's household. 19 If any one goes out of the doors of your house into the street, his blood shall be upon his head, and we shall be guiltless; but if a hand is laid upon any one who is with you in the house, his blood shall be on our head. 20 But if you tell this business of ours, then we shall be guiltless with respect to your oath which you have made us swear." 21 And she said, "According to your words, so be it." Then she sent them away, and they departed; and she bound the scarlet cord in the window.

[31]

returned to Jericho. 23 Then the two spies came down from the hills, crossed the river, and went back to Joshua. They told him everything that had happened, 24 and then said, "We are sure that the LORD has given us the whole country. All the people there are terrified of us."

22 They departed, and went into the hills, and remained there three days, until the pursuers returned; for the pursuers had made search all along the way and found nothing. 23 Then the two men came down again from the hills, and passed over and came to Joshua the son of Nun; and they told him all that had befallen them. 24 And they said to Joshua, "Truly the LORD has given all the land into our hands; and moreover all the inhabitants of the land are fainthearted because of us."

Verses 15-24 narrate the final conversation between Rahab and the Israelite spies, and their departure from Jericho. Following her advice, they hide in the hill country west of the Jordan until they are sure that the messengers of the king of Jericho have given up the search for them, and then they cross the Jordan and return to camp, where they report to Joshua.

If a separate section heading is felt necessary for these verses, one may say "The spies return to camp" or "The two Israelite spies return to their camp."

2.15   Rahab lived in a house built into the city wall, so she let the men down from the window by a rope.

A house built into the city wall: archaeological excavations reveal that at one time Jericho had two city walls, an inner one and an outer one, separated by a space of some 3.5 to 4.5 meters. Houses were built on heavy timbers laid from one wall to the other: the window through which Rahab let the men down looked out from the outer wall (see Bright). The phrase a house built into the city wall could possibly be unclear; it may be more satisfactory to translate "a section of the city wall formed the outside wall of Rahab's house." Moreover, it may even be necessary to include a footnote, indicating more precisely the relation between the house and the city wall. Finally, to restructure so she let...by a rope as an explanation rather than as the next event in a sequence may help to resolve the flashback problem of verses 17-21. That is, one may translate either "that is why Rahab was able to let the men down..." or "so Rahab was able to let the men down...." Such restructuring does not do harm to the text, and it will benefit the reader.

2.16   "Go into the hill country," she said, "or the king's men will find you. Hide there for three days until they come back. After that, you can go on your way."

The hill country would be the region on the west side of the Jordan River.

It may be more effective to place the two commands Go...Hide in closer relation to one another; for example, "Go into the hill country and hide, so that the king's men will not find you. Stay (hidden) there...."

As the spies leave, she advises them to stay hidden in the hills for three days, that is, until two days later (see 1.11). For three days until they come back may be translated, "They will look for you for three days, and then they will come back."

After that, you can go on your way may be translated "After they return, you can go safely back to your camp."

2.17   The men said to her, "We will keep the promise
         that you have made us give.

It is pointed out that the dialogue in verses 17-21 must have taken place before Rahab let the men down out of the window of her house (verse 15); it is hardly imaginable that all of this would have been said by the Israelite spies outside the city walls to Rahab in her house. A temporal marker at the beginning of verse 17 may resolve or at least ease the problem of the sequence of events: "Before the men left, they said to Rahab...."

We will keep the promise translates the Hebrew "we (will be) guiltless from this vow of yours," that is, they would discharge their responsibility and do what they had promised to do. In order to represent the chronological sequence of events, it is possible to invert the order of the two clauses in the sentence, We will keep the promise that you have made us give. It may then be translated, "You made us give you a promise, and we will keep it." Many languages will have idiomatic ways of saying We will keep the promise, and in some instances a negative form may be stronger: "We will not break the promise...."

2.18   This is what you must do. When we invade your land,
         tie this red cord to the window you let us down
         from. Get your father and mother, your brothers, and
         all your father's family together in your house.

The two Israelites impose three conditions which Rahab must keep: (1) tie the red cord to the window (verse 18a); (2) gather all the family in the house and keep them there during the fighting (verses 18b-19); and (3) keep the whole arrangement a strict secret (verse 20).

When we invade your land is more literally "When we come into the land," but the obvious reference is to an attack by the Israelites on the land and its people. Some translators prefer to leave the entire clause implicit.

Red cord translates the Hebrew phrase "cord of red thread"; in the Old Testament the Hebrew word translated "cord" occurs only here and in verse 21.

Some languages may require that the text specify whether the cord
was supplied by the Israelite spies or whether it already belonged to
Rahab. If it is assumed that the cord was given to her by the two men,
one may translate "We are giving you this red cord for you to tie to
your window when we invade your land." In the report of how Rahab and
her family were spared (6.22-25), no mention is made of the cord.

2.19   If anyone goes out of the house, his death will be
        his own fault, and we will not be responsible; but if
        anyone in the house with you is harmed, then we will
        be responsible.

The expression "his blood shall be upon his (our) head" (see RSV)
is a way of saying "he (we) will be responsible for that person's
death." Every member of Rahab's family will be safe during the attack
on Jericho so long as he or she stays in Rahab's house; and, in fact,
they were all spared (see 6.23,25). His death will be his own fault
may be restructured as either "he will be killed, and it will be his
own fault" or "we will kill him, and...." The spies are affirming that
everyone except the persons found in Rahab's house will be put to
death.

2.20   However, if you tell anyone what we have been doing,
        then we will not have to keep our promise which you
        have made us give you."

The third condition is that Rahab must say nothing about what we
have been doing (literally "this matter of ours"). It may be both unnecessary and unnatural to repeat in such close sequence the information which you have made us give you, since this is given in verse 17.
Instead one may translate "(our promise) which we made to you" or even
"(our promise) to you."

2.21   She agreed and sent them away. When they had gone,
        she tied the red cord to the window.

Rahab agreed to the three conditions, and after the Israelites
left she tied the cord to the window. According to verse 18 the Israelite spies instructed Rahab to tie the red cord to her window when we
invade your land. But the present verse states When they had gone, she
tied the red cord to the window. The problem may be resolved by leaving
implicit When we invade your land of verse 18. It is also legitimate
to render verse 18 "When we invade your land, be sure this red cord is
tied to the window."

2.22   The spies went into the hills and hid. The king's
        men looked for them all over the countryside for three
        days, but they did not find them, so they returned to
        Jericho.

After a fruitless search lasting three days, the king of Jericho's men return to the city; the Israelite spies come down out of the hills, cross the Jordan to the east side, return to the Israelite camp at Acacia, and report to Joshua. They conclude their report by saying that victory is assured: everyone in Jericho is terrified of the Israelites.

The directions and the movement of events in this verse are somewhat difficult. The hills suggest that these spies went and hid themselves in the hills west of Jericho, while their pursuers went searching for them eastward, in the direction of the Jordan River. On the other hand, it is possible that the hills is intended to contrast with travel along the roads. The Hebrew phrase "in all the way" is somewhat ambiguous and may mean either "everywhere" (as in TEV all over the countryside) or "every road." Accordingly the verse may be translated, "The two men hid themselves in the hills for three days, until their pursuers returned to the city. The guards had searched along every road in the region, but had found no one."

2.23   Then the two spies came down from the hills, crossed
        the river, and went back to Joshua. They told him
        everything that had happened,

Came down from the hills may be taken to mean "went down into the Jordan Valley."

The Hebrew of this verse contains four verbs of motion ("returned"; "came down"; "crossed"; "came to"). TEV combines the force of the first ("returned") and last ("came to") verbs in the series by rendering went back.

Everything that had happened is more literally "everything that had happened to them"; the clause may also be translated "everything that they had done" or "everything that they had experienced."

2.24   and then said, "We are sure that the LORD has given
        us the whole country. All the people there are ter-
        rified of us."

The first part of verse 24 may be slightly restructured as follows: "and they assured him, 'The LORD has placed this entire country in our hands....'"

All the people there may be translated "All the people of that land" or "All the people who live there."

Terrified translates the second verb of fear used in verse 9, literally "melt away" (RSV); AT has "losing heart"; NEB "panic-stricken"; NAB "overcome with fear."

Chapter 3

The People of Israel Cross the Jordan

1 The next morning Joshua and all the people of Israel got up early, left the camp at Acacia, and went to the Jordan, where they camped while waiting to cross it. 2 Three days later the leaders went through the camp 3 and told the people, "When you see the priests carrying the Covenant Box of the LORD your God, break camp and follow them. 4 You have never been here before, so they will show you the way to go. But do not get near the Covenant Box; stay about half a mile behind it."

1 Early in the morning Joshua rose and set out from Shittim, with all the people of Israel; and they came to the Jordan, and lodged there before they passed over. 2 At the end of three days the officers went through the camp 3 and commanded the people, "When you see the ark of the covenant of the LORD your God being carried by the Levitical priests, then you shall set out from your place and follow it, 4 that you may know the way you shall go, for you have not passed this way before. Yet there shall be a space between you and it, a distance of about two thousand cubits; do not come near it."

At Joshua's command all necessary preparations are made, and the Israelites cross to the west bank of the Jordan River and so set foot on Canaan, the promised land. The passage is accomplished by a miraculous cessation of the flow of the river, recalling the drying up of the Sea of Reeds at the departure from Egypt. Memorial stones in the Jordan and at Gilgal, on the west side of the river, mark the event. Everything is ready for the conquest of the land.

Preparations are begun the day after the spies return to camp; the Israelites make their way to the east bank of the Jordan, and three days later are told that on the following day the crossing will begin. The narrative leaves the impression that the crossing was accomplished in one day, the 10th of Abib (4.19), which would be around March 25, in the spring (see 3.14-15). The Israelites leave Acacia on the 8th of Abib, one week before Passover.

The section heading, The People of Israel Cross the Jordan, may be rendered "How the people of Israel crossed the Jordan River" or "How God enabled (helped) the people of Israel to cross the Jordan River." If an additional section heading is included before 4.10b (see comment there), it may be appropriate to translate this heading as either "The people of Israel prepare to cross the Jordan River" or "...get ready to cross the Jordan."

<u>3.1</u>　　　　The next morning Joshua and all the people of
Israel got up early, left the camp at Acacia, and
went to the Jordan, where they camped while waiting
to cross it.

<u>The next morning</u>, after the two spies return to camp, the Israel-
ites leave the camp at Acacia (see 2.1).

In Hebrew the verb "got up" is singular, with <u>Joshua</u> as the subject, while the other verbs (left...went...camped) are plural, including <u>all the people of Israel</u>. However, the use of a singular verb,
later followed by a larger group of subjects, is a typical Hebraism
and is not to be imitated in translation. For example, in the New Testament one frequently encounters a structure such as "Jesus left, and his
disciples," the meaning of which is "Jesus and his disciples left" or
"Jesus left with his disciples." It is obvious that all the Israelites
did get up (unless everyone else except Joshua had stayed up all
night!), and in many languages this information must be included.

The verb rendered <u>left the camp</u> technically means "broke camp,"
and the clause may then be rendered "moved their camp from Acacia."
Translators should be careful not to imply that the people of Israel
were merely going outside their camp. This information does, of course,
become clear later in the verse, but the possibility of any misunderstanding should be avoided.

<u>While waiting to cross it</u> translates the Hebrew "before they
crossed over." It is also possible to leave this information implicit
and render the last clause of this verse as a separate sentence: "There
they set up camp." The entire verse may easily be broken into several
units. For example, "The next day Joshua and all the people of Israel
got up early. They left the camp at Acacia and traveled west to the
Jordan River. There they set up camp and waited until it was time to
cross the river."

<u>3.2-3</u>　　　Three days later the leaders went through the camp
3 and told the people, "When you see the priests
carrying the Covenant Box of the LORD your God,
break camp and follow them.

For <u>Three days later</u> see 1.11; for <u>the leaders</u> see 1.10.

<u>When you see the priests carrying the Covenant Box of the LORD
your God</u> translates the Hebrew "When you see the Covenant Box of the
LORD your God and the Levitical priests carrying it." This is structure
that occurs quite frequently in Hebrew, and it is technically known as
a hendiadys, or the conveying of one idea through two coordinate structures. In the hendiadys the "and" functions to unite the two thoughts
into one, as can be seen in most translations. For further discussion
of this type of construction, see comments on <u>prosperous and successful</u>
at 1.8.

<u>The priests</u> represents the Hebrew "the Levitical priests" (see
RSV), a typical formula for referring to the Israelite priests. In the
thinking of the editor of this material (see Deut 18.1) there is only
one priesthood, that is, there are no regular priests other than those

[37]

of the tribe of Levi. So TEV has the priests, since "the Levitical priests" implies that there were priests who were not Levites (but see TEV in 8.33). It is important in translation not to convey the false notion that some priests were not Levites, as "the Levitical priests" might suggest. The Hebrew is in fact literally "the priests, the Levites," in which "the Levites" is an appositional. The term was important to the final editor of the Joshua text, but it is quite capable of being misunderstood by readers other than those for whom the text was originally intended.

The Covenant Box of the LORD (traditionally called "the ark of the covenant"; so King James Version [KJV], RSV, NEB, NAB, JB) was the portable chest in which were kept the two stone tablets on which were inscribed the Ten Commandments. On top of the chest were the winged creatures representing the earthly throne of God (see the description of the Covenant Box in Exo 25.10-22; 37.1-9). It was called the Covenant Box becasue the Ten Commandments represented the agreement, pact, covenant that the Lord made with the people of Israel at Mount Sinai (see Deut 29.1-15). The Covenant Box of the LORD should be rendered in such a way as to indicate that its primary function is to serve as a witness to the covenant between God and his people. One may translate "the Box of (or, containing) God's Laws and Promises."

It may be useful or even necessary to indicate the place to which the priests were carrying the Covenant Box, for example, "out of the camp." One may also translate "in the direction of the Jordan River," or even combine the two, "out of the camp in the direction of the Jordan River."

3.4   You have never been here before, so they will show you
           the way to go. But do not get near the Covenant Box;
           stay about half a mile behind it."

Verse 4 in Hebrew gives first the instruction for the people to stay a certain distance away from the Covenant Box, after which comes the explanation of why they were to follow the Box. For clarity and ease of understanding, TEV and RSV have reversed the order. The priests carrying the Covenant Box would lead the way, and the people were to follow at a distance of 2,000 cubits, about 3,000 feet (a little more than half a mile) or 914 meters (almost one kilometer). This care was needed because of the holiness of the Box; it was dangerous for ordinary people to be exposed to its holiness (see 2 Sam 6.6-7).

It may make a more natural arrangement if the two clauses in the first sentence of this verse are inverted. For example, "3...and follow them. 4 They will show you the way to go, since you have never been here before." Show you the way to go may be translated, "lead you where you are to go," since show you might imply that the priests are standing along the road and pointing the way.

About half a mile may be rendered "about a kilometer" or even "about a thousand steps." Many languages have idiomatic ways of expressing distance (for example, "the distance that one can walk in the time it takes a pot of bananas to boil"), and the translator should look for a term that is neither a modern term not appropriate for that time, nor a term outside the cultural expectations of the readers.

TEV	3.5-8	RSV

5 Joshua told the people, "Purify yourselves, because tomorrow the LORD will perform miracles among you." 6 Then he told the priests to take the Covenant Box and go with it ahead of the people. They did as he said.

7 The LORD said to Joshua, "What I do today will make all the people of Israel begin to honor you as a great man, and they will realize that I am with you as I was with Moses. 8 Tell the priests carrying the Covenant Box that when they reach the river, they must wade in and stand near the bank."

5 And Joshua said to the people, "Sanctify yourselves; for tomorrow the LORD will do wonders among you." 6 And Joshua said to the priests, "Take up the ark of the covenant, and pass on before the people." And they took up the ark of the covenant, and went before the people.

7 And the LORD said to Joshua, "This day I will begin to exalt you in the sight of all Israel, that they may know that, as I was with Moses, so I will be with you. 8 And you shall command the priests who bear the ark of the covenant, 'When you come to the brink of the waters of the Jordan, you shall stand still in the Jordan.'"

3.5   Joshua told the people, "Purify yourselves, because tomorrow the LORD will perform miracles among you."

Purify yourselves translates the reflexive form of the Hebrew verb "be holy"; so "make yourselves holy"—that is, ritually pure, by undergoing some sort of ceremony which would effect the forgiveness of sins and remove all ritual impurity. This was a preparation for a cultic procession or a holy war (see similar instruction in Exo 19.10,14-15). The concept of ritual or cultic purity is well-known in many cultures but unknown in many others. And even in cultures where this belief is found, the presuppositions may be quite different from those of the ancient Israelites. Therefore a footnote may be necessary. The translation may be handled quite well by going from general to specific, and then by following this with an explanation of the specific command: "Get yourselves ready! Be sure that you are pure, as the LORD demands of his people."

Tomorrow appears strange in the context, since the narrative itself makes no mention of a day's interval between the order for the people to purify themselves and the actual crossing. However, it is an evident part of the text and must be retained in translation. It was at the crossing that the Lord performed a miracle, namely, stopping the flow of the river.

Miracles translates a word meaning "wonderful things, extraordinary deeds." Although the Hebrew does use the plural form "miracles," this is probably done solely for the sake of intensifying the miraculous aspect of what the Lord was going to do. Since only one miracle is involved, it may be better to render "Tomorrow the LORD will work a miracle for you." Or, if it is felt that the impact of the Hebrew plural form is not adequately conveyed by "a miracle," one may render "a great miracle."

3.5

Among you, which represents the form of the Hebrew, may be more
effectively rendered "for you," or better "for us," to include Joshua.
The phrase will perform miracles among you could convey the incorrect
picture of the Lord as a miracle worker among the people of Israel,
and that on the next day he would perform miracles among them in a
number of different places.

3.6   Then he told the priests to take the Covenant Box
             and go with it ahead of the people. They did as he
             said.

In verse 6 the procession actually begins, but verses 7-13 contain more instructions. For stylistic reasons TEV shifts to indirect
discourse for Joshua's address to the priests, whereas Hebrew prefers
direct discourse. Other languages may also prefer direct discourse.
Take the Covenant Box may be translated "Place the Covenant Box upon
your shoulders," since this is the manner in which the Covenant Box
was carried by the priests. Or, if Joshua's directive to the priests
is given in indirect discourse, the verb "take" can be used of Joshua's
instructions, and the next sentence can say "The priests placed the
Covenant Box upon their shoulders and went ahead of the rest of the
people, just as he had commanded."
    Ahead of the people may imply that Joshua will not take part in
the procession. He is automatically included, however, if this phrase
is rendered "ahead of us." The movements of the priests may also be
given with more precision if the phrase is translated "and cross the
Jordan ahead of us."

3.7   The LORD said to Joshua, "What I do today will
             make all the people of Israel begin to honor you as
             a great man, and they will realize that I am with
             you as I was with Moses.

Today perhaps may imply a day after the events of verse 6; more
probably the use of different sources explains the discrepancy (see
Soggin). The Lord promises to be with Joshua as he had been with Moses
(see 1.5), and in this way honor him in the sight of all the Israelites.
What I do...as a great man may also be translated to mean, "Today I
will confirm you as the leader of all the people of Israel." As the
context makes clear, the "greatness" involved concerns Joshua's capacity to lead the people as God's appointed man. The honor refers to the
recognition and acceptance of Joshua in this capacity. More specifically,
the miraculous crossing of the Jordan River will confirm Joshua as God's
chosen man and at the same time confirm him in the minds of the people
as their leader.
    Will realize may be translated "will know for sure."
    I am with you may be rendered "I am at your side" or "I stand with
you."

3.8   Tell the priests carrying the Covenant Box that when
they reach the river, they must wade in and stand
near the bank."

Here again it may be more effective to shift back to the direct
discourse of the Hebrew. For example, "Tell the priests who carry the
Covenant Box, 'When you....'" Joshua's command to the priests may be
translated, "As soon as all of you have gone a few steps into the water, stop and stand there." Or, "As soon as you have taken your first
steps into the water...."

The instruction to the priests is a bit unclear in Hebrew, but it
seems to mean what TEV says, namely, that they were to enter the Jordan
only a few feet and then stop. See also the discussion on 3.17.

<table>
<tr><td>TEV</td><td>3.9-13</td><td>RSV</td></tr>
</table>

9 Then Joshua said to the people, "Come here and listen to what the LORD your God has to say. 10 As you advance, he will surely drive out the Canaanites, the Hittites, the Hivites, the Perizzites, the Girgashites, the Amorites, and the Jebusites. You will know that the living God is among you 11 when the Covenant Box of the Lord of all the earth crosses the Jordan ahead of you. 12 Now choose twelve men, one from each of the tribes of Israel. 13 When the priests who carry the Covenant Box of the LORD of all the earth put their feet in the water, the Jordan will stop flowing, and the water coming downstream will pile up in one place."

9 And Joshua said to the people of Israel, "Come hither, and hear the words of the LORD your God." 10 And Joshua said, "Hereby you shall know that the living God is among you, and that he will without fail drive out from before you the Canaanites, the Hittites, the Hivites, the Perizzites, the Girgashites, the Amorites, and the Jebusites. 11 Behold, the ark of the covenant of the Lord of all the earth is to pass over before you into the Jordan. 12 Now therefore take twelve men from the tribes of Israel, from each tribe a man. 13 And when the soles of the feet of the priests who bear the ark of the LORD, the Lord of all the earth, shall rest in the waters of the Jordan, the waters of the Jordan shall be stopped from flowing, and the waters coming down from above shall stand in one heap."

3.9   Then Joshua said to the people, "Come here and
listen to what the LORD your God has to say.

Come here may be included outside the direct discourse; for example, "Then Joshua called the people to himself and said, 'Listen
to....'"

And listen to what the LORD your God has to say may be rendered
"and I will tell you what the LORD your God has said he will do." The
problem is that Joshua is not directly quoting the Lord, but rather is
informing the Israelites of what the Lord has said he will do for them.

[41]

3.10   As you advance, he will surely drive out the Canaan-
        ites, the Hittites, the Hivites, the Perizzites, the
        Girgashites, the Amorites, and the Jebusites. You will
        know that the living God is among you

In verse 10 Joshua transmits to the people the message from the
Lord that he will surely drive out all the native inhabitants of the
land they are about to enter. Seven different ethnic groups are listed;
see the identical list in Deuteronomy 7.1 and similar lists in Exodus
3.8,17 and Deuteronomy 20.17. For the possible distinctions among the
seven, see commentaries or dictionaries. Nothing is known of the Perizzites and the Girgashites; the Jebusites were associated with Jerusalem
(see 15.63).
        It is possible to rearrange verses 10-13 in a more or less chrono-
logical order and simultaneously delete the problematic verse 12. It
is true that this same information is repeated again in 4.2, but this
does raise a question of how one deals with so-called "seams" in the
text (see "A Note on Two Special Translation Problems," page 5). For
example, here is a place where the writer of the Joshua text found no
difficulty in retaining a statement which appears totally out of place.
Is it legitimate, then, to delete such information when it is included
later at a place where it fits more logically? It could be argued that
as far as translation is concerned the real problem is that of verse
numbers. That is to say, if translators were not required to include
verse numbers in the rendering of this story, they could easily conclude
that the giving of the information in 4.2 is sufficient, without repeat-
ing it here at a place where it does not seem to fit properly. This may
in fact be considered an excellent example of how a text must be dealt
with at a total discourse level, beyond the sentence and paragraph. No
information is really left out, and the meaning of the text is in no
way twisted by rendering in this manner. If, on the other hand, it is
felt that deleting verse 12 here is not being faithful to the text,
then verses 10-13 may still be arranged in a chronological order with
verse 12 (without the verse number) placed in parentheses at the end
of the paragraph.
        As an example of how this reordering might be done, compare:
        10-13 The Covenant Box of the Lord, who rules the entire
        earth, will go ahead and prepare a way for you through the
        Jordan. As soon as the priests who are carrying it place their
        feet into the waters of the Jordan, the water will stop flow-
        ing. The water upstream will pile up as it does before a dam.
        Thereby you will know that your God is a living God. He will
        keep his promise and drive the Canaanites, the Hittites, the
        Hivites, the Perizzites, the Girgashites, the Amorites, and
        the Jebusites out of the land before you.
If it is felt necessary, then as mentioned above, one may include verse
12 in parentheses at the end: "(The LORD also has said that he wants
you to choose twelve men, one from each of the tribes of Israel.)"
        The living God characterizes the Lord as one who lives and acts,
contrasted with the pagan gods, who are "dead," that is, unable to act
and save their peoples.

3.11-12   when the Covenant Box of the Lord of all the earth
           crosses the Jordan ahead of you. 12 Now choose twelve
           men, one from each of the tribes of Israel.

In some languages it may be impossible to say when the Covenant...
crosses, since inanimate objects cannot "cross." If this is the case,
the clause may be translated, "when the priests carrying the Covenant
Box cross..." or "when the priests cross over with the Covenant Box...."

The Lord of all the earth translates the title of God, not the
proper name "Yahweh."[2] The phrase may be rendered, "the Lord who rules
all the earth" or "the Lord who rules all people on earth."

For choose twelve men, one from each of the twelve tribes of Israel
see comments at verse 10. Nothing more is said of them until 4.1-8.

3.13   When the priests who carry the Covenant Box of the
           LORD of all the earth put their feet in the water,
           the Jordan will stop flowing, and the water coming
           downstream will pile up in one place."

Joshua announces the miracle that is described in verses 14-17.
The Hebrew text has "(the ark of) Yahweh, the Lord of all the earth,"
using both the name and the title of God. For the LORD of all the earth
see the comment at verse 11.

Will pile up in one place translates what is literally "will stand
in one heap" (see RSV); the word translated "heap" occurs here and in
verse 16, and is also used of the crossing of the Sea of Reeds in Exodus
15.8; Psalm 78.13. The picture is that of the waters solidified into a
barrier or dam. This verb phrase may be rendered "will pile up (or,
stand up) like waters behind a dam."

TEV	3.14-17	RSV

14-15 It was harvest time, and the river was in flood.

When the people left the camp to cross the Jordan, the priests went ahead of them, carrying the Covenant Box. As soon as the priests stepped into the river, 16 the water stopped flowing and piled up, far upstream at Adam, the city beside Zarethan. The flow downstream to the Dead Sea was completely cut off, and the people were able to cross over near Jericho. 17 While the people walked across on dry ground, the priests carrying the LORD's Covenant Box stood on dry ground in the middle of the Jordan until all the people had crossed over.

14 So, when the people set out from their tents, to pass over the Jordan with the priests bearing the ark of the covenant before the people, 15 and when those who bore the ark had come to the Jordan, and the feet of the priests bearing the ark were dipped in the brink of the water (the Jordan overflows all its banks throughout the time of harvest), 16 the waters coming down from above stood and rose up in a heap far off, at Adam, the city that is beside Zarethan, and those flowing down toward the sea of the Arabah, the Salt Sea, were wholly cut off; and the people passed over opposite Jericho. 17 And while all Israel

> were passing over on dry ground,
> the priests who bore the ark of
> the covenant of the LORD stood on
> dry ground in the midst of the
> Jordan, until all the nation fin-
> ished passing over the Jordan.

Verses 14-17 describe the crossing of all the people; in 4.10b-11 the priests carrying the Covenant Box also cross to the west bank.

3.14-15   It was harvest time, and the river was in flood.
            When the people left the camp to cross the Jordan,
        the priests went ahead of them, carrying the Covenant
        Box. As soon as the priests stepped into the river,

TEV has rearranged the material in verses 14-15 in order to place first the comment about the time when the crossing took place; in the Hebrew text the time is mentioned at the end of verse 15 (see RSV). The exact date of the crossing is given in 4.19. This is harvest time, in the spring of the year, the season when the Jordan overflows its banks because of the melting snow of Mount Hermon.
It is helpful to rearrange the material of 14-15 as TEV has done, so as to place first the information It was harvest time, and the river was in flood. But it is also possible to retain the verse sequence, and to move this information from the end of verse 15 up to the beginning of the verse. For example:
        14 The people left the camp to cross the Jordan River,
        and the priests went ahead of them with the Covenant Box.
        15 It was harvest time (or springtime), the time of the
        year that the Jordan River floods its banks. As soon as the
        priests stepped into the river....
There is indeed nothing sacred about the verse numbering, though it is less disturbing to some readers if the verse sequence can be preserved wherever possible.

3.16   the water stopped flowing and piled up, far upstream
        at Adam, the city beside Zarethan. The flow downstream
        to the Dead Sea was completely cut off, and the people
        were able to cross over near Jericho.

The Hebrew text defines Adam as a "city," and TEV translates this part of the verse at Adam, the city beside Zarethan. In restructuring, however, it may be simpler not to follow the appositional form of TEV; for example, "at the city of Adam, which is beside Zarethan" (see RSV). In translation it may also be necessary to mark Zarethan as a city. In languages which differentiate sharply between "city," "town," and "vil-lage," it is certainly inaccurate to speak of either of these places as a "city." Probably "town" is closer to the meaning, though a generic expression such as "place" may even be better.

[44]

In verse 14 the people left the camp (Hebrew "their tents"), following behind the priests. The miracle occurred just as the priests
stepped into the river: the water stopped flowing at Adam, which was
far upstream.⁵ Adam is about 30 kilometers north of Jericho; Zarethan
is usually located about 20 kilometers farther north, but as Soggin
points out, this makes it difficult to explain the events. In any case,
the Hebrew text says that Adam was "beside, close to, near" Zarethan.
It has been suggested by W. F. Albright (see reference in Bright) that
the text is meant to say that the flow was blocked at Adam and the water backed up as far upstream as Zarethan.

The waters "stopped (stood)...(and) rose up in one heap" (verse
16); the same expression is used in verse 13.⁴ Here also one may render
"stood up (or, piled up) like waters behind a dam."

The flow...was completely cut off may be stated as an active
clause: "No more water flowed downstream to the Dead Sea" or "The river
completely stopped flowing downstream to the Dead Sea." Since the Lord
caused this to happen, it may be translated, "The LORD cut off the
flow...."

The Dead Sea is in Hebrew called "the sea of the Arabah, the Salt
Sea" (RSV). "Arabah" designates the extensive geological depression,
a rift, in which the Jordan River and the Dead Sea are located, and
which extends farther south. It is called "Salt Sea" because of the
heavy concentration of minerals left by the evaporating water; no water flows out of the Dead Sea.

3.17   While the people walked across on dry ground, the
         priests carrying the LORD's Covenant Box stood on
         dry ground in the middle of the Jordan until all
         the people had crossed over.

Verse 17 completes the narrative: the priests, carrying the Covenant Box, stood on dry ground in the middle of the Jordan. The Hebrew
text has a second verb form going with the main verb "they stood." It
may be understood as an infinitive of the verb "be firm," thus they
"stood firm" (KJV, NEB); or it may be taken as a composite form of the
adverb "there": "they stood right there" (see AT "right in the middle
of the Jordan"). Most translations take it in the first sense; so NIV
"stood firm"; TEV and RSV have simply "stood," which is quite adequate.
There is a slight discrepancy here, since in verse 8 the priests
were told to stand near the bank (that is, on the east side), but here
they are standing in the middle of the Jordan. It may be, however, that
the phrase in the middle of does not necessarily refer to the geographical center of the Jordan River, but may mean rather that they were
"completely in the riverbed."

It is not the role of the translator to attempt a harmonization
of the text at points where it is obviously at variance. However, the
directions in verse 8 are themselves somewhat ambiguous. The priests
are commanded to stand "in the Jordan River" when they have come to the
"edge of the Jordan River" (see RSV, verse 8). This command is not
necessarily contradictory to what the priests are described as having
done here in verse 17, especially if in the middle of the Jordan may
be taken in a broader sense of "in the Jordan."

Chapter 4

Memorial Stones Are Set Up

1 When the whole nation had crossed the Jordan, the LORD said to Joshua, 2 "Choose twelve men, one from each tribe, 3 and command them to take twelve stones out of the middle of the Jordan, from the very place where the priests were standing. Tell them to carry these stones with them and to put them down where you camp tonight."

4 Then Joshua called the twelve men he had chosen, 5 and he told them, "Go into the Jordan ahead of the Covenant Box of the LORD your God. Each one of you take a stone on your shoulder, one for each of the tribes of Israel. 6 These stones will remind the people of what the LORD has done. In the future, when your children ask what these stones mean to you, 7 you will tell them that the water of the Jordan stopped flowing when the LORD's Covenant Box crossed the river. These stones will always remind the people of Israel of what happened here."

1 When all the nation had finished passing over the Jordan, the LORD said to Joshua, 2 "Take twelve men from the people, from each tribe a man, 3 and command them, 'Take twelve stones from here out of the midst of the Jordan, from the very place where the priests' feet stood, and carry them over with you, and lay them down in the place where you lodge tonight.'" 4 Then Joshua called the twelve men from the people of Israel, whom he had appointed, a man from each tribe; 5 and Joshua said to them, "Pass on before the ark of the LORD your God into the midst of the Jordan, and take up each of you a stone upon his shoulder, according to the number of the tribes of the people of Israel, 6 that this may be a sign among you, when your children ask in time to come, 'What do those stones mean to you?' 7 Then you shall tell them that the waters of the Jordan were cut off before the ark of the covenant of the LORD; when it passed over the Jordan, the waters of the Jordan were cut off. So these stones shall be to the people of Israel a memorial for ever."

There are two sets of twelve stones in this chapter, which may be due to two different traditions which are here combined. The first set (4.1-8) are the twelve stones which were set up at the place where the Israelites camped on the night after crossing the Jordan. They were placed either on the west bank or at Gilgal (4.19), which is about 4 kilometers west of the river. The second set of twelve stones are those which Joshua placed in the Jordan at the very place where the priests had stood while the people crossed (4.9).

The memorial stones are designed to keep alive in Israel the memory of the miracle wrought by the Lord: when the Covenant Box crossed the Jordan into Canaan, the Jordan stopped flowing and the people crossed on dry land. They did as their fathers had done when they crossed the Sea of Reeds on dry land as they left Egypt (see verses 21-23).

It may be advisable to translate Memorial Stones in the heading as a complete statement. For example, "The people (of Israel) set up (twelve) stones to remind them of what the LORD had done."

4.1   When the whole nation had crossed the Jordan, the LORD said to Joshua,

The whole nation translates the same Hebrew phrase which in the preceding verse (3.17b) TEV translates all the people; RSV has "all the nation" in both places. This may also be rendered either "all (the) Israelites" or "all the people of Israel." Since a new section is introduced here, the reader (or persons being read to) may not know immediately that it is the nation of Israel which is being referred to. Therefore the phrase may be translated "the whole nation of Israel."

4.2-3   "Choose twelve men, one from each tribe, 3 and command them to take twelve stones out of the middle of the Jordan, from the very place where the priests were standing. Tell them to carry these stones with them and to put them down where you camp tonight."

The verbs choose and command in Hebrew are plural, as in 3.12 where Joshua speaks to the people, and not singular; the TOB footnote suggests that originally the order was given to the leaders, not just to Joshua alone. English versions do not reflect this difference between singular and plural imperative forms. Choose twelve men, one from each tribe may be rendered "Choose one man from each of the twelve tribes of Israel." The twelve men, representatives of the twelve tribes, are to take one stone each from the Jordan, from the very place where the priests were standing, and take them to the place where the people will spend the first night on the west side of the river.[5]

Command them to take twelve stones could possibly be ambiguous, suggesting that each of the men was to take twelve stones. To avoid this ambiguity one may render "Command them each to take a stone." For some languages it may be necessary to include a verb of motion, which may involve a slight reordering of the command: "command them to go to the place where the priests were standing in the middle of the Jordan River. Tell each of them to take a stone from there and carry it to the place where you will camp tonight." In this restructuring, put them down is left implicit, but in some languages this aspect of the command may also need to be stated explicitly.

[47]

4.4-5 Then Joshua called the twelve men he had chosen, 5 and he told them, "Go into the Jordan ahead of the Covenant Box of the LORD your God. Each one of you take a stone on your shoulder, one for each of the tribes of Israel.

Joshua does as the Lord commands: he chooses twelve men and gives them their instructions. They are to enter the Jordan ahead of the priests carrying the Covenant Box. The difficulty here is that in the final text of the book the crossing has already taken place (3.17; 4.1). Accordingly, Soggin takes these instructions to mean that the twelve men were to carry twelve stones from the east bank of the Jordan into the river and place them there for the priests to stand on; but certainly the Hebrew text as it now stands does not say this. Some scholars have suggested that the confusion arises because the writer joined two separate traditions about two different sets of twelve stones. The translator, however, can only translate the text as we have it.

Frequently the translator is torn between the desire to maintain the integrity of the text as it stands and the desire to "make sense" of the text (either logically, chronologically, or historically). Upon close reading, one discovers a "gap" between the end of verse 3 and the beginning of verse 4. In verses 1-3 the Lord commands Joshua to choose twelve men, but there is no statement in the text indicating that Joshua did choose these men. Then verse 4 begins "Then Joshua called the twelve men he had chosen.... The sequence of events which is suggested is that somewhere between verses 3 and 4 Joshua did choose the twelve men, but as of verse 4 he still had not called them together to give them their orders. For some readers this lack of connection between verses 3 and 4 can be quite confusing.

The translator may solve this problem by simply stating at the end of verse 3 "Joshua did as the LORD had commanded him," since it is stated explicitly in verse 4 that Joshua did choose twelve men according to the Lord's command. The dilemma may otherwise be resolved by placing together verses 4-5 and beginning the paragraph, "Joshua chose twelve men, one from each tribe of Israel...." An alternative solution, and one which may be less problematic, is to retain the text as it is, except for inverting the order of the verbs in verse 4. This verse may then be translated, "Then Joshua chose the twelve men and called them together."

4.6-7 These stones will remind the people of what the LORD has done. In the future, when your children ask what these stones mean to you, 7 you will tell them that the water of the Jordan stopped flowing when the LORD's Covenant Box crossed the river. These stones will always remind the people of Israel of what happened here."

Verses 6-7 give the reason for setting up these twelve stones at Israel's lodging place that first night in Canaan. They will serve (verse 6) as "a sign" (RSV), "a memorial" (NEB); they will remind (TEV). The noun "memorial" in verse 7 (RSV) defines the precise nature of "the sign" in verse 6; for all time to come the people of Israel will be reminded of what happened at the Jordan River.

By placing together verses 6 and 7 it is possible to avoid the repetition contained in the first part of verse 6 (These stones will remind the people of what the LORD has done) and in the last part of verse 7 (These stones will always remind the people of Israel of what happened here). If this adjustment is made to the text, then the first sentence of verse 6 may be combined with the last sentence of verse 7 and placed as Joshua's concluding statement: "These stones will always remind the people of Israel of what the LORD did here."

Whereas the repetition found in the Hebrew text may cause one kind of problem, a much more severe problem may possibly result from the failure to mark explicitly certain events. For example, a potentially comical situation could result from the information in verses 5 and 6: Each one of you take a stone on your shoulder.... In the future, when your children ask what these stones mean to you.... The reader may well be left with the impression that the children of these Israelite men will in the future ask them why they are carrying these stones about on their shoulders. Therefore it may be necessary to make explicit in verse 5 some of the information found in verse 8. For example, "Each one of you twelve men take a stone on your shoulder, one for each of the tribes of Israel. Then carry these stones to the camping place, and put them down there." The repetition of this information toward the end of verse 8 (especially if done in a slightly different manner) will certainly not stand out as awkward to the reader.

When the LORD's Covenant Box crossed the river may need to be stated somewhat differently, since the Lord's Covenant Box is not an animate being which may move on its own (see also go...ahead of the Covenant Box of verse 5). One may translate "when the priests carried the LORD's Covenant Box across (or, into) the river."

TEV	4.8-10a	RSV

8 The men followed Joshua's orders. As the LORD had commanded Joshua, they took twelve stones from the middle of the Jordan, one for each of the tribes of Israel, carried them to the camping place, and put them down there. 9 Joshua also set up twelve stones in the middle of the Jordan, where the priests carrying the Covenant Box had stood. (Those stones are still there.) 10 The priests stood in the middle of the Jordan until everything had been done that the LORD ordered Joshua to tell the people to do. This is what Moses had commanded.

8 And the men of Israel did as Joshua commanded, and took up twelve stones out of the midst of the Jordan, according to the number of the tribes of the people of Israel, as the LORD told Joshua; and they carried them over with them to the place where they lodged, and laid them down there. 9 And Joshua set up twelve stones in the midst of the Jordan, in the place where the feet of the priests bearing the ark of the covenant had stood; and they are there to this day. 10 For the priests who bore the ark stood in the midst of the Jordan, until

everything was finished that the
LORD commanded Joshua to tell the
people, according to all that Moses
had commanded Joshua.

4.3   The men followed Joshua's orders. As the LORD
         had commanded Joshua, they took twelve stones from
         the middle of the Jordan, one for each of the tribes
         of Israel, carried them to the camping place, and
         put them down there.

Verse 8 reports that Joshua's order was obeyed, and the twelve
stones were taken from the middle of the Jordan and placed at the camping place. Translators often find it difficult to place the clause As
the LORD had commanded Joshua in a satisfactory position in the text.
Grammatically it may be less complicated to include it as a coordinate
clause in the first sentence: "The men followed Joshua's orders and
did as the LORD had commanded him."
    Difficult also is the positioning of one for each of the tribes
of Israel. It may be less difficult if placed at the end of the verse
as a separate statement: "They took twelve stones from the middle of
the Jordan, carried them to the camping place, and put them down there.
These twelve stones represented the twelve tribes of Israel." Or "...Each
of these stones represented one of the twelve tribes of Israel."

4.9   Joshua also set up twelve stones in the middle of
         the Jordan, where the priests carrying the Covenant
         Box had stood. (Those stones are still there.)

Verse 9 deals with another set of twelve stones, which Joshua
placed in the river exactly where the priests...had stood. The writer
of the account added the note: "And they are there to this day"—that
is, to the time when this comment was written.
    Joshua also set up twelve stones must not be interpreted to mean
that Joshua himself did this particular work. Joshua is the one responsible for having it done, but the implication is that he gave the orders
and others did the work. One may need to translate "Joshua also commanded (or, caused) the men to set up twelve stones...." Or, if one
assumes that the men who set up the stones in the middle of the Jordan
were not the same as the ones who had carried the stones to the camping
place, one may translate "Joshua also had some men to set up twelve
stones...."
    TEV places the last sentence of this verse, (Those stones are
still there), within parentheses in order to indicate that this is an
added comment. The force of the parentheses may be lost on readers who
are lacking a certain degree of sophistication, and most translations
do not use parentheses here.

4.10a   The priests stood in the middle of the Jordan until
          everything had been done that the LORD ordered Joshua
          to tell the people to do. This is what Moses had
          commanded.

Verse 10a finishes the account of the crossing. Everything was
done just as the LORD ordered Joshua to tell the people to do, and also
as "Moses had commanded Joshua" (RSV). This reference to two sets of
instructions to Joshua, the Lord's and Moses', is not smooth and reflects one of the "seams" in the text, according to many scholars. The
Septuagint simplifies considerably by having only "until Joshua did
everything that the Lord had ordered him to tell the people." NEB follows the Septuagint, but the HOTTP committee believes that the shorter
reading reflects an attempt to simplify the text and should not be
followed.

This is what Moses had commanded is literally "according to all
that Moses had commanded Joshua" (RSV). It may also be rendered, "Moses
had already given these instructions to Joshua," or, "Moses himself
had given these same instructions to Joshua."

At least two factors complicate the restructuring of 10a. First,
there is the problem of "seams" in the text, already referred to; second, there is the series of commands (the Lord commands Joshua; Joshua
commands the people; Moses commands Joshua).

It may be necessary to shift the impersonal passive structure
until everything had been done to an active construction: "until the
people had done everything." The last part of the sentence may then be
translated, "that the LORD, speaking through Joshua, had commanded them
to do" or "that the LORD had ordered Joshua to tell them to do."

TEV   4.10b-18   RSV

10b The people hurried across the river. 11 When they were all on the other side, the priests with the LORD's Covenant Box went on ahead of the people. 12 The men of the tribes of Reuben and Gad and of half the tribe of Manasseh, ready for battle, crossed ahead of the rest of the people, as Moses had told them to do. 13 In the presence of the LORD about forty thousand men ready for war crossed over to the plain near Jericho. 14 What the LORD did that day made the people of Israel consider Joshua a great man. They honored him all his life, just as they had honored Moses.

15 Then the LORD told Joshua 16 to command the priests carrying

10b The people passed over in haste; 11 and when all the people had finished passing over, the ark of the LORD and the priests passed over before the people. 12 The sons of Reuben and the sons of Gad and the half-tribe of Manasseh passed over armed be- fore the people of Israel, as Moses had bidden them; 13 about forty thousand ready armed for war passed over before the LORD for battle, to the plains of Jer- icho. 14 On that day the LORD exalted Joshua in the sight of all Israel; and they stood in awe of him, as they had stood in awe of Moses, all the days of his life.

15 And the LORD said to Joshua,

[51]

the Covenant Box to come up out
of the Jordan. 17 Joshua did so,
18 and when the priests reached
the riverbank, the river began
flowing once more and flooded
its banks again.

16 "Command the priests who bear
the ark of the testimony to come
up out of the Jordan." 17 Joshua
therefore commanded the priests,
"Come up out of the Jordan."
18 And when the priests bearing
the ark of the covenant of the
LORD came up from the midst of
the Jordan, and the soles of the
priests' feet were lifted up on
dry ground, the waters of the Jordan returned to their place and
overflowed all its banks, as before.

Chapter 4.10b—5.1 completes the narrative of the crossing of the
Jordan; the Israelites are now in Canaan, ready to begin the conquest
of the land. The news of how the Lord had brought his people across
the river on dry land has reached the ears of the kings in the land
and they are filled with fear.

4.10b-11   The people hurried across the river. 11 When
                they were all on the other side, the priests with
                the LORD's Covenant Box went on ahead of the people.

Some translators prefer to close the paragraph at the end of verse
11, forming verses 12-14 into a separate paragraph. TEV and RSV separate
the last part of verse 10 from the preceding section and join it to the
following section; BJ, JB join the whole verse to the following section.

TEV does not have a section heading at 4.10b, but one may be useful so as to break the long narrative. The difficulty is in finding a
wording which is not merely a repetition of the section heading at 3.1.
"The crossing completed" is satisfactory for translations where an incomplete statement is sufficient, but it is inadequate for readers who
expect a complete statement in a section heading. Further complications
arise because this entire passage is heavily repetitious of events beginning in 3.1. Perhaps a section heading such as "The people of Israel
set up camp at Gilgal" (see verse 19) may best satisfy the needs of the
reader.

The people hurried across the river may also be translated, "The
people crossed the river as fast as they could."

On the other side refers to the western shore of the Jordan River.
The sentence may be translated, "When the people of Israel had crossed
over to the west bank of the river."

As soon as all the Israelites had reached the west bank, the
priests with the LORD's Covenant Box ("the priests who were carrying
the LORD's Covenant Box") left the river and took their customary position ahead of the people. So TEV went on ahead; but the Hebrew can be
understood "and the Covenant Box of the LORD and the priests crossed
ahead of the people," since the same verb "to pass over" is used of
the priests as of the people. This, however, is quite confusing; NEB

[52]

consequently omits "before the people," which makes sense. But the
HOTTP says that the second time "to cross over" is used it means "to
pass by," that is, to move up to the head of the column (so NAB, TOB).
The text may then be rendered, "When everyone had reached the other
bank, the priests with the Covenant Box went over and took their place
at the head of the procession."

One must be careful not to translate went on ahead with the meaning "went on ahead and left the people behind." It is possible to translate, following TEV exegesis, "...took their place at the head of the
people and led them on."

4.12   The men of the tribes of Reuben and Gad and of half
            the tribe of Manasseh, ready for battle, crossed
            ahead of the rest of the people, as Moses had told
            them to do.

Verses 12-13 report the fulfillment of the agreement described in
1.12-15 (see also Deut 3.18-20). Verse 12 of TEV has a complex structure. As Moses had told them to do represents a flashback which in some
languages may be better introduced at the beginning of the verse. For
example, "Moses had told the men of the tribes of Reuben and Gad and
of the half tribe of Manasseh to cross ahead of the rest of the people.
So they did this. They got themselves ready for battle and crossed ahead
of the rest of the people." For ready for battle see the similar expression in 1.14.

4.13   In the presence of the LORD about forty thousand
            men ready for war crossed over to the plain near
            Jericho.

In the presence of the LORD probably refers to the Covenant Box,
which symbolized the Lord's earthly throne. Since the more likely interpretation is that this phrase is a reference to the Covenant Box, one
may translate "About forty thousand men ready for war crossed over to
the plain near Jericho, and the LORD was with them because his Covenant
Box was there among them." If, on the other hand, in the presence of the
LORD is not specifically related to the Covenant Box, one may translate
"and the LORD was with them" or "under the leadership of the LORD."

The number about forty thousand refers to the warriors of the two
and one-half eastern tribes. In translation one should avoid the possibility that the reader may understand about forty thousand men to include the total number of Israelites who crossed over. Therefore one
may render "about forty thousand men from these two and one-half tribes
crossed over to the plain near Jericho, and they were all ready for
war."

In verse 13 ready for war (RSV "ready armed for war") translates
a Hebrew verb which means "stripped," a reference to discarding for
work or battle those garments which were ordinarily worn.

<u>4.14</u>   What the LORD did that day made the people of Israel
consider Joshua a great man. They honored him all his
life, just as they had honored Moses.

Verse 14 tells how the promise made in 3.7 is fulfilled (see also
1.5,17). The Hebrew verb translated <u>honored</u> means basically "to fear,
to be in awe of"; RSV "stood in awe <u>of</u>"; AT, NEB "revered"; NAB "respected." The first sentence of this verse in TEV represents considerable restructuring of the text, which in Hebrew is more literally rendered by RSV, "On that day the LORD exalted Joshua in the sight of all
Israel." The means by which the Lord "exalted" Joshua (RSV) was the
miraculous act of bringing the people of Israel across the Jordan River,
and the TEV restructuring represents an attempt to make this meaning
explicit. The verb "exalted" is represented in TEV by <u>made...consider
...a great man</u>. One may translate the first part of the verse "On that
day the LORD placed Joshua in high esteem among the Israelites."

<u>4.15-16</u>   Then the LORD told Joshua 16 to command the
priests carrying the Covenant Box to come up out
of the Jordan.

The Hebrew text of verses 15-18 is quite wordy (see RSV), and
TEV has reduced the number of words in the interests of ease of reading and understanding. At the Lord's command Joshua orders the priests
to come out of the water onto the west bank of the Jordan, and they do
so. (Verse 11 has already told the reader that the priests had left the
river and taken their place ahead of the people.)
In Hebrew the Lord's command is given in direct discourse (see
RSV), and for many languages it will be more natural to retain the
direct discourse form.
In verse 16 <u>Covenant Box</u> translates a different Hebrew expression,
literally "ark of the testimony (or instruction)" (see RSV). The Hebrew
word "testimony" is used in wisdom literature as one of the several
words for the Torah or its specific ordinances. NEB "Ark of the Tokens"
is a meaningless phrase in English. In verse 18 the usual phrase "ark
of the covenant" (RSV) is used. Although the Hebrew does use a slightly
different term for <u>Covenant Box</u>, it is probably better in translation
to maintain the continuity of the story by using the same term that has
been used previously in the account. This is especially true for a common language translation, though for a translation at a literary level
one may want to reflect the difference in the Hebrew form.

<u>4.17-18</u>   Joshua did so, 18 and when the priests reached the
riverbank, the river began flowing once more and
flooded its banks again.

In verse 17 <u>Joshua did so</u> is literally "Joshua therefore commanded
the priests, 'Come up out of the Jordan'" (RSV). It is possible to
shorten and combine as "Joshua gave the command." One may also translate "Joshua did what the LORD had commanded him to do."

Verse 18, as indicated in the introduction to this section, is much more wordy in Hebrew than in TEV. Whereas Hebrew repeats the full phrase "the priests carrying the Covenant Box," TEV has shortened this to the priests, since the full information was given in verse 16. Reached the riverbank represents the repetitious "came up from the midst of the Jordan, and the soles of the priests' feet were lifted up on dry ground" (RSV). Here again, one may shorten by combining: "and hardly had the priests left the riverbed." For English speakers "riverbed" is not too frequently used, and so instead of "came up out of the riverbed," TEV has reached the riverbank. But one may translate "as soon as the priests got out on the other side of the riverbed" or "as soon as the priests had crossed the riverbed."

As soon as the priests reached the west bank of the Jordan, the water started flowing again and overflowed its banks as before (see 3.14-15).

TEV   4.19—5.1   RSV

19 The people crossed the Jordan on the tenth day of the first month and camped at Gilgal, east of Jericho. 20 There Joshua set up the twelve stones taken from the Jordan. 21 And he said to the people of Israel, "In the future, when your children ask you what these stones mean, 22 you will tell them about the time when Israel crossed the Jordan on dry ground. 23 Tell them that the LORD your God dried up the water of the Jordan for you until you had crossed, just as he dried up the Red Sea for us. 24 Because of this everyone on earth will know how great the LORD's power is, and you will honor the LORD your God forever."

5.1 All the Amorite kings west of the Jordan and all the Canaanite kings along the Mediterranean Sea heard that the LORD had dried up the Jordan until the people of Israel had crossed it. They became afraid and lost their courage because of the Israelites.

19 The people came up out of the Jordan on the tenth day of the first month, and they encamped in Gilgal on the east border of Jericho. 20 And those twelve stones, which they took out of the Jordan, Joshua set up in Gilgal. 21 And he said to the people of Israel, "When your children ask their fathers in time to come, 'What do these stones mean?' 22 then you shall let your children know, 'Israel passed over this Jordan on dry ground.' 23 For the LORD your God dried up the waters of the Jordan for you until you passed over, as the LORD your God did to the Red Sea, which he dried up for us until we passed over, 24 so that all the peoples of the earth may know that the hand of the LORD is mighty; that you may fear the LORD your God for ever."

5.1 When all the kings of the Amorites that were beyond the Jordan to the west, and all the kings of the Canaanites that were by the sea, heard that the LORD had dried up the waters of the Jordan for the people of Israel until they had crossed over, their heart melted, and

[55]

> there was no longer any spirit
> in them, because of the people
> of Israel.

4.19-20   The people crossed the Jordan on the tenth day
of the first month and camped at Gilgal, east of
Jericho. 20 There Joshua set up the twelve stones
taken from the Jordan.

Crossed is literally "came up out of" (RSV). Many languages will
have specialized terms for "crossing a river" or for "coming up out of
a valley onto level land." One must avoid a term which would suggest
the crossing of the river in a boat or by some other water vehicle.
For that reason the word generally used for "crossing" may not be satisfactory, and one may do better to select a term which means "cross
a valley by foot."
    The day the people crossed into Canaan is given as the tenth day
of the first month, that is, of Abib (later called Nisan). This month
began with the first new moon occurring after the modern March 11, so
the crossing occurred between March 21 and April 18, in modern terms.
(Passover falls on 14 Nisan; see Exo 12.18.) Problems related to the
months of the year are sometimes highly complex, and it may be useful
to provide a cultural note, indicating that the reference is to the
first month of the Jewish calendar year and to define it in terms of
the international (or local) calendar year.
    Gilgal is usually located about 4 kilometers east (really north-
east) of Jericho (RSV "on the east border of Jericho"). It may be useful to mark Gilgal as a "town"; if so, one would then translate "camped
near the town of Gilgal."
    The Hebrew phrase translated "the east border" by RSV probably
indicates the eastern edge of the territory controlled by Jericho.
Jericho was a walled city, and the text does not mean that the Israelites were camped right outside the city walls.
    There at Gilgal Joshua set up the twelve stones taken from the
Jordan (see 4.8). As at 4.8, so here also it is necessary to clarify
that Joshua himself was not the one who set up the twelve stones. Moreover, the indefinite passive taken from may be a problem. One may then
need to translate "There Joshua caused (or, commanded) the men to set
up the twelve stones which they had taken from the Jordan."

4.21-24   And he said to the people of Israel, "In the future,
when your children ask you what these stones mean,
22 you will tell them about the time when Israel
crossed the Jordan on dry ground. 23 Tell them that
the LORD your God dried up the water of the Jordan
for you until you had crossed, just as he dried up
the Red Sea for us. 24 Because of this everyone on
earth will know how great the LORD's power is, and
you will honor the LORD your God forever."

Verses 21-24 repeat in an expanded form the instructions contained in 4.6-7. In verse 21 the Hebrew has "When in the future your children ask their fathers," which TEV renders when your children ask you. This would apply, of course, to all succeeding generations. In verse 23 is the explicit comparison with what the Lord did at the Sea of Reeds. At the end of verse 23 the Hebrew has "just as the LORD your God dried up the Sea of Reeds for us until we crossed over." (It should be noted that TEV omits "until we crossed over" as being redundant; however, it should be included in translation.) The adult generation that departed from Egypt had died during the forty years of wandering in the wilderness, but the younger generation, of course, had survived (see 5.4-7, below).

In some languages it will be more natural to shift what these stones mean (verse 21) to direct discourse: "'What do these stones mean?'" (see RSV). This will involve a direct quotation within a direct quotation, but for many readers this will be easier to handle than an indirect quotation within a direct quotation, especially when the first indirect quotation is followed by a second indirect quotation containing a lengthy answer to the first: you will tell them...just as he dried up the Red Sea for us. So the following restructuring may be used:

"In the future, your children will ask you, 'What do these stones mean?' 22 Tell them, 'These stones are to remind us of the time when we crossed the Jordan on dry ground. 23 The LORD our God dried up the water of the Jordan River for us until we had crossed, just as he dried up the Sea of Reeds for our ancestors until they crossed.'...."

Because of this introduces the twofold result of the instruction. It does so in the form of a confession of faith: all the Gentiles will know of the Lord's mighty power (literally "the hand of the LORD is mighty"), and the Israelites will honor[6] (or be in awe of, respect, revere; see verse 14 for the same verb) him forever. In place of beginning the verse with Because of this, it may be more appropriate to translate "Teach your children these things so that...."

<u>5.1</u>   All the Amorite kings west of the Jordan and all the Canaanite kings along the Mediterranean Sea heard that the LORD had dried up the Jordan until the people of Israel had crossed it. They became afraid and lost their courage because of the Israelites.

The people of Israel crossed represents one form of the Masoretic text ("they crossed over"). Another form of the text has "we crossed over" (NAB), but the choice represented in TEV seems preferable. In the telling of this story, it was customary for later generations to identify themselves with the generation that crossed over, as it was in the telling of the exodus event. It is probably this tendency that accounts for the two variant readings.

In this verse the kings in Canaan are described as being overcome with fear: "their heart melted" (see 2.11) and "there was no spirit in them" (also in 2.11, see RSV). These two idiomatic expressions for extreme fear are perhaps best understood as synonyms; in Hebrew the use of two or more synonymous expressions serves to intensify the degree of fear. In some languages, on the other hand, the use of two or more synonymous expressions tends rather to negate (as with a double negative in English). TEV has changed the metaphors to nonfigurative language (afraid...lost their courage), but other languages will find it more expressive to seek out metaphors that come from their own culture.

Chapter 5

The Circumcision at Gilgal

2 Then the LORD told Joshua, "Make some knives out of flint and circumcise the Israelites." 3 So Joshua did as the LORD had commanded, and he circumcised the Israelites at a place called Circumcision Hill. 4-6 When the people of Israel left Egypt, all the males were already circumcised. However, during the forty years the people spent crossing the desert, none of the baby boys had been circumcised. Also, by the end of that time all the men who were of fighting age when they left Egypt had died because they had disobeyed the LORD. Just as he had sworn, they were not allowed to see the rich and fertile land that he had promised their ancestors. 7 The sons of these men had never been circumcised, and it was this new generation that Joshua circumcised.

8 After the circumcision was completed, the whole nation stayed in the camp until the wounds had healed. 9 The LORD said to Joshua, "Today I have removed from you the disgrace of being slaves in Egypt." That is why the place was named Gilgal,^{b} the name it still has.

^{b}GILGAL: *This name sounds like the Hebrew for "removed."*

2 At that time the LORD said to Joshua, "Make flint knives and circumcise the people of Israel again the second time." 3 So Joshua made flint knives, and circumcised the people of Israel at Gibeathhaaraloth.^{a} 4 And this is the reason why Joshua circumcised them: all the males of the people who came out of Egypt, all the men of war, had died on the way in the wilderness after they had come out of Egypt. 5 Though all the people who came out had been circumcised, yet all the people that were born on the way in the wilderness after they had come out of Egypt, had not been circumcised. 6 For the people of Israel walked forty years in the wilderness, till all the nation, the men of war that came forth out of Egypt, perished, because they did not hearken to the voice of the LORD; to them the LORD swore that he would not let them see the land which the LORD had sworn to their fathers to give us, a land flowing with milk and honey. 7 So it was their children, whom he raised up in their stead, that Joshua circumcised; for they were uncircumcised, because they had not been circumcised on the way. 8 When the circumcising of all the nation was done, they remained in their places in the camp till they were healed. 9 And the LORD said to Joshua, "This day I have

rolled away the reproach of Egypt
from you." And so the name of that
place is called Gilgal*b* to this
day.

*a*That is *the hill of the foreskins*

*b*From Heb *galal* to roll

This chapter provides an interlude before the conquest of Jericho.
It narrates three events: (1) the circumcision of all male Israelites
(verses 2-9); (2) the celebration of Passover (verses 10-12); and
(3) the appearance of the commander of the LORD's army (verses 13-15).
The section heading The Circumcision at Gilgal may be rendered,
"The LORD commands Joshua to circumcise the Israelite men." The reason
for the mass circumcision of all male Israelites is given in verses
6-7. The boys born during the forty years' travel through the wilderness had not been circumcised, and now Joshua is ordered to circumcise
them in preparation for the coming celebration of Passover on 14 Nisan
(see verses 10-12; Exo 12.43-39). Circumcision is the cutting off of
the foreskin from the penis. It was the sign of the covenant that God
made with Abraham (Gen 17.9-14).

5.2   Then the LORD told Joshua, "Make some knives out
           of flint and circumcise the Israelites."

It is in light of the historical circumstances that we must understand the wording of the Lord's order to circumcise the Israelites
"again the second time" (RSV). Obviously it does not mean to circumcise
the same individuals again (which would be impossible), but to perform
the rite once again. NEB translates "make Israel a circumcised people
again." TEV gives the meaning without trying to represent "again the
second time," since this would be apt to mislead the reader.[7] The
problem with TEV restructuring is that information is deleted from
the text, though with good reason. The Living Bible (LB) moves in the
right direction by including this information as a parenthetical statement: "(It was the second time in Israel's history that this was done)."
One may restructure entirely: "I commanded all the Israelite men to be
circumcised before they left Egypt. Now make some knives out of flint
and circumcise the Israelites who were born since you left Egypt."
Flint is a quartz, noted for its hardness.[8]

5.3   So Joshua did as the LORD had commanded, and he
           circumcised the Israelites at a place called Circum-
           cision Hill.

Did as the LORD had commanded, and he may be omitted from translation on the grounds that the information is clearly implicit. One may
render "So Joshua circumcised...." Although in verse 2 the command is
to Joshua (Make some knives) and in the present verse it is stated

that Joshua <u>circumcised the Israelites</u>, it is difficult to imagine
that he alone <u>did these actions</u>. Rather one must assume that he was
the responsible person, given the command by God to see that it was
done. If the language has a causative form, then it is possible to
render "Cause (some men) to make some knives (of flint) and cause them
to circumcise the Israelites" or "...and cause the Israelites to be
circumcised." Otherwise one may render

"Command some men to make knives out of flint and circumcise those Israelites who have not yet been circumcised."
3 So Joshua obeyed the LORD's command, and the place where
the Israelites were circumcised is now called Circumcision
Hill.

<u>A place called Circumcision Hill</u> obviously means that the place
got its name from this event, not that it was called that before the
mass circumcision of the Israelites. RSV, NEB, NAB transliterate the
Hebrew name; BJ, JB, TOB translate "the Hill of the Foreskins." In
order to indicate that this place was not previously called <u>Circumci-
sion Hill</u>, one may translate "a place which since that time <u>has been</u>
<u>called Circumcision Hill</u>."

<u>5.4-6</u>   When the people of Israel left Egypt, all the males
              were already circumcised. However, during the forty
              years the people spent crossing the desert, none of
              the baby boys had been circumcised. Also, by the end
              of that time all the men who were of fighting age
              when they left Egypt had died because they had dis-
              obeyed the LORD. Just as he had sworn, they were not
              allowed to see the rich and fertile land that he had
              promised their ancestors.

The explanation of why the rite of circumcision was necessary is
given in verses 4-7; TEV has endeavored to rearrange the material in
verses 4-6 for ease of understanding. The Hebrew expression "the men
of war" (RSV) in verses 4,6 means males twenty years and older who were
eligible for military duty. All those male adults had died during the
forty years spent in going from Egypt to Canaan, and the new male generation now had to be circumcised.

Although TEV restructuring of verses 4-6 does make the understanding of the text somewhat easier, certain difficulties still exist. For
example, the first sentence begins with a temporal clause that describes
an event which took place subsequent to the action of the main clause.
This problem is easily solved by inverting the two clauses: "All the
Israelite men and boys were circumcised before the people of Israel
left Egypt." The next sentence can then begin "However, they did not
circumcise any of the baby boys who were born during the forty years
that the people spent crossing the desert."

The next sentence is highly complex, and some restructuring may
be necessary. For example,

Also, by the end of that time all the men who were of fighting age when they left Egypt had died. They had disobeyed the
LORD, and the LORD had sworn that he would not let them see
the rich and fertile land that he had promised their ancestors.

Or, one may shift to direct discourse: "They had not obeyed the LORD, and so the LORD had sworn, 'You will not see the rich and fertile land that I promised your ancestors.'"

Just as he had sworn: Numbers 14.28-35 reports the Lord's vow not to allow any male Israelite over twenty years of age to enter Canaan; all of them except Caleb and Joshua would die during the wanderings in the wilderness, and only their children would enter the promised land.

The rich and fertile land (RSV "a land flowing with milk and honey") is a set phrase to describe Canaan (see Exo 3.8; Num 14.8) as opposed to the wilderness where the Israelites had wandered for forty years. A number of translations maintain the Hebraism. This may be an effective device in cultures where the idiom has already become a part of the active vocabulary of the majority of speakers. However, this would certainly not be the case for many languages. In America, for example, church people and people who know certain biblical metaphors through English literature might understand the meaning, but it would otherwise be unclear for the average reader. On the other hand, a number of languages will have their own metaphors which will very effectively carry the meaning of the biblical expression.

He had promised their ancestors represents the Hebrew "The LORD had promised their ancestors (fathers) to give to us." Here "us" refers to the generation of the writer of the account and the people of his time, who live many years after these historic events. He sees Israel in his own time as the recipients of God's promise to the ancestors. In order to include the meaning of "us" of the Hebrew text, one may translate

The LORD had promised our ancestors that he would give this land to them, and to us, their descendants. But these men who left Egypt did not obey the LORD, and so the LORD said to them, "You will never live in the land which I promised your ancestors...."

5.7   The sons of these men had never been circumcised, and it was this new generation that Joshua circumcised.

It is important that these men not be taken as a reference back to ancestors of the previous verse, as may be suggested by TEV restructuring. In order to ease the situation, one may render "these men who had disobeyed the LORD" or "these men whom the LORD had brought out of Egypt."

This new generation represents the Hebrew "those whom he (the LORD) raised up in their place." A literal rendering of the text, such as RSV, may suggest that the focus is upon the action of the Lord in raising up a new generation. Actually the real focus is upon the new generation which now takes the place of the previous one, "In the meantime the sons had taken the place of their fathers."

The meaning of Joshua circumcised is "(whom) Joshua caused (or, commanded) to be circumcised." Direct discourse is also possible: "It was this generation to whom Joshua said, 'Get yourselves circumcised.'"

[62]

<u>5.8</u>   After the circumcision was completed, the whole
          nation stayed in the camp until the wounds had healed.

<u>After the circumcision was completed</u> may be translated "After all
the men had been circumcised." It may be necessary to translate "After
Joshua had circumcised all the men" or "...had caused (commanded) all
the men to be circumcised."
<u>The whole nation</u> is a reference to the men of Israel, as the He-
brew form of the verb <u>stayed</u> (masculine plural) clarifies. The verse
may then be rendered, "After all the men of Israel had been circumcised, they stayed in the camp until their wounds had healed."

<u>5.9</u>   The LORD said to Joshua, "Today I have removed from you
          the disgrace of being slaves in Egypt." That is why the
          place was named Gilgal,^{b} the name it still has.

          ^{b}GILGAL: *This name sounds like the Hebrew for "removed."*

The Lord says to Joshua that he has, by this act of mass circumcision, <u>removed from you the disgrace of being slaves in Egypt</u> (RSV
"rolled away the reproach of Egypt from you"). It was not the fact that
these Israelites were now circumcised; the Egyptians themselves prac-
ticed circumcision. It was their slavery which had been the "reproach
of Egypt." But BJ, JB suppose that "the reproach" was in being uncircumcised; the writer of this statement apparently thought that the
Egyptians did not practice circumcision. This is possible and may perhaps be the best explanation of the phrase.
It may be useful to invert the order of the information flow in
the Lord's words to Joshua. For example, "It was a disgrace for my
people to be slaves in Egypt. But today I have removed this disgrace
from you." Or, "It was a disgraceful thing for my people to be slaves
in Egypt...."
The place-name <u>Gilgal</u> is similar in sound to the Hebrew verb
translated <u>removed</u>, which is the basis for the remark <u>That is why the</u>
<u>place was named Gilgal</u>. This clause may become an active: "That is why
the people (of Israel) named that place Gilgal." <u>The name it still has</u>
may be restructured as "And that is what people still call it today"
or "And people still call it Gilgal today."
It is absolutely imperative that a footnote follow <u>Gilgal</u>; otherwise the reader will have no clue as to the relation between the Lord's
words to Joshua and the explanation given by the author of the text.
One proposal for a note is "Gilgal in Hebrew sounds like 'remove';
literally: 'roll away.'"

TEV	5.10-12	RSV
10 While the Israelites were camping at Gilgal on the plain near Jericho, they observed Pass-over on the evening of the		10 While the people of Israel were encamped in Gilgal they kept the passover on the fourteenth day of the month at evening in the

[63]

forteenth day of the month. 11 The
next day was the first time they
ate food grown in Canaan: roasted
grain and bread made without
yeast. 12 The manna stopped falling then, and the Israelites no
longer had any. From that time on
they ate food grown in Canaan.

plains of Jericho. 11 And on the
morrow after the passover, on
that very day, they ate of the
produce of the land, unleavened
cakes and parched grain. 12 And
the manna ceased on the morrow,
when they ate of the produce of
the land; and the people of
Israel had manna no more, but
ate of the fruit of the land of
Canaan that year.

5.10   While the Israelites were camping at Gilgal on
the plain near Jericho, they observed Passover on the
evening of the fourteenth day of the month.

On the evening of 14 Nisan (or Abib; see 4.19) the Israelites
celebrated the Passover for the first time in Canaan. This festival
commemorated their deliverance from slavery in Egypt (see Exo 12.1-14).
The Jewish day began at sunset, and so the time notice, on the
evening, is important. In some cultures there is a distinction between
"on the evening of the fourteenth day" (meaning "the evening before
the fourteenth day") and "the fourteenth day evening" (meaning "the
evening of the fourteenth day," as we would understand it in English).
If such a distinction does exist in the receptor language, it should
be taken into consideration in the translation. The Festival of Unleavened Bread lasted a week (15-22 Nisan; see Exo 12.14-20); here the
text does not explicitly say that the Israelites also celebrated this
festival, but the mention of unleavened bread implies it (verse 11).

5.11   The next day was the first time they ate food grown
in Canaan: roasted grain and bread made without yeast.

This was the first time they ate food grown in Canaan; the roasted
grain they ate was barley. And on that same day, the first day they ate
food grown in Canaan, the manna stopped falling (see verse 12). Some
languages may distinguish between unprepared food and prepared food.
It is obvious that food grown in Canaan means here the grain, which the
Israelites made into bread. It may be necessary in translation to indicate more precisely the series of events:
    The next day they gathered grain (barley) from the grain
    fields in Canaan. They roasted part of the grain and made
    bread without yeast from part of it. This was the first
    time they had eaten food from any of the crops grown in
    Canaan.
Bread made without yeast is a plural form in Hebrew (RSV "unleavened cakes"); the Hebrew is still preserved in English as "matzo" or
"matzoth."

5.12   The manna stopped falling then, and the Israelites
         no longer had any. From that time on they ate food
         grown in Canaan.

Then is literally "on the morrow" (RSV); it is not the day after
the "on the morrow after the passover" of verse 11, but is the same
day, that is, the day after the Passover Day in verse 10. So TEV has
then; it could better be expressed by "that same day."
     For a description of manna see Exodus 16.14,31; the Israelites
had eaten it for forty years (Exo 16.35). The manna stopped falling
then may need to be restructured so as not to suggest that manna had
been constantly falling from the skies. One may translate "From that
day on no more manna fell...." If this shift is made, then for stylistic reasons From that time on of the last sentence may be changed to
"After that...."

              TEV   5.13-15   RSV

         Joshua and the Man
            with a Sword

     13 While Joshua was near   13 When Joshua was by Jericho,
Jericho, he suddenly saw a man   he lifted up his eyes and looked,
standing in front of him, holding   and behold, a man stood before
a sword. Joshua went up to him   him with his drawn sword in his
and asked, "Are you one of our   hand; and Joshua went to him and
soldiers, or an enemy?"   said to him, "Are you for us, or
     14 "Neither," the man an-   for our adversaries?" 14 And he
swered. "I am here as the com-   said, "No; but as commander of
mander of the LORD's army."   the army of the LORD I have now
     Joshua threw himself on the   come." And Joshua fell on his
ground in worship and said, "I   face to the earth, and worshiped,
am your servant, sir. What do you   and said to him, "What does my
want me to do?"   lord bid his servant?" 15 And
     15 And the commander of the   the commander of the LORD's army
LORD's army told him, "Take your   said to Joshua, "Put off your
sandals off; you are standing on   shoes from your feet; for the
holy ground." And Joshua did as   place where you stand is holy."
he was told.   And Joshua did so.

     The section heading Joshua and the Man with a Sword may be ren-
dered "The LORD sends a mighty helper" or "Joshua talks with the commander of the LORD's army." It is possible also to translate "The commander of the LORD's army appears to Joshua."
     The report of Joshua's encounter with what is obviously a heavenly
messenger is brief, and in the narrative itself no obvious purpose is
given. The only thing that is revealed is that the spot on which the
heavenly messenger stands is holy ground. In the context in which this
event is placed, however, it seems that its purpose is to assure Joshua
that the Lord is with him, and the heavenly army will help him conquer
Jericho and the land of Canaan. So BJ, JB connect this incident with

                         [65]

what follows, as a prelude to the actual conquest of Jericho. This may
be the best way to handle this short narrative.

5.13   While Joshua was near Jericho, he suddenly saw
    a man standing in front of him, holding a sword.
    Joshua went up to him and asked, "Are you one of
    our soldiers, or an enemy?"

Near Jericho represents the Hebrew "in Jericho," which is also
the translation of the Septuagint.[9] The Latin Vulgate has "in the field
of the city of Jericho," and the Syriac has "in the plain of Jericho."
Most modern translations have "near" or "by," since the Hebrew preposition "in" may also have this meaning. But even if one follows the rendering of most modern translations, this event still seems to interrupt
the flow of the narrative. In order to make a proper transition, it may
be necessary to translate "One day while Joshua and the people of Israel
were still camped near Jericho, Joshua suddenly saw...."
  The oral reading of this verse may present a difficulty. That is,
one may hear "...a man standing in front of him. Holding a sword, Joshua
went up to him and asked...." To avoid this ambiguity one may translate
"Holding a sword" as either a separate sentence ("The man was holding
a sword") or a coordinate clause ("..., and he was holding a sword").
  The heavenly messenger is called a man, as is the case in other
angelic visitations in the Old Testament. Joshua naturally asks him
on whose side he is. The question may be phrased succinctly: "Friend
or foe?"

5.14   "Neither," the man answered. "I am here as the
    commander of the LORD's army."
    Joshua threw himself on the ground in worship and
    said, "I am your servant, sir. What do you want me to
    do?"

Neither is literally "No" (RSV), an answer which is difficult to
understand; does the "No" apply to the first part or to the second
part of Joshua's question?[10] It hardly seems possible that the meaning
is "I'm neither a friend nor a foe," as NAB, TEV interpret it.[11] It is
inconceivable that the commander of the LORD's army should have been
on the side of Israel's adversaries. But however difficult the answer
Neither may be, it is the clear meaning of the Hebrew text and should
be followed in translation. The Septuagint and some Hebrew manuscripts
have "to him," which sounds like "no" in Hebrew. However, this probably represents an attempt on the part of some scribes to resolve this
difficulty.
  I am here as the commander of the LORD's army may perhaps be rendered more forcefully as two sentences: "I am the commander of the
LORD's army. And now I am here." The noun commander may be shifted to
a verb phrase: "I am the one who commands" or "I command."
  The Hebrew word for army is the same word which in the plural
form is sometimes used with the divine name in the construction
"Yahweh of armies" (the traditional translation in English being "the
LORD of hosts").

Joshua threw himself on the ground in worship is more literally
rendered as "Joshua fell down before him, face to the ground." The
phrase in worship interprets for English readers the meaning of
Joshua's actions. In many cultures this act of prostrating himself on
the ground would be easily understood, but for many modern readers of
the western world its significance may be lost without making explicit
the meaning of the action. But it may be that in worship implies too
much. There are places in the Old Testament where the angel of the
Lord is quickly identified as the Lord himself. But up to this point
in the passage the person is not even explicitly referred to as an
angel, but only as a man (verse 13). And it may be that even in verse
15 this person stands only as the representative of the Lord and not
as the Lord himself. A more accurate rendering may therefore be "in
awe," or "in reverence," or "with great respect." One may translate
"Joshua threw himself face down on the ground in order to show his
respect for the man. Then he said...."

I am your servant may be translated "I am here to serve you" or
"I will do whatever you command." The question What do you want me to
do? may be altered to a statement, "Tell me what you want me to do" or
"Give a command, and I will obey it."

5.15   And the commander of the LORD's army told him,
            "Take your sandals off; you are standing on holy
            ground." And Joshua did as he was told.

In some languages it may be preferable not to repeat the full
title the commander of the LORD's army. One may translate either "he"
or "the man." If either of these is used of the commander of the Lord's
army, then one may want to mention Joshua by name: "He said to Joshua."

Take your sandals off; you are standing on holy ground are exactly
the same instructions as those given by the Lord to Moses at the burning bush (Exo 3.5). The ground on which Joshua is standing is holy because of the presence of the commander of the Lord's army. The order
of the words may need to be inverted in translation: "You are standing
on holy ground. So take off your sandals." The phrase holy ground may
not be understood; or worse, it may be misunderstood as "ground that is
taboo," or in a negative sense as "ground that defiles people who touch
it." One may even be compelled to dispense with the "ground" imagery
and translate "You are standing in the presence of the LORD." If the
imagery is maintained one may translate "You are standing on ground
where the LORD has chosen to be worshiped."

Chapter 6

The Fall of Jericho

1 The gates of Jericho were kept shut and guarded to keep the Israelites out. No one could enter or leave the city. 2 The LORD said to Joshua, "I am putting into your hands Jericho, with its king and all its brave soldiers. 3 You and your soldiers are to march around the city once a day for six days. 4 Seven priests, each carrying a trumpet, are to go in front of the Covenant Box. On the seventh day you and your soldiers are to march around the city seven times while the priests blow the trumpets. 5 Then they are to sound one long note. As soon as you hear it, all the men are to give a loud shout, and the city walls will collapse. Then the whole army will go straight into the city."

6 Joshua called the priests and told them, "Take the Covenant Box, and seven of you go in front of it, carrying trumpets." 7 Then he ordered his men to start marching around the city, with an advance guard going on ahead of the LORD's Covenant Box.

1 Now Jericho was shut up from within and from without because of the people of Israel; none went out, and none came in. 2 And the LORD said to Joshua, "See, I have given into your hand Jericho, with its king and mighty men of valor. 3 You shall march around the city, all the men of war going around the city once. Thus shall you do for six days. 4 And seven priests shall bear seven trumpets of rams' horns before the ark; and on the seventh day you shall march around the city seven times, the priests blowing the trumpets. 5 And when they make a long blast with the ram's horn, as soon as you hear the sound of the trumpet, then all the people shall shout with a great shout; and the wall of the city will fall down flat, and the people shall go up every man straight before him." 6 So Joshua the son of Nun called the priests and said to them, "Take up the ark of the covenant, and let seven priests bear seven trumpets of rams' horns before the ark of the LORD." 7 And he said to the people, "Go forward; march around the city, and let the armed men pass on before the ark of the LORD."

The story of the fall of Jericho to the Israelites emphasizes that it was not military might that defeated the enemy but the Lord's power; he is in absolute control of the events, and as long as his people follow his commands they will prosper and succeed.

The section heading <u>The Fall of Jericho</u> may be rendered, "The walls of Jericho fall down" or "The people of Israel capture the city of Jericho."

In verses 1-7 the Lord gives instructions to Joshua about the capture of Jericho; it is the Lord's doing (verse 2), and the city walls will fall without the use of human force (verses 3-5). Joshua tells the Lord's instructions to the priests (verse 6) and to the people (verse 7), and all is ready. Jericho is in a state of siege (verse 1), which may indicate that considerable time has passed since the Israelites encamped at Gilgal.

6.1   The gates of Jericho were kept shut and guarded to keep the Israelites out. No one could enter or leave the city.

The city is described as being completely closed to all outgoing or incoming traffic. Were kept shut and guarded translates two verbal participles, one active and the other passive; a literal rendering would be "had shut and was shut." This suggests that a siege has been going on for some time as the narrative begins. It may be necessary to indicate who shut and guarded the gates of Jericho. For example, "The men of Jericho kept the city gates shut and guarded so that the Israelites could not get in."

Similarly the second sentence may be rendered, "The men would not let anyone enter or leave the city." A literal rendering of the text such as RSV ("none went out, and none came in"), if interpreted according to strict rules of English grammar, would mean "none of the people of Israel went out or came in." But the reference is to the people of the city, as NEB also makes explicit: "No one went out, no one came in."

6.2   The LORD said to Joshua, "I am putting into your hands Jericho, with its king and all its brave soldiers.

Beginning with verse 2 the Lord gives Joshua his instructions, with the assurance that he, God, is handing the city of Jericho and all its inhabitants into the power of Joshua. The victory will be the Lord's doing; the Israelites are not to mount a military campaign against the city but are to engage in a religious procession around the city. The instructions are explicit: once a day, for six consecutive days, the Israelite army is to march around the city; seven priests, followed by the Covenant Box, will lead the procession. Each priest is to carry a trumpet, an instrument made of a ram's horn. It seems quite clear in verse 4 that only on the seventh day were the priests to blow the trumpets; in contrast, the single march around the city on each of the six preceding days was to be made in silence. But in the execution of the plan (verses 8-14) the trumpets are blown every time the Israelites march around the city.

A transitional marker may be required at the beginning of this verse; Luther Rev has "But"; others may prefer "Then." It is also possible to translate "But one day" or "Then one day."

Putting into your hands translates the Hebrew idiom "given into your hand" (RSV). In some languages it may be necessary either to utilize a known idiom or else to translate without the use of an idiomatic expression. Moreover, it may be useful, if not obligatory, to use two verbs in the place of this one. For example, "I will let you conquer the city of Jericho. You will defeat its king and all its brave soldiers." Or "I am placing in your power the city of Jericho with its king and all its men of war." It is legitimate to translate brave soldiers (RSV "men of valor") as "men of war," since the Hebrew expression focuses more upon their strength than upon their bravery. A literal rendering of the Hebrew would be more nearly "strong men of war."

In Hebrew the conjunction and is lacking in the phrase with its king and all its brave soldiers. For this reason NEB assumes that all its brave soldiers is not an original part of the Hebrew text, and drops it in translation. JB, on the other hand, transfers it into verse 3, as subject of the verb rendered march around by TEV. There is no textual evidence for its omission, and the HOTTP indicates that it should be retained in its present position. They assume that the elliptical (that is, abbreviated) form of the Hebrew actually means "although they are mighty warriors."

6.3 You and your soldiers are to march around the city once a day for six days.

You and your soldiers are to march around translates a plural form of the Hebrew verb "march around" (RSV "You shall march around"). TEV has translated this way in order to indicate that the form of the verb is plural and that the reference is to Joshua and his men. But even for languages which distinguish between the singular and plural forms of "you," it still may be helpful to mark explicitly the participants: "You with your battle-ready men."

The verb march around is here used of a religious or cultic procession, which would have been formal and solemn, but which would not have required strict marching in step such as in a modern day parade or military procession. One may wish to translate "I command you and your fighting men to go in procession around...."

For six days may require a separate statement: "Do this for six days," or "...for six consecutive days," or "...for six days in a row."

6.4 Seven priests, each carrying a trumpet, are to go in front of the Covenant Box. On the seventh day you and your soldiers are to march around the city seven times while the priests blow the trumpets.

The use of the appositional each carrying a trumpet may be avoided if the first sentence of this verse is either broken into two sentences or else made into two coordinate clauses joined by "and." For example, "Seven priests are to go in front of the Covenant Box. Each one of them is to carry a trumpet." Or "Seven priests are to go in front of the Covenant Box, and each of them is to carry a trumpet." It may even be advisable to translate "Seven priests are to go with you each time you

march around the city. Each one of them is to carry a trumpet, and
they are to go immediately in front of the Covenant Box."
  On the seventh day (verses 4b-5) the march is to be made seven
times; the priests are to blow the trumpets; and at the end of the
seventh march, one long note is to be sounded, at which time the soldiers are to give a loud shout, and Jericho's walls will collapse.
  The reader may get a false assumption from the statement that
your soldiers are to march around the city seven times while the priests
blow the trumpets. That is, it is possible to conclude that only Joshua
and the soldiers are to march around the city, while the priests stand
aside, blowing the trumpets. To avoid this misunderstanding, one may
translate "On the seventh day all of you are to march around the city
seven times while the priests blow the trumpets." Or "On the seventh
day you, your soldiers, and the priests are to march around the city
seven times. While all of you are marching around the city, the priests
are to blow the trumpets."
  Since in the last sentence the text mentions soldiers before
priests, the reader may automatically assume that in the order of the
march the soldiers went ahead of the priests. But this is not the case;
only an advance guard marched ahead of the priests (verse 7). The
order of this procession would have been: an advance guard of soldiers,
the priests, the Covenant Box, and then the rest of the soldiers. This
is basically a religious procession, though the ancient Israelites would
hardly have distinguished between a religious and a military procession.
To help the reader understand the order of the procession, one may
translate "On the seventh day all of you are to march around the city
seven times. The priests will march in front of the Covenant Box and
blow the trumpets, and you will march behind the Covenant Box." The
information regarding the advance guard can then be delayed until verse
7, where it is given in the Hebrew text.

6.5   Then they are to sound one long note. As soon as
          you hear it, all the men are to give a loud shout,
          and the city walls will collapse. Then the whole
          army will go straight into the city."

  Depending upon the restructuring of the last sentence in verse 4,
they may need to be rendered "the priests." In fact the first sentence
of this verse may need to be made more explicit: "When everyone has
marched around the city seven times, the priests are to sound one long
note on their trumpets."
  As soon as you hear it, all the men are... may need to be translated "As soon as you and the men hear it, all of them are..." or
"...all of you are...."
  It may be more effective to indicate the fall of the city walls
by a new sentence: "The city walls will collapse, and the whole army
will go straight into the city." The whole army is the same group as
all the men, and some languages may require clear identification. The
Hebrew is something like RSV, "and the people shall go up every man
straight before him," which seems to focus more upon the individuals
within the groups than upon the group acting together. Accordingly the

[71]

text may be translated, "Then the walls will collapse, and every man can go up into the city from the place where he happens to be standing."

6.6   Joshua called the priests and told them, "Take the Covenant Box, and seven of you go in front of it, carrying trumpets."

In this verse Joshua delivers the Lord's instructions to the priests, and in the following verse to the Israelite soldiers. Joshua is literally "Joshua son of Nun," but in English, as in many other languages, it is unnatural to repeat the qualifying phrase every time it occurs in the Hebrew.

Called may better be rendered "called together" or "assembled."
The command for the priests to take the Covenant Box is qualified by the second command for seven of them to go in front of it, carrying trumpets. One may therefore need to render "Some of you are to march along carrying the Covenant Box, and seven others are to go in front of it, carrying trumpets." Or the order of the command may be inverted: "Seven of you are to carry trumpets and march in front of the Covenant Box. The rest of you are to carry the Covenant Box and march behind the priests who are carrying trumpets."

6.7   Then he ordered his men to start marching around the city, with an advance guard going on ahead of the LORD's Covenant Box.

In addition to the instructions to the priests, Joshua orders an advance guard to march in front of the Covenant Box. This group of "armed men" (RSV) is described in Hebrew by the same verb that in 4.13 is used of the forty thousand men from the two and one-half eastern tribes who crossed the Jordan ahead of the other Israelites. So NEB takes the Hebrew here to refer to those men and translates accordingly. JB follows the same exegesis as TEV and refers to a "vanguard" which goes before the Covenant Box, and to a "rearguard" which marches behind the Covenant Box. Others prefer to translate "The most experienced fighters will go before the Covenant Box as an advance guard." RSV makes it appear that all "the armed men" went ahead of the Covenant Box.

It may be best to render Joshua's orders to his men in direct discourse, as was done with the instructions to the priests in the previous verse. For example, "Then Joshua said to his men, 'Start marching around the city. Some of you are to form an advance guard and march in front of the LORD's Covenant Box.'" Or, in order to clarify the relationship between the advance guard and the priests carrying trumpets, one may translate "...ahead of the seven priests who march in front of the Covenant Box and carry trumpets."

8-9 So, just as Joshua had ordered, an advance guard started out ahead of the priests who were blowing trumpets; behind these came the priests who were carrying the Covenant Box, followed by a rear guard. All this time the trumpets were sounding. 10 But Joshua had ordered his men not to shout, not to say a word until he gave the order. 11 So he had this group of men take the LORD's Covenant Box around the city one time. Then they came back to camp and spent the night there.

12-13 Joshua got up early the next morning, and for the second time the priests and soldiers marched around the city in the same order as the day before: first, the advance guard; next, the seven priests blowing the seven trumpets; then, the priests carrying the LORD's Covenant Box; and finally, the rear guard. All this time the trumpets were sounding. 14 On this second day they again marched around the city one time and then returned to camp. They did this for six days.

8 And as Joshua had commanded the people, the seven priests bearing the seven trumpets of rams' horns before the LORD went forward, blowing the trumpets, with the ark of the covenant of the LORD following them. 9 And the armed men went before the priests who blew the trumpets, and the rear guard came after the ark, while the trumpets blew continually. 10 But Joshua commanded the people, "You shall not shout or let your voice be heard, neither shall any word go out of your mouth, until the day I bid you shout; then you shall shout." 11 So he caused the ark of the LORD to compass the city, going about it once; and they came into the camp, and spent the night in the camp.

12 Then Joshua rose early in the morning, and the priests took up the ark of the LORD. 13 And the seven priests bearing the seven trumpets of rams' horns before the ark of the LORD passed on, blowing the trumpets continually; and the armed men went before them, and the rear guard came after the ark of the LORD, while the trumpets blew continually. 14 And the second day they marched around the city once, and returned into the camp. So they did for six days.

According to verses 8-14, the routine is followed for six days; once each day, in the prescribed order, the Israelites march around Jericho. The order of the procession seems fairly clear: the advance guard went first, followed by the seven priests who were blowing trumpets; next were the priests who were carrying the Covenant Box, and at the end of the procession came the rear guard.

6.8-9   So, just as Joshua had ordered, an advance guard started out ahead of the priests who were blowing trumpets; behind these came the priests who were carrying the Covenant Box, followed by a rear guard. All this time the trumpets were sounding.

In verse 8 TEV as Joshua had ordered translates the Masoretic text (so most translations); some Hebrew manuscripts have "when Joshua ordered," which seems to be the text translated by Soggin, "And as Joshua was addressing the people." The Hebrew text in verse 8 has "before the LORD" and then "the ark of the covenant of the LORD following" (see RSV); these appear to say the same thing and are combined into one statement by TEV, since "before the LORD" is obviously a way of saying "ahead of the Covenant Box."

So, just as Joshua had ordered may be translated as a separate sentence: "Everyone obeyed Joshua's commands" or "Everyone did as Joshua had ordered." Since a number of groups are involved in the procession, it may promote clarity to describe the actions of each group by a separate sentence:

A select group of fighting men went first. They were followed by the seven priests who constantly blew the trumpets. The priests who carried the Covenant Box came next. A second group of fighting men marched behind the Covenant Box.

Contrary to what is implicit in verse 4a, here in verse 9 the priests keep blowing the trumpets during the whole march around the city; the soldiers, however, are emphatically told not to make a sound (verse 10).

6.10   But Joshua had ordered his men not to shout, not to say a word until he gave the order.

A shift may be made to indirect discourse: "But Joshua had told his men, 'Do not shout or say a word until I give the order.'" The two expressions not to shout, not to say a word of TEV represent a combining and shortening of the Hebrew "not shout or let your voice be heard, neither shall any word go out of your mouth" (RSV). Further combining is possible: "But Joshua had told his men, 'Do not say a word until I give the order for you to shout.'"

6.11   So he had this group of men take the LORD's Covenant Box around the city one time. Then they came back to camp and spent the night there.

The Hebrew of verse 11 begins literally "And he caused 'the ark of the LORD' to go around the city"; at Joshua's order the procession begins, and the most important part of the procession is the LORD's Covenant Box, which symbolizes the presence of the Lord with his people. It is he who gives victory to the Israelites. The Hebrew is repetitious, as can be seen from RSV ("and they came into the camp, and spent the night in the camp"). In TEV, NEB, JB the adverb there substitutes for "in the camp" of the Hebrew text (see RSV, end of verse 11). The march accomplished, the Israelites return to camp, where they spent the night.

Although the Lord's Covenant Box is in focus in the first sentence of this verse, it will be obligatory in most languages (as in English) to indicate how the Covenant Box went around the city. Implied in the verse is an agent or agents who see to it that Joshua's command to carry the Covenant Box around the city is obeyed. This is the basis for TEV So he had this group of men take the LORD's Covenant Box around the city one time. Without the specific mention of the persons who transported the Lord's Covenant Box, it is possible that the translation may sound somewhat ridiculous: "At Joshua's command, the ark of Yahweh went around the town and made the circuit once" (JB). Moreover, in the second half of the verse the pronoun they is without clear antecedent, unless the people who carried the Covenant Box are mentioned in the first half of the verse. Note, for example, the rendering of the verse in RSV.

6.12-13   Joshua got up early the next morning, and for
            the second time the priests and soldiers marched
            around the city in the same order as the day before:
            first, the advance guard; next, the seven priests
            blowing the seven trumpets; then, the priests carry-
            ing the LORD's Covenant Box; and finally, the rear
            guard. All this time the trumpets were sounding.

TEV has attempted to combine these two verses, but the result is not very satisfactory. For example, the reader searches in vain for the relation between Joshua's getting up early the next morning and the marching of the priests and the soldiers around the city for a second time. If the purpose of Joshua's getting up early the next morning is made explicit in translation, then it is possible to retain the verse sequence without placing together verses 12-13. For example:
Early the next morning Joshua got up and gave the same com-
mand to the priests and to his men. So the priests who had
been commanded to carry the Covenant Box placed it upon their
shoulders. 13 Then they all marched around the city in the
same order as the day before: first, the advance guard; next,
the seven priests who blew the trumpets all the time that
they were marching; then, the priests who carried the LORD's
Covenant Box; and finally, the rear guard.

6.14   On this second day they again marched around the
         city one time and then returned to camp. They did
         this for six days.

The same order of march is followed by the Israelites for the next five days; the same groups maintain the same order in line as had been done the first day. In verses 12-13 TEV adds and for the second time, which makes On this second day they again marched unnecessarily repetitious. But the proposed restructuring of verses 12-13 may help to alleviate this difficulty. Moreover, the first sentence of this verse may be rendered, "They marched around the city on this second day, just as they had done on the first day. Then they returned to camp." On the assumption that it is the march around the city that is in focus, some translators choose to delete and then returned to camp

[75]

from their rendering. This information would remain implicit, since the reader would assume that the Israelites did return to camp after going around the city, and the omission of it from translation may tend to bring into sharper focus the march around the city.

The final statement They did this for six days includes, of course, the first day's march (verses 8-11). It may be helpful to indicate that They includes "Joshua's men and the priests."

By adding "including the first day" or "counting the first day" after for six days, any problem of misunderstanding is immediately removed.

TEV	6.15-21	RSV

15 On the seventh day they got up at daybreak and marched seven times around the city in the same way—this was the only day that they marched around it seven times. 16 The seventh time around, when the priests were about to sound the trumpets, Joshua ordered his men to shout, and he said, "The LORD has given you the city! 17 The city and everything in it must be totally destroyed as an offering to the LORD. Only the prostitute Rahab and her household will be spared, because she hid our spies. 18 But you are not to take anything that is to be destroyed; if you do, you will bring trouble and destruction on the Israelite camp. 19 Everything made of silver, gold, bronze, or iron is set apart for the LORD. It is to be put in the LORD's treasury."

20 So the priests blew the trumpets. As soon as the men heard it, they gave a loud shout, and the walls collapsed. Then all the army went straight up the hill into the city and captured it. 21 With their swords they killed everyone in the city, men and women, young and old. They also killed the cattle, sheep, and donkeys.

15 On the seventh day they rose early at the dawn of day, and marched around the city in the same manner seven times: it was only on that day that they marched around the city seven times. 16 And at the seventh time, when the priests had blown the trumpets, Joshua said to the people, "Shout; for the LORD has given you the city. 17 And the city and all that is within it shall be devoted to the LORD for destruction; only Rahab the harlot and all who are with her in her house shall live, because she hid the messengers that we sent. 18 But you, keep yourselves from the things devoted to destruction, lest when you have devoted them you take any of the devoted things and make the camp of Israel a thing for destruction, and bring trouble upon it. 19 But all silver and gold, and vessels of bronze and iron, are sacred to the LORD; they shall go into the treasury of the LORD." 20 So the people shouted, and the trumpets were blown. As soon as the people heard the sound of the trumpet, the people raised a great shout, and the wall fell down flat, so that the people went up into the city, every man straight before him, and they took the city. 21 Then they utterly destroyed all in the city, both men and women,

> young and old, oxen, sheep, and
> asses, with the edge of the sword.

On the seventh day, at the seventh march around the city, Jericho's walls fell and the Israelites swarmed into the city. They slaughtered all living beings, human and animal alike, with the exception of
Rahab and her family. From the way in which the matter is described,
it would appear that only at the seventh march around did the priests
blow their trumpets (verses 16,20). It was then that the Israelites
shouted for the first time, and at once the city's walls fell.

6.15   On the seventh day they got up at daybreak and
            marched seven times around the city in the same way—
            this was the only day that they marched around it
            seven times.

It is specified that everyone rose at daybreak of the seventh day
for the day's activities (as in verse 12; see also 3.1); that day they
marched around Jericho seven times. Although TEV has once again considerably shortened the text from that of the Hebrew (see RSV), it is possible to make it even shorter. The verse may be translated, "On the
seventh day they got up at daybreak and marched around the city in the
same way. Only on this day they marched around it seven times."
In the same way translates the Hebrew "according to this manner
(or, rule)"; they followed the pattern described in verses 8-9.

6.16   The seventh time around, when the priests were about
            to sound the trumpets, Joshua ordered his men to shout,
            and he said, "The LORD has given you the city!

Because of the way in which the story is told (see RSV), it may
appear that after the priests blew their trumpets, at the finish of
the seventh march around the city (verse 16), Joshua gave the people
their instructions (verses 16b-19); then the people shouted, the
priests blew their trumpets, the people shouted again, and the walls
fell in (verse 20). But it seems better to understand the text as NEB,
TEV have done: just before the priests blew their trumpets, Joshua
gave his order; the trumpets were blown, the people shouted, and the
walls fell in.[12]
The seventh time around (Hebrew "And it happened on the seventh
time") is difficult, because it contains a hidden subject and predicate. The phrase may need to be translated, "When they had gone around
the city seven times...." If this shift is made, then the sentence may
continue: "..., the priests got ready to blow their trumpets. So Joshua
said to his men, 'Shout! the LORD has given you the city!'" It may be
preferable to translate the pronoun you as "us" (inclusive form), so
as to indicate that Joshua and the other Israelites were also to share
in the victory.

6.17   The city and everything in it must be totally destroyed
        as an offering to the LORD. Only the prostitute Rahab
        and her household will be spared, because she hid our
        spies.

The city and everything in it must be totally destroyed may require
the shift to an active construction, identifying the persons who are to
destroy the city: "You must totally destroy the city and everything in
it. In this way you will dedicate it to the LORD." Or "...In this way
you will show that it is an offering to the LORD." The reader may find
it difficult to reconcile the giving of the city to the people by the
Lord with the requirement to give it to him as an offering. Therefore
it would help at the end of verse 16 to translate "The LORD will let
you conquer the city" or "The LORD has placed the city in your power."
    The noun everything may also be misunderstood to include only in-
animate objects. But the word is intended to be comprehensive, to include buildings, people, and animals. It may then be translated, "Destroy every building in the city, and kill all its people and their
animals." Or "Completely destroy the city, and kill every living thing
in it, people and animals alike."
    Must be totally destroyed as an offering translates the Hebrew
expression "shall be a dedicated offering" (RSV "shall be devoted...for
destruction"); the Hebrew noun "dedicated offering" qualifies an object
(or a person) that has been dedicated exclusively to the Lord's use;
and since it cannot be used for ordinary purposes it can only be completely destroyed (see Lev 27.28-29). So all the inhabitants and all
the animals in Jericho are killed (verse 21), with the exception of
Rahab and her family (verses 17b,22-25).
    The last sentence of this verse may need to be inverted and her
household made explicit: "But remember that the prostitute Rahab hid
our spies. So we promised to spare her and everyone who is in her
house."

6.18   But you are not to take anything that is to be destroyed;
        if you do, you will bring trouble and destruction on the
        Israelite camp.

The order to destroy everything and everyone in the city is re-
inforced with the warning that unless the Israelites do so the Israelite camp itself will have to be destroyed.[13] But you translates a
strongly emphatic form in Hebrew.
    That is to be destroyed may be translated "that I have told you
to destroy." This dreadful warning of destruction is followed in Hebrew by another verbal phrase which RSV translates "and bring trouble
upon it." This seems rather anticlimactic; the JB rendering is more
effective, "bring disaster on it." For the sake of making the passage
more climactic, TEV inverts the order of the Hebrew nouns "trouble"
and "destruction." It is possible to take the noun phrase trouble and
destruction as meaning "great trouble" or "terrible destruction." With
this in mind, and representing the two nouns as verbs, one may translate "If you do take anything that belongs to the LORD, he will totally

destroy everyone in our camp. And it will be your own fault." It should
be observed that in this restructuring the Israelite camp of TEV is rendered "our camp," since Joshua himself is included in the group. This
is also in keeping with the use of our spies of verse 17. The Hebrew
verb translated bring trouble...on is used also in 7.25, in connection
with Achan's disregard of this very order requiring the destruction of
all the enemy loot.

6.19   Everything made of silver, gold, bronze, or iron is
              set apart for the LORD. It is to be put in the LORD's
              treasury."

     All the metal objects were to be placed in the LORD's treasury
(see verse 24). TEV is set apart for the LORD translates the Hebrew
phrase "is holy to the LORD," which means that all those metal uten-
sils were to be used in the Israelite worship ceremonies; they were
sacred vessels and were not to be used for ordinary purposes. A translation should make clear the distinction between "be holy to the LORD"
and "be devoted (for destruction) to the LORD."
     Everything made of...is set apart for the LORD may be translated
as an active: "Set apart for the LORD everything made of...." The passive structure It is to be put... may also be rendered as an active
"We will put it...."

6.20   So the priests blew the trumpets. As soon as the
              men heard it, they gave a loud shout, and the walls
              collapsed. Then all the army went straight up the hill
              into the city and captured it.

     In verse 16 it is stated that "the priests were about to sound
the trumpets," which was then followed by Joshua's detailed instructions to the people (verses 17-19). It is therefore possible that the
reader will have forgotten the precise setting by the time that the
priests are mentioned again at the beginning of this verse. Since this
possibility exists, a more specific transitional than So may be required at the beginning of the verse. For example, "When Joshua finished giving these instructions to the people, the priests blew the
trumpets."
     As RSV shows, the Hebrew text says that the people shouted, the
priests blew the trumpets, and then the people shouted again, this
time "a great shout," at which the walls fell down. TEV and NEB eliminate the repetition in the Hebrew text on the grounds that it is a
stylistic matter, possibly reflecting the use of different sources. In
the light of the whole event it seems impossible to believe that the
Israelites shouted twice, although the HOTTP supports this as one possible way of understanding the text. Assuming that a single shout is
intended, one may translate loud shout as "battle cry."
     Jericho had a double wall; at one time in its history[14] the outer
wall fell outward and the inner wall collapsed into the space between
the two walls.

[79]

TEV <u>went straight up the hill</u> makes explicit what is implicit in
the Hebrew "went up" (see RSV); Jericho was built on a hill. The expression "every man straight before him" (RSV) indicates that there
was no opposition to the attack (see also verse 5). The victory was
the Lord's doing; it was his power that caused Jericho to fall.

<u>6.21</u>   With their swords they killed everyone in the city,
         men and women, young and old. They also killed the
         cattle, sheep, and donkeys.

The first sentence of this verse may be broken into two sentences
as follows: "They took their swords and killed everyone in the city.
They killed all the men, women, and children." All living things, human
and animal, are put to death; logically this would seem to include
Rahab and her family, but verses 22-25 narrate how they were spared.

"Utterly destroyed" (RSV; TEV <u>killed everyone</u>) translates a verb
which comes from the same stem as the noun that RSV translates "destruction" in verse 17 and "things devoted to destruction," "devoted
things," and "a thing for destruction" in verse 18; see comments there.

| TEV | 6.22-27 | RSV |

22 Joshua then told the two
men who had served as spies, "Go
into the prostitute's house, and
bring her and her family out, as
you promised her." 23 So they went
and brought Rahab out, along with
her father and mother, her brothers, and the rest of her family.
They took them all, family and
slaves, to safety near the Israelite camp. 24 Then they set fire
to the city and burned it to the
ground, along with everything in
it, except the things made of
gold, silver, bronze, and iron,
which they took and put in the
LORD's treasury. 25 But Joshua
spared the lives of the prostitute Rahab and all her relatives,
because she had hidden the two
spies that he had sent to Jericho.
(Her descendants have lived in
Israel to this day.)
26 At this time Joshua issued a solemn warning: "Anyone
who tries to rebuild the city of
Jericho will be under the LORD's
curse.

22 And Joshua said to the two
men who had spied out the land,
"Go into the harlot's house, and
bring out from it the woman, and
all who belong to her, as you
swore to her." 23 So the young
men who had been spies went in,
and brought out Rahab, and her
father and mother and brothers
and all who belonged to her; and
they brought all her kindred, and
set them outside the camp of
Israel. 24 And they burned the
city with fire, and all within
it; only the silver and gold, and
the vessels of bronze and of iron,
they put into the treasury of the
house of the LORD. 25 But Rahab
the harlot, and her father's
household, and all who belonged
to her, Joshua saved alive; and
she dwelt in Israel to this day,
because she hid the messengers
whom Joshua sent to spy out Jericho.
26 Joshua laid an oath upon
them at that time, saying,
"Cursed before the LORD be the

| Whoever lays the foundation will lose his oldest son; Whoever builds the gates will lose his youngest." 27 So the LORD was with Joshua, and his fame spread through the whole country. | man that rises up and rebuilds this city, Jericho. At the cost of his first-born shall he lay its foundation, and at the cost of his youngest son shall he set up its gates." 27 So the LORD was with Joshua; and his fame was in all the land. |

What follows describes how Rahab and all her family escaped death (verses 22-25); and the account of the fall of Jericho ends with the solemn vow that anyone who should attempt to rebuild the city would be punished by the Lord (verses 26-27). Since there is something of a transition in the narrative at this point, it may be important to introduce a new section heading, such as "Rahab and her family are spared" or "The Israelites spare Rahab and her family."

6.22   Joshua then told the two men who had served as spies, "Go into the prostitute's house, and bring her and her family out, as you promised her."

Joshua instructs the two spies to go to Rahab's house and bring her and her family out to safety. It is to be assumed that this happened while the killing was going on in the city; it could not have been after all the city's other inhabitants had been put to death (verse 21). It may be important translationally to shift from Joshua then told to "Joshua had told," indicating a previous command given before the beginning of the battle. The Hebrew will support either rendering, and this would tend to provide a less complicated sequence of events.

Nothing is gained in translation by continually emphasizing Rahab's profession. Go into the prostitute's house may then be translated "Go into Rahab's house." Moreover, the events may be arranged in chronological sequence: "You promised Rahab that we would not harm her or the people in her house. So go to her house and bring them out here to safety." Direct discourse may be preferable for the promise made by the spies: "You promised Rahab, 'We will not harm you or anyone in your house.' So go....'"

6.23   So they went and brought Rahab out, along with her father and mother, her brothers, and the rest of her family. They took them all, family and slaves, to safety near the Israelite camp.

They is literally "young men" (RSV), which may be taken to mean that they were in their early twenties; the Hebrew word is used sometimes of unmarried males, but it does not necessarily imply that the young male so indicated is in fact a bachelor. However, if the receptor language requires a choice between "unmarried young men" and

"married young men," it would be better to use "unmarried young men."
There are indications elsewhere in the Old Testament that married men,
or men with families, were occasionally released from the responsibilities of warfare. In the Hebrew text an appositional is attached to
"young men" so that the text is literally "the young men, the spies."
However, they were identified as spies in verse 22, and many languages
will prefer not to repeat this information so soon. Here, as elsewhere,
one must be alert to the demands of the larger discourse unit, and not
merely to the sentence as an isolated entity.

Rahab and all her family are brought out of Jericho and taken to
a place near the Israelite camp. The significance of their being brought
near, that is, not into the camp, is that they are all Gentiles and
cannot enter the camp of Israel, which is holy.

All, family and slaves translates two phrases in Hebrew, "and all
who belonged to her and all her group (or, clan)"; most translations,
like RSV, translate the second phrase "and all her kindred," thus taking this Hebrew phrase to be completely equivalent in meaning to the
preceding phrase. Some take it to be a summary statement (see NEB),
"so they took out all her family (clan)." TEV has made explicit the
fact that the slaves would also be included in the group; but no other
translation uses the word "slaves" here.

6.24   Then they set fire to the city and burned it to the
        ground, along with everything in it, except the things
        made of gold, silver, bronze, and iron, which they
        took and put in the LORD's treasury.

The destruction of the city by fire follows the slaughter of all
its inhabitants and animals; only the objects of gold, silver, bronze,
and iron are spared, and they are placed in the LORD's treasury, according to instructions (see verse 19). The Hebrew text says "the
treasury of the house of the LORD" (see RSV), a phrase which ordinarily
means the Jerusalem Temple. Most take this to be an anachronism; the
Septuagint omits "the house of" (possibly to ease the problem of the
Hebrew text); Soggin suggests it could refer to the sanctuary in Gilgal, which does not seem very likely.

The pronoun they is ambiguous, since in verse 23 TEV twice used
"they" to refer to the two men who had served as spies. Here the reference is to the entire army of Israel which has invaded the city. The
verse may be translated,

        Then the Israelite soldiers set fire to the city. They burned
        it to the ground, and they burned everything in it, except
        the things made of gold, silver, bronze, and iron. They took
        these things and put them in the LORD's treasury.
Or, in keeping with the form of the Hebrew, the LORD's treasury may be
translated "the treasury which was in the shrine dedicated to the LORD"
or "the treasury which was kept in the place where the people of Israel
worshiped the LORD."

6.25   But Joshua spared the lives of the prostitute Rahab
   and all her relatives, because she had hidden the
   two spies that he had sent to Jericho. (Her descendants have lived in Israel to this day.)

Verse 25 brings the matter to a close, with a summary statement
of how and why the lives of Rahab and all her family were spared. TEV
and a number of other translations begin this verse with a conjunction
equivalent to But in order to make an immediate contrast between the
fate of Rahab and her family and the rest of the people of Jericho.
Here again it may not be necessary to refer to Rahab as the prostitute;
the emotive impact of this upon modern day readers may be quite different from the connotation it carried among the original readers. Because she had hidden the two spies may be better rendered as a complete
statement: "Joshua did this because she had hidden the two spies."

Before giving the reason why (because she hid the Israelite spies),
the writer inserts "and she has lived in Israel to this day." This obviously does not mean that Rahab herself was alive at the time of the
writing of the account; it means, as TEV expresses it, Her descendants
have lived in Israel to this day. Rahab is usually identified as Rahab
the mother of Boaz, and so the great-great-grandmother of King David
(Matt 1.5-6; see Ruth 4.18-22; and see also references to her in Heb
11.31; James 2.25). In translating the sentence which TEV places in
parentheses, one should be careful not to leave the impression that
the writer himself was not an Israelite. For example, one modern translation renders "Her descendants still live today among the Israelites,"
from which the reader could assume that the writer is disassociating
himself from the people called Israelites. It is probably better also
not to introduce the parentheses as TEV has done. If it is felt necessary to separate this statement from what precedes, it can be made into
a separate paragraph in place of putting it within parentheses.

6.26   At this time Joshua issued a solemn warning:
   "Anyone who tries to rebuild the city of Jericho
   will be under the LORD's curse.
     Whoever lays the foundation will lose
      his oldest son;
     Whoever builds the gates will lose his
      youngest."

At this time may need to be made more specific: "After Joshua and
his men had destroyed the city of Jericho, Joshua...." This may be
particularly important, especially in light of the intervening reference to the day in which the book is being written.

It may be obligatory to indicate the persons to whom Joshua gave
the warning, and other languages will require that issued a solemn
warning be translated solely as a verb instead of a verb (issued) fol-
by an object (solemn warning). Moreover, the fact that it is a solemn
warning may have to be brought out in the manner in which the warning
is stated, since this phrase may be difficult, if not impossible, to
render into many languages. For example, "Joshua warned the people of

Israel never to try to rebuild the city of Jericho" or "Joshua warned the people of Israel, 'You must never try to rebuild the city of Jericho.'"

The story of the fall of Jericho ends with the solemn curse pronounced by Joshua. The Hebrew "cursed before the LORD" (see RSV) means, as TEV has it, under the LORD's curse (see also NEB). The Hebrew word translated curse means the object of the Lord's anger and punishment. Joshua was not merely predicting what would happen, but as a spokesman for the Lord he was causing the disaster to occur which he had described. The fulfillment of this curse is reported in 1 Kings 16.34 (during the reign of King Ahab of Israel, 874-853 B.C.).

Instead of the passive Anyone...will be under the LORD's curse, a shift to an active structure may be more effective: "The LORD will place a curse upon anyone who tries to rebuild the city of Jericho."

The last two statements of this verse indicate the content of the curse, but the relation between under the LORD's curse and these two statements may need to be stated clearly: "under the LORD's curse. And this is what the curse will be:...."

Contemporary cities do not have a foundation, and neither did ancient cities. The reference is to the foundation for the city walls, as the mention of gates in the last statement indicates. Moreover, maintaining the two parallel statements of the curse may well lead to a misunderstanding of its content. In fact, it is probably much better to combine than to retain the parallel curses. The meaning is that whoever attempts to rebuild the city of Jericho will lose all of his children, from the oldest to the youngest. The curse may then be stated, "Whoever starts to rebuild the city walls will lose all of his children," or even "If a man even starts to rebuild the city of Jericho, the LORD will take the lives of all of his children."

6.27   So the LORD was with Joshua, and his fame spread
           through the whole country.

So the LORD was with Joshua may be translated "The LORD stood beside Joshua" or "The LORD helped Joshua in everything he did."

As the Lord had promised (compare 3.7; 4.14), Joshua's fame spread through the whole country. Or, expressed in a less abstract manner, "everyone in the whole country heard what a great man Joshua was." Or in still a different way, "everyone in the whole country told their friends what a great man Joshua was."

Chapter 7

Achan's Sin

1 The LORD's command to Israel not to take from Jericho anything that was to be destroyed was not obeyed. A man named Achan disobeyed that order, and so the LORD was furious with the Israelites. (Achan was the son of Carmi and grandson of Zabdi, and belonged to the clan of Zerah, a part of the tribe of Judah.)

2 Joshua sent some men from Jericho to Ai, a city east of Bethel, near Bethaven, with orders to go and explore the land. When they had done so, 3 they reported back to Joshua: "There is no need for everyone to attack Ai. Send only about two or three thousand men. Don't send the whole army up there to fight; it is not a large city." 4 So about three thousand Israelites made the attack, but they were forced to retreat. 5 The men of Ai chased them from the city gate as far as some quarries and killed about thirty-six of them on the way down the hill. Then the Israelites lost their courage and were afraid.

1 But the people of Israel broke faith in regard to the devoted things; for Achan the son of Carmi, son of Zabdi, son of Zerah, of the tribe of Judah, took some of the devoted things; and the anger of the LORD burned against the people of Israel.

2 Joshua sent men from Jericho to Ai, which is near Bethaven, east of Bethel, and said to them, "Go up and spy out the land." And the men went up and spied out Ai. 3 And they returned to Joshua, and said to him, "Let not all the people go up, but let about two or three thousand men go up and attack Ai; do not make the whole people toil up there, for they are but few." 4 So about three thousand went up there from the people; and they fled before the men of Ai, 5 and the men of Ai killed about thirty-six of them, and chased them before the gate as far as Shebarim, and slew them at the descent. And the hearts of the people melted, and became as water.

Chapter 7 serves to connect the fall of Jericho (6.1-27) to the capture and destruction of Ai (8.1-29). There is first an unsuccessful attempt to capture the city (verses 2-5); Israel's failure to take the city is explained as being the consequence of Achan's sin in disobeying the Lord's command not to keep anything valuable found in Jericho (verse 1). The Israelite leaders complain to God about the defeat of Israel (verses 6-9), and God reveals the reason for their defeat and the method for discovering the guilty one (verses 10-15). The plan is put into effect: Achan is indicated as the guilty man (verses 16-19), he confesses his sin (verses 20-21), and is immediately executed (verses 22-26). The people are now able to launch a successful attack on Ai because the sin has been purged from Israel.

The section heading, <u>Achan's Sin</u>, may be rendered as a complete statement: "Achan disobeys the LORD's command" or "Achan takes some of the things from Jericho for himself." The chapter may be subdivided for easier comprehension: "The fortunes of war turn against Israel" (1-9); "The cause: disobedience" (10-15); "The sin is removed" (16-26). If this proposal is followed, the section headings may require a complete sentence: "The people in the city of Ai defeat the Israelite army" (1-9); "Someone in Israel disobeyed the LORD's command" (10-15); and "The guilty man is punished" or "The people of Israel punish the guilty man" (16-26).

7.1　　　　The LORD's command to Israel not to take from Jericho anything that was to be destroyed was not obeyed. A man named Achan disobeyed that order, and so the LORD was furious with the Israelites. (Achan was the son of Carmi and grandson of Zabdi, and belonged to the clan of Zerah, a part of the tribe of Judah.)

This verse is not simply the statement about one man's sin; all the Israelites suffer as a consequence of his sin: <u>The LORD was furious with the Israelites.</u>
The first sentence of TEV is difficult because it contains (a) two negatives (<u>not to take; was not obeyed</u>) and (b) a series of four events: command, take, destroy, and obey. The complexity may be somewhat eased as follows: "The LORD commanded the people of Israel to destroy Jericho and everything in it. But a man named Achan did not obey the LORD's command, and so the LORD was very angry with the people of Israel." Or, if repetition is more effective: "...but not everyone obeyed this command. A man named Achan disobeyed what the LORD had said...." Direct discourse may be employed for the Lord's command: "The LORD had told the people of Israel, 'Destroy Jericho and everything in it.'...."

Achan's disobedience is spoken of as treachery, as "an act of unfaithfulness" (TOB). He defied the Lord's explicit command and "took some of the devoted things" (RSV), that is, "things devoted to destruction." Achan's lineage is given: <u>Carmi, Zabdi, Zerah</u>, and <u>tribe of Judah</u> (see verses 16-18). In identifying <u>Achan</u> TEV follows the order of the Hebrew: <u>son of...grandson of...clan of...tribe of</u>.... Some languages may prefer to go from the larger units of tribe and clan to that of the family.

7.2　　　　Joshua sent some men from Jericho to Ai, a city east of Bethel, near Bethaven, with orders to go and explore the land. When they had done so,

After the encouraging report brought back by his spies, Joshua sends a relatively small force (some three thousand men) to attack Ai, a city on a mountain ridge some 24 kilometers northwest of Jericho.

Of course neither Joshua nor the rest of the Israelites know that the Lord is angry with them because of what Achan has done, and so they are surprised and terrified by the defeat they suffer.

The location of Ai is given in relation to Bethel; it was about 2.5 kilometers east (or better, southeast) of Bethel, which is easily identified and located on biblical maps. It is not easy, however, precisely to identify Bethaven, which in the text is said to be a separate locality, not far from Bethel.[15]

The initial sentence of verse 2 is difficult for at least two reasons. First, it contains a series of two appositionals, which separate by some distance the subject men from the verbs go and explore. Second, it implies discourse (with orders to go and explore). Some of these difficulties may be made easier if the following restructuring is accepted as a guideline:

> Joshua sent some men from Jericho to the city of Ai. Ai was east of the city of Bethel and not far from the city of Bethaven. Joshua told the men, "Go and find out what you can about the city of Ai and the land around it."

When they had done so is literally "And the men went up and spied out Ai" (RSV). The sentence may be translated "The men obeyed Joshua's command" or "The men did what Joshua told them to do."

7.3　　they reported back to Joshua: "There is no need for everyone to attack Ai. Send only about two or three thousand men. Don't send the whole army up there to fight; it is not a large city."

As in the case of Jericho (2.1), Joshua sends spies to find out what they can about the land. On their return, they report that Ai is not a large city and can easily be taken by some two or three thousand men.[16]

In verse 3 RSV "do not make the whole people toil up there" translates a verb which means "to have trouble, to be difficult." The meaning could be expressed by "Don't go to the trouble of having the whole army go up there."

Both the Hebrew (note RSV) and TEV contain a considerable amount of repetition in verse 3. In order to avoid the redundancy, one may render the words of the spies: "Ai is not a large city. There is no need to send all our men to attack it. Send only about two or three thousand men."

7.4-5　　So about three thousand Israelites made the attack, but they were forced to retreat. 5 The men of Ai chased them from the city gate as far as some quarries and killed about thirty-six of them on the way down the hill. Then the Israelites lost their courage and were afraid.

In order to make a tighter connection between this and the previous verse, one may translate "So Joshua sent about three thousand
Israelite men to attack the city." The second clause (but they were
forced to retreat) may be shifted to an active: "but the people of the
city forced them to retreat."

The Israelites were not able to force their way into Ai; they were
repulsed at the city gate, and fled down the hill. The place name "Shebarim" (AT, RSV, JB) in Hebrew means "quarries" and has been translated
that way by TEV, NEB; Soggin translates "ravines"; the Septuagint seems
to have understood the Hebrew text to mean, "and they defeated them."

The sequence of events in this verse is not entirely clear in TEV.
One could assume that the sequence is (1) from the city gate, (2) as
far as some quarries, and then (3) down the hill. However, the proper
sequence seems to be: (1) from the city gate, (2) down the hill, and
then (3) as far as some quarries. The verse may need to be restructured:
"The men of Ai chased them from the city gate and all the way down the
hill as far as some quarries. On the way down the hill they killed
about thirty-six of the Israelite men." Following a slightly different
interpretation of the text, one may translate "The men of Ai chased
them from the city gate to the place where the rock makes a steep slope,
and they killed about thirty-six of the Israelite men."

Before this unexpected defeat, the Israelites lost their courage
and were afraid (literally "their hearts melted, and became like water,"
see RSV). Lost their courage and were afraid may sound either redundant or anticlimactic. The Hebrew in fact indicates only a single re-
action, although two figures of speech are used ("hearts melted" and
"like water"). Many languages will have idiomatic ways of expressing
fear; moreover, it is also possible to translate either lost their
courage or were afraid, without utilizing both figures of speech.

TEV	7.6-9	RSV

6 Joshua and the leaders of
Israel tore their clothes in grief,
threw themselves to the ground before the LORD's Covenant Box, and
lay there till evening, with dust
on their heads to show their sorrow. 7 And Joshua said, "Sovereign
LORD! Why did you bring us across
the Jordan at all? To turn us over
to the Amorites? To destroy us?
Why didn't we just stay on the
other side of the Jordan? 8 What
can I say, O Lord, now that Israel
has retreated from the enemy? 9 The
Canaanites and everyone else in
the country will hear about it.
They will surround us and kill
every one of us! And then what
will you do to protect your
honor?"

6 Then Joshua rent his clothes,
and fell to the earth upon his
face before the ark of the LORD
until the evening, he and the
elders of Israel; and they put
dust upon their heads. 7 And
Joshua said, "Alas, O Lord GOD,
why hast thou brought this people
over the Jordan at all, to give
us into the hands of the Amorites,
to destroy us? Would that we had
been content to dwell beyond the
Jordan! 8 O Lord, what can I say,
when Israel has turned their backs
before their enemies! 9 For the
Canaanites and all the inhabitants
of the land will hear of it, and
will surround us, and cut off our
name from the earth; and what wilt
thou do for they great name?"

The shock of defeat was so great that Joshua and the other leaders of Israel lay prostrate in grief in front of the Covenant Box until evening. Joshua's anguished questions to the Lord reveal the enormity of the shock. The previous experience at Jericho had led the Israelites to believe that they were invincible, because their God, the Lord, was with them, and he was more powerful than the gods of the Canaanites. How, then, could his people be defeated? The Lord replies that it was Israel's sin that caused the defeat (verses 11-13), and he gives Joshua instructions on how to discover the guilty one, who is to be put to death by fire (verses 14-15).

<u>7.6</u>   Joshua and the leaders of Israel tore their clothes in grief, threw themselves to the ground before the LORD's Covenant Box, and lay there till evening, with dust on their heads to show their sorrow.

Here and in 8.10 mention is made of <u>the leaders</u> of Israel as "the elders" (RSV). They should be thought of as <u>older men</u> who helped Joshua in administrative matters.

The tearing of clothes, the lying on the ground, and the throwing of dust on the head, all indicate humiliation and mourning. The clothes were not torn so completely as to become useless; probably only a tear along the edge of the outer garment was made. Some languages have verb forms which indicate either intentional tearing or unintentional tearing. Here the tearing of the clothes by Joshua and the leaders of Israel is obviously intentional.

The prepositional phrase <u>in grief</u> may need to be treated more fully: "because of their grief" or "to show their grief," or even "They did this to show that they were sorry for what had happened."

<u>Threw themselves to the ground</u> must be understood to mean "threw themselves face downward on the ground." The position would be the same as that of 5.14, only this time the purpose is not for worship.

<u>Before the LORD's Covenant Box</u> means "with their heads in the direction of the LORD's Covenant Box." It is impossible to define with precision the exact sequence of events as described in this verse. Several things happened: (1) they tore their clothes; (2) they threw themselves to the ground; (3) they approached the Lord's Covenant Box; (4) they lay on the ground until evening; and (5) they placed dust on their heads. It is obvious that event (3) precedes event (2), and that event (4) is last in the sequence. But beyond this it is impossible to state dogmatically the order of the occurrences. One possibility would be:

Joshua and the leaders of Israel approached the LORD's Covenant Box. There they tore their clothes and threw dust on their heads to show their sorrow. Then they threw themselves face downward to the ground and lay there until evening.

For the <u>Covenant Box</u> see comments at 3.3.

7.7   And Joshua said, "Sovereign LORD! Why did you bring us
       across the Jordan at all? To turn us over to the Amo-
       rites? To destroy us? Why didn't we just stay on the
       other side of the Jordan?

And Joshua said introduces a prayer and may be translated "Joshua
prayed." In order to indicate more precisely the temporal relation between the time of Joshua's prayer and the events of the previous verse,
one may translate "While they lay on the ground, Joshua prayed...." If
there is a distinction in the language between silent prayer and oral
prayer, the prayer is best understood as oral.

Sovereign LORD translates the Hebrew phrase "Lord Yahweh"—the
title and the personal name of God (KJV, RSV, AT, NEB, NAB "Lord GOD";
compare TOB Seigneur DIEU). TEV has followed the KJV tradition of translating "Yahweh" by LORD, but it has not used the form GOD. In a number
of languages the word for "God" will be "Lord," and so the combination
"Lord God" will be impossible. To translate as Sovereign LORD with TEV
may also be impossible, for both the modifier Sovereign and the noun
LORD imply rulership. Some translations render the double expression
as merely "Lord." If this is felt inadequate, one may render "LORD,
who rules over all" or "LORD of all peoples."

In this verse the translator does not face the problem of breaking
TEV up into smaller units, but rather of creating larger pieces out of
the smaller units of TEV. In Joshua's prayer the first question (Why
did you bring us across the Jordan at all?) is answered by two other
questions (To turn us over to the Amorites? To destroy us?). The two
questions which answer the first question are both abbreviated in that
they leave implicit the first part of each question, which is "Did you
bring us across the Jordan...?" If the question form is retained, then
this information may need to be built into the responses. On the other
hand, it is possible to shift from a question to a strongly affirmative
statement: "LORD! You surely did not bring us across the Jordan just
to turn us over to the Amorites and let them destroy us."

"Alas" (RSV, NEB, NAB, JB) translates a Hebrew expression used
infrequently in the Old Testament to denote sorrow or remorse (see
Judges 6.22; 2 Kings 3.10; 6.5,15). BJ has Helas, TOB Ah. Joshua's
questions imply that the Lord is responsible for Israel's defeat.

The Amorites probably refers in a general way to all the inhabi-
ants of Canaan, equivalent to Canaanites (see 3.10 for the list of
seven peoples of the land); Gray suggests that here Amorites may mean
specifically those who lived in the hills (see Num 13.29).

Why didn't we just stay translates an idiomatic Hebrew phrase
"Would that we had persisted and remained"; compare NEB "If only we
had been content to settle." "Why weren't we satisfied to remain" would
represent the meaning well, as would "I wish that we had stayed on the
other side of the Jordan."

7.8   What can I say, O Lord, now that Israel has retreated
       from the enemy?

The question What can I say...? may be restructured as a statement: "I do not know what to say...." The order may be inverted: "O Lord, our army has retreated from the enemy, and I do not know what to say." Or "O Lord, the men of Ai made our men turn and run, and I do not know what to say."

7.9
The Canaanites and everyone else in the country will hear about it. They will surround us and kill every one of us! And then what will you do to protect your honor?"

The Canaanites and everyone else in the country is literally "the Canaanites and all the inhabitants of the land" (RSV). But in such a context Hebrew will often use "all" in the sense of "all the others" or "everyone else," not excluding the group joined to "all" by the conjunction "and." In many languages, such as English, a literal rendering of the Hebrew will convey a wrong sense.

Kill every one of us translates the Hebrew "cut off our name from the earth" (RSV). It may be that the intent of the verb is to focus more upon the removal of the Israelites from the land than upon the slaughter of them. Accordingly one may render "drive us from the land"; the verb surround may then be translated either "come and attack us" or merely "come."

This use of "name" leads to the final question in Joshua's lament, 'What will you do for your great name?" (see RSV). Here the Lord's "name" stands for his reputation, his honor; the defeat of his people would bring shame on him, for pagan Canaanites and all the others in the land would conclude that the God of the Hebrews was weak and had less power than their own gods. A god's good reputation depended on the success of his people.

To protect your honor may need to be stated in a less abstract manner: "to keep people from saying evil things about you" or "to keep people from saying that you are not a great God." The meaning may even be expressed "to keep people from saying that you could not protect your people."

TEV	7.10-15	RSV

10 The LORD said to Joshua, "Get up! Why are you lying on the ground like this? 11 Israel has sinned! They have broken the agreement with me that I ordered them to keep. They have taken some of the things condemned to destruction. They stole them, lied about it, and put them with their own things. 12 This is why the Israelites cannot stand against their enemies. They retreat from

10 The LORD said to Joshua, "Arise, why have you thus fallen upon your face? 11 Israel has sinned; they have transgressed my covenant which I commanded them; they have taken some of the devoted things; they have stolen, and lied, and put them among their own stuff. 12 Therefore the people of Israel cannot stand before their enemies; they turn their backs before their enemies,

them because they themselves have now been condemned to destruction! I will not stay with you any longer unless you destroy the things you were ordered not to take! 13 Get up! Purify the people and get them ready to come before me. Tell them to be ready tomorrow, because I, the LORD God of Israel, have this to say: 'Israel, you have in your possession some things that I ordered you to destroy! You cannot stand against your enemies until you get rid of these things!' 14 So tell them that in the morning they will be brought forward, tribe by tribe. The tribe that I pick out will then come forward, clan by clan. The clan that I pick out will come forward, family by family. The family that I pick out will come forward, man by man. 15 The one who is then picked out and found with the condemned goods will be burned, along with his family and everything he owns, for he has brought terrible shame on Israel and has broken my covenant."

because they have become a thing for destruction. I will be with you no more, unless you destroy the devoted things from among you. 13 Up, sanctify the people, and say, 'Sanctify yourselves for tomorrow; for thus says the LORD, God of Israel, "There are devoted things in the midst of you, O Israel; you cannot stand before your enemies, until you take away the devoted things from among you." 14 In the morning therefore you shall be brought near by your tribes; and the tribe which the LORD takes shall come near by families; and the family which the LORD takes shall come near by households; and the household which the LORD takes shall come near man by man. 15 And he who is taken with the devoted things shall be burned with fire, he and all that he has, because he has transgressed the covenant of the LORD, and because he has done a shameful thing in Israel.'"

As indicated at the beginning of this chapter, it may be appropriate to introduce a new section heading at this point where the Lord reveals to Joshua the reason why Israel was defeated. It was Israel's sin, as described by the biblical writer in verse 1.

7.10   The LORD said to Joshua, "Get up! Why are you lying on the ground like this?

Why are you lying on the ground like this? is literally 'Why have you fallen on your face?" The reference is to the actions described in verse 6, and whereas Hebrew focuses upon the initiation of the action (the falling), TEV describes the result (lying on the ground). It may be better to invert the order of the Lord's two remarks so that Get up follows the question. One may even shift the question to a command: "Quit lying on the ground like this! Get up!"

7.11   Israel has sinned! They have broken the agreement with me that I ordered them to keep. They have taken some of the things condemned to destruction. They stole them, lied about it, and put them with their own things.

Israel has sinned may be translated "The people of Israel have sinned." Achan's disobedience involved all Israel, and as a result Israel suffered defeat.

The Lord's accusation, then, is that the Israelites have broken the agreement and have taken some of the things condemned to destruction; they stole,...lied, and hid those things among their own belongings. In this context the agreement (RSV "covenant") refers specifically to the Lord's command about the attack on Jericho (6.17-18); it does not refer to the basic covenant at Mount Sinai.

In order to indicate specifically that the agreement refers to the Lord's command not to take anything from the city of Jericho, considerable restructuring may be necessary. For example, They have broken... condemned to destruction may be translated, "I commanded them to destroy everything in the city of Jericho. This was my agreement with them. But they kept back for themselves some of the things from the city." Moreover, if it is felt that the agreement (the agreement with me) and the command (I ordered them to keep) are synonymous, one may even render "I commanded them to destroy everything in the city. But they disobeyed my command and kept back some of the things for themselves."

The three events described in the last sentence of this verse (stole...lied...put them with) may need to be arranged in chronological sequence: "They stole them, put them with their own things, and then lied about what they had done."

7.12   This is why the Israelites cannot stand against
        their enemies. They retreat from them because
        they themselves have now been condemned to de-
        struction! I will not stay with you any longer
        unless you destroy the things you were ordered
        not to take!

As a consequence of taking things condemned to destruction, Israel herself has become condemned to destruction. Achan's sin has placed him under the Lord's curse, and the curse is now communicated to all Israel. That is why the Israelites can no longer defeat their enemies. And the Lord threatens to withdraw his help and protection from them unless they destroy what has been devoted to him.

It may be good to unite This is why with because they themselves have now been condemned to destruction: "The people of Israel have themselves been condemned to destruction. This is why they cannot stand against their enemies and must retreat." Since cannot stand against their enemies is implicit in retreat from them, the two may be combined: "This is why they retreat from their enemies."

In the Lord's address to Joshua the shift from they to you (plural) may be somewhat confusing. This problem of the shift from a third person plural to a second person plural in Hebrew has been noted several times previously, and it will frequently occur in the book of Joshua. The translator should be constantly alert to any sort of stylistic adjustments which must be made in the receptor language.

Stay with you is literally "be with you" (RSV). The meaning may be rendered as either "stand beside you" or "help you."

[93]

7.12

Not stay with you any longer may be expressed as either "will
stop being with you" or "will stop helping you."

The negative unless you destroy the things may be translated by
a nonnegative construction if the shift to "will stop being with you"
is made; for example, "until you destroy the things."

You were ordered not to take may take the shape of an active
clause with the Lord as subject: "which I ordered you not to take."
Direct discourse may even be substituted: "of which I said, 'Do not
take.'"

7.13   Get up! Purify the people and get them ready to come
            before me. Tell them to be ready tomorrow, because I,
            the LORD God of Israel, have this to say: 'Israel, you
            have in your possession some things that I ordered
            you to destroy! You cannot stand against your enemies
            until you get rid of these things!'

Israel has now become ritually impure, and so the Lord orders
Joshua to rise and to purify the people. This will involve a confession of sin and a ritual whereby Israel's guilt will be removed and
the people will be able to appear before the Lord (that is, at the
place of worship). Only by locating and destroying the objects which
have been kept by Achan will Israel be able again to defeat her
enemies.[17]

The repetition of the command Get up may imply for some readers
that Joshua did not obey the Lord the first time he gave the command
(verse 10). In Hebrew the verb "get up" is frequently used in conjunction with a verb that follows, so that it means "begin to do the verb
that follows." That may also be the meaning here. Get up! Purify the
people may then mean "Go and purify the people" or merely "Purify the
people."

Purify the people and get them ready to come before me translates
"Purify the people" (RSV "sanctify the people") of the Hebrew text. The
lengthy rendering of TEV is intended to interpret for the reader the
purpose of the purification ceremony. It may also be effectively translated as "Stand up and prepare the people for the meeting with me!" In
a number of languages a causative verb may be necessary: "cause the
people to purify themselves...."

Tell them to of TEV represents a shift from the direct discourse
of Hebrew to indirect discourse. As a rule, TEV prefers to use indirect discourse so as never to go beyond a quotation within a quotation.
This is primarily for the sake of avoiding double quotation marks,
within single quotation marks, within double quotation marks. But the
direct discourse of the Hebrew may be retained without introducing a
third layer of quotation marks, if it is not felt necessary to enclose
the Lord's quoting of himself within separate quotation marks. RSV in
fact does punctuate in precisely this manner, though TEV introduces a
separate layer of quotation marks.

Be ready tomorrow refers back to "ready to come before me." Once
again some of the redundancy of the Hebrew and of TEV could be avoided
if the command for Joshua to purify the people and the command for him

[94]

to tell the people to purify themselves are combined into one:
"Go tell the people to purify themselves and get ready to
come before me tomorrow. Tell them that I, the LORD God
of Israel, say 'People of Israel, I ordered you to destroy
everything in the city of Jericho. But you kept back some
of the things that I ordered you to destroy! ...'"
Or,
"Go tell the people that I, the LORD God of Israel, say to
them, 'Purify yourselves and get ready to come before me
tomorrow. I ordered you to destroy everything in the city
of Jericho, but you kept back some of the things that I
ordered you to destroy! ...'"
You cannot stand...until may be restructured as a coordinate construction: "Get rid of these things, and then you will be able to oppose your enemies and defeat them."

7.14   So tell them that in the morning they will be brought
            forward, tribe by tribe. The tribe that I pick out
            will then come forward, clan by clan. The clan that
            I pick out will come forward, family by family. The
            family that I pick out will come forward, man by man.

     All of the people are to be brought forward (RSV "brought near");
here and throughout these two verses this probably means to be brought
near the Covenant Box, which represented the throne of the Lord. He
himself will make the decision—that I pick out; this would probably
be done by the casting (or drawing) of lots to indicate which one of
the units (tribe, clan, family, man) was indicated. See 1 Samuel
14.41-43 for a more detailed description of this method of learning
to know God's will.
     A tribe is made up of several clans which trace their origins back
to a common ancestor, and which have in common a language, culture, and
name. A clan consists of a number of families which have a common ancestor and other close ties. Thus the Lord is narrowing the choice down
from the larger units of tribe and clan to the smaller unit of family,
and finally to the individual man.
     The third personal pronouns them and they represent second per-
sonal pronouns ("you") of the Hebrew text. So tell...that is merely a
stylistic device of TEV to make possible the shift from the second
personal pronouns of the previous verse to the third personal pronoun
of the present verse. It will probably simplify translation of this
verse if the second person is maintained: "So in the morning you will
come and stand before me, one tribe at a time...."
     In order to indicate the manner in which the Lord makes his
choice, The tribe that I pick out may be translated, "The tribe that
I cause the lot to fall upon." This same form may then be maintained
throughout the verse, or after its first usage a shift may be made
back to the form of TEV.
     Come forward continues the scene indicated by "be brought forward"
in the first part of the verse. All the tribes are now standing and
facing the Lord's Covenant Box, waiting for him to point out the guilty

[95]

person. The way that the Lord will do this is to have the guilty tribe to step out in front of all the other tribes. Then the guilty clan will be told to step out in front of the tribe. After that the guilty person's family will be told to step out in front of the clan, and finally the guilty person himself will be commanded to step out in front of his family. In this way the guilty person will be left standing alone in front of all the people. He will also be standing closest to the Covenant Box, which symbolizes the Lord's presence.

7.15   The one who is then picked out and found with the
        condemned goods will be burned, along with his
        family and everything he owns, for he has brought
        terrible shame on Israel and has broken my cove-
        nant."

The one who is then picked out and found with the condemned goods may be translated, "The man whom I pick out is the one who has the condemned goods." Or "The man on whom I cause the lot to fall...." If this restructuring is followed, then will be burned may be rendered "Burn him,..." It will probably be best also to render for he...my covenant as a separate sentence.

When the guilty man is exposed, then he, his family, and all his possessions are to be burned; they are all condemned to destruction, and anything condemned to destruction has to be completely destroyed by fire (6.24). Will be burned may possibly be misunderstood. That is, it may be taken to mean either burned as a means of torture or burned alive, neither of which is the meaning in the context. One may need to translate "Kill him and everyone in his family. Then burn their bodies together with everything he owns."

The Hebrew word translated terrible shame (RSV "a shameful thing") is used of particularly odious sins, such as rape (Gen 34.7; Judges 20.6) and adultery (Deut 22.21); sometimes it means "a fool, foolish" (see Nabal in 1 Sam 25.25). At the end of verse 15 covenant translates the same Hebrew word translated agreement in verse 11, and means the same thing.

The order brought terrible shame...broken my covenant represents the opposite sequence from the Hebrew text (RSV "transgressed the covenant...done a shameful thing"). As in verse 11, broken my covenant is best taken as a specific reference to the command not to take anything from the city of Jericho. It may be more effectual to maintain the order of the Hebrew and translate "He disobeyed my command not to take anything from the city of Jericho, and his disobedience brought terrible shame on Israel."

TEV	7.16-21	RSV
16 Early the next morning Joshua brought Israel forward, tribe by tribe, and the tribe of Judah was picked out. 17 He brought		16 So Joshua rose early in the morning, and brought Israel near tribe by tribe, and the tribe of Judah was taken; 17 and he

the tribe of Judah forward, clan by clan, and the clan of Zerah was picked out. Then he brought the clan of Zerah forward, family by family, and the family of Zabdi was picked out. 18 He then brought Zabdi's family forward man by man, and Achan, the son of Carmi and grandson of Zabdi, was picked out. 19 Joshua said to him, "My son, tell the truth here before the LORD, the God of Israel, and confess. Tell me now what you have done. Don't try to hide it from me."

20 "It's true," Achan answered. "I have sinned against the LORD, Israel's God, and this is what I did. 21 Among the things we seized I saw a beautiful Babylonian cloak, about five pounds of silver, and a bar of gold weighing over one pound. I wanted them so much that I took them. You will find them buried inside my tent, with the silver at the bottom."

brought near the families of Judah, and the family of the Zerahites was taken; and he brought near the family of the Zerahites man by man, and Zabdi was taken; 18 and he brought near his household man by man, and Achan the son of Carmi, son of Zabdi, son of Zerah, of the tribe of Judah, was taken. 19 Then Joshua said to Achan, "My son, give glory to the LORD God of Israel, and render praise to him; and tell me now what you have done; do not hide it from me." 20 And Achan answered Joshua, "Of a truth I have sinned against the LORD God of Israel, and this is what I did: 21 when I saw among the spoil a beautiful mantle from Shinar, and two hundred shekels of silver, and a bar of gold weighing fifty shekels, then I coveted them, and took them; and behold, they are hidden in the earth inside my tent, with the silver underneath."

The story is quickly told of how Achan was exposed as the guilty man, followed by the immediate execution not only of him but also of his whole family and all his animals; his other possessions were destroyed by fire (verse 25). And so the Lord stopped being angry with his people.

The story also serves to explain the origin of the name Trouble Valley (verses 24-25).

7.16-18   Early the next morning Joshua brought Israel
               forward, tribe by tribe, and the tribe of Judah was
               picked out. 17 He brought the tribe of Judah forward,
               clan by clan, and the clan of Zerah was picked out.
               Then he brought the clan of Zerah forward, family by
               family, and the family of Zabdi was picked out. 18 He
               then brought Zabdi's family forward, man by man, and
               Achan, the son of Carmi and grandson of Zabdi, was
               picked out.

The process of selection, by means of drawing lots, starts early the following morning. Early the next morning translates "So Joshua rose early in the morning" (RSV). One may even translate "The next morning."

All the twelve tribes of Israel are "brought near" the Covenant Box, and the tribe of Judah is indicated (verse 16). Then all the clans of Judah are brought near, and the clan of Zerah is indicated (verse 17a); next all the families of the clan of Zerah are brought near, and the family of Zabdi is indicated (verse 17b).[18] Zabdi's family is brought near, man by man, and his grandson Achan is indicated. Thus by the long process of elimination Achan is exposed as the guilty man.

Brought Israel forward, tribe by tribe (verse 16) may be translated "made all the tribes of Israel come into the LORD's presence, one tribe at a time."

The tribe of Judah was picked out may be translated "The lot fell upon the tribe of Judah" or "The LORD picked out the tribe of Judah." It is obvious that in such a context picked out must not imply favorable choice.

The restructuring of verses 17-18 will be similar to the pattern followed for verse 16.

7.19   Joshua said to him, "My son, tell the truth here before the LORD, the God of Israel, and confess. Tell me now what you have done. Don't try to hide it from me."

Joshua, in a rather kindly manner (My son), urges Achan to tell the truth. My son must not imply a parent—child relation between Joshua and Achan. In many languages it will be more satisfactory not to include any noun of address. Other languages will have their own ways of introducing address in polite and kind manner when a person of higher rank speaks to one of lower rank.

The Hebrew "give glory to the Lord" (see RSV) is a way of demanding the truth before God (see John 9.24), in much the same way that a modern witness in court (in the U.S.A.) is called upon to place his hand on the Bible and promise to tell the truth. The next demand, "render praise to him" (RSV), is taken by some to mean that Achan is to thank God for making his will known through the drawing of the lots (see Gray, Bright). So most translations agree with RSV. TEV, NEB, however, have confess (NEB "make your confession"; see also KJV).[19] One of the standard Hebrew lexicons explains "the song of thanksgiving... develops into confession," and cites this passage and Ezra 10.11, where the context demands the sense "confess" (see RSV). Certainly confess better fits the context here, and is recommended. It is difficult to visualize Joshua demanding that Achan break into a song of thanksgiving.

Since tell the truth and confess carry basically the same meaning, it is possible to translate them by a single verb: "confess to the LORD, the God of Israel, what you have done." Or a negative and a positive form may be used: "Do not lie to the LORD, the God of Israel. Tell him what you have done."

Tell me now what you have done indicates the manner in which Achan confesses his sin to the Lord, the God of Israel. He stands near the Lord's Covenant Box and tells Joshua, the Lord's representative, what he has done. The translation should not imply that more than one confession is involved; to make open confession to Joshua is the manner in which Achan tells the truth to the Lord.

[98]

7.20   "It's true," Achan answered. "I have sinned
            against the LORD, Israel's God, and this is what
            I did.

I have sinned against the LORD may need to be rendered "I did not
obey the LORD" or "I did what the LORD said not to do."
And this is what I did may not be necessary to include in the
translation, since the following verse immediately explains what Achan
did.

7.21   Among the things we seized I saw a beautiful Baby-
            lonian cloak, about five pounds of silver, and a
            bar of gold weighing over one pound. I wanted them
            so much that I took them. You will find them buried
            inside my tent, with the silver at the bottom."

In this verse Achan tells what he took: a beautiful...cloak from
Babylonia ("Shinar" [RSV] is Babylonia; see Gen 10.10); "two hundred
shekels of silver"; and a bar of gold weighing "fifty shekels." A
shekel at that time was a weight, not a coin; the best estimate is
that it was equal in weight to 11.424 grams (0.4 ounces avoirdupois),
and so two hundred shekels would be over two kilograms in the metric
system (see British TEV) and five pounds in the English system. These
were silver pieces, not bullion or coins. The bar of gold weighed one-
fourth the amount of the silver (over 0.5 kilogram, metric; over one
pound, English).
      Achan ends his confession by telling where he has hidden his loot.

           TEV   **7.22-26**   RSV

TEV	RSV
22 So Joshua sent some men, who ran to the tent and found that the condemned things really were buried there, with the silver at the bottom. 23 They brought them out of the tent, took them to Joshua and all the Israelites, and laid them down in the presence of the LORD. 24 Joshua, along with all the people of Israel, seized Achan, the silver, the cloak, the bar of gold, together with Achan's sons and daughters, his cattle, donkeys, and sheep, his tent, and everything else he owned; and they took them to Trouble Valley. 25 And Joshua said, "Why have you brought such trouble on us? The LORD will now bring trouble on you!" All the people then stoned	22 So Joshua sent messengers, and they ran to the tent; and behold, it was hidden in his tent with the silver underneath. 23 And they took them out of the tent and brought them to Joshua and all the people of Israel; and they laid them down before the LORD. 24 And Joshua and all Israel with him took Achan the son of Zerah, and the silver and the mantle and the bar of gold, and his sons and daughters, and his oxen and asses and sheep, and his tent, and all that he had; and they brought them up to the Valley of Achor. 25 And Joshua said, "Why did you bring trouble on us? The LORD brings trouble on you today." And all Israel stoned him with stones;

Achan to death; they also stoned and burned his family and posses- sions. 26 They put a huge pile of stones over him, which is there to this day. That is why that place is still called Trouble Valley.	they burned them with fire, and stoned them with stones. 26 And they raised over him a great heap of stones that remains to this day; then the LORD turned from his burning anger. Therefore to this day the name of that place is called the Valley of Achor.*c*

Then the LORD was no longer furious.

*c*That is *Trouble*

7.22   So Joshua sent some men, who ran to the tent
and found that the condemned things really were
buried there, with the silver at the bottom.

So Joshua sent some men, who ran to the tent translates a coordi- nate construction in Hebrew; literally "So Joshua sent messengers, and they ran to the tent" (RSV). It may be useful in translation to connect the phrase to the tent with the verb sent: "So Joshua sent some men to Achan's tent."
RSV "it was hidden" is difficult to understand. What is meant is "the things were hidden." And "behold" indicates the surprise the men felt when they found the things; TEV expresses this by really (were buried there).
The last part of this verse (and found...at the bottom) may be handled much more economically: "and they found everything just as Achan had described it."

7.23   They brought them out of the tent, took them to
Joshua and all the Israelites, and laid them down
in the presence of the LORD.

The objects are brought out of Achan's tent and placed in the presence of the LORD, that is, in front of the Covenant Box (see com- ment on verse 14).[20] These are all condemned to destruction and so are presented to the Lord.
It is difficult to determine with precision the exact number of actions narrated in this verse. But the following reconstruction seems possible. The men bring the items dedicated for destruction immediately back to Joshua who is standing in the presence of the Covenant Box. By this action both Joshua and all the people of Israel who are gathered there see the items. Then, without change of location, the men lay the goods down beside where Joshua is standing. It is best in translation not to imply that the goods were carried in sequence to Joshua, the people, and then finally taken and placed in the presence of the Cove- nant Box.

7.24   Joshua, along with all the people of Israel, seized
        Achan, the silver, the cloak, the bar of gold, to-
        gether with Achan's sons and daughters, his cattle,
        donkeys, and sheep, his tent, and everything else
        he owned; and they took them to Trouble Valley.

   In TEV this verse consists of one rather lengthy sentence, which
may need to be divided into at least two smaller units. For example,
"Then Joshua and all the people of Israel took Achan and the things
that he had stolen down to Trouble Valley. They also took his sons and
daughters, his cattle, donkeys, and sheep, his tent, and everything
else he owned."21

7.25   And Joshua said, "Why have you brought such trouble on
        us? The LORD will now bring trouble on you!" All the
        people then stoned Achan to death; they also stoned and
        burned his family and possessions.

   In place of And Joshua said, it may be better to translate "When
they got there, Joshua said."
   Why have you brought such trouble on us? may be more effective if
rendered as a statement and combined with the following statement: "You
have brought trouble on us, and now the LORD will bring trouble on
you!"
   Although the Hebrew does not state that the people burned Achan
after stoning him, it is implicit and should be clearly indicated: "So
all the people stoned Achan and his family to death. Then the people
burned up the bodies together with all Achan's possessions."
   The Hebrew text has two different verbs for "to stone"; first,
"they stoned Achan" and then "they burned them with fire" and then
(another verb) "they stoned them with stones." Many scholars believe
that the writer used two different sources, in one of which only Achan
was stoned, and the other in which all his family were stoned. It is
unlikely that the Israelites first burned them (the people and the
animals) to death and then stoned them (as the RSV literal translation
of the Hebrew says). NEB, NAB, following the Septuagint, omit "they
burned them with fire and stoned them with stones." The HOTTP retains
the Hebrew, but it translates the second verb as "heap stones upon."22
This may be correct but does not relieve the text of difficulties,
since the following verse begins "and they also placed a heap of stones
on them." Bright would omit the first "they stoned him," so that the
text would mean that Achan, his family, animals, and belongings were
all destroyed by fire, after which a huge pile of stones was heaped
over the charred remains.
   Whereas TEV interprets them to mean "Achan's family and possessions," it is possible also to limit it to his family: "All Israel
stoned Achan and his relatives to death, and then they burned their
bodies." Either this translation or that of TEV may be followed.

7.26   They put a huge pile of stones over him, which is
there to this day. That is why that place is still
called Trouble Valley.
     Then the LORD was no longer furious.

Achan's sin has made him and his family and everything he owns
devoted to destruction; so he, his family, and his animals are all
stoned to death, while his belongings are all burned. Thus the Lord's
order is finally obeyed, and he was no longer furious.

The execution takes place in Trouble Valley (RSV "Valley of
Achor"). The Hebrew noun *akor* means "trouble." Joshua's words in
verse 25 contain a play on words: Achan has brought...trouble (Hebrew
verb *akar*) on Israel, and now the Lord will...bring trouble on him.

As in the case of Circumcision Hill (5.3), the name Trouble Valley
here was given to the valley as a result of the execution of Achan. At
the time of the writing of this account, the place still had that name
and the pile of stones was still there.

In the phrase over him Achan is in focus; however, the meaning is
surely "over them," including everything that was burned, especially
Achan and his relatives.

Then the LORD was no longer furious may need to be translated,
"After the death of Achan, the LORD was no longer furious with the
people of Israel." Or "After the people of Israel had put Achan to
death, the LORD was no longer angry with them."

Chapter 8

The Capture and Destruction of Ai

1 The LORD said to Joshua, "Take all the soldiers with you and go on up to Ai. Don't be afraid or discouraged. I will give you victory over the king of Ai; his people, city, and land will be yours. 2 You are to do to Ai and its king what you did to Jericho and its king, but this time you may keep its goods and livestock for yourselves. Prepare to attack the city by surprise from the rear." 3 So Joshua got ready to go to Ai with all his soldiers. He picked out thirty thousand of his best troops and sent them out at night 4 with these orders: "Hide on the other side of the city, but not too far away from it; be ready to attack. 5 My men and I will approach the city. When the men of Ai come out against us, we will turn and run, just as we did the first time. 6 They will pursue us until we have led them away from the city. They will think that we are running from them, as we did before. 7 Then you will come out of hiding and capture the city. The LORD your God will give it to you. 8 After you have taken the city, set it on fire, just as the LORD has commanded. These are your orders." 9 So Joshua sent them out, and they went to their hiding place and waited there, west of Ai, between Ai and Bethel. Joshua spent the night in camp.

1 And the LORD said to Joshua, "Do not fear or be dismayed; take all the fighting men with you, and arise, go up to Ai; see, I have given into your hand the king of Ai, and his people, his city, and his land; 2 and you shall do to Ai and its king as you did to Jericho and its king; only its spoil and its cattle you shall take as booty for yourselves; lay an ambush against the city, behind it." 3 So Joshua arose, and all the fighting men, to go up to Ai; and Joshua chose thirty thousand mighty men of valor, and sent them forth by night. 4 And he commanded them, "Behold, you shall lie in ambush against the city, behind it; do not go very far from the city, but hold yourselves all in readiness; 5 and I, and all the people who are with me, will approach the city. And when they come out against us, as before, we shall flee before them; 6 and they will come out after us, till we have drawn them away from the city; for they will say, 'They are fleeing from us, as before.' So we will flee from them; 7 then you shall rise up from the ambush, and seize the city; for the LORD your God will give it into your hand. 8 And when you have taken the city, you shall set the city on fire, doing as the LORD has bidden; see, I have commanded you." 9 So Joshua sent them forth; and

> they went to the place of ambush,
> and lay between Bethel and Ai, to
> the west of Ai; but Joshua spent
> that night among the people.

The section heading, The Capture and Destruction of Ai, may be rendered as a statement: "Joshua and the people of Israel capture and destroy the city of Ai" or "The people of Israel capture and destroy the city of Ai." Since the actual capture of Ai is not narrated until verses 18-29, it is possible to give separate section headings to verses 1-17 and 18-29. If that is done, the section heading which TEV places for the entire division would be placed before verses 18-29. The first part of the chapter would then be called "How Joshua planned to capture the city of Ai" or "Joshua makes plans to capture the city of Ai."

8.1   The LORD said to Joshua, "Take all the soldiers
       with you and go on up to Ai. Don't be afraid or dis-
       couraged. I will give you victory over the king of
       Ai; his people, city, and land will be yours.

Now that Israel has been purged of sin, the Lord is ready to allow the Israelites to capture the city of Ai. He orders Joshua to proceed (verses 1-2). Joshua explains his strategy to his troops (verses 3-9), and the next day the campaign against the city is successfully executed. The city is captured and destroyed, and all its inhabitants, including the king, are killed (verses 10-29). Thus the Lord again demonstrates his invincible power, to which the ruins of the city and the huge pile of stones over the king's grave are eloquent if mute witnesses.

TEV rearranges the sequence of God's instructions to Joshua by placing the command Take all the soldiers with you and go on up to Ai as the first part of God's instructions. For the actual order of the Hebrew, see RSV, which begins with the command for Joshua not to be afraid.

All the soldiers may be translated "all the soldiers of Israel" or "all your soldiers." And the command go on up to Ai may need to be more specific: "attack the city of Ai a second time." In Hebrew the natural way of saying this would be to use the directive "go up," because the cities of Ancient Palestine were customarily built on hills or mountains for the sake of protection.

The Lord says to Joshua, Don't be afraid or discouraged (as in 1.9), for he, the Lord, will give Joshua and his men victory. The Hebrew verbs translated be afraid and discouraged are virtually synonyms, except that the verb translated discouraged literally means "be shattered" or "be filled with terror." This is a very strong formula in Hebrew, and it should be rendered in a way which is most effective in the receptor language, whether with a single verb or with two verbs. If the pattern of TEV is followed, one may translate "Do not be afraid of the people of Ai! Do not be discouraged because of what happened before!" Using a single verb one may render "Do not be frightened!" or "Do not be the least bit frightened!"

[104]

The city, its king, his people, and all his land will be handed over to Joshua (RSV "I have given into your hand"). <u>Give you victory over</u> and <u>will be yours</u> translate the one verb rendered "given into your hand" by RSV. Many languages will have quite vivid idioms for describing power over one's enemies. It may be more effective if a single verb is used; for example, "I have placed in your power the king of Ai, his people, his city, and his land."

8.2   You are to do to Ai and its king what you did to
         Jericho and its king, but this time you may keep
         its goods and livestock for yourselves. Prepare
         to attack the city by surprise from the rear."

<u>Ai and its king</u> are to be completely destroyed, as were Jericho and its king. (It should be noticed that the story of the fall of Jericho [6.20-25] does not expressly state that its king was put to death, but it is implied in 6.21.) This time, however, the Israelites will be allowed to keep <u>its goods and livestock</u>. The Hebrew noun translated <u>goods</u> is literally "plunder" and may refer to any removable goods taken in battle, including prisoners (see 1 Sam 30.19). In the present context it would refer to any physical objects which may be hauled away, but not to prisoners, since all the people of the city are condemned to destruction. The word translated <u>livestock</u> refers basically to cattle, though sheep and other domesticated animals would also be included. However, one should be careful not to select a term which specifically indicates unclean animals such as pigs.

The Lord tells Joshua the strategy he is to follow: the Israelites are to lie in ambush behind the city, that is, to the west of it (see verses 9,12), so as to <u>attack it by surprise</u>. The translation should not imply that Joshua is commanded to line up all his men behind the city to attack it by surprise. As the unfolding of the account will indicate, only part of Joshua's force was placed behind the city in ambush. In order to make this clear one may translate "Secretly place some of your men behind the city, so that they can come out and attack it by surprise at the right time."

8.3-4   So Joshua got ready to go to Ai with all his
         soldiers. He picked out thirty thousand of his best
         troops and sent them out at night 4 with these
         orders: "Hide on the other side of the city, but
         not too far away from it; be ready to attack.

<u>Got ready</u> translates the Hebrew verb "rise" (see RSV). This verb is often used in the Old Testament as an auxiliary which means to prepare to do something or to begin doing something; it does not mean, as the English verb "arise" implies, that the subject has been sitting or lying down (see also in verse 1 "and arise, go up to Ai," RSV; TEV <u>go on up to Ai</u>). See 1.2.

<u>So Joshua got ready to go to Ai with all his soldiers</u> may give two false implications: (1) <u>got ready to go</u> may imply that he made

preparations but did not go; and (2) <u>with all his soldiers</u> could suggest that Joshua himself was leading the entire force as a unit to attack the city. Since, as indicated in the previous paragraph, the Hebrew verb rendered <u>got ready</u> frequently functions merely as an auxiliary of the main verb, it is not necessary always to represent it in translation. Therefore "got ready to go up" may even mean "went up" (see the comment on "go up" in verse 1). These two potential problems may be resolved, and a smooth transition made from the previous verse, if this verse is begun as follows: "So before Joshua went up against Ai with his main force, he picked out thirty thousand of his best troops. Then he sent them out at night 4 and told them...."

Joshua selects thirty thousand of his best soldiers and tells them to lie in ambush west of the city, not very far from it. This seems to be a very large number (see in verse 12 where only about five thousand men are actually stationed there). Gray thinks that thirty thousand may be a scribal error for three thousand, and a few translations place three thousand in the text, with a footnote: "Hebrew thirty thousand." From the Israelite camp at Gilgal to Ai was about 25 kilometers.

<u>8.5</u>   My men and I will approach the city. When the men
       of Ai come out against us, we will turn and run,
       just as we did the first time.

Joshua himself, with his men, will attack Ai frontally, that is, from the east, and when its soldiers come out to fight the Israelites, Joshua and his men will flee, as they did in the first attempt to capture the city (7.4-5). This will draw the soldiers of Ai away from the city, and then the Israelite soldiers who have been in ambush west of the city will be able to capture it unopposed; it will be the Lord's victory (verse 7). The city is to be set on fire (verse 8).

<u>My men and I</u> may be more clearly translated "The rest of the men and I" or "The men who are with me."

<u>Will approach the city</u> may need to be further described by "from the front."

<u>Come out against us</u> means "come out and attack us." Instead of beginning this sentence with a subordinate temporal clause (<u>When...</u>), it is possible to begin "The men of Ai will come out and attack us, but we will turn and run, just as we did the first time."

<u>8.6</u>   They will pursue us until we have led them away
       from the city. They will think that we are run-
       ning from them, as we did before.

It may be better to invert the order of the two sentences in this verse. To do so will have two advantages: (1) the first sentence leads more naturally into verse 7, and (2) the second sentence ties closely with the last part of verse 5. Moreover, <u>that we are running from them as we did before</u> may need to be shifted back to the direct discourse of the Hebrew (see RSV).[23] Following these suggestions, the verse may be translated, "They will think, 'Those Israelites are running from us, as they did before.' Then they will pursue us, and we will lead them away from the city."

8.7   Then you will come out of hiding and capture the
          city. The LORD your God will give it to you.

Then you will come out of hiding translates "then you shall rise up from the ambush" (RSV). The verb "rise up" is the same one discussed in verse 3; here the meaning is "come up from" or "come out from."
     It may be better to translate your God as "our God," so as not to exclude Joshua.
     Will give it to you is literally "will give it into your hand" (RSV). This translates the same expression used in verse 1. It may be translated, "will place it in your power."

8.8   After you have taken the city, set it on fire,
          just as the LORD has commanded. These are your
          orders."

The first sentence of this verse in TEV is very similar in struc- ture to that of the Hebrew. The order is both logical and chronological, and in this respect should cause no basic translational difficulties.
     These are your orders is literally "see, I have commanded you" (RSV). The meaning may also be rendered, "strictly obey my orders!"

8.9   So Joshua sent them out, and they went to their
          hiding place and waited there, west of Ai, between
          Ai and Bethel. Joshua spent the night in camp.

In the clause So Joshua sent them out, it may be beneficial to remind the reader that them refers back to the thirty thousand of his best troops mentioned in verse 3. One may then translate "So Joshua sent out the thirty thousand men." Assuming that the information of this clause is clearly implicit, one may also translate "According to Joshua's instructions, they went...."
     Because of the two appositional statements (west of Ai and between Ai and Bethel) it may be to the readers' advantage if the sentence is divided into two parts and somewhat restructured: "So Joshua sent the men out to their hiding place, which was west of Ai in the direction of Bethel. The men went there and waited all night." Joshua spends the night "among the people" (RSV), that is, in camp (TEV).[24]

	TEV	8.10-17	RSV

10 Early in the morning, Joshua got up and called the sol- diers together. Then he and the

10 And Joshua arose early in the morning and mustered the peo- ple, and went up, with the elders

leaders of Israel led them to Ai.
11 The soldiers with him went toward the main entrance to the
city and set up camp on the north
side, with a valley between themselves and Ai. 12 He took about
five thousand men and put them in
hiding west of the city, between
Ai and Bethel. 13 The soldiers
were arranged for battle with the
main camp north of the city and
the rest of the men to the west.
Joshua spent the night in the valley. 14 When the king of Ai saw
Joshua's men, he acted quickly.
He and all his men went out toward
the Jordan Valley to fight the
Israelites at the same place as
before, not knowing that he was
about to be attacked from the rear.
15 Joshua and his men pretended
that they were retreating, and
ran away toward the barren country.
16 All the men in the city had
been called together to go after
them, and as they pursued Joshua,
they kept getting farther away
from the city. 17 Every man in
Ai*c* went after the Israelites,
and the city was left wide open,
with no one to defend it.

cOne ancient translation Ai; *Hebrew* Ai and Bethel.

of Israel, before the people to
Ai. 11 And all the fighting men
who were with him went up, and
drew near before the city, and
encamped on the north side of Ai,
with a ravine between them and Ai.
12 And he took about five thousand
men, and set them in ambush between
Bethel and Ai, to the west of the
city. 13 So they stationed the
forces, the main encampment which
was north of the city and its
rear guard west of the city. But
Joshua spent that night in the valley. 14 And when the king of Ai
saw this he and all his people,
the men of the city, made haste
and went out early to the descent*d*
toward the Arabah to meet Israel
in battle; but he did not know
that there was an ambush against
him behind the city. 15 And Joshua
and all Israel made a pretense of
being beaten before them, and fled
in the direction of the wilderness.
16 So all the people who were in
the city were called together to
pursue them, and as they pursued
Joshua they were drawn away from
the city. 17 There was not a man
left in Ai or Bethel, who did not
go out after Israel: they left
the city open, and pursued Israel.

dCn: Heb *appointed time*

The plan is carried out and works perfectly (verses 10-29). The
city is captured and all its inhabitants are killed. It should be
noticed that the account contains difficulties and is not completely
clear. Some scholars believe there is evidence that the writer mixed
together two or more different accounts, so that there are what appear
to be discrepancies and doublets, that is, two accounts of the same
event. In any case, the translator should not attempt to "correct" the
text.

8.10   Early in the morning Joshua got up and called
            the soldiers together. Then he and the leaders of
            Israel led them to Ai.

The following morning (TEV <u>in the morning</u> means "the next morning") the plan is put into operation: <u>Joshua and the leaders of Israel</u> lead the troops from the camp at Gilgal to the city of Ai (about 25 kilometers). For <u>the leaders of Israel</u> see 7.6. It should be noted that TEV <u>soldiers</u> translates a Hebrew noun which RSV and others translate "people." But in a context such as this, "the people" are not all the individuals, men, women, and children, but the fighting men (NEB, NAB "the army"). <u>Called...together</u> (RSV "mustered") translates a Hebrew verb which has many meanings: here with <u>soldiers</u> as object, it means to group together in military fashion.

In order to avoid a misunderstanding, it may be necessary to state explicitly that the leaders of Israel were included in this group of fighting men: "the leaders of Israel and the fighting men" or "all the fighting men of Israel and their leaders." Some languages will require explicit mention of the people's response to Joshua's call: 'When they had all come together, he and the leaders of Israel led the fighting men to Ai."

<u>8.11</u>   The soldiers with him went toward the main entrance
             to the city and set up camp on the north side, with
             a valley between themselves and Ai.

<u>The soldiers with him</u> includes all the men mentioned in the previous verse. The reading of TEV is ambiguous; it suggests that there was another group or other groups led by someone else. In order to avoid this ambiguity, at least two solutions are possible: (1) The last part of the previous verse may be connected with the first part of this verse: "Then he and the leaders of Israel led the fighting men 11 up toward the main entrance to the city of Ai." (2) The other solution would be to begin verse 11 with the pronoun "They," referring back to Joshua, the leaders of Israel, and the fighting men: "They went up toward the main entrance to the city...."

The main body took up its position <u>north</u> of the city, where it would be in plain sight of the enemy (verse 11); between the Israelite army and the city was <u>a valley</u>. The explanation <u>with a valley between themselves and Ai</u> may fare better as a separate statement: "Only a valley separated them from the city of Ai" or "There was a valley between their camp and the city of Ai."

In translating verses 11-13 one should not attempt either to "sew up the seams" or to remove what seem to be contradictions between verses 10-12 and verses 3-9. JB places verses 11-13 together in such a manner as to make them agree with the earlier account, while LB even adds a footnote with an explanation which assumes that one person must have written the narrative in a singular and consistent manner. This is dishonest; the translator's first duty is to be honest with the text.

<u>8.12</u>   He took about five thousand men and put them in
             hiding west of the city, between Ai and Bethel.

8.12

Joshua placed a smaller group of five thousand men in ambush west
of Ai, between it and Bethel, which was 3 kilometers west of Ai. The
account of the ambush found here is distinct from that of verse 3.
Whereas verse 3 speaks of thirty thousand men, this verse is more
modest and speaks of only five thousand. It is not being true to the
text to translate "another five thousand men" (LB). The translator
must always be conscious of the problems keeping parts of a discourse
consistent with each other; however, one must never employ translational techniques as a means of covering over obvious textual difficulties.

He took...and put must not be understood to imply that Joshua accompanied the men. The meaning is "Joshua ordered about five thousand
of his men to hide west of the city...."

8.13   The soldiers were arranged for battle with the main
          camp north of the city and the rest of the men to
          the west. Joshua spent the night in the valley.

Verse 13 repeats the information in verses 11-12; the main body
of troops is north of Ai, and the smaller body (literally "the heel")
is west of the city. NEB, following the Septuagint, omits verse 13. At
the end of the verse the Masoretic text has "and Joshua went that night
into the valley"; some Hebrew manuscripts, however, have the verb "to
spend the night," which is preferred by most translations. HOTTP, however, prefers to follow the Masoretic text, in which case one may
translate "Joshua himself returned during the night to the Jordan Valley."

8.14   When the king of Ai saw Joshua's men, he acted
          quickly. He and all his men went out toward the
          Jordan Valley to fight the Israelites at the
          same place as before, not knowing that he was
          about to be attacked from the rear.

The following morning (as is implied by spent the night in verse
13), as soon as the king of Ai saw what was happening, he took action.
The Hebrew text says simply "when the king of Ai saw" (RSV), the implied
object being, most likely, the main Israelite force north of the city.
TEV supplies Joshua's men as object of the verb saw; "the main Israelite force north of the city" or "the Israelite army north of the city"
will also suffice as object.

The Hebrew text of verse 14 is wordy and none too clear; a literal
translation would be as follows:
      And it was when the king of Ai saw (it), and they hurried and
      were eager and went out, the men of the city, to encounter
      Israel in battle, he and all his people, for the appointed
      time (or, place) facing the valley, and he did not know that
      (there was) an ambush for him behind the city.
He acted quickly of TEV combines two Hebrew verbs ("hurried and
were eager"); one may combine the two: "he did not hesitate long."

[110]

The Jordan Valley translates "the Arabah" (RSV), which was east of the city.

NEB, following the Septuagint, omits the Hebrew phrase represented in the literal translation above by "for the appointed time (place) facing the valley." HOTTP prefers the Hebrew and translates the phrase as "for the encounter," saying it "can refer to an agreement, whether of place, time, tactic or sign." The BJ footnote translates "place of meeting" (*lieu de rendez-vous*); TOB has "a certain place" (*un lieu fixé*). NAB, RSV follow a conjecture "to the descent" (as in 7.5). TEV takes the Hebrew to mean "appointed place," which it interprets to refer to the place of the previous encounter between the forces of Ai and the Israelites, at the same place as before. This problematic phrase may also be represented by the adverb "there": "to attack them there."

Not knowing that...from the rear may be better rendered as a complete sentence: "he did not know that other Israelite soldiers were going to attack him from the rear" or "...that Joshua had laid an ambush for him."

8.15   Joshua and his men pretended that they were retreating, and ran away toward the barren country.

Joshua and his men pretended that they were retreating is literally "Joshua and all Israel were beaten (defeated) before them"; in the context it means that "they pretended they were beaten" (see RSV).
The barren country is the land between Ai and the Jordan Valley. One may translate "in the direction of the Jordan Valley."

8.16   All the men in the city had been called together to go after them, and as they pursued Joshua, they kept getting farther away from the city.

Joshua's plan worked: "all the people" (RSV) of Ai joined in the pursuit of the fleeing Israelites. ("All the people," of course, means all the men, that is, all who were fit and able for battle.) It is possible to translate this first clause by an active construction: "The leaders of the city had called together all the men of the city to go after them."
They kept getting farther away from the city represents a slight shift in focus from the Hebrew, which indicates that the Israelite men intentionally drew the men of Ai away from the city. The entire verse may be translated more economically than TEV. For example, "The leaders of the city had commanded all the men in the city to go after the Israelites. And the Israelites led them farther and farther away from the city."

8.17   Every man in Ai*c* went after the Israelites, and the city was left wide open, with no one to defend it.

cOne ancient translation Ai; *Hebrew* Ai and Bethel.

The Hebrew of this verse speaks of "Ai and Bethel" (see RSV; TEV footnote); the Septuagint omits "and Bethel," which TEV, NEB, JB follow; there seems to be no reason for supposing that the men of Bethel were involved in this campaign. HOTTP favors the Hebrew text, and a translator should feel free to follow it. Ai was left unprotected, an easy target for the Israelite troops lying in ambush west of the city.

Went after represents two verbs in Hebrew (RSV "go out after...pursued"). Some languages will require the retention of two verbs, one indicating departure from the city and the other the actual pursuit of the Israelites.

The city was left wide open refers specifically to the city gates. One may then translate the verse "Every man in Ai left the city and ran after the Israelites. There was no one left to defend the city, and the gates of the city were left wide open." Or "...and the men of the city had left the gates wide open."

TEV   8.18-23   RSV

TEV	RSV
18 Then the LORD said to Joshua, "Point your spear at Ai; I am giving it to you." Joshua did as he was told, 19 and as soon as he lifted his hand, the men who had been hiding got up quickly, ran into the city and captured it. They immediately set the city on fire. 20 When the men of Ai looked back, they saw the smoke rising to the sky. There was no way for them to escape, because the Israelites who had run toward the barren country now turned around to attack them. 21 When Joshua and his men saw that the others had taken the city and that it was on fire, they turned around and began killing the men of Ai. 22 The Israelites in the city now came down to join the battle. So the men of Ai found themselves completely surrounded by Israelites, and they were all killed. No one got away, and no one lived through it 23 except the king of Ai. He was captured and taken to Joshua.	18 Then the LORD said to Joshua, "Stretch out the javelin that is in your hand toward Ai; for I will give it into your hand." And Joshua stretched out the javelin that was in his hand toward the city. 19 And the ambush rose quickly out of their place, and as soon as he had stretched out his hand, they ran and entered the city and took it; and they made haste to set the city on fire. 20 So when the men of Ai looked back, behold, the smoke of the city went up to heaven; and they had no power to flee this way or that, for the people that fled to the wilderness turned back upon the pursuers. 21 And when Joshua and all Israel saw that the ambush had taken the city, and that the smoke of the city went up, then they turned back and smote the men of Ai. 22 And the others came forth from the city against them; so they were in the midst of Israel, some on this side, and some on that side; and Israel smote them, until there was left none that survived or escaped. 23 But the king of Ai they took alive, and brought him to Joshua.

Joshua, at the Lord's command, points his spear at Ai, and immediately the Israelites lying in ambush west of the city advance, capture Ai, and set it on fire. This assumes that Joshua is located at a place where those Israelites could see him; in verse 15, however, he is portrayed as fleeing with his troops eastward of Ai. Some scholars suppose that the writer's source of information for verse 18 had Joshua still north of the city, where he and the main force had camped the night before (verse 13).

8.18-19   Then the LORD said to Joshua, "Point your spear at Ai; I am giving it to you." Joshua did as he was told, 19 and as soon as he lifted his hand, the men who had been hiding got up quickly, ran into the city and captured it. They immediately set the city on fire.

The spear that Joshua points at the city is more precisely a "javelin" (AT, RSV, NAB, TOB), which is a smaller weapon; Gray defines it as a weapon that is thrown, not thrust; Soggin says that in the Qumran literature it means "sword" (so BJ). He keeps his weapon pointed toward Ai until the destruction and slaughter are complete (verse 26). So this is not just a signal for the troops lying in ambush but a gesture whereby the Lord enables his people to win (see Moses at the battle of Rephidim, Exo 17.11-13).

In the statement I am giving it to you the pronoun "it" refers back to Ai of the previous clause. It is possible, however, that the reader might take this to mean the spear. It may therefore be helpful to translate "I am giving the city to you." Or it may be expressed, "I am placing the city in your power," by which "in your power" substitutes for "in your hand" of the Hebrew (see RSV).

Joshua did as he was told may be translated with even more brevity ("Joshua did it") or more explicitness ("Joshua pointed his spear at the city"). One may also translate "Joshua did what the LORD told him to do."

Verse 19 either assumes or narrates six separate events. Although these events are described in an orderly manner, it may be to the readers' advantage if a new sentence is used to begin the verse. Moreover, depending upon the expectations of the receptor language, the verse allows itself to be broken into sentence units at various places. For example, "The men who had been hiding saw Joshua lift up his spear. So they immediately got up and ran into the city. They captured the city and quickly set it on fire."

8.20   When the men of Ai looked back, they saw the smoke rising to the sky. There was no way for them to escape, because the Israelites who had run toward the barren country now turned around to attack them.

This verse depicts the confusion of the men of Ai; seeing the city in flames, they know that the enemy is there, so that retreat to the city is impossible; and now the main Israelite force turns around and attacks them: there was no way for them to escape.

When the men of Ai looked back, they saw the smoke rising avoids
the problem of RSV: "So when the men of Ai looked back, behold, the
smoke of the city went up...." That is, RSV assumes the sequence:
(1) the men looked back; (2) the smoke went up. However, the sequence
is more naturally assumed to be: (1) the smoke went up; (2) the men
looked back.

There was no way for them to escape may be translated "There was
no place for them to run" or "...where they could run for safety."

8.21   When Joshua and his men saw that the others had
        taken the city and that it was on fire, they
        turned around and began killing the men of Ai.

Verse 21 essentially repeats the information in verse 20, but this
time the focus is on the Israelites, while in verse 20 it is on the
enemy.

Because of the duplication of information in verses 20-21, the two
may be translated as a unit. Such restructuring may be advisable, since
there is already a good deal of repetition in the narrative. One pattern might be:

When the men from Ai looked back, they saw the smoke from
their city rising to the sky. Joshua and his men also saw
the smoke, and they knew that the other Israelite soldiers
had captured the city and set it on fire. Now there was no
place where the men of Ai could run for safety. So Joshua
and his men turned around and began killing them.

8.22-23   The Israelites in the city now came down to join
           the battle. So the men of Ai found themselves
           completely surrounded by Israelites, and they
           were all killed. No one got away, and no one
           lived through it 23 except the king of Ai. He
           was captured and taken to Joshua.

Verses 22-23 describe the complete annihilation of the enemy
force: the Israelites who have set Ai on fire leave the city and advance against the enemy. The men of Ai are caught between the two
Israelite bodies, and they are all killed, with the exception of the
king, who is taken alive and delivered to Joshua.

The Israelites in the city now came down to join the battle translates "And the others came forth from the city against" (RSV). It may
be necessary to be even more explicit: "The Israelite men who had gone
into the city and had set it on fire now came out and attacked the men
of Ai."

The second sentence of TEV (So the men...were all killed) may be
formulated as an active sentence: "So the Israelite army completely
surrounded the men of Ai and killed every one of them."

No one got away, and no one lived through it translates "until
there was left none that survived or escaped" (RSV). It may also be
translated, "None of them escaped with his life" or "All the men of
Ai were killed."

He was captured and taken to Joshua may also be changed into an active: "The men of Israel captured him and took him to Joshua."

TEV	8.24-29	RSV

24 The Israelites killed every one of the enemy in the barren country where they had chased them. Then they went back to Ai and killed everyone there. 25-26 Joshua kept his spear pointed at Ai and did not put it down until every person there had been killed. The whole population of Ai was killed that day—twelve thousand men and women. 27 The Israelites kept for themselves the livestock and goods captured in the city, as the LORD had told Joshua. 28 Joshua burned Ai and left it in ruins. It is still like that today. 29 He hanged the king of Ai from a tree and left his body there until evening. At sundown Joshua gave orders for the body to be removed, and it was thrown down at the entrance to the city gate. They covered it with a huge pile of stones, which is still there today.

24 When Israel had finished slaughtering all the inhabitants of Ai in the open wilderness where they pursued them, and all of them to the very last had fallen by the edge of the sword, all Israel returned to Ai, and smote it with the edge of the sword. 25 And all who fell that day, both men and women, were twelve thousand, all the people of Ai. 26 For Joshua did not draw back his hand, with which he stretched out the javelin, until he had utterly destroyed all the inhabitants of Ai. 27 Only the cattle and the spoil of that city Israel took as their booty, according to the word of the LORD which he commanded Joshua. 28 So Joshua burned Ai, and made it for ever a heap of ruins, as it is to this day. 29 And he hanged the king of Ai on a tree until evening; and at the going down of the sun Joshua commanded, and they took his body down from the tree, and cast it at the entrance of the gate of the city, and raised over it a great heap of stones, which stands there to this day.

The account ends with the hanging of the king of Ai and with the pile of stones which are heaped over his body.

8.24   The Israelites killed every one of the enemy in the barren country where they had chased them. Then they went back to Ai and killed everyone there.

Verse 24a again reports the complete slaughter of the men of Ai by the Israelite forces; the Israelites then advance on the city and kill all its inhabitants (verse 24b).

As a comparison of TEV and RSV indicates, TEV is considerably shorter than the Hebrew. Moreover, there is some ambiguity about the clause rendered where they had chased them. According to TEV, they would seem to refer to the Israelites, while them points back to the men of Ai. However, it is possible to understand the men of Ai as subject of the clause: "when the Israelites had slaughtered all the men of Ai who had pursued them...." The ambiguity of the Hebrew text allows either interpretation, though according to verse 20 it was the men of Ai who had pursued the Israelites in the direction of the barren country.

8.25-26   Joshua kept his spear pointed at Ai and did not put
           it down until every person there had been killed.
           The whole population of Ai was killed that day—twelve
           thousand men and women.

TEV combines verses 25 and 26 in order to give the information about Joshua first. However, it is not obligatory to give the information in this order, and the narrative may flow even more smoothly if verses 25 and 26 are retained in their proper order. For example, "On that day the men of Israel killed everyone in the city of Ai. They killed twelve thousand men and women, and Joshua kept his spear pointed toward the city until they had killed them all." If the restructuring of TEV is maintained, it should be noted that until every person there had been killed is literally "until he had caused to be killed all the people of Ai." Either the use of the causative, or the shift to a plural subject ("Joshua's men") will be necessary in some languages. For example, "That is how Joshua caused his men to kill all the people of Ai on that day. There were twelve thousand men and women in the city, and Joshua's men killed every one of them."

In verse 26 (RSV) "utterly destroyed" translates the same verb discussed at 2.10 (see comments on 2.10). From the biblical point of view this is not mindless slaughter but is a religious act of destroying completely what has been dedicated to the Lord; it is a "holy war."

All the citizens of Ai are killed—a total of twelve thousand; no specific mention is made of the children, but it is assumed that they are included.

8.27   The Israelites kept for themselves the livestock and
           goods captured in the city, as the LORD had told
           Joshua.

Only the livestock and goods in the city are spared, and these are kept as loot by the victorious Israelites, as the Lord had instructed Joshua (verse 2). It is possible to render part of this verse as direct discourse: "The LORD had told Joshua, 'The people of Israel may keep the livestock and the goods captured in the city.' So the Israelites kept these for themselves."

8.28   Joshua burned Ai and left it in ruins. It is still
           like that today.

Joshua burned Ai may be a summary of the narrative and not an
additional action on the part of Joshua (see verse 19). This may also
be translated as either "Joshua caused the city of Ai to be burned" or
"Joshua and his men burned the city of Ai." The translation should not
leave the impression that Joshua alone burned the city.

The city was left...in ruins, a condition which persisted to the
time the account was written (today). It is important that the reader
not confuse today, the time of the writing of the book, with "today,"
the time of the reading of the book. To avoid this possibility of misunderstanding, one may translate "The city is still in ruins today, as
I write this story to tell you about it." If this restructuring is followed, it is obvious that the word chosen for "story" should suggest a
"true story" as opposed to an invented story.

8.29   He hanged the king of Ai from a tree and left his
           body there until evening. At sundown Joshua gave
           orders for the body to be removed, and it was thrown
           down at the entrance to the city gate. They covered
           it with a huge pile of stones, which is still there
           today.

The text says simply that Joshua "hanged the king of Ai on a tree
until evening" (RSV). It is probable that first he was killed and then
his body was impaled on a stake (see 10.26; Deut 21.22-23), and some
languages will require that the translation be explicit; for example,
"They killed the king of Ai and hanged his body on a tree."

The Hebrew word translated tree means also a pole or a stake; accordingly, one may translate "They killed the king of Ai, and then they
impaled his body on a pole."

At sundown his body was removed, buried near the city gate, and
stones piled over it. But this formulation may leave too many gaps.
That is, it may be necessary to state explicitly that the body was removed before it was thrown down at the entrance to the city gate. For
example:

           At sundown Joshua told his men to remove the body and to
           throw it down at the entrance to the city gate. He also
           told them to cover it with a huge pile of stones. They
           obeyed Joshua's command, and the pile of stones is still
           there as I write this story.

Or the command may be given in direct discourse:

           At sundown Joshua told his men, "Take the body down from
           the tree and throw it down at the entrance to the city
           gate. Then cover it with a huge pile of stones." Joshua's
           men did what he told them, and the pile of stones is still
           there today.

That huge pile of stones was still there when the account was written.

The Law Is Read at Mount Ebal

30 Then Joshua built on Mount Ebal an altar to the LORD, the God of Israel. 31 He made it according to the instructions that Moses, the LORD's servant, had given the Israelites, as it says in the Law of Moses: "an altar made of stones which have not been cut with iron tools." On it they offered burnt sacrifices to the LORD, and they also presented their fellowship offerings. 32 There, with the Israelites looking on, Joshua made on the stones*d* a copy of the Law which Moses had written. 33 The Israelites, with their leaders, officers, and judges, as well as the foreigners among them, stood on two sides of the LORD's Covenant Box, facing the levitical priests who carried it. Half of the people stood with their backs to Mount Gerizim and the other half with their backs to Mount Ebal. The LORD's servant Moses had commanded them to do this when the time came for them to receive the blessing. 34 Joshua then read aloud the whole Law, including the blessings and the curses, just as they are written in the book of the Law. 35 Every one of the commandments of Moses was read by Joshua to the whole gathering, which included women and children, as well as the foreigners living among them.

30 Then Joshua built an altar on Mount Ebal to the LORD, the God of Israel, 31 as Moses the servant of the LORD had commanded the people of Israel, as it is written in the book of the law of Moses, "an altar of unhewn stones, upon which no man has lifted an iron tool"; and they offered on it burnt offerings to the LORD, and sacrificed peace offerings. 32 And there, in the presence of the people of Israel, he wrote upon the stones a copy of the law of Moses, which he had written. 33 And all Israel, sojourner as well as homeborn, with their elders and officers and their judges, stood on opposite sides of the ark before the Levitical priests who carried the ark of the covenant of the LORD, half of them in front of Mount Gerizim and half of them in front of Mount Ebal, as Moses the servant of the LORD had commanded at the first, that they should bless the people of Israel. 34 And afterward he read all the words of the law, the blessing and the curse, according to all that is written in the book of the law. 35 There was not a word of all that Moses commanded which Joshua did not read before all the assembly of Israel, and the women, and the little ones, and the sojourners who lived among them.

*d*the stones; *or* stones

This section interrupts the narrative, which continues from 8.29 directly to 9.1. The locale is Shechem Valley, about 32 kilometers north of Ai, with Mount Ebal on the north side of the pass and Mount Gerizim on the south side. Scholars generally connect this incident with the events at Shechem in chapter 24 (see Bright, Gray, Soggin, Smith). The Septuagint places this section between 9.2 and 9.3.

In any case, this section describes the renewal of the covenant between the Lord and the people of Israel: an altar is built, sacrifices are offered, and the Law is read, including the blessings and the curses; presumably the people respond to the reading (see Deut 27.11-26), but the text does not expressly state this.

It may be to the benefit of the reader to restructure the section heading so that both the reader and the hearers are clearly indicated: "Joshua reads the Law of God (or, of Moses) to the people of Israel at Mount Ebal."

8.30-31   Then Joshua built on Mount Ebal an altar to
               the LORD, the God of Israel. 31 He made it accord-
               ing to the instructions that Moses, the LORD's
               servant, had given the Israelites, as it says in
               the Law of Moses: "an altar made of stones which
               have not been cut with iron tools." On it they
               offered burnt sacrifices to the LORD, and they
               also presented their fellowship offerings.

As indicated in the general introduction to this section, the event described here presupposes a separation of time and place from that of the previous narrative. Therefore in place of the transitional Then, which may suggest immediate succession of events, it may be better to translate "Some time later."

Although the Hebrew does say Joshua built, the meaning is certainly "Joshua caused to be built" or "Joshua commanded his men to build, and they built."

A stone altar is built, and the instructions written in Exodus 20.25 are followed: If you make an altar of stone for me, do not build it out of cut stones, because when you use a chisel on the stones, you make them unfit for my use (TEV); see also Deuteronomy 27.5-6. In translation one must take care to select a verb for "build" which will not contradict these instructions.

It is possible to combine verses 30-31 and to shift Joshua's commands to direct discourse:

               Some time later Joshua and the people of Israel came to
               Mount Ebal. When they got there, Joshua told some of the men,
               "Build an altar to the LORD our God. Build it according to
               the teaching in the Law of Moses. Moses, the LORD's servant,
               said to build an altar made of stones which have not been
               cut with iron tools." So the men built the altar. Then all
               the people offered burnt sacrifices to the LORD, and they
               also presented their fellowship offerings to him.

No indication is given of the size of this stone altar, but it was large enough to accomodate the sacrifice of a large number of animals. Burnt sacrifices were those in which the whole animal was consumed by the fire; fellowship offerings were sacrifices in which only a part of the animal was burned, and the rest was eaten by the worshipers. Burnt sacrifices may then be translated "those sacrifices which must be completely burned on the altar," and fellowship offerings may be rendered "those sacrifices that you are allowed to eat a part of."

For the Law of Moses see 1.7,8.

<u>8.32</u>   There, with the Israelites looking on, Joshua
made on the stones^d a copy of the Law which
Moses had written.

^{d}the stones; *or* stones.

<u>With the Israelites looking on</u> is literally "in the presence of
the people of Israel" (RSV); many languages will have idiomatic formu-
las for "in the presence of," as, for example, "before all eyes."
It is not certain whether the text means that Joshua inscribed <u>a</u>
<u>copy of the Law</u> on <u>the stones</u> of the altar or on some other stones (see
TEV text and footnote; see NEB text and footnote). The instructions in
Deuteronomy 27.1-8 distinguish between the altar (made of undressed
stones) and the stones, covered with plaster, on which the Law was to
be written. It is not to be thought that the area of the stones would
be large enough to allow all the instructions and laws to be written;
either the Ten Commandments or some other short section of the Law
would be inscribed.
<u>The Law which Moses had written</u> is literally "the law of Moses"
(RSV); for English readers the "of" phrase may imply ownership rather
than authorship.

<u>8.33</u>   The Israelites, with their leaders, officers, and
judges, as well as the foreigners among them, stood
on two sides of the LORD's Covenant Box, facing the
levitical priests who carried it. Half of the people
stood with their backs to Mount Gerizim and the other
half with their backs to Mount Ebal. The LORD's servant Moses had commanded them to do this when the time
came for them to receive the blessing.

In verses 33-35 of this section the people are evidently assembled
in Shechem Valley, between Mount Ebal and Mount Gerizim. They are all
there, including the resident aliens (TEV <u>the foreigners among them</u>;
RSV "sojourner").
Three groups of leaders are specifically named (RSV): "the elders"
(see 7.6; 8.10); "the officers" (see 1.10; 3.2); and "the judges." It
is difficult to distinguish precisely among them. The <u>officers</u> probably
had military responsibilities (see 1.10), and the <u>judges</u> were responsible for judicial matters; but the precise role of the <u>leaders</u> (RSV
"the elders") is not clear.
The people stand in two groups, facing each other, with the Covenant Box and the priests in between. The priests stand at either end
of <u>the LORD's Covenant Box</u>, which was carried by means of poles which
went through the rings on the sides of the Box (see Exo 37.3-5). In
TEV the geographical relationship between the people and the levitical
priests is less than clear, if <u>facing</u> is understood to mean that the
people and the priests faced each other. How can the people stand on
two sides of the Covenant Box and at the same time face the levitical
priests who carried it? A few minor adjustments in the order of presentation results in a somewhat more simplified arrangement:

The Israelites stood in two groups and faced the Covenant Box, which was placed between them. Their leaders, officers, judges, and the foreigners who lived among them stood in these two groups with them. One group of Israelites stood with their backs to Mount Gerizim, while the other group stood with their backs to Mount Ebal. The levitical priests who carried the Covenant Box took their places on each side of it.

The levitical priests is a rather unusual phrase, since it seems to imply that there were also nonlevitical priests. As a matter of fact all priests were Levites (that is, of the tribe of Levi), but not all Levites were priests (see comments on 3.3). The ritual proceeds according to the instructions recorded in Deuteronomy 27.11-13.

At the end of this verse the Hebrew text has "at the first"; it is not clear what this modifies. TEV takes it to modify the time when Moses issued the command: Moses had commanded; similarly RSV "as Moses...had commanded at the first" (so JB); following the cue of RSV, it may be translated "according to the instructions which Moses had given." Bright takes it to go with the action of blessing: "that they should bless the people of Israel first of all," that is, before the reading of the blessings and curses (verse 34). NEB is similar, translating "that the blessing should be pronounced first" (also BJ, TOB); NAB "for the blessing of the people of Israel on this first occasion." Everything considered, it would seem that the interpretation of NEB, BJ, TOB is to be preferred; the opening words of verse 34 "And afterward" (RSV) seem to support this interpretation.

In verse 31 Moses was referred to as the Lord's Servant; therefore it may not be necessary so soon to refer to him again as the LORD's servant Moses. The verse is otherwise complicated, and some of the difficulties may be lessened if he is referred to merely as "Moses." If the exegesis of TEV is followed concerning the phrase "at the first," one may then translate "Moses had told them to stand this way so that the priests could pronounce God's blessing on the people." Or, if the interpretation of NEB is pursued, "Moses had told them to stand this way, and have the priests pronounce God's blessings upon them before Joshua read the Law of Moses to them."

8.34 Joshua then read aloud the whole Law, including the blessings and the curses, just as they are written in the book of the Law.

Joshua then reads the whole Law, including the blessings and the curses. It is important to translate read aloud, as with TEV, to make clear that an oral reading to the people is indicated. RSV ("And afterward he read all the words of the law") does not require that the reading be oral, though "before all the assembly" of the following verse does clarify the situation. Another translation may still be clearer: "Then Joshua read (aloud) the whole Law to all the people."

As elsewhere in this book, the Law is probably part if not all of what is now the book of Deuteronomy. It is, of course, not possible to make this identity in translation. Nor would a comment of this nature be appropriate in Bible Society publications.

8.35   Every one of the commandments of Moses was read by
        Joshua to the whole gathering, which included women
        and children, as well as the foreigners living among
        them.

Every one of the commandments of Moses was read by Joshua may be
simplified: "Joshua read every one of the commandments that Moses had
written" or "Joshua read every word that Moses had written." A negative
form is permissible: "He did not leave out a word that Moses had said."
The whole gathering translates the Hebrew "all the assembly of
Israel" (RSV). In the Septuagint the Hebrew noun "assembly" is translated by a noun which in the New Testament usually means "church." The
Hebrew word itself in the Old Testament is used of a formal coming together of the people of Israel for cultic purpose. Here the biblical
writer emphasizes the participation of all the people by explicitly
mentioning women and children, and the resident aliens as well. Was
read by Joshua to the whole gathering may be stated quite differently:
"The entire Israelite community heard it, including the women and children, and also the foreigners who lived with them."
The clause which included women and children may seem redundant,
but it reflects the organization of the ancient Israelite society in
which women and children played a secondary role. Therefore in order
to reflect the cultural situation, this clause should be maintained.
In translating the phrase among them, one should take care that
the pronoun them is not taken to refer back to women and children; it
refers, of course, to the whole gathering.

Chapter 9

The Gibeonites Deceive Joshua

1 The victories of Israel became known to all the kings west of the Jordan—in the hills, in the foothills, and all along the coastal plain of the Mediterranean Sea as far north as Lebanon; these were the kings of the Hittites, the Amorites, the Canaanites, the Perizzites, the Hivites, and the Jebusites. 2 They all came together and joined forces to fight against Joshua and the Israelites.

3 But the people of Gibeon, who were Hivites, heard what Joshua had done to Jericho and Ai, 4 and they decided to deceive him. They went and got some food and loaded their donkeys with worn-out sacks and patched-up wineskins. 5 They put on ragged clothes and worn-out sandals that had been mended. The bread they took with them was dry and moldy. 6 Then they went to the camp at Gilgal and said to Joshua and the men of Israel, "We have come from a distant land. We want you to make a treaty with us."

7 But the men of Israel said, "Why should we make a treaty with you? Maybe you live nearby."

8 They said to Joshua, "We are at your service."

Joshua asked them, "Who are you? Where do you come from?"

1 When all the kings who were beyond the Jordan in the hill country and in the lowland all along the coast of the Great Sea toward Lebanon, the Hittites, the Amorites, the Canaanites, the Perizzites, the Hivites, and the Jebusites, heard of this, 2 they gathered together with one accord to fight Joshua and Israel.

3 But when the inhabitants of Gibeon heard what Joshua had done to Jericho and to Ai, 4 they on their part acted with cunning, and went and made ready provisions, and took worn-out sacks upon their asses, and wineskins, worn-out and torn and mended, 5 with worn-out patched sandals on their feet, and worn-out clothes; and all their provisions were dry and moldy. 6 And they went to Joshua in the camp at Gilgal, and said to him and to the men of Israel, "We have come from a far country; so now make a covenant with us." 7 But the men of Israel said to the Hivites, "Perhaps you live among us; then how can we make a covenant with you?" 8 They said to Joshua, "We are your servants." And Joshua said to them, "Who are you? And where do you come from?"

This chapter tells how the people of Gibeon, a city some 11 kilometers southwest of Ai, tricked the Israelites into making a treaty with them. Their plan worked, and even when the Israelites discovered that they had been deceived they could not kill them; the treaty was binding, and all the Israelites could do was to subject them to the status of slavery, a condition which was still in force when the account was written.

The section heading, The Gibeonites Deceive Joshua, may be translated, "The people from the town of Gibeon deceive Joshua and the people of Israel." Or, "The people of Israel agree not to kill the people
from the town of Gibeon." Or even, "The people of Gibeon make a peace
treaty with Joshua and the people of Israel."

9.1-2   The victories of Israel became known to all the
             kings west of the Jordan—in the hills, in the foot-
             hills, and all along the coastal plain of the Mediterra-
             nean Sea as far north as Lebanon; these were the kings
             of the Hittites, the Amorites, the Canaanites, the Per-
             izzites, the Hivites, and the Jebusites. 2 They all
             came together and joined forces to fight against Joshua
             and the Israelites.

These two verses describe how the natives of Canaan, alarmed by
the news of Israel's victories, banded together to fight the Israelites.
The victories of Israel became known to all the kings west of the
Jordan is more literally "And it happened when all the kings who were
beyond the Jordan heard." The TEV restructuring takes two stages:
(1) The victories of Israel is supplied as object of the verb "heard"
(RSV); and (2) the shift is made from an active to a passive construction by use of the verb became known. Together with English, most other
languages will also require that the verb "heard" receive an object
(RSV supplies "of this"). But many languages will prefer to retain an
active where TEV has became known: "All the kings west of the Jordan
heard about the victories of Israel" or "...heard that the people of
Israel had defeated their enemies." Verse 1 may even begin with a general statement ("The victories of Israel were spoken of everywhere in
the land"), followed with a more specific one: "All the kings...heard
of it."
The geographical data in verse 1 are given following a westerly
direction: the central mountain range (the hills), the lowlands (the
foothills), and then the coastal plain along the Mediterranean Sea.
It is possible that some languages might prefer the geographical
data to be given in an easterly direction. If this is so, then the
necessary adjustments must be made. It is quite possible also that
verse 1 should be broken into several sentences. For example,
             All the kings west of the Jordan River heard of the way that
             the people of Israel had defeated their enemies. The kings in
             the hills and in the foothills of central Palestine heard
             about it. And the kings along the coastal plain of the Med-
             iterranean Sea also heard about it. Even the kings as far
             north as Lebanon heard about the victories of Israel. These
             kings who heard about the victories of Israel were the kings
             of the Hittites, the Amorites, the Canaanites, the Perizzites,
             the Hivites, and the Jebusites.
For the list of the peoples, see 3.10; for kings see 2.2.
Alarmed at the news of Israel's victories at Jericho and Ai, the
rulers of these peoples form an alliance to fight the invading Israelites. "With one accord" (RSV) indicates the unanimous purpose of them

all; they were all together in this. It is possible to make this emphasis as follows: "All these kings brought their armies together with one
purpose in mind. They wanted to defeat Joshua and the people of Israel.

9.3   But the people of Gibeon, who were Hivites,
          heard what Joshua had done to Jericho and Ai,

It would appear that the explanation of the trick used by the
Gibeonites to secure a treaty with the Israelites is to be found in
the regulation recorded in Deuteronomy 20.10-18. This regulation allowed the Israelites to spare the lives of their enemies who lived a
great distance away, but required that they put to death all enemies
nearby, in order to eliminate any possibility of apostasy on the part
of the Israelites. The trick makes sense only on the assumption that
the Gibeonites knew this Israelite rule.
   But the story also serves to explain the reason why these people,
at the time the account was written, provided certain menial services
in the Temple (verse 27).
   Gibeon, some 11 kilometers southwest of Ai, was about 30 kilometers west of the Israelite camp at Gilgal. TEV inserts who were
Hivites, which in Hebrew comes only at verse 7 (see RSV). There is
no certainty about the particular designation Hivites; commentaries
and dictionaries offer a variety of definitions.[25]
   This verse may be made into a separate sentence: "But the people
from the town of Gibeon, who belonged to the tribe of the Hivites,
heard what Joshua had done to the cities of Jericho and Ai." Verse 4
would then begin: "So they decided to deceive him." Or one may render
"So they decided to deceive Joshua and the people of Israel."

9.4-5   and they decided to deceive him. They went and got
          some food and loaded their donkeys with worn-out
          sacks and patched-up wineskins. 5 They put on ragged
          clothes and worn-out sandals that had been mended.
          The bread they took with them was dry and moldy.

In verse 4 They...got some food (RSV "made ready provisions")
translates a Hebrew verb found in some Hebrew manuscripts and the ancient versions (and also in verse 12 in the Masoretic text); the Masoretic text has a verb found only here in the Old Testament, and it
seems to mean here "disguise oneself as messenger" (Soggin; see KJV
"made as if they had been ambassadors"); BJ says the form is unintelligible. NEB, TOB prefer Masoretic text; RSV, TEV, NAB, BJ, JB translate the textual variant. HOTTP also prefers the Masoretic text but
evaluates its choice a "C" rating, indicating "considerable doubt."
   The two occurrences of the pronoun they in this verse do not refer
absolutely to the same people. In its first occurrence (they decided)
the reference is to all the people of Gibeon; its second occurrence
(They went), however, refers to only a part of the people of Gibeon
(see verse 11). Therefore They went may be translated, "Some of them
went."

[125]

Verses 4-5 give in detail the elaborate trick they used: worn-out sacks (in which they placed their provisions) on their donkeys; they wore ragged clothes and worn-out sandals that had been mended, and supplied themselves with bread that was dry and moldy. All of this would give the impression that they had finished a long, arduous journey from some far-off place.

By placing items of food and clothing in two separate groups, it is possible to translate verses 4-5 as a unit. This can be done with either exegesis: (1) By accepting the textual variant with TEV and RSV ("made ready provisions"), and by equating food (verse 4) with bread (verse 5):

They put on ragged clothes and worn-out sandals that had been mended. Then they loaded their donkeys with worn-out sacks and patched-up wineskins, and took along bread that was dry and moldy.

(2) By accepting the alternative textual possibility ("disguise oneself as a messenger"):

Several of them dressed themselves as messengers from a distant land. They put on ragged clothes and worn-out sandals that had been mended. They loaded their donkeys with worn-out sacks and patched up wineskins, and they took along bread that was dry and moldy.

9.6 Then they went to the camp at Gilgal and said to Joshua and the men of Israel, "We have come from a distant land. We want you to make a treaty with us."

The camp at Gilgal may be specified as "the Israelite camp at Gilgal"; or, since the last place mentioned for the Israelites was in the valley between Mount Ebal and Gerizim, "the Israelite camp, which was now near the town of Gilgal." A treaty (RSV "covenant") is an agreement that is made between two groups, usually in order to ensure peace between them.

The request of the Gibeonites may be stated: "We have come from a distant land, and we would like for you to make a treaty with us."

9.7-8 But the men of Israel said, "Why should we make a treaty with you? Maybe you live nearby."

8 They said to Joshua, "We are at your service."

Joshua asked them, "Who are you? Where do you come from?"

It is interesting to note that in verse 6 the Gibeonites address Joshua and the men of Israel; in verse 7 the men of Israel speak, and in verse 8 the Gibeonites address Joshua, and he answers.

Verse 7 indicates that the Israelites are suspicious. TEV inverts the order of their response (compare RSV) so that the question (Why should we make a treaty with you?) comes first. The question may also be expressed as a statement: "We cannot make a treaty with you as easily as that!"

<u>Maybe you live nearby</u> (literally "among us"—see RSV); if this is the case, the Israelites cannot make a peace treaty with them. The response of the Israelites implies shared information; it intimates that the strangers already knew that the Israelites were not allowed to make a treaty with people who lived in the same vicinity. This may be expressed as a direct statement: "We are not allowed to make a treaty with people who live nearby, and we do not know where you come from." This would in fact suffice for the rendering of the entire response of the Israelites.

They then speak to Joshua: "We are your servants" (RSV), indicating at once that they do not presume to be treated as equals but as inferiors. It may be necessary to translate <u>They said</u> as "The men from Gibeon said." It is Joshua, then, who asks the <u>obvious</u> questions: "<u>Who are you? Where do you come from?</u>"

TEV	9.9-15	RSV

9 Then they told him this story: "We have come from a very distant land, sir, because we have heard of the LORD your God. We have heard about everything that he did in Egypt 10 and what he did to the two Amorite kings east of the Jordan: King Sihon of Heshbon and King Og of Bashan, who lived in Ashtaroth. 11 Our leaders and all the people that live in our land told us to get some food ready for a trip and to go and meet you. We were told to put ourselves at your service and ask you to make a treaty with us. 12 Look at our bread. When we left home with it and started out to meet you, it was still warm. But look! Now it is dry and moldy. 13 When we filled these wineskins, they were new, but look! They are torn. Our clothes and sandals are worn out from the long trip."

14 The men of Israel accepted some food from them, but did not consult the LORD about it. 15 Joshua made a treaty of friendship with the people of Gibeon and allowed them to live. The leaders of the community of Israel gave their solemn promise to keep the treaty.

9 They said to him, "From a very far country your servants have come, because of the name of the LORD your God; for we have heard a report of him, and all that he did in Egypt, 10 and all that he did to the two kings of the Amorites who were beyond the Jordan, Sihon the king of Heshbon, and Og king of Bashan, who dwelt in Ashtaroth. 11 And our elders and all the inhabitants of our country said to us, 'Take provisions in your hand for the journey, and go to meet them, and say to them, "We are your servants; come now, make a covenant with us."' 12 Here is our bread; it was still warm when we took it from our houses as our food for the journey, on the day we set forth to come to you, but now, behold, it is dry and moldy; 13 these wineskins were new when we filled them, and behold, they are burst; and these garments and shoes of ours are worn out from the very long journey." 14 So the men partook of their provisions, and did not ask direction from the LORD. 15 And Joshua made peace with them, and made a covenant with them, to let them live; and the leaders of the congregation swore to them.

9.9-10   Then they told him this story: "We have come
            from a very distant land, sir, because we have heard
            of the LORD your God. We have heard about everything
            that he did in Egypt 10 and what he did to the two
            Amorite kings east of the Jordan: King Sihon of
            Heshbon and King Og of Bashan, who lived in Ashtaroth.

The Gibeonites reply that it was because of all that they had
heard about the Lord, the God of the Israelites, that they had come on
a peace mission (see also verse 24). Because we have heard of the LORD
your God is literally "because of the name of the LORD your God." In
such a context "name" would refer to the reputation of the Lord, and
so it is possible to translate "because of the fame of the LORD your
God." Since "fame" is abstract, it may even be better to shift to a
verb formation: "because we have heard of the great things that the
LORD your God has done."
      As they tell what they have heard, they mention only what the Lord
has done in Egypt, when he freed Israel from bondage, and what he has
done to King Sihon of Heshbon (see Num 21.21-32) and to King Og of
Bashan (see Num 21.33-35), whose territories were on the east side of
the Jordan River. Heshbon was the capital city of Sihon's kingdom (see
Num 21.27), and Ashtaroth was the capital city of Og's kingdom. Both
can be located with a fairly high degree of certainty (see maps). The
Gibeonites do not refer to the Israelite victories at Jericho and Ai,
since a knowledge of these recent campaigns would be inconsistent with
their claim that they lived far away from Canaan.
      Verse 10 may also need to begin with a new sentence: "We also
heard what he did to...Jordan. We heard how he defeated King Sihon...."

9.11   Our leaders and all the people that live in our land
          told us to get some food ready for a trip and to go
          and meet you. We were told to put ourselves at your
          service and ask you to make a treaty with us.

Leaders (RSV "elders") indicates that the Gibeonites did not have
a king as their ruler (see 10.2). The Gibeonites tell their elaborate
story, seeking to convince the Israelites that indeed they have come
from a very distant land.
      The instructions given the men by their leaders and by all the
people of Gibeon may be made into direct discourse: "Our leaders and
everyone in our country told us, 'Get some food ready for a trip and
go meet the people of Israel. Put yourselves at their service, and ask
them to make a treaty with us.'"

9.12-13   Look at our bread. When we left home with it and
           started out to meet you, it was still warm. But
           look! Now it is dry and moldy. 13 When we filled
           these wineskins, they were new, but look! They
           are torn. Our clothes and sandals are worn out
           from the long trip."

Look at our bread translates "Here is our bread" (RSV), a Hebraism for calling attention to the bread.
The second sentence of verse 12 (When we left home...it was still
warm) may be inverted and made shorter, since and started out to meet
you was mentioned in the previous verse: "It was still warm when we
left home with it."
But look translates a Hebraism (RSV "behold") used as an attention
getter. It is possible to translate accurately without using a word to
express it in the text. In fact, for some languages But look! Now...
may result in overemphasis, which would have negative effects.
Similarly, verse 13 may be translated, "The same is true of these
wineskins. When we filled them they were new, but now they are torn...."

9.14-15   The men of Israel accepted some food from
           them, but did not consult the LORD about it.
           15 Joshua made a treaty of friendship with the
           people of Gibeon and allowed them to live. The
           leaders of the community of Israel gave their
           solemn promise to keep the treaty.

The trick worked; the Israelites partook of the food of the Gibeonites (even though it was dry and moldy!); this meal was part of the
ceremony by which a treaty was ratified.26 Therefore accepted some food
from them is inadequate as a translation, since the reader does not
know (1) that the men of Israel actually ate the food, and (2) that
the act of eating was the means by which the treaty was ratified. It
will help to translate "The Israelites ate some of their provisions as
a sign of fellowship" or "...as a sign that they had agreed to the
treaty."
The reason why the Israelites were deceived is given in verse 14:
they did not consult the LORD, as they should have done. This would be
done by the use of the sacred lots, the Urim and Thummim (see comments
on 7.14). This clause may be translated as a complete sentence: "They
agreed to this before they asked the LORD about it." Or, in chronological order, "They should have consulted the LORD about this, but they
did not do so."
In verse 15 the Hebrew noun means not only "peace" (RSV) as the
absence of armed conflict, but friendship, thereby guaranteeing their
safety (allowed them to live; NEB is better: "promising to spare their
lives"). If the matter of making a treaty is mentioned in verse 14,
then the first sentence of this verse may be translated, "Joshua promised the people of Gibeon that the Israelites would let them live in
peace."

[129]

The treaty was ratified also by the leaders of the community,[27] who are not otherwise identified; they gave their solemn promise to keep the treaty. The concept of a solemn promise may be too abstract. One may translate either "took an oath and promised" or "promised with an oath." Many languages will also have idiomatic ways of describing a binding oath, such as the Hebrew, which frequently uses "place one's hands between another's thighs."

TEV	9.16-21	RSV

16 Three days after the treaty had been made, the Israelites learned that these people did indeed live nearby. 17 So the people of Israel started out and three days later arrived at the cities where these people lived: Gibeon, Chephirah, Beeroth, and Kiriath Jearim. 18 But the Israelites could not kill them, because their leaders had made a solemn promise to them in the name of the LORD, Israel's God. All the people complained to the leaders about this, 19 but they answered, "We have made our solemn promise to them in the name of the LORD God of Israel. Now we cannot harm them. 20 We must let them live because of our promise; if we don't, God will punish us. 21 Let them live, but they will have to cut wood and carry water for us." This was what the leaders suggested.

16 At the end of three days after they had made a covenant with them, they heard that they were their neighbors, and that they dwelt among them. 17 And the people of Israel set out and reached their cities on the third day. Now their cities were Gibeon, Chephirah, Beeroth, and Kiriath-jearim. 18 But the people of Israel did not kill them, because the leaders of the congregation had sworn to them by the LORD, the God of Israel. Then all the congregation murmured against the leaders. 19 But all the leaders said to all the congregation, "We have sworn to them by the LORD, the God of Israel, and now we may not touch them. 20 This we will do to them, and let them live, lest wrath be upon us, because of the oath which we swore to them." 21 And the leaders said to them, "Let them live." So they became hewers of wood and drawers of water for all the congregation, as the leaders had said of them.

It may benefit the reader if a section heading is introduced at this point. It may be "The Israelites discover that the Gibeonites have tricked them" or "The Israelites punish the Gibeonites for tricking them."

9.16-17   Three days after the treaty had been made, the Israelites learned that these people did indeed live nearby. 17 So the people of Israel started out and three days later arrived at the cities where these people lived: Gibeon, Chephirah, Beeroth, and Kiriath Jearim.

The text does not say how the Israelites discovered that they had
been deceived, but the intimation is that they learned by accident;
this would seem the better alternative in translation, if a choice must
be made between intentional and unintentional learning. In any case,
they set out at once and went to the four centers of the Gibeonites,
but because of their treaty with them they could not kill them. Instead,
the Gibeonites became slaves of the Israelites.

Three days later (in both 16 and 17) means "the day after tomorrow"
(see comments on 1.11).28 Many languages will have idiomatic ways of
describing such short periods of time. Concerning the possibility of
understanding three days later of both verses as a reference to the
same time period, see below.

After the treaty had been made may be restructured as an active
clause: either "after the Israelites had made the treaty with the Gibeonites" or "after the Israelites and the Gibeonites had made a treaty."

The Israelites learn the truth about the Gibeonites, that they did
indeed live nearby (the Hebrew is quite repetitious: "they were neighbors to them and in their neighborhood they lived"). At once the Israelites set out and arrive at Gibeon on the third day (Gibeon was only 30
kilometers from the Israelite camp at Gilgal; and notice that in 10.9
the Israelites are able to cover the distance in a nightlong forced
march). The four cities were quite close together: Beeroth was about
7 kilometers northeast of Gibeon; Chephirah was about 7 kilometers
southwest of Gibeon, and Kiriath Jearim a bit farther away in the same
direction.

The Hebrew text of verse 16 reads "At the end of three days,"
while in verse 17 it reads "on the third day." There is the possibility
that the same period of time is designated by each of these temporal
phrases. If that is the case, then the text would appear to mean that
three days after the treaty was signed the people of Israel happened
to arrive in the area where the Gibeonites' cities were. It was at this
time that they learned that they had been tricked. HOTTP recognizes
the problem and recommends that these three-day periods be identified
as one in translation. If the translator follows the HOTTP recommenda-
tion, verses 16-17 may then become a unit:

> After making the treaty with the Gibeonites, the Israelites
> broke camp and were on the move again. At the end of the
> third day, they arrived in the vicinity of the cities of
> Gibeon, Chephirah, Beeroth, and Kiriath Jearim. It was then
> that the Israelites learned that the Gibeonites did indeed
> live nearby.

9.18   But the Israelites could not kill them, because
          their leaders had made a solemn promise to them
          in the name of the LORD, Israel's God. All the
          people complained to the leaders about this,

Because of the promise that their leaders had made (verse 15),
the Israelites were not allowed to kill the Gibeonites. This caused a
general protest, which the leaders settled by reminding the people of
their solemn promise. Even though the friendship treaty had been the

result of a falsehood (on the part of the Gibeonites), nevertheless it could not be annulled; it had been made <u>in the name of the LORD, Israel's God.</u>

To begin the verse <u>But the Israelites could not kill them</u> may sound somewhat strange to the reader, for it may leave the impression that there was some magical power protecting these people. A more sequential arrangement of the events may be advisable:

> But the leaders had made a solemn promise to the Gibeonites in the name of the LORD, Israel's God. And so the people of Israel were not permitted to kill the Gibeonites. When they complained about this to the leaders, 19 the leaders answered . . . .

9.19-20   but they answered, "We have made our solemn promise to them in the name of the LORD God of Israel. Now we cannot harm them. 20 We must let them live because of our promise; if we don't, God will punish us.

<u>We</u> (also <u>us</u>) of this and the following two verses must be translated as an inclusive first personal pronoun, in those languages that make a distinction between inclusive and exclusive forms. The leaders are saying that no one in Israel is allowed to harm these people. Although the Hebrew text has "touch" (RSV), it is used in the sense of bringing harm to the persons touched, and so the basis for TEV.

<u>God will punish us</u> translates the Hebrew "anger will be upon us" (see RSV), a reference to God's anger.

It is possible to place verses 19-20 together and so translate "19-20 But they answered, 'We have promised them freedom in the name of the LORD, the God of Israel. Therefore we must let them live. Otherwise the LORD will punish us severely.'"

9.21   Let them live, but they will have to cut wood and carry water for us." This was what the leaders suggested.

<u>They will have to cut wood and carry water for us</u> puts into direct discourse what in Hebrew is part of the narrative (see RSV, and see comments by Soggin). NEB is like TEV. Similarly, the text may be translated, "They must take over the work of cutting wood and carrying water for all Israel." In this proposed restructuring <u>Let them live</u> is deleted from verse 21, since it is unnecessary on the basis of its inclusion in verse 20.

"Hewers of wood and drawers of water" (the quaint KJV language is still preserved in RSV) may have been a picturesque way of describing the low social class of those who performed menial tasks (see Deut 29.11). But verses 23,27 seem to take the expression quite literally, implying that these two tasks were performed particularly in connection with the Temple services.[29]

22 Joshua ordered the people of Gibeon to be brought to him, and he asked them, "Why did you deceive us and tell us that you were from far away, when you live right here? 23 Because you did this, God has condemned you. Your people will always be slaves, cutting wood and carrying water for the sanctuary of my God."

24 They answered, "We did it, sir, because we learned that it was really true that the LORD your God had commanded his servant Moses to give you the whole land and to kill the people living in it as you advanced. We did it because we were terrified of you; we were in fear of our lives. 25 Now we are in your power; do with us what you think is right." 26 So this is what Joshua did: he protected them and did not allow the people of Israel to kill them. 27 But at the same time he made them slaves, to cut wood and carry water for the people of Israel and for the LORD's altar. To this day they have continued to do this work in the place where the LORD has chosen to be worshiped.

22 Joshua summoned them, and he said to them, "Why did you deceive us, saying, 'We are very far from you,' when you dwell among us? 23 Now therefore you are cursed, and some of you shall always be slaves, hewers of wood and drawers of water for the house of my God." 24 They answered Joshua, "Because it was told to your servants for a certainty that the LORD your God had commanded his servant Moses to give you all the land, and to destroy all the inhabitants of the land from before you; so we feared greatly for our lives because of you, and did this thing. 25 And now, behold, we are in your hand: do as it seems good and right in your sight to do to us." 26 So he did to them, and delivered them out of the hand of the people of Israel; and they did not kill them. 27 But Joshua made them that day hewers of wood and drawers of water for the congregation and for the altar of the LORD, to continue to this day, in the place which he should choose.

9.22   Joshua ordered the people of Gibeon to be brought to him, and he asked them, "Why did you deceive us and tell us that you were from far away, when you live right here?

Joshua now summons the Gibeonites and reprimands them for deceiving the Israelites. In Hebrew Joshua ordered the people of Gibeon to be brought to him is literally "Joshua called them." The verb "called" in such a context may have the meaning of "sent for" or "caused someone to bring to." The latter meaning is probably intended here. That is, Joshua sent some of the men of Israel to bring the Gibeonites to him. The pronoun "them" of the Hebrew text also causes complications. TEV suggests that the whole group of Gibeonites are summoned before Joshua, but it is more likely that the reference is limited to the messengers who came from the Gibeonites to Joshua. Joshua calls them and announces to them what will happen to all the Gibeonites. A shift may also be made to direct discourse: "Joshua told some of his men, 'Bring to me the messengers who came to us from the Gibeonites.'"

Joshua's remarks to the men of Gibeon may be restructured, "You deceived us. You live right here near us, and you said, 'We are from far away.'" Or, if indirect discourse is retained, "Why did you deceive us? You told us that you were from far away, when you live right here."

9.23   Because you did this, God has condemned you. Your people will always be slaves, cutting wood and carrying water for the sanctuary of my God."

Because of their lie, God has condemned them (literally "you are accursed"). In order to make immediately clear the connection between God's condemnation of the Gibeonites and their punishment, this portion of the verse may be translated, "God has condemned you, and this will be your punishment: your people will always...." From then on the Gibeonites would be slaves for the Israelites, cutting wood and carrying water for the sanctuary of the Lord.

It is not certain where this sanctuary is to be located, if, in fact, the writer had a particular place in mind. It could be in Gilgal or in Gibeon itself (see 1 Kgs 3.4; Gibeon is an important religious center in the time of King Solomon), or it could be taken to refer to the Jerusalem Temple.[30] Sanctuary may be translated either "house of worship" or "Temple." And the modifier (of my God) may be rendered "of the God of Israel."

9.24-25   They answered, "We did it, sir, because we learned that it was really true that the LORD your God had commanded his servant Moses to give you the whole land and to kill the people living in it as you advanced. We did it because we were terrified of you; we were in fear of our lives. 25 Now we are in your power; do with us what you think is right."

In a redundant manner the writer brings the account to a close with a final dialogue between Joshua and the Gibeonites. Once more they explain the reason for their deceptive conduct (verse 24): it was only in order to avoid being killed that they had lied to the Israelites.

The use of sir in TEV is to indicate the tone of the men's response to Joshua. In languages where honorifics are obligatory, or where there is a definite distinction made between a lower and a higher person in conversation, special attention should be given to the proper categories of language to be used in the dialogue. It is obvious, of course, that the men of Gibeon would be addressing a superior, while Joshua would be speaking to persons of lower status than himself.

We learned translates an emphatic Hebrew idiomatic phrase: "we were told repeatedly" (see TOB), "were fully informed" (NAB).

In translation it may be more effective to invert the order of the men's explanation to Joshua. For example:

'We did it, sir, because we feared for our lives. Moses served the LORD your God, and we know what the LORD promised to him

and to all the people of Israel. He promised to give you the
whole land, and he commanded you to kill the people in it."

Or:

"...feared for our lives. We know that the LORD your God will
make true his promise to Moses his servant. He told Moses,
'I command you to take the whole land and to kill all the
people living there.'"

They throw themselves on Joshua's mercy (verse 25), and he pro-
tects them from the Israelites, who want to kill them (verse 26).
Right (verse 25) translates two Hebrew nouns (RSV "good and right").
In such a context the two nouns are basically synonymous, and the use
of a single noun is perhaps more effective in contemporary English.
For other languages it may be more natural to maintain the two synonyms
or else shift to an idiom.

9.26-27   So this is what Joshua did: he protected them and did
           not allow the people of Israel to kill them. 27 But
           at the same time he made them slaves, to cut wood and
           carry water for the people of Israel and for the LORD's
           altar. To this day they have continued to do this work
           in the place where the LORD has chosen to be worshiped.

In verse 26 the use of a colon makes TEV unnecessarily cumbersome.
For economy of words it may be translated, "So Joshua protected the
Gibeonites and did not allow the people of Israel to kill them."

Once again the Gibeonites' punishment is described: to cut wood
and carry water for the people of Israel and for the LORD's altar. In
place of this infinitive clause, a new sentence may be more natural:
"But at the same time he made them slaves. They had to cut wood...."

To this day refers to the time when the account was written, and
the standard phrase the place where the LORD has chosen to be worshiped
(see Deut 12.11,14,26; 15.20; 17.8; 31.11) is a way of speaking of Jerusalem, the city which the Lord chose as the place where his Temple would
be built. In the place may be better expressed as "for the place." The
Gibeonites would have cut the wood before bringing it to the place where
the Lord was worshiped, and they would have carried the water to the
place.

Where the LORD has chosen to be worshiped may be otherwise formulated: "where the LORD has chosen for his people to worship him." Or,
if the author of the book does have in mind the Temple: "the place
which the LORD has chosen for his sanctuary (or, Temple)."

Chapter 10

The Amorites Are Defeated

1 Adonizedek, the king of Jerusalem,e heard that Joshua had captured and totally destroyed Ai and had killed its king, just as he had done to Jericho and its king. He also heard that the people of Gibeon had made peace with the Israelites and were living among them. 2 The people of Jerusalem were greatly alarmed at this because Gibeon was as large as any of the cities that had a king; it was larger than Ai, and its men were good fighters. 3 So Adonizedek sent the following message to King Hoham of Hebron, King Piram of Jarmuth, King Japhia of Lachish, and to King Debir of Eglon: 4 "Come and help me attack Gibeon, because its people have made peace with Joshua and the Israelites." 5 These five Amorite kings, the kings of Jerusalem, Hebron, Jarmuth, Lachish, and Eglon, joined forces, surrounded Gibeon, and attacked it.

eJERUSALEM: *At that time it was a Jebusite city.*

1 When Adonizedek king of Jerusalem heard how Joshua had taken Ai, and had utterly destroyed it, doing to Ai and its king as he had done to Jericho and its king, and how the inhabitants of Gibeon had made peace with Israel and were among them, 2 hex feared greatly, because Gibeon was a great city, like one of the royal cities, and because it was greater than Ai, and all its men were mighty. 3 So Adonizedek king of Jerusalem sent to Hoham king of Hebron, to Piram king of Jarmuth, to Japhia king of Lachish, and to Debir king of Eglon saying, 4 "Come up to me, and help me, and let us smite Gibeon; for it has made peace with Joshua and with the people of Israel." 5 Then the five kings of the Amorites, the king of Jerusalem, the king of Hebron, the king of Jarmuth, the king of Lachish, and the king of Eglon, gathered their forces, and went up with all their armies and encamped against Gibeon, and made war against it.

xHeb *they*

The first part of the book (1.1—12.24), which deals with the conquest of Canaan, is now drawing to a close. Having secured the central section of the land (Jericho, Ai, Gibeon), Joshua now strikes south and captures important cities and strongholds. In chapter 11 Joshua's campaigns in the northern part of Canaan are reported, and chapter 12 brings the first half of the book to a close with a summary statement of the victories of Moses and Joshua.

At the initiative of the king of Jerusalem, the forces of five
cities (Jerusalem, Hebron, Jarmuth, Lachish, and Eglon) join together
and attack the Israelites at Gibeon. Word is sent to Joshua at the camp
at Gilgal, and he immediately marches out with his men and attacks the
enemy forces by surprise, routing them and chasing them as far south as
Azekah and Makkedah. Two significant miracles enable the Israelites to
defeat their enemies. The victory won, the Israelites return to camp
at Gilgal.

A translator should by all means locate on a map all the places
mentioned in this passage so as to have a clear notion of the movement
of the Israelite forces as they overrun the southern part of Canaan.

The passive form of the section heading (The Amorites Are Defeated)
may be altered to an active: "Joshua and the Israelites defeat the Amorites" or "The Israelites defeat the Amorites."

10.1   Adonizedek, the king of Jerusalem,*e* heard that
                Joshua had captured and totally destroyed Ai and
                had killed its king, just as he done to Jericho and
                its king. He also heard that the people of Gibeon
                had made peace with the Israelites and were living
                among them.

        *e*JERUSALEM: *At that time it was a Jebusite city.*

The news of Joshua's victories reaches Adonizedek, the king of
Jerusalem (for king see 2.2), which at that time was a Jebusite city
(TEV footnote).31 Again (see 8.2), mention is expressly made of the
death of the king of Jericho; this will occur later on in this chapter
(see verses 28,30).

Two translational adjustments may be necessary in order to give
this verse maximum readability. (1) A link, showing time relationships,
may be established between this chapter and the preceding chapter: "At
that time Adonizedek was king of Jerusalem." (2) The events in this
verse may be narrated in a somewhat more chronological order:
        He heard that Joshua had captured and destroyed the cities
        of Jericho and Ai, and he heard that Joshua had killed the
        kings of these two cities. He also heard that the people of
        Gibeon....
Or:
        He heard that Joshua had captured and destroyed the city of
        Jericho and had killed its king. And he heard that Joshua
        had done the same thing to the city of Ai and its king. He
        also heard that the people of Gibeon....
Or:
        Joshua had captured and destroyed the city of Ai just as he
        had done with the city of Jericho. The city had been burned
        to the ground, and the king and all the people who lived
        there had been killed. After that the people of Gibeon had
        made peace with the Israelites and were living among them.
        When king Adonizedek of Jerusalem learned of this, 2 all
        the people of Jerusalem became greatly alarmed....

<u>10.2</u>   The people of Jerusalem were greatly alarmed
        at this because Gibeon was as large as any of
        the cities that had a king; it was larger than
        Ai, and its men were good fighters.

The people of Jerusalem[32] are alarmed at the alliance which the
Gibeonites had made with the invaders, especially since Gibeon was a
large city and its men had the reputation of being good fighters. It
should be noticed that Gibeon is not included among cities that had
a king (see 9.11, where they refer to "Our leaders").
        The beginning of this verse will depend upon the way in which the
last part of verse 1 is translated. On the assumption that a new sentence begins with this verse, one may want to translate:
        When the people of Jerusalem heard that the people of Gibeon
        had made peace with the Israelites, they became greatly
        alarmed. Gibeon was larger than Ai, and it was as large as
        any of the cities that were ruled by a king. Moreover, its
        men were good fighters.

<u>10.3</u>   So Adonizedek sent the following message to
        King Hoham of Hebron, King Piram of Jarmuth,
        King Japhia of Lachish, and to King Debir of
        Eglon:

We learn from verse 5 that the four kings to whom Adonizedek sent
the message were Amorite kings, as was King Adonizedek himself. It may
be useful to introduce that information at the beginning of this verse,
and to indicate that the four kings to whom the message was sent were
neighboring kings of Adonizedek. For example:
        At that time there were four other Amorite kings in the
        region besides King Adonizedek. They were King Hoham of
        Hebron, King Piram of Jarmuth, King Japhia of Lachish,
        and King Debir of Eglon. So Adonizedek sent a message to
        each of them. 4 He said....
        Four cities are listed: Hebron, about 32 kilometers south of Jeru-
salem; Eglon, about 56 kilometers southwest of Jerusalem; Jarmuth and
Lachish were between Eglon and Jerusalem, Lachish being nearer to
Eglon. The word Amorite (verse 5) is equivalent to Canaanite; it may
be that the term was especially used of the native peoples in the hill
country (verse 6; see 3.10).

<u>10.4</u>   "Come and help me attack Gibeon, because its
        people have made peace with Joshua and the
        Israelites."

Adonizedek proposes they attack Gibeon for having made peace, that
is, an alliance, with the Israelites. It may be beneficial to reverse
the order of the two clauses: "The people of Gibeon have made peace
with Joshua and the Israelites. So come and help me attack them."

[138]

10.5   These five Amorite kings, the kings of Jerusalem,
        Hebron, Jarmuth, Lachish, and Eglon, joined forces,
        surrounded Gibeon, and attacked it.

The four kings comply with Adonizedek's proposal, and the combined
armies of the five city-states march to Gibeon, surround it, and attack
it. The repetition of the names of the cities, combined with the distance between the subject (kings) and the verbs (joined forces, surrounded, and attacked) may make it advisable to delete the repetition
of the names "Then these five kings joined forces. They surrounded the
city of Gibeon and attacked it." The verb surrounded (RSV "encamped")
represents a method of ancient warfare known as "siege warfare." In
order to weaken a city's resistance the enemy army would set up camp
around the city. This would make it impossible for the people of the
city to send for or to receive help from the outside. When the people
of the city were weakened from a lack of food and water, the enemy army
would then launch its attack. The presence of the enemy army outside
the city walls also had the psychological advantage of putting fear
into the hearts of the people in the city.

	TEV	10.6-11	RSV

TEV

6 The men of Gibeon sent word
to Joshua at the camp in Gilgal:
"Do not abandon us, sir! Come at
once and help us! Save us! All the
Amorite kings in the hill country
have joined forces and have attacked us!"

7 So Joshua and his whole
army, including the best troops,
started out from Gilgal. 8 The
LORD said to Joshua, "Do not be
afraid of them. I have already
given you the victory. Not one of
them will be able to stand against
you." 9 All night Joshua and his
army marched from Gilgal to Gibeon,
and they made a surprise attack on
the Amorites. 10 The LORD made the
Amorites panic at the sight of
Israel's army. The Israelites
slaughtered them at Gibeon and
pursued them down the mountain
pass at Beth Horon, keeping up the
attack as far south as Azekah and
Makkedah. 11 While the Amorites
were running down the pass from
the Israelite army, the LORD made
large hailstones fall down on them
all the way to Azekah. More were

RSV

6 And the men of Gibeon sent
to Joshua at the camp in Gilgal,
saying, "Do not relax your hand
from your servants; come up to us
quickly, and save us, and help us;
for all the kings of the Amorites
that dwell in the hill country
are gathered against us." 7 So
Joshua went up from Gilgal, he and
all the people of war with him, and
all the mighty men of valor. 8 And
the LORD said to Joshua, "Do not
fear them, for I have given them
into your hands; there shall not
a man of them stand before you."
9 So Joshua came upon them suddenly, having marched up all night
from Gilgal. 10 And the LORD threw
them into a panic before Israel,
who slew them with a great slaughter at Gibeon, and chased them by
the way of the ascent of Beth-
horon, and smote them as far as
Azekah and Makkedah. 11 And as
they fled before Israel, while
they were going down the ascent
of Beth-horon, the LORD threw
down great stones from heaven
upon them as far as Azekah, and

killed by the hailstones than by
the Israelites.

they died; there were more who
died because of the hailstones
than the men of Israel killed with
the sword.

10.6   The men of Gibeon sent word to Joshua at the
        camp in Gilgal: "Do not abandon us, sir! Come at
        once and help us! Save us! All the Amorite kings
        in the hill country have joined forces and have
        attacked us!"

The Gibeonites immediately send a call for help to Joshua at the
Israelite camp at Gilgal. The Hebrew text of this verse is quite wordy.
Do not abandon translates the Hebrew idiomatic expression "Do not relax
your hand" (RSV). Sir represents the relationship expressed by the Hebrew "your servants." The language is designed to remind Joshua of the
treaty between them; as his subjects they are entitled to his protection
from their enemies. The idea may also be expressed, 'We are your subjects! Please do not abandon us!" Or, "We have surrendered ourselves
to you and placed ourselves under your protection! Do not abandon us!"
    In the Hebrew text there are also two synonymous verbs, which TEV
translates help and save. In some languages these will be better rendered as a single verb.

10.7-8   So Joshua and his whole army, including the
          best troops, started out from Gilgal. 8 The LORD
          said to Joshua, "Do not be afraid of them. I have
          already given you the victory. Not one of them
          will be able to stand against you."

Joshua responds immediately (verse 7), having been assured by the
Lord that victory would be his (verse 8).
    His whole army (RSV "All the people of war") and the best troops
(RSV "all the mighty men of valor") could possibly be taken as synonyms. However, the present context seems to distinguish between the
mass of soldiers (his whole army) and the best fighters among them
(the best troops). In translation it may be necessary to indicate that
Joshua called together his troops before they started out: "So Joshua
called together his whole army. Then he, his best troops, and all the
other soldiers started out from Gilgal."
    It may be useful to indicate the relationship in time between
verses 7 and 8. If this is the case, one may translate "At that time
the LORD said to Joshua..." or "Before Joshua and his army started out,
the LORD said to him...."
    In the command Do not be afraid of them, the pronoun them may need
to be qualified as "the Amorite kings and their armies."
    I have already given may be difficult in a number of languages,
and the victory may be too abstract. Therefore one may translate "I
will certainly cause you to defeat them (or, the Amorite kings and their
armies)." Given you the victory is literally "given them into your hands"

(RSV). As previously indicated, where this phrase occurs one may translate "will certainly place them in your power.

10.9   All night Joshua and his army marched from Gilgal
        to Gibeon, and they made a surprise attack on the
        Amorites.

A new section heading, such as "God helps the Israelites defeat their enemies," may be introduced at this point. If this is done, then verse 9 will have to be a new paragraph.

In a forced all-night march up steep mountain trails, Joshua and his men cover the 30 kilometers from Gilgal to Gibeon. Soggin comments that this is difficult "but not impossible and can be carried out in 8-10 hours."

The verb chosen to translate marched should be suitable for a military group, though it should not necessarily imply keeping in step. See comments at 6.4.

And they made a surprise attack on the Amorites may be rendered as a separate sentence: "So the Israelite army was able to attack the Amorites before the Amorites knew they were there."

10.10   The LORD made the Amorites panic at the sight of
        Israel's army. The Israelites slaughtered them at
        Gibeon and pursued them down the mountain pass at
        Beth Horon, keeping up the attack as far south as
        Azekah and Makkedah.

In Hebrew all the verbs of this verse are in the singular, and the most natural understanding of the text is to take The LORD as the subject throughout (so BJ, JB, TOB; see Bright). NEB introduces Joshua as the subject after the first verb; RSV has "Israel," and TEV, NAB have The Israelites. The Hebrew text is concerned to show that the victory, as always, is really the Lord's; the Israelites are able to win because he gives them the victory (verse 8).

Panic may be rendered "run away in fear" or "become afraid and start running in all directions."

At the sight of Israel's army may be translated "when they saw Israel's army attacking them."

In Hebrew the verb slaughtered translates a Hebrew idiomatic expression which signifies a great defeat (RSV "slew them with a great slaughter"). In translation it may be necessary to provide slaughtered and pursued with two objects: "slaughtered some of them at Gibeon, and pursued the rest of them...."

Keeping up the attack may be better rendered as a complete sentence: "They kept on attacking the Amorites until they had gone as far south as the cities of Azekah and Makkedah."

Beth Horon is northwest of Gibeon; there was a mountain pass there that led from the highlands to the flat country.[33] The Israelites kept pursuing the enemy, who fled south toward Azekah and Makkedah. Since the Hebrew does indicate that the Lord is the subject throughout, one

[141]

may want to stress this in translation:

> The LORD caused the Amorites to become afraid and run when
> they saw Israel's army approaching. Then the LORD caused
> the Israelites to slaughter some of the Amorites at Gibeon,
> and he caused them to pursue the rest of the Amorites down
> the mountain pass at the city of Beth Horon. He gave the
> Israelites the power to keep on attacking the Amorites as
> far south as the cities of Azekah and Makkedah.

10.11   While the Amorites were running down the pass
         from the Israelite army, the LORD made large
         hailstones fall down on them all the way to
         Azekah. More were killed by the hailstones
         than by the Israelites.

The first divine intervention, in verse 10, is the panic that the
Lord brought on the enemy. The second one occurs during the chase down
the mountain pass: large hailstones (literally "large stones from
heaven") came down and killed more of the enemy than were killed by
the Israelites. Hailstones are frozen drops of rain or snow; sometimes
they can be almost as large as hens' eggs.

In the Hebrew text the Amorites are not expressly mentioned by
name, but in the restructuring of TEV it was felt helpful to do so.
The clause While...army may be inverted: "While the Israelite army was
chasing the Amorites down the pass...." The main clause of this first
sentence (the LORD...to Azekah) may be divided into two parts: "the
LORD caused large hailstones to fall down on the Amorites. This happened all the way to the city of Azekah."

The passive construction (More were...than by the Israelites) may
be stated as an active: "The hailstones killed more of the enemy than
the Israelite army did."

TEV	10.12-15	RSV

12 On the day that the LORD
gave the men of Israel victory
over the Amorites, Joshua spoke
to the LORD. In the presence of
the Israelites he said,
    "Sun, stand still over
        Gibeon;
    Moon, stop over Aijalon
        Valley."
13 The sun stood still and the
moon did not move until the nation
had conquered its enemies. This
is written in *The Book of Jashar*.
The sun stood still in the middle
of the sky and did not go down
for a whole day. 14 Never before,

12 Then spoke Joshua to the
LORD in the day when the LORD gave
the Amorites over to the men of
Israel; and he said in the sight
of Israel,
    "Sun, stand thou still at
        Gibeon,
    and thou Moon in the valley
        of Aijalon."
13 And the sun stood still,
        and the moon stayed,
    until the nation took venge-
        ance on their enemies.
Is this not written in the Book
of Jashar? The sun stayed in the
midst of heaven, and did not

and never since, has there been a day like it, when the LORD obeyed a human being. The LORD fought on Israel's side!	hasten to go down for about a whole day. 14 There has been no day like it before or since, when the LORD hearkened to the voice of a man; for the LORD fought for Israel.
15 After this, Joshua and his army went back to the camp at Gilgal.	15 Then Joshua returned, and all Israel with him, to the camp at Gilgal.

The Lord provided more help: an extraordinarily long day, providing twice the usual amount of daylight, gave the Israelites the necessary time to pursue and slaughter the enemy. The emphasis is, as always, on the Lord's power; he gave the victory to the Israelites.

10.12   On the day that the LORD gave the men of Israel
        victory over the Amorites, Joshua spoke to the LORD.
        In the presence of the Israelites he said,
            "Sun, stand still over Gibeon;
            Moon, stop over Aijalon Valley."

Joshua's command (or prayer) in the last half of this verse is in poetic language and poetic form. Whatever the original meaning, it is taken literally by the writer of the account, who quotes from _The Book of Jashar_ (verse 13); this book is referred to also in 2 Samuel 1.18 and nowhere else. It was probably a collection of ancient war songs.

The clause On the day that...over the Amorites may be more effective as a complete sentence: "So the LORD gave the men of Israel victory over the Amorites on that day." If the initial clause becomes a sentence, then it is possible to remove the potential confusion of TEV, which uses two verbs of a single event (spoke to the LORD and In the presence of the Israelites he said). One can then translate "On that same day, Joshua stood up in the presence of the Israelites and prayed to the LORD. He said...." Or, if Joshua's words to the Lord are understood as a command rather than a prayer, "On that same day Joshua stood up in the presence of the Israelites and said to the LORD...."

But whether Joshua's words to the Lord are conceived of as a prayer or a command, a problem still remains, for Joshua addresses the sun and moon directly, not the Lord. This difficulty may be resolved, however, if the prayer (or command) begins "LORD, cause the sun to stand still...."

Aijalon Valley is some 6.5 kilometers south of the lower (western) end of the mountain pass at Beth Horon.

10.13   The sun stood still and the moon did not move until
        the nation had conquered its enemies. This is written
        in _The Book of Jashar_. The sun stood still in the
        middle of the sky and did not go down for a whole day.

[143]

The sun stood still and the moon did not move need not be translated as a causative ("So the LORD caused the sun..."), since this will already be implicit on the basis of verse 12.

Had conquered translates a Hebrew verb which is translated "took vengeance" by RSV and most other translations. In many places the Hebrew verb does express the idea of retaliation, or getting even with someone, which is the normal meaning of "vengeance" in English. But when used of warfare, its main area of meaning is that of punishment (see the *Translator's Handbook on Psalms*, Psa 18.47).

For *The Book of Jashar* see comments at verse 12. This is written in *The Book of Jashar* may be translated "You can read about this in *The Book of Jashar*" or "...in the book that Jashar wrote."

Since the last sentence of this verse repeats the information contained in the first sentence, the entire verse may be translated:

The sun stood still in the middle of the sky and did not go down for a whole day. And the moon did not move until the Israelites had conquered their enemies. You can read about this in *The Book of Jashar*.

Or, if the first sentence of verse 13 is understood as a quotation from *The Book of Jashar*, and it may be more effectively rendered in poetic form:

The sun stood still,
and the moon did not move,
until Israel had conquered its enemies.

You may read this in *The Book of Jashar*. For a whole day the sun stood still in the middle of the sky and did not go down.

It would seem that For a whole day (or "for about a whole day" RSV) means the twelve-hour period of daylight and not a twenty-four-hour period.

10.14   Never before, and never since, has there been a
day like it, when the LORD obeyed a human being.
The LORD fought on Israel's side!

An extraordinary statement is made: the Lord obeyed Joshua's command; that is, he caused the sun to stand still in the sky for a whole day.

A day like it most probably means a day such as this, when the Lord responded to a person in such a manner. This meaning may be translated more clearly: "Never before and never since, has the LORD answered a person's prayer in that way." Or, if Joshua is conceived of as giving a command to the Lord, "...has the LORD done what a person commanded him to do."

10.15   After this, Joshua and his army went back to
the camp at Gilgal.

As commentators point out, verse 15 does not fit here. The campaign against the Amorite forces is still going on and ends only in verse 39. After the summary statement in verses 40-42, the Israelites return to camp at Gilgal (verse 43, which is identical with verse 15). Bright thinks that by mistake a copyist included the statement in verse 43 here after verse 14 because the endings of verses 14 and 42 are similar. Both verses 15 and 43 are omitted from the Septuagint.

Although this verse may not fit well here, it is obviously a part of the text and must remain. Its absence from the Septuagint represents an attempt of the Greek translators to smooth over the problem. However, if After this is translated more specifically, the problem is at least minimized: "After their victory" or "After Joshua and his men had defeated the Amorites.

TEV	10.16-21	RSV

Joshua Captures the Five
    Amorite Kings

16 The five Amorite kings, however, had escaped and were hiding in the cave at Makkedah.
17 Someone found them, and Joshua was told where they were hiding.
18 He said, "Roll some big stones in front of the entrance to the cave. Place some guards there,
19 but don't stay there yourselves. Keep on after the enemy and attack them from the rear; don't let them get to their cities! The LORD your God has given you victory over them." 20 Joshua and the men of Israel slaughtered them, although some managed to find safety inside their city walls and were not killed. 21 Then all of Joshua's men came back safe to him at the camp at Makkedah.

No one in the land dared even to speak against the Israelites.

16 These five kings fled, and hid themselves in the cave at Makkedah. 17 And it was told Joshua, "The five kings have been found, hidden in the cave at Makkedah." 18 And Joshua said, "Roll great stones against the mouth of the cave, and set men by it to guard them; 19 but do not stay there yourselves, pursue your enemies, fall upon their rear, do not let them enter their cities; for the LORD your God has given them into your hand." 20 When Joshua and the men of Israel had finished slaying them with a very great slaughter, until they were wiped out, and when the remnant which remained of them had entered into the fortified cities, 21 all the people returned safe to Joshua in the camp at Makkedah; not a man moved his tongue against any of the people of Israel.

The five Amorite kings had escaped, but they were eventually found and taken to Joshua, who put them to death. Their bodies were thrown into the cave at Makkedah, where they had been hiding, and the pile of stones in front of the cave was still there at the time of the writing of the account.

The section heading, Joshua Captures the Five Amorite Kings, is a simple statement and will perhaps not be a problem in translation. However, one may wish either to expand ("Joshua captures and puts to death the five Amorite kings") or, if a passive structure is stylistically better, to translate "The five Amorite kings are captured and put to death."

[145]

<u>10.16-17</u>   The five Amorite kings, however, had escaped
and were hiding in the cave at Makkedah. 17 Some-
one found them, and Joshua was told where they were
hiding.

The narrative in these verses is simple and clear: the five kings
hide in the cave at Makkedah, they are discovered, and the news is taken
to Joshua. Notice that Joshua is in the camp near Makkedah itself (verse
21), not in Gilgal (see verse 15).

Although the text seems clear enough, it may be helpful to indicate from whom the five Amorite kings <u>had escaped</u>: "had escaped from
Joshua and the Israelite men." The passive <u>were hiding</u> may be changed
to a reflexive: "They had run away to the cave near the city of Makkedah and had hidden themselves there."

If there is felt to be a conflict between <u>Someone found them</u> and
<u>Joshua was told</u>, the text may be restructured to say "Someone found
them and told Joshua."

<u>10.18</u>   He said, "Roll some big stones in front of the
entrance to the cave. Place some guards there,

If the restructuring suggested above is followed ("someone...told
Joshua"), then <u>He said</u> should be translated "So Joshua said."

Joshua orders the entrance of the cave to be blocked with huge
stones and has guards stationed there, to prevent the five kings from
escaping. Then he orders his troops to pursue the enemy and kill them
all before they can reach their fortified cities.

Joshua's two commands (<u>Roll some big stones in front of the en-</u>
<u>trance to the cave</u> and <u>Place some guards there</u>) were apparently di-
rected to his soldiers. But then there is a distinction made between
the persons whom Joshua addresses and the persons who are to be stationed as guards (see verse 19). Who then are these guards (RSV "men")
stationed at the entrance to the cave? Is this a distinction, for example, between Joshua's "best troops" and the rest of his men (see
verse 7)? Or is this a distinction between Joshua's men and local
citizens? It seems quite possible that some local citizen (or perhaps
even a Gibeonite) may have found where the kings were hiding and sub-
sequently informed Joshua. Given the circumstances, most any of the
local citizens could be trusted at this point to stand guard before
the mouth of the sealed-up cave. The verse may therefore be translated, "Joshua said to his men, 'Roll some big stones in front of the
entrance to the cave. Then place some men there to guard it....'"

<u>10.19</u>   but don't stay there yourselves. Keep on after
the enemy and attack them from the rear; don't
let them get to their cities! The LORD your God
has given you victory over them."

Attack them from the rear translates a verb found only here and in Deuteronomy 25.18. The sense in this context is better expressed by Soggin: "cut off their retreat" (so JB "cut off their line of retreat"). The enemy would obviously be fleeing in retreat back to their fortified cities, where they would be safe, and Joshua orders his men to prevent them from reaching their cities, not simply to harass them from the rear.

The entire sentence (Keep on after the enemy and attack them from the rear; don't let them get to their cities!) may be more briefly translated, "Keep on pursuing the rest of the enemy. Do not let them escape to their cities!"

Has given you victory over them once again translates the Hebrew idiom "has given them into your hand" (RSV). The terminology of TEV may be less abstractly translated as "has placed them in your power" or "will cause you to defeat them."

10.20　　Joshua and the men of Israel slaughtered them, although some managed to find safety inside their city walls and were not killed.

Verse 20 is quite wordy (see RSV), emphasizing the great victory won by the Israelites.

As a reading of RSV will indicate, the structure of this verse is similar in some respects to that of verse 10, especially the Hebrew expression translated slaughtered. The reader may benefit if slaughtered them, although some is translated "slaughtered most of them, although some," since only some of the enemy managed to reach their walled cities and escape the slaughter.

10.21　　Then all of Joshua's men came back safe to him at the camp at Makkedah. No one in the land dared even to speak against the Israelites.

Safe translates the Hebrew "in peace"; see JB "safe and sound." The section (10.16-21) ends with a graphic statement of the fear all the Canaanites felt. Not only did active opposition against the Israelites cease, but even criticism of them; "not a man moved his tongue" (RSV). The verb translated "moved" means literally "to sharpen."[34] TEV, by rendering dared even to speak against, removes the metaphor of the Hebraic expression. Although it is doubtful if many languages can use the Hebrew idiom very effectively, it is quite possible that a number of languages will have their own idiomatic expressions which might be very effective. For example, "No one dared even to cast a glance toward the Israelites" or "...squint at the Israelites."

22 Then Joshua said, "Open
the entrance to the cave and bring
those five kings out to me." 23 So
the cave was opened, and the kings
of Jerusalem, Hebron, Jarmuth,
Lachish, and Eglon were brought
out 24 and taken to Joshua. Joshua
then called all the men of Israel
to him and ordered the officers
who had gone with him to come and
put their feet on the necks of the
kings. They did so. 25 Then Joshua
said to his officers, "Don't be
afraid or discouraged. Be determined and confident because this
is what the LORD is going to do to
all your enemies." 26 Then Joshua
killed the kings and hanged them
on five trees, where their bodies
stayed until evening. 27 At sundown Joshua gave orders, and their
bodies were taken down and thrown
into the same cave where they had
hidden earlier. Large stones were
placed at the entrance to the cave,
and they are still there.

22 Then Joshua said, "Open
the mouth of the cave, and bring
those five kings out to me from
the cave." 23 And they did so,
and brought those five kings out
to him from the cave, the king of
Jerusalem, the king of Hebron, the
king of Jarmuth, the king of Lachish, and the king of Eglon.
24 And when they brought those
kings out to Joshua, Joshua summoned all the men of Israel, and
said to the chiefs of the men of
war who had gone with him, "Come
near, put your feet upon the
necks of these kings." Then they
came near, and put their feet on
their necks. 25 And Joshua said
to them, "Do not be afraid or
dismayed; be strong and of good
courage; for thus the LORD will
do to all your enemies against
whom you fight." 26 And afterward
Joshua smote them and put them to
death, and he hung them on five
trees. And they hung upon the
trees until evening; 27 but at
the time of the going down of the
sun, Joshua commanded, and they
took them down from the trees,
and threw them into the cave
where they had hidden themselves,
and they set great stones against
the mouth of the cave, which remain to this very day.

<u>10.22-24</u>   Then Joshua said, "Open the entrance to the
cave and bring those five kings out to me." 23 So
the cave was opened, and the kings of Jerusalem,
Hebron, Jarmuth, Lachish, and Eglon were brought
out 24 and taken to Joshua. Joshua then called all
the men of Israel to him and ordered the officers
who had gone with him to come and put their feet
on the necks of the kings. They did so.

After defeating the armies of the five kings, Joshua ordered that
the five kings themselves be brought from the cave in which they had
been trapped (verses 16-18). In the presence of all the Israelite soldiers, Joshua ordered <u>the officers</u> who had taken part with him in the

campaign to place their feet on the necks of the prostrate kings. As
commentators point out, this gesture of domination was widespread at
that time (see 1 Kgs 5.3, RSV; Psa 110.1).

Then Joshua said may be translated more specifically as "Then
Joshua commanded his men."

Inasmuch as the break between verses 23 and 24 comes at an unusual place, the two verses may be translated as a unit. Moreover, the
two passive verbs (was opened and were brought out) may be transformed
into active constructions: "So Joshua's men opened the cave and brought
to Joshua the kings of Jerusalem, Hebron, Jarmuth, Lachish, and Eglon."

The officers who had gone with him may imply that some officers
had not gone with Joshua. To translate "his (or, their) officers" would
avoid this wrong implication.

10.25   Then Joshua said to his officers, "Don't be
afraid or discouraged. Be determined and
confident because this is what the LORD is
going to do to all your enemies."

For the language of this verse, see 8.1 and 1.9. At the beginning
of the verse the Hebrew has "And Joshua said to them"; this "them"
could be all the men of Israel, but more probably it refers to the officers, who are the nearest antecedents.

Because this is...to all your enemies may be made into a separate
sentence and translated, "The LORD is going to do this same thing to
all your enemies."

10.26-27   Then Joshua killed the kings and hanged them
on five trees, where their bodies stayed until
evening. 27 At sundown Joshua gave orders, and
their bodies were taken down and thrown into the
same cave where they had hidden earlier. Large
stones were placed at the entrance to the cave,
and they are still there.

After executing the five kings, Joshua had their bodies strung up
on five trees (or impaled on five posts; see comments on 8.29), where
they stayed until sundown—as was done to the king of Ai (8.29). Their
bodies were then thrown back into the cave where they had hidden themselves, and the pile of huge stones placed at the entrance of the cave
was still there at the time of the writing of the account (verse 27).

Whereas 8.29 leaves open the possibility that the king of Ai was
killed by being impaled on a tree or a post, it is now specifically
stated that the five kings were killed before their bodies were hanged
on five trees. So the problem of the sequence of events is here resolved for the translator. It may well be that Joshua killed the kings,
but it is quite unlikely that he alone hanged them on the five trees.
One may then translate either "Then Joshua killed the kings and ordered
his men to hang them on five trees" or "Then Joshua ordered his men to
kill the kings and hang them on five trees." For economy's sake verses
26-27 may be placed together:

Then Joshua killed the kings and ordered his men to hang
their bodies on five trees. In the evening he gave orders
for their bodies to be taken down and to be thrown into
the same cave where they had hidden earlier.
If direct discourse is preferable, two options are available:
(1) Joshua killed the kings. Then he told his men, "Hang
their bodies on five trees." At sunset Joshua gave his
men further orders. He said, "Take their bodies down and
throw them into the cave where they hid themselves earlier."
(2) Joshua told his men, "Kill the kings and hang their
bodies on five trees."...

TEV   <u>10.28-35</u>   RSV

Joshua Captures More Amorite Territory

28 Joshua attacked and captured Makkedah and its king that
day. He put everyone in the city
to death; no one was left alive.
He did to the king of Makkedah
what he had done to the king of
Jericho.
29 After this, Joshua and
his army went on from Makkedah to
Libnah and attacked it. 30 The
LORD also gave the Israelites
victory over this city and its
king. They spared no one, but
killed every person in it. They
did to the king what they had done
to the king of Jericho.
31 After this, Joshua and his
army went on from Libnah to Lachish, surrounded it and attacked
it. 32 The LORD gave the Israelites
victory over Lachish on the second
day of the battle. Just as they had
done at Libnah, they spared no one,
but killed every person in the
city. 33 King Horam of Gezer came
to the aid of Lachish, but Joshua
defeated him and his army and left
none of them alive.
34 Next, Joshua and his army
went on from Lachish to Eglon, surrounded it and attacked it. 35 They
captured it the same day and put
everyone there to death, just as
they had done at Lachish.

28 And Joshua took Makkedah
on that day, and smote it and its
king with the edge of the sword;
he utterly destroyed every person
in it, he left none remaining;
and he did to the king of Makkedah
as he had done to the king of Jericho.
29 Then Joshua passed on from
Makkedah, and all Israel with him,
to Libnah, and fought against Libnah; 30 and the LORD gave it also
and its king into the hand of
Israel; and he smote it with the
edge of the sword, and every person in it; he left none remaining
in it; and he did to its king as
he had done to the king of Jericho.
31 And Joshua passed on from
Libnah, and all Israel with him,
to Lachish, and laid siege to it,
and assaulted it; 32 and the LORD
gave Lachish into the hand of
Israel, and he took it on the
second day, and smote it with the
edge of the sword, and every person in it, as he had done to
Libnah.
33 Then Horam king of Gezer
came up to help Lachish; and
Joshua smote him and his people,
until he left none remaining.
34 And Joshua passed on with

all Israel from Lachish to Eglon;
and they laid siege to it, and
assaulted it; 35 and they took it
on that day, and smote it with the
edge of the sword; and every person
in it he utterly destroyed that
day, as he had done to Lachish.

Verses 28-43 describe the Israelite conquest of six important
cities in the southern part of Canaan: Makkedah, Libnah, Lachish, Eglon,
Hebron, and Debir. The section heading is rather simple, with subject
(Joshua), verb (Captures), and object (More Amorite Territory). It may
also be translated, "Joshua and the people of Israel capture more Amorite territory" or "Joshua leads the people of Israel to capture more
Amorite cities."

10.28   Joshua attacked and captured Makkedah and its
             king that day. He put everyone in the city to death;
             no one was left alive. He did to the king of Makkedah
             what he had done to the king of Jericho.

Joshua attacked may need to be enlarged to "Joshua and his troops
attacked."
Joshua first attacks Makkedah, a city in the lowlands, about 25
kilometers southwest of Gibeon. In place of Makkedah one may want to
translate "the Amorite city of Makkedah." The adverbial modifier that
day may be more satisfactory if placed in a different position in some
languages: "That same day Joshua also attacked and captured the Amorite
city of Makkedah and its king."
Put...to death (RSV "utterly destroyed") translates the Hebrew
verb discussed at 2.10. The text is very emphatic: "killed...utterly
destroyed...left no survivor"—indicating the complete slaughter of
all the inhabitants. This is a holy war. Notice that the phrase "(struck
it) with the edge of the sword" (see RSV, verses 28,30,32,35,37,39) is
a way of saying "killed in battle" or "executed."
Joshua of course did not attack, capture, and kill all these inhabitants by himself. In most languages it will be necessary to say
"Joshua and his men...," or it may even be necessary to state explicitly that Joshua gave certain commands before the battle began.
Although repetition is forceful in Hebrew, it may lessen the impact in other languages. One may reduce the length:
He told his men to put to death everyone in the city. Then
he killed the king of Makkedah, just as he had killed the
king of Jericho.
Or, somewhat longer,
Before they attacked the city, Joshua told his men, "Put to
death everyone in the city." So Joshua's men killed all the
people of the city. Then after the city was completely destroyed, Joshua killed the king of Makkedah, just as he had
killed the king of Jericho.

10.29-30   After this, Joshua and his army went on from
              Makkedah to Libnah and attacked it. 30 The LORD
              also gave the Israelites victory over this city
              and its king. They spared no one, but killed every
              person in it. They did to the king what they had
              done to the king of Jericho.

After this, Joshua and his army went on from Makkedah may be translated "From Makkedah Joshua and his army went on to." From Makkedah
Joshua goes about 11 kilometers southwest to Libnah, where the same
thing happens. By this time in the narrative most readers should expect
the place-names to be those of cities, but for some languages it may
be important to say "to the city of Libnah."
     The language is stylized; in verse 30 the statement is made again
that the Lord gave...victory to the Israelites (literally "gave...into
the hand of," RSV), as at verse 19 and elsewhere.
     The verbs continue in the singular, without an explicit change of
subject, and "he smote...he left...he did" (RSV) could be read as having
the Lord as subject. Probably Joshua or the Israelite army is to be
understood as the subject.
     They spared no one, but killed every person in it may be translated
without the repetition of information: "They killed everyone in the
city."
     Here, as in verse 39, the statement is made that the king of Lib-
nah was put to death, just as the king of Jericho had been (see 8.2).
The last sentence of verse 30 may be translated, "They killed the king
of Libnah, just as they had killed the king of Jericho."

10.31-33   After this Joshua and his army went on from
              Libnah to Lachish, surrounded it and attacked it.
              32 The LORD gave the Israelites victory over Lachish
              on the second day of the battle. Just as they had
              done at Libnah, they spared no one, but killed every
              person in the city. 33 King Horam of Gezer came to
              the aid of Lachish, but Joshua defeated him and his
              army and left none of them alive.

     Verse 31 may begin in the same way as verse 29 (see comments).
     The capture of Lachish, about 17 kilometers south of Libnah, seems
to have been more difficult, since it is said that only on the second
day was the city taken. Surrounded it and attacked it may be made into
a separate sentence: "They surrounded the city and attacked it."
     Gave...victory over once again translates "put into the hands of"
(see 10.8). This sentence may be translated, "On the second day of the
battle the LORD put the city of Lachish in the power of the Israelites."
     The sentence Just as...in the city may be rephrased with more
simplicity and reduced length: "They killed every person in the city,
just as they had killed everyone in the city of Libnah."
     The city of Gezer is usually located 35 kilometers north of Lachish
(but Soggin says its location is still uncertain). Its king came to the
aid of Lachish, but he and his army were also destroyed. The city of
Gezer itself was not taken until the time of Solomon (see 16.10; 1 Kgs
9.16).

In verse 33 several translational adjustments may be made. First, King Horam of Gezer may be rendered "King Horam, who ruled the city of Gezer." Second, to the aid of Lachish may need to be rendered "to the aid of the people of Lachish." Third, the last clause of this verse (but Joshua...them alive) may need to be translated either as a complete sentence or else as two complete sentences: "But Joshua and his army defeated King Horam and his army. Not one of King Horam's men got away alive."

10.34-35   Next, Joshua and his army went on from Lachish to Eglon, surrounded it and attacked it. 35 They captured it the same day and put everyone there to death, just as they had done at Lachish.

From Lachish the Israelite army proceeded to Eglon, about 16 kilometers west of Lachish. There the capture of the city and the slaughter of its people took only one day. "That day" (RSV) is said twice and should be emphatically stated in translation. Again the verb meaning "condemn to destruction" is used. The destruction and slaughter in Eglon are compared to that inflicted on Lachish.

The restructuring of verse 34 will be similar to that of 31, as will the restructuring of verse 35 be somewhat similar to the last part of verse 32. The Hebrew readers would have found these accounts of the destruction of the various cities exciting, because it was their ancestors who had won these important victories. But this is not the case with the contemporary reader, for whom the repetition may tend to be boring. Therefore, without adding to or deleting from the accounts of defeat of the cities, one should aim to translate as interestingly as possible.

TEV	10.36-43	RSV

36 After this Joshua and his army went from Eglon up into the hills to Hebron, attacked it 37 and captured it. They killed the king and everyone else in the city as well as in the nearby towns. Joshua condemned the city to total destruction, just as he had done to Eglon. No one in it was left alive.

38 Then Joshua and his army turned back to Debir and attacked it. 39 He captured it, with its king and all the nearby towns. They put everyone there to death. Joshua did to Debir and its king what he had done to Hebron and to Libnah and its king.

36 Then Joshua went up with all Israel from Eglon to Hebron; and they assaulted it, 37 and took it, and smote it with the edge of the sword, and its king and its towns, and every person in it; he left none remaining, as he had done to Eglon, and utterly destroyed it with every person in it.

38 Then Joshua, with all Israel, turned back to Debir and assaulted it, 39 and he took it with its king and all its towns; and they smote them with the edge of the sword, and utterly destroyed every person in it; he left none remaining; as he had done to Hebron

40 Joshua conquered the whole land. He defeated the kings of the hill country, the eastern slopes, and the western foothills, as well as those of the dry country in the south. He spared no one; everyone was put to death. This was what the LORD God of Israel had commanded. 41 Joshua's campaign took him from Kadesh Barnea in the south to Gaza near the coast, including all the area of Goshen, and as far north as Gibeon. 42 Joshua conquered all these kings and their territory in one campaign because the LORD, Israel's God, was fighting for Israel. 43 After this, Joshua and his army went back to the camp at Gilgal.

and to Libnah and its king, so he did to Debir and to its king. 40 So Joshua defeated the whole land, the hill country and the Negeb and the lowland and the slopes, and all their kings; he left none remaining, but utterly destroyed all that breathed, as the LORD God of Israel commanded. 41 And Joshua defeated them from Kadesh-barnea to Gaza, and all the country of Goshen, as far as Gibeon. 42 And Joshua took all these kings and their land at one time, because the LORD God of Israel fought for Israel. 43 Then Joshua returned, and all Israel with him, to the camp at Gilgal.

10.36-37   After this, Joshua and his army went from Eglon up into the hills to Hebron, attacked it 37 and captured it. They killed the king and everyone else in the city as well as in the nearby towns. Joshua condemned the city to total destruction, just as he had done to Eglon. No one in it was left alive.

Joshua and his army may be translated by the pronoun "they," since they are fully identified in verse 34.

Went...up into the hills to Hebron translates "went up to Hebron" of the Hebrew text. The verb "went up" is the normal one used of attacking cities, since cities were generally placed on the highest geographical point possible. Here, however, TEV attempts to indicate that Hebron is in the highlands; it is some 36 kilometers from Eglon.

The same language is used; there is complete slaughter and destruction, as is indicated by the use once again of the verb meaning condemned...to total destruction. The king is killed; either he is the successor of the former king executed by Joshua (verses 23-25), or (as some scholars think is likely) there is an inconsistency in the two accounts.

The size and importance of Hebron are emphasized by the mention of the nearby towns. As well as in the nearby towns may be translated as a complete statement: "They also captured the nearby towns, and killed everyone in them as well."

Joshua condemned the city to total destruction may be too abstract for many readers. It is possible to translate "Joshua told his men, 'Completely destroy the city, just as you completely destroyed the city of Eglon. Kill everyone in it.'"

10.38-39   Then Joshua and his army turned back to Debir
and attacked it. 39 He captured it, with its king
and all the nearby towns. They put everyone there
to death. Joshua did to Debir and its king what he
had done to Hebron and to Libnah and its king.

Finally the Israelites advance on Debir, also in the highlands,
20 kilometers southwest of Hebron. They take the city and all the nearby towns. The language is the same: he "utterly destroyed" (RSV) everyone, and Joshua did to Debir and its king what he had done to Hebron
and Libnah.35

Turned back to Debir must not be translated so as to imply that
Joshua and his army had previously been to Debir. The verb turned back
to in the present context is best taken to mean "turned and went to."
As a glance at the location of the cities on a map will indicate, Debir
is actually farther south than Joshua and his army had previously gone.

He captured it may be translated, "They captured it," with Joshua
and his army as the antecedent. Moreover, it is perhaps unnecessary to
mention with its king at this place, since the king is also brought
into focus in the second sentence of this verse. One may then translate
the verse:

They captured the city of Debir and all the small towns
around it. Then they put to death everyone they captured,
just as they had put to death everyone in the city of
Hebron. They did the same thing to the city of Debir and
its king that they had done to Libnah and its king.

10.40-41   Joshua conquered the whole land. He defeated
the kings of the hill country, the eastern slopes,
and the western foothills, as well as those of the
dry country in the south. He spared no one; everyone was put to death. This was what the LORD God of
Israel had commanded. 41 Joshua's campaign took him
from Kadesh Barnea in the south to Gaza near the
coast, including all the area of Goshen, and as far
north as Gibeon.

Verses 40-43 summarize Joshua's conquest of the whole land (verse
40), by which is meant the southern part of Canaan. Again the statement
is made (verse 42) that the victories were due to the Lord, the God of
Israel.

The area conquered by Joshua is divided into four regions (verse
40). Following RSV, these regions are called: (1) "the hill country,"
by which is meant the central highlands; (2) "the Negeb," or Negev,
which is the southern region, the semiarid country southwest of the
Dead Sea; (3) "the lowland" translates "The Shephelah"; this is the
region of the western foothills, between the central highlands and the
coastal plain; (4) "the slopes" refers to the region between the central
highlands and the Dead Sea; the land falls steeply and there are high
cliffs. See 12.8, where these four geographical terms, and others, are
also used.

Again the explicit statement is made that Joshua "utterly destroyed" (RSV) all living beings (literally "all breath" or "life"),
which refers only to people, not to animals as well. As Bright notes,
this is exaggerated language. Joshua did this in obedience to the
Lord's command.

The whole area conquered by Joshua is further defined (verse 41)
as going from Kadesh Barnea (which lies 88 kilometers south of Beersheba) in the south, to Gaza, the Philistine city near the Mediterranean coast. Goshen is "an undetermined area in southern Palestine"
(Bright), not to be confused with Goshen in the Nile Delta, in Egypt.
The town of Goshen is located about 7 kilometers southeast of Debir.
Gibeon is the northernmost city captured, the place where the campaign
began (10.6-9).

Verses 40-41 may be translated as a unit by separating between
the geographical references and the references to the slaughtering
of the kings and the inhabitants of their territories. For example:

> Joshua conquered the whole land: the hill country, the
> eastern slopes, the western foothills, and the dry country
> in the south. Joshua led his army from Kadesh Barnea in
> the south to Gaza near the coast. He led them across the
> area of Goshen, and as far north as Gibeon.

Since there is the possibility of confusing the Goshen of this account
with that of Egypt, it may be wise to supply a footnote indicating
which Goshen is here intended.

After describing the territories conquered by Joshua, one may then
proceed to relate its effects: "Joshua defeated every king in the land
and put to death all its people. He spared no one, because the LORD,
the God of Israel, had commanded him to kill them all."

10.42-43   Joshua conquered all these kings and their territory
           in one campaign because the LORD, Israel's God, was
           fighting for Israel. 43 After this, Joshua and his
           army went back to the camp at Gilgal.

All this area was conquered in one campaign (verse 42; RSV "at
one time") because the Lord was fighting for Israel. The impression is
left that it was all done in a short period of time. Unless readers
are familiar with military terminology, in one campaign may be unsatisfactory. If this phrase is rendered "at this time," then verse 42 may
be translated so as to follow immediately after the suggested restructuring of verse 41: "At this time Joshua conquered all these kings and
their territory. He was able to do this because the LORD, the God of
Israel, was fighting for his people."

The campaign successfully accomplished, Joshua and his men returned to the Israelite camp at Gilgal. For verse 43, see comments at
verse 15.

Chapter 11

Joshua Defeats Jabin and His Allies

1 When the news of Israel's victories reached King Jabin of Hazor, he sent word to King Jobab of Madon, to the kings of Shimron and Achshaph, 2 and to the kings in the hill country in the north, in the Jordan Valley south of Lake Galilee, in the foothills, and on the coast near Dor. 3 He also sent word to the Canaanites on both sides of the Jordan, to the Amorites, the Hittites, the Perizzites, and the Jebusites in the hill country, as well as to the Hivites who lived at the foot of Mount Hermon in the land of Mizpah. 4 They came with all their soldiers—an army with as many men as there are grains of sand on the seashore. They also had many horses and chariots. 5 All of these kings joined forces and came together and set up camp at Merom Brook to fight against Israel.

1 When Jabin king of Hazor heard of this, he sent to Jobab king of Madon, and to the king of Shimron, and to the king of Achshaph, 2 and to the kings who were in the northern hill country, and in the Arabah south of Chinneroth, and in the lowland, and in Naphoth-dor on the west, 3 to the Canaanites in the east and the west, the Amorites, the Hittites, the Perizzites, and the Jebusites in the hill country, and the Hivites under Hermon in the land of Mizpah. 4 And they came out, with all their troops, a great host, in number like the sand that is upon the seashore, with very many horses and chariots. 5 And all these kings joined their forces, and came and encamped together at the waters of Merom, to fight with Israel.

This chapter reports Joshua's campaign in the northern part of the country (verses 1-15). The narrative is very brief and leaves the impression that the whole territory was conquered quickly and easily. But the note in verse 18 of a long time (and in 13.1 Joshua was now very old) shows that it was not a matter of weeks or only of months.

The summary statement (verses 16-23) reviews all the territory conquered by Joshua.

In the northern campaign, as in the southern one, the rulers of the region form an alliance against the invading Israelites, but they are defeated. The Lord is with the Israelites (verse 8), and their enemies cannot defeat them. Joshua follows the instructions he has received from Moses, to whom the Lord had given commands (verses 12,15). For all his greatness, Joshua is not the equal of Moses, to whom the Lord made known his will.

In order to indicate precisely the geographical location of Joshua's next series of victories, the section heading may be rendered "Joshua defeats the kings in the north" or "Joshua defeats King Jabin and the other kings of the north."

11.1-2   When the news of Israel's victories reached King Jabin of Hazor, he sent word to King Jobab of Madon, to the kings of Shimron and Achshaph, 2 and to the kings in the hill country in the north, in the Jordan Valley south of Lake Galilee, in the foothills, and on the coast near Dor.

When the news of Israel's victories reached King Jabin may not be possible in languages where news does not "reach" someone, but rather a person hears the news. If such is the case, one may translate "King Jabin of Hazor heard that the Israelite army had conquered all this territory." Or "King Jabin of Hazor heard about the victories of Israel's army."

King Jabin of Hazor heard of Israel's victories in the south, and immediately he sent messengers to the rulers in the northern part of the country proposing they all join forces against the invaders. Hazor is in Galilee, about 15 kilometers north of the northern end of Lake Galilee. It was a large and important city-state, and mention of it is made in nonbiblical texts.

Before listing the kings to whom Jabin addressed his message, it may be wise both to indicate that they were neighboring kings and to specify the reason for this message. In verses 4 and 5 the reason does become clear, but it could be very helpful to indicate from the outset the nature of the communication. For example,

So King Jabin sent a message to the neighboring kings and asked them to bring their armies together to fight against Israel. He sent this message to King Jobab of Madon, to... near Dor.

Madon is 30 kilometers southeast of Hazor, and 4 kilometers west of Lake Galilee.[36]

There is considerable uncertainty over the identification and location of Shimron and Achshaph.[37] On the maps Shimron is located in Zebulun (see 19.15), about 51 kilometers southwest of Hazor; and Achshaph is located about 42 kilometers southwest of Hazor. But the location of these places is far from certain.

In verse 2 "the Arabah" (RSV) is the Jordan Valley, and "Chinneroth" (RSV) is Lake Galilee.[38] The hill country in the north is the highlands of Galilee.

On the coast near Dor translates the Hebrew *naphothdor* (see RSV). It is not quite certain what the Hebrew *naphoth* means; perhaps "the coast" (Bright), referring to the Mediterranean coastal plains south of Mount Carmel, of which Dor was the chief city. BJ, JB have "the hillsides of Dor"; AT "the uplands of Dor"; also TOB. Gray defines it as "the foothills of Carmel."[39]

11.3   He also sent word to the Canaanites on both sides
of the Jordan, to the Amorites, the Hittites, the
Perizzites, and the Jebusites in the hill country,
as well as to the Hivites who lived at the foot of
Mount Hermon in the land of Mizpah.

For the people listed see 3.10. So as to distinguish this group
from the neighboring kings, verse 3 may open with "He also sent the
same message to...." Moreover it may be advisable to break verse 3
somewhere, for example, "...in the hill country. He sent the message
to the Hivites...of Mizpah." Finally, it may be better to substitute
the pattern "to the kings of the Canaanites..." for to the Canaanites;
otherwise, a problem will arise in verse 5 (see comments there).
    Mount Hermon lies northeast of Lake Huleh, toward Damascus. A
land of Mizpah east of the Jordan is not known; perhaps it is the same
place as "the valley of Mizpeh" (RSV) in verse 8. The Hebrew word, as
a common noun, means "watchtower."

11.4   They came with all their soldiers—an army with
as many men as there are grains of sand on the
seashore. They also had many horses and chariots.

The huge size of the enemy army is described in the common expression, "as many as the grains of sand on the seashore." Readers who know
anything about an ocean would have no difficulty understanding this figure of speech. However, even though it may be understood, many cultures
will have expressions of their own which are more meaningful. For example, "as many men as there are trees in the jungle."
    The Hittite chariot was pulled by two horses and carried the driver
and two warriors. It is possible to mention in one sentence the soldiers, horses, and chariots, and then to make the comparison in a separate sentence: "They brought together many foot soldiers and also a
large number of war chariots that were drawn by horses. They had as
many soldiers as there are grains of sand on the seashore."

11.5   All of these kings joined forces and came together
and set up camp at Merom Brook to fight against
Israel.

All of these kings may cause some difficulty, since there are no
kings mentioned in verse 3 for the Canaanites, Amorites, Hittites,
Perizzites, Jebusites, and Hivites. Therefore in verse 3 it may be
advisable to follow the pattern "To the Canaanite kings..." (see comment
at verse 3).
    Merom Brook ran southward from the mountains of Galilee into the
upper northwest corner of Lake Galilee.
    This verse is short, but it can be divided into two segments: "All
of these kings came together and set up camp at Merom Brook. There they
joined forces to fight against Israel."

TEV	11.6-9	RSV

6 The LORD said to Joshua, "Do not be afraid of them. By this time tomorrow I will have killed all of them for Israel. You are to cripple their horses and burn their chariots." 7 So Joshua and all his men attacked them by surprise at Merom Brook. 8 The LORD gave the Israelites victory over them; the Israelites attacked and pursued them as far north as Misrephoth Maim and Sidon, and as far east as the valley of Mizpah. The fight continued until none of the enemy was left alive. 9 Joshua did to them what the LORD had commanded: he crippled their horses and burned their chariots.

6 And the LORD said to Joshua, "Do not be afraid of them, for tomorrow at this time I will give over all of them, slain, to Israel; you shall hamstring their horses, and burn their chariots with fire." 7 So Joshua came suddenly upon them with all his people of war, by the waters of Merom, and fell upon them. 8 And the LORD gave them into the hand of Israel, who smote them and chased them as far as Great Sidon and Misrephoth-maim, and eastward as far as the valley of Mizpeh; and they smote them, until they left none remaining. 9 And Joshua did to them as the LORD bade him; he hamstrung their horses, and burned their chariots with fire.

11.6-7   The LORD said to Joshua, "Do not be afraid of them. By this time tomorrow I will have killed all of them for Israel. You are to cripple their horses and burn their chariots." 7 So Joshua and all his men attacked them by surprise at Merom Brook.

The Lord assures Joshua that he, the Lord will provide the victory; all the enemy will be killed by the next day. Joshua is told to cripple their horses and burn their chariots. To "hamstring" (RSV) an animal is to cut the large sinew of the back legs, leaving the animal unable to walk. Although the events of verse 6 are narrated in chronological sequence, the use of the future perfect (will have killed) and of the imperative (You are to) may cause some confusion of time sequence. Moreover, in Hebrew the personal pronoun "I" (of the Lord) is emphatic. The Lord's instructions to Joshua may then be translated, "Do not be afraid of them, because I, the LORD, will kill them all. By this time tomorrow they will all be dead. After the battle, cripple their horses and burn their war chariots."

Joshua attacked the enemy by surprise (perhaps by night, verse 7), routed them and killed them all (verse 8). As a comparison of TEV and RSV will indicate, the Hebrew (represented by the formal structure of RSV) is somewhat more lengthy than TEV. If there is a problem with the pronoun them, it may be rendered either "the enemy camp" or "the enemy." By surprise may be translated, "before the enemy knew they were there."

11.8   The LORD gave the Israelites victory over them; the
        Israelites attacked and pursued them as far north
        as Misrephoth Maim and Sidon, and as far east as
        the valley of Mizpah. The fight continued until
        none of the enemy was left alive.

In order to show the immediate causal relations between verses 7
and 8, it may be advisable to make the first clause of verse 8 a continuation of the last sentence in verse 7: "at Merom Brook, 8 and the
LORD...over them."
    Gave the Israelites victory over them may need to be less abstract:
"caused the Israelite army to defeat their enemies" (see comment at
10.8).
    The remainder of this verse may be restructured as two sentences:
"Part of the Israelite army attacked and pursued the enemy as far north
as the cities of Misrephoth Maim and Sidon. The rest of the Israelite
army pursued the enemy as far east as the valley of Mizpah."
    Misrephoth Maim is near the Mediterranean coast, and Sidon (in He-
brew "Great Sidon") is the important Phoenician city much farther north,
on the Mediterranean Sea. To the east the Israelites chase the fleeing
enemy as far as the valley of Mizpah (see verse 3); RSV follows the
spelling "Mizpeh," which represents the Masoretic text.
    The fight continued...left alive may be translated in the active:
"Joshua's men fought the enemy until they had killed them all" or
"...until they had killed everyone of them."

11.9   Joshua did to them what the LORD had commanded: he
        crippled their horses and burned their chariots.

Joshua obeyed the Lord's command: he crippled their horses and
burned their chariots.
    Some languages may require that a portion of this verse be given
in direct discourse: "'After you defeat your enemies, cripple their
horses and burn their war chariots.' So Joshua did as the LORD had
commanded." It may be preferable to describe Joshua's actions in the
same terms as the command: "...so Joshua did as the LORD had commanded.
He crippled their horses and burned their chariots."

           TEV   11.10-15   RSV

    10 Joshua then turned back,   10 And Joshua turned back at
captured Hazor and killed its king. that time, and took Hazor, and
(At that time Hazor was the most   smote its king with the sword; for
powerful of all those kingdoms.)   Hazor formerly was the head of all
11 They put everyone there to   those kingdoms. 11 And they put to
death; no one was left alive, and   the sword all who were in it, ut-
the city was burned.   terly destroying them; there was
    12 Joshua captured all these   none left that breathed, and he
cities and their kings, putting   burned Hazor with fire. 12 And all
everyone to death, just as Moses,   the cities of those kings, and all

                          [161]

the LORD's servant, had commanded.
13 However, the Israelites did not
burn any of the cities built on
mounds, except Hazor, which Joshua
did burn. 14 The people of Israel
took all the valuables and livestock from these cities and kept
them for themselves. But they put
every person to death; no one was
left alive. 15 The LORD had given
his commands to his servant Moses,
Moses had given them to Joshua,
and Joshua obeyed them. He did
everything that the LORD had commanded Moses.

their kings, Joshua took, and smote
them with the edge of the sword,
utterly destroying them, as Moses
the servant of the LORD had commanded. 13 But none of the cities
that stood on mounds did Israel
burn, except Hazor only; that
Joshua burned. 14 And all the
spoil of these cities and the cattle, the people of Israel took for
their booty; but every man they
smote with the edge of the sword,
until they had destroyed them,
and they did not leave any that
breathed. 15 As the LORD had commanded Moses his servant, so
Moses commanded Joshua, and so
Joshua did; he left nothing undone
of all that the LORD had commanded
Moses.

11.10   Joshua then turned back, captured Hazor and
           killed its king. (At that time Hazor was the most
           powerful of all those kingdoms.)

After routing and killing the enemy forces, Joshua turned back to
Hazor, captured the city, and killed its king. The note that follows
about Hazor's importance is written from the point of view of the
writer's time: At that time refers to the time of Joshua; it does not
mean, as RSV might be understood, that before Joshua's time Hazor had
been (but no longer was) the most powerful of all those kingdoms.
    The translation of this verse presents several difficulties. First,
the verb turned back may suggest that Joshua had previously been to the
city of Hazor. Second, the presence of the parenthetical statement makes
the comprehension difficult. Third, in verse 10 it is Joshua who turns
back, captures Hazor, and kills its king. In verse 11 the subject
shifts to They, for which the only immediate antecedent is Joshua of
this verse. These difficulties may be overcome by translating as follows:
    At that time the city of Hazor and its king ruled over all
    the other kingdoms in the territory. So after the battle,
    Joshua and his men went and attacked the city of Hazor. They
    captured the city, killed its king, and 11 put everyone there
    to death....

11.11   They put everyone there to death; no one was left
           alive, and the city was burned.

They put everyone there to death represents "And they put to the
sword all who were in it, utterly destroying them" (RSV) of the Hebrew

text. The verb which RSV renders "utterly destroying" is the same Hebrew verb discussed at 2.10, which means "dedicate to God (for complete
destruction)."

While the Hebrew text uses three verbs to describe the slaughter
of the people, TEV uses only two. If the form of TEV is followed, then
no one was left alive may be translated either "they did not leave anyone alive" or "they killed everyone there." And the city was burned may
also be translated as an active: "and they burned the city."

Recent excavations have dated the destruction of Hazor around
1225 B.C. The city was rebuilt by Solomon (1 Kgs 9.15).

11.12   Joshua captured all these cities and their kings,
           putting everyone to death, just as Moses, the LORD's
           servant, had commanded.

Verses 12-15 summarize the campaigns in the north. Verse 12 emphasizes the complete massacre of all the population. In Hebrew all these
cities and their kings are placed in emphatic position, followed by the
subject and verb Joshua captured. RSV represents fairly well the inverted
form of the Hebrew text.

Putting everyone to death translates "and smote them with the edge
of the sword, utterly destroying them" (RSV). The verb "utterly destroying" translates once again the Hebrew verb which means "condemn to total
destruction." In translation a new sentence may begin here: "He put
everyone to death, just as Moses, the LORD's servant, had commanded him
to do." The verb "put...to death" may be translated as a causative, "He
caused his men to put everyone to death." Or direct discourse may be
used: "Joshua and his men captured all these cities and their kings. He
told his men, 'Put everyone to death, just as Moses, the LORD's servant
commanded us to do.'"

11.13   However, the Israelites did not burn any of the cities
           built on mounds, except Hazor, which Joshua did burn.

Cities built on mounds were walled cities built on the ruins or
debris of previous settlement—as such cities were customarily built.
Hazor was the only one of those cities that Joshua set on fire.

Which Joshua did burn may be omitted from explicit mention in translation, since the phrase except Hazor clearly implies that Joshua and
his army did burn that city. In fact, in light of verse 11, this verse
may be translated, "However, Joshua and his men did not burn any of
these cities. They left them standing on the mounds where they were
built."

11.14   The people of Israel took all the valuables and live-
           stock from these cities and kept them for themselves.
           But they put every person to death; no one was left
           alive.

[163]

The Israelites kept all the valuables and livestock, but they killed all the people. They put every person to death; no one was left alive is similar in Hebrew to what occurs in 10.40 and 11.11.

The word translated valuables (RSV "spoil") refers to any kind of loot taken from a captured city; it is the same word translated goods at 8.27. Livestock is also the same word translated livestock in 8.27.

But they put every person to death; no one was left alive translates "but every man they smote with the edge of the sword, until they had destroyed them, and they did not leave any that breathed" (RSV). One may further shorten the statement: "But they put every person in the city to death."

11.15   The LORD had given his commands to his servant
         Moses, Moses had given them to Joshua, and Joshua
         obeyed them. He did everything that the LORD had
         commanded Moses.

All this was done in obedience to the Lord's command to Moses, which Moses passed on to Joshua. In fact, the entire purpose of this verse is to underline the absolute obedience of Joshua in doing everything that Moses had commanded him to do.

The LORD had given his commands may be taken as a reference to an indefinite number of general commands. However, in context the reference is to the specific command to destroy the inhabitants of the land. The relation between the last part of verse 14 and the first part of verse 15 becomes clearer if translated,

         That is what the LORD had commanded his servant Moses to do.
         Moses had told Joshua what the LORD had commanded, and Joshua
         obeyed the LORD's commands. Joshua did everything that the
         LORD had commanded Moses.
Or,
         ...Joshua completely obeyed the LORD's command. He did
         everything that Moses had told him to do.

                 TEV   11.16-20   RSV

The Territory Taken by Joshua

16 Joshua captured all the land—the hill country and foothills, both north and south, all the area of Goshen and the dry country south of it, as well as the Jordan Valley. 17-18 The territory extended from Mount Halak in the south near Edom, as far as Baalgad in the north, in the valley of Lebanon south of Mount Hermon. Joshua was at war with the kings of this territory for a long time,

16 So Joshua took all that land, the hill country and all the Negeb and all the land of Goshen and the lowland and the Arabah and the hill country of Israel and its lowland 17 from Mount Halak, that rises toward Seir, as far as Baal-gad in the valley of Lebanon below Mount Hermon. And he took all their kings, and smote them, and put them to death. 18 Joshua made

[164]

but he captured them all and put them to death. 19 The only city that made peace with the people of Israel was Gibeon, where some of the Hivites lived. All the others were conquered in battle. 20 The LORD had made them determined to fight the Israelites, so that they would be condemned to total destruction and all be killed without mercy. This was what the LORD had commanded Moses.

war a long time with all those kings. 19 There was not a city that made peace with the people of Israel, except the Hivites, the inhabitants of Gibeon; they took all in battle. 20 For it was the LORD's doing to harden their hearts that they should come against Israel in battle, in order that they should be utterly destroyed, and should receive no mercy but be exterminated, as the LORD commanded Moses.

This section summarizes all the conquests of the Israelites in Canaan (verses 16-20), and adds a note about the defeat of the giants in the land (verses 21-22). The battles won, the people now experience a time of peace (verse 23).

The section heading, The Territory Taken by Joshua (equivalent of a passive construction), may be reformulated as an active clause in keeping with verses 16 and 23: either "Joshua captures all the land" or "Joshua captures all the land that the LORD told him to capture." For English readers the verb "take" could imply "take for yourself," which explains the shift to "capture" in these proposed restructurings.

11.16   Joshua captured all the land—the hill country and foothills, both north and south, all the area of Goshen and the dry country south of it, as well as the Jordan Valley.

Verses 16-17 (see RSV) list the area conquered by the Israelites; see comments on 10.40-41 for "the hill country," "the Negeb," "the land of Goshen," "the lowland"; and for "the Arabah" see comments on 11.2. The hill country and foothills both north and south translates "the hill country...and the lowland" (of Judah, in the first part of verse 16), and "the hill country of Israel and its lowland" (at the end of verse 16). In this section Judah and Israel (see verse 21) are used of the two parts of the country, the south and the north.

This verse may require some modification in translation. For example, the subject Joshua may need to be enlarged to "Joshua and his army," and the phrase all the land may need further definition: "Joshua and his army captured all the land from north to south. They captured the hill country and foothills, all the area of Goshen and the dry country south of it, as well as the Jordan Valley."

11.17-18 The territory extended from Mount Halak in the south near Edom, as far as Baalgad in the north, in the valley of Lebanon south of Mount Hermon. Joshua was at war with the kings of this territory for a long time, but he captured them all and put them to death.

[165]

TEV places verses 17-18 together because verse 18 merely repeats
the last part of verse 17, except for the additional information "made
war a long time" (see RSV). It is possible, however, to translate these
verses in a way that sounds natural without joining them together:
"17...Joshua and his army finally captured and put to death all the kings
of this territory, 18 even though the war against the kings took a
long time." Verse 18 may also be translated either "even though the
war lasted a long time" or "even though it took them a long time (to
defeat the kings)."

The limits of the territory are given in verse 17: the southern
limit was Mount Halak, near Edom, south of the Dead Sea; the northern
limit was the town of Baalgad, not far from Mount Hermon.

The territory extended from of TEV translates the preposition
"from" of the Hebrew text. In Hebrew verse 17a continues the listing
of territories begun in verse 16, and the restructuring of TEV is
necessary only because TEV breaks the sentence at the end of verse 16.
A sentence break may still be maintained, and the relationship between
the two verses made even clearer, if verse 17 begins: "They captured all
the territory from Mount Halak in the south near Edom and as far north
as the city of Baalgad, in the valley of Lebanon south of Mount Hermon."
Or, 16-17a may be translated as a unit:

Joshua and his army captured all the land as far south as
Mount Halak near Edom and as far north as the city of Baalgad in the valley between Mount Hermon and the Lebanon Mountains. They captured the central hill country, the western
slopes, the dry country in the south, and the Jordan Valley.

Although all the area of Goshen is not mentioned explicitly in this restructuring, it is included in the phrase "all the dry country to the
south."

11.19   The only city that made peace with the people of
            Israel was Gibeon, where some of the Hivites lived.
            All the others were conquered in battle.

Only Gibeon made peace with the Israelites; again, as in 9.3 (TEV),
it is said that they were Hivites.

All the others were conquered in battle may be translated "The
people of Israel conquered all the other cities."

11.20   The LORD had made them determined to fight the
            Israelites, so that they would be condemned to
            total destruction and all be killed without mercy.
            This was what the LORD had commanded Moses.

Verse 20 provides the theological justification for the wholesale
massacre of the people: the Lord "hardened their hearts" (see RSV),
that is, made them proud and stubborn (TEV determined to fight). Again
the Hebrew verb condemned to total destruction is used, and it is said
that this was done in obedience to the Lord's command to Moses.

Many languages will have idiomatic expressions equivalent to "harden their hearts" of the Hebrew; for example, "stiffen their necks" or "make their eyes glare." If idiomatic expressions do exist, then one will have to decide whether it is more effective to introduce an indigenous idiom or to translate in plain language, without a metaphor, as in TEV.

So that they would be condemned to total destruction and all be killed without mercy may be changed to an active construction and translated as a separate sentence: "He did this so that the people of Israel would condemn them to total destruction and kill them all without mercy."

This was what is somewhat ambiguous in TEV. It actually refers only to the clause which begins so that; it does not refer back to the entire previous sentence. One may then translate "The LORD had commanded Moses to kill all the people of the land."

	TEV	11.21-23	RSV

21 At this time Joshua went and destroyed the race of giants called the Anakim who lived in the hill country—in Hebron, Debir, Anab, and in all the hill country of Judah and Israel. Joshua completely destroyed them and their cities. 22 None of the Anakim were left in the land of Israel; a few, however, were left in Gaza, Gath, and Ashdod.
23 Joshua captured the whole land, as the LORD had commanded Moses. Joshua gave it to the Israelites as their own and divided it into portions, one for each tribe.
So the people rested from war.

21 And Joshua came at that time, and wiped out the Anakim from the hill country, from Hebron, from Debir, from Anab, and from all the hill country of Judah, and from all the hill country of Israel; Joshua utterly destroyed them with their cities. 22 There was none of the Anakim left in the land of the people of Israel; only in Gaza, in Gath, and in Ashdod, did some remain. 23 So Joshua took the whole land, according to all that the LORD had spoken to Moses; and Joshua gave it for an inheritance to Israel according to their tribal allotments. And the land had rest from war.

11.21   At this time Joshua went and destroyed the race of giants called the Anakim who lived in the hill country—in Hebron, Debir, Anab, and in all the hill country of Judah and Israel. Joshua completely destroyed them and their cities.

Joshua went and destroyed may be better rendered as "Joshua also destroyed," since in Hebrew the use of the verb went (RSV "came") in such a context indicates continuation of action rather than movement.

With less complication than TEV, the object of destroyed may be translated, "...the race of giants called the Anakim who lived in the cities of Hebron, Debir, Anab, and in all the rest of the hill country of Judah and Israel." Or, "...Anakim. They lived in the cities of...." Either of these proposals would avoid the complications involved with the use of a dash.

[167]

11.21

The race of giants wiped out by Joshua are called the Anakim, that is, the descendants of Anak (see Num 13.33); and for the other names used of the Canaanite giants, see Deuteronomy 2.10-11. Of the places mentioned in the highlands of the south, Hebron and Debir are already known (see 10.36-39); Anab is located about 8 kilometers southeast of Debir. Again the verb completely destroyed is used.

Judah and Israel refer to the southern and the northern parts of the country.

11.22   None of the Anakim were left in the land of Israel;
            a few, however, were left in Gaza, Gath, and Ashdod.

Israel (literally "the land of the descendants of Israel") means the whole country and includes the same territory referred to as Judah and Israel in the previous verse. Therefore it would be less confusing not to mention Israel by name in this verse. Accordingly one may translate "He killed all of the Anakim who lived in the land, except for a few who lived in Gaza, Gath, and Ashdod.

Gaza, Gath, and Ashdod were Philistine cities on the Mediterranean coastal plain.

11.23   Joshua captured the whole land, as the LORD had
            commanded Moses. Joshua gave it to the Israelites as
            their own and divided it into portions, one for each
            tribe.
            So the people rested from war.

The whole land conquered, Joshua proceeded to divide it among the tribes (see chapters 13-21). For "inheritance" (RSV) see 1.6; "according to their tribal allotments" (RSV) means that each tribe received a share of the land (see NEB "allotting to each tribe its share"). At long last there was a period of peace.

One for each tribe, a phrase hanging on at the end of the second sentence, may tend to confuse the meaning. This potential difficulty may be avoided if the sentence is shortened and translated, "Joshua divided the land up among the tribes of Israel" or "...among the tribes of Israel and gave each tribe its share."

So the people rested from war is literally "And the land had rest from war." An idiomatic expression will be appropriate in many languages. Otherwise, it is possible to translate "The Israelites then lived in peace (throughout the land)."

Chapter 12

The Kings Defeated by Moses

1 The people of Israel had already conquered and occupied the land east of the Jordan, from the Arnon Valley up the Jordan Valley and as far north as Mount Hermon. They defeated two kings. 2 One was Sihon, the Amorite king who ruled at Heshbon. His kingdom included half of Gilead: from Aroer (on the edge of the Arnon Valley) and from the city in*f* the middle of that valley, as far as the Jabbok River, the border of Ammon; 3 it included the Jordan Valley from Lake Galilee south to Beth Jeshimoth (east of the Dead Sea) and on toward the foot of Mount Pisgah.

4 They also defeated King Og of Bashan, who was one of the last of the Rephaim; he ruled at Ashtaroth and Edrei. 5 His kingdom included Mount Hermon, Salecah, and all of Bashan as far as the boundaries of Geshur and Maacah, as well as half of Gilead, as far as the territory of King Sihon of Heshbon.

6 These two kings were defeated by Moses and the people of Israel. Moses, the LORD's servant, gave their land to the tribes of Reuben and Gad and to half the tribe of Manasseh, to be their possession.

*f*Probable text (see 13.16; Dt 2.36) the city in; Hebrew does not have these words.

1 Now these are the kings of the land, whom the people of Israel defeated, and took possession of their land beyond the Jordan toward the sunrising, from the valley of the Arnon to Mount Hermon, with all the Arabah eastward: 2 Sihon king of the Amorites who dwelt at Heshbon, and ruled from Aroer, which is on the edge of the valley of the Arnon, and from the middle of the valley as far as the river Jabbok, the boundary of the Ammonites, that is, half of Gilead, 3 and the Arabah to the Sea of Chinneroth eastward, and in the direction of Beth-Jeshimoth, to the sea of the Arabah, the Salt Sea, southward to the foot of the slopes of Pisgah; 4 and Og*e* king of Bashan, one of the remnant of the Rephaim, who dwelt at Ashtaroth and at Edre-i 5 and ruled over Mount Hermon and Salecah and all Bashan to the boundary of the Geshurites and the Ma-acathites, and over half of Gilead to the boundary of Sihon king of Heshbon. 6 Moses, the servant of the LORD, and the people of Israel defeated them; and Moses the servant of the LORD gave their land for a possession to the Reubenites and the Gadites and the half-tribe of Manasseh.

*e*Gk: Heb the boundary of Og

With this chapter the first half of the book comes to an end. First the conquest of the land east of the Jordan is recalled (verses 1-6), and then the conquest of the land west of the Jordan (verses 7-24).

This section recalls the victories won by the Israelites under the leadership of Moses in the land east of the Jordan. The two kings, Sihon of Heshbon and Og of Bashan, were defeated and their land was given to the two and one-half tribes that settled in the east.

The section heading, The Kings Defeated by Moses, may be slightly restructured as "A list of the kings whom Moses defeated." Or, if a complete statement is more appropriate, "These are the kings whom Moses defeated."

12.1 The people of Israel had already conquered and occupied the land east of the Jordan, from the Arnon Valley up the Jordan Valley and as far north as Mount Hermon. They defeated two kings.

The land conquered on the east side of the Jordan had for its southern limit the Arnon Valley; the Arnon River flows into the Dead Sea about halfway between the southern and northern ends of the sea; and the city of Aroer (verse 2) is on the Arnon River. The northern limit was Mount Hermon (see 11.3).

The verb tense had already conquered and occupied may leave the reader guessing as to the time reference intended, especially if the reading is begun with this chapter. In order to help the reader, and on the basis of verse 6, one may translate "Moses had (already) led the people of Israel to conquer and occupy...."

They defeated two kings may easily be fitted into the earlier part of the verse,

Moses had led the people of Israel to defeat two kings east of the Jordan and to take over their territory, which went from the Arnon Valley up the Jordan River and as far north as Mount Hermon.

Or, if two sentences are more satisfactory,

Moses had already led the people of Israel to conquer two kings east of the Jordan and to take over their territory. The territory of these two kings ran from the Arnon Valley up the Jordan River and as far north as Mount Hermon.

12.2-3 One was Sihon, the Amorite king who ruled at Heshbon. His kingdom included half of Gilead: from Aroer (on the edge of the Arnon Valley) and from the city in*f* the middle of that valley, as far as the Jabbok River, the border of Ammon; 3 it included the Jordan Valley from Lake Galilee south to Beth Jeshimoth (east of the Dead Sea) and on toward the foot of Mount Pisgah.

*f*Probable text (see 13.16; Dt 2.36) the city in; Hebrew does not have these words

[170]

One was Sihon...at Heshbon may be somewhat clearer if translated, "One of the kings whom Moses defeated was King Sihon. He was an Amorite king who ruled at the city of Heshbon."

The geographical data in verses 2-3 relating to the kingdom of Sihon are not very clear in Hebrew. For the defeat of Sihon, see Numbers 21.21-30; Deuteronomy 2.26-37.

Heshbon, the capital of Sihon, was about 25 kilometers northeast of the northern end of the Dead Sea. The southern limit of Sihon's kingdom was Aroer (that is, the Arnon Valley); the northern limit was the Jabbok River, which flows into the Jordan. The river formed the boundary with Ammon, which lay to the east (a look at a map in *The New Oxford Annotated Bible*, RSV, will show how the river runs north and then turns west to the Jordan). Sihon's kingdom occupied (the southern) half of Gilead.

TEV and from the city in the middle of that valley attempts to make sense of the Hebrew, which has "from Aroer, on the edge of the Arnon Valley, and the middle of the valley and half of Gilead and to the Jabbok River, the border of the Ammonites." JB, NEB, NAB, BJ, TOB, in different ways, translate "and the valley (or, riverbed) itself"; RSV "from the middle of the valley" involves a slight alteration of the Masoretic text. TEV has taken its clue from 13.9,16, "the city that is in the middle of the valley" (see also Deut 2.36), on the assumption that the city in has dropped out from the text here.

In verse 3, RSV "the Arabah" and "the Sea of Chinneroth" are the Jordan Valley and Lake Galilee. Beth Jeshimoth lies slightly northeast of the Dead Sea, about 20 kilometers west of Heshbon, the capital of Sihon's kingdom. Mount Pisgah is between Heshbon and Beth Jeshimoth. RSV translates the Hebrew "the sea of the Arabah, the Salt Sea," which is a way of speaking of the Dead Sea.[40]

A clear and simple presentation of the geographical data contained in this and the following verse will be extremely difficult. At the least it will require constant reference to a map and careful consideration of the most natural order in which to present the material in the receptor language. Following the interpretation of TEV, one method of presentation would be:

2 King Sihon ruled the southern half of the land of Gilead, which was the territory between the Jabbok River valley in the north and the Arnon River valley in the south. His kingdom extended southeast as far as the city of Aroer on the edge of the Arnon Valley. In the southwest it extended as far as the town in the Arnon Valley halfway between Aroer and the Dead Sea. 3 The western boundary of his kingdom was the Jordan River valley from Lake Galilee in the north to the Dead Sea in the south. Included in his territory was the area east of the Dead Sea as far as the town of Beth Jeshimoth and Mount Pisgah.

Since Mount Pisgah is less well known than Mount Nebo, the neighboring mountain, it would also be proper to use the better known term for the geographical description.

12.4   They also defeated King Og of Bashan, who was
one of the last of the Rephaim; he ruled at Ashtaroth
and Edrei.

Og is called <u>one of the last of the Rephaim</u>, another name for the
race of giants (see <u>Deut 2.10-11</u>). For Og himself see Deuteronomy 3.11.
For the defeat of King Og of Bashan, see Numbers 21.33-35; Deuteronomy
3.1-11.[41]
The pronoun <u>they</u> may be better rendered "Moses and the people of
Israel," because a great deal of information has intervened since the
previous mention of Moses in verse 1 (see suggested translation model).
Moreover, inasmuch as the book speaks primarily about the exploits of
Joshua and the Israelites, it may easily be forgotten by the reader
that in this instance the reference is to Moses.
Finally, the first sentence of verse 4 may be divided into two
parts: "Moses and the Israelites also defeated King Og of Bashan. He
was one of the last of the giants called Rephaim, and he ruled from the
cities of Ashtaroth and Edrei." <u>Ashtaroth and Edrei</u> are two cities to
the east and southeast of Lake Galilee, about 25 kilometers distance
from one another.

12.5   His kingdom included Mount Hermon, Salecah, and all
of Bashan as far as the boundaries of Geshur and
Maacah, as well as half of Gilead, as far as the
territory of King Sihon of Heshbon.

<u>Bashan</u> is the region east and northeast of Lake Galilee. The north-
ern limit of Og's territory was <u>Mount Hermon</u>. <u>Salecah</u> lay about 100
kilometers east of Lake Galilee. <u>Geshur and Maacah</u> were not well-de-
fined territories; they lay east and northeast of Lake Galilee, beyond
the territory conquered by the Israelites, and were inhabited by tribal
groups. Og ruled over (the northern) <u>half of Gilead</u>. The southern limit
of his kingdom was the border with <u>Sihon's territory</u>.
It is possible to translate this verse so that the geographical
directions are more explicit:
He ruled land as far north as Mount Hermon and as far east
as the city of Salecah. He also ruled all of Bashan, as far
as the territories of Geshur and Maacah to the east. In addition he ruled the northern half of Gilead, as far south
as the territory of King Sihon of Heshbon.

12.6   These two kings were defeated by Moses and the
people of Israel. Moses, the LORD's servant, gave
their land to the tribes of Reuben and Gad and to
half the tribe of Manasseh, to be their possession.

This verse is a summary statement of the conquest of the land east
of the Jordan, and the division of the territory among the two and one-
half eastern tribes (see detailed account in 13.8-32).
<u>These two kings were defeated by Moses and the people of Israel</u>
may be stated in the active: "Moses and the people of Israel defeated
these two kings."

For most readers, <u>gave...to</u> and <u>to be their possession</u> will be synonymous in meaning. Therefore the meaning may be expressed, "Moses, the LORD's servant, divided their land among the tribes of Reuben, Gad, and the half tribe of Manasseh."

TEV	12.7-24	RSV

The Kings Defeated by Joshua

7 Joshua and the people of Israel defeated all the kings in the territory west of the Jordan, from Baalgad in the valley of Lebanon to Mount Halak in the south near Edom. Joshua divided this land among the tribes and gave it to them as a permanent possession. 8 This portion included the hill country, the western foothills, the Jordan Valley and its foothills, the eastern slopes, and the dry country in the south. This land had been the home of the Hittites, the Amorites, the Canaanites, the Perizzites, the Hivites, and the Jebusites. 9 The people of Israel defeated the kings of the following cities: Jericho, Ai (near Bethel), 10 Jerusalem, Hebron, 11 Jarmuth, Lachish, 12 Eglon, Gezer, 13 Debir, Geder, 14 Hormah, Arad, 15 Libnah, Adullam, 16 Makkedah, Bethel, 17 Tappuah, Hepher, 18 Aphek, Lasharon, 19 Madon, Hazor, 20 Shimron Meron, Achshaph, 21 Taanach, Megiddo, 22 Kedesh, Jokneam (in Carmel), 23 Dor (on the coast), Goiim (in Galilee*g*), 24 and Tirzah—thirty-one kings in all.

gOne ancient translation Galilee; *Hebrew* Gilgal.

7 And these are the kings of the land whom Joshua and the people of Israel defeated on the west side of the Jordan, from Baalgad in the valley of Lebanon to Mount Halak, that rises toward Seir (and Joshua gave their land to the tribes of Israel as a possession according to their allotments, 8 in the hill country, in the lowland, in the Arabah, in the slopes, in the wilderness, and in the Negeb, the land of the Hittites, the Amorites, the Canaanites, the Perizzites, the Hivites, and the Jebusites): 9 the king of Jericho, one; the king of Ai, which is beside Bethel, one; 10 the king of Jerusalem, one; the king of Hebron, one; 11 the king of Jarmuth, one; the king of Lachish, one; 12 the king of Eglon, one; the king of Gezer, one; 13 the king of Debir, one; the king of Geder, one; 14 the king of Hormah, one; the king of Arad, one; 15 the king of Libnah, one; the king of Adullam, one; 16 the king of Makkedah, one; the king of Bethel, one; 17 the king of Tappuah, one; the king of Hepher, one; 18 the king of Aphek, one; the king of Lasharon, one; 19 the king of Madon, one; the king of Hazor, one; 20 the king of Shimron-meron, one; the king of Achshaph, one; 21 the king of Taanach, one; the king of Megiddo, one; 22 the king of Kedesh, one; the king of Jokne-am in Carmel, one; 23 the king of Dor in Naphath-dor, one; the king of Goiim in Galilee,*f* one; 24 the king of Tirzah, one:

in all, thirty-one kings.

fGk: Heb *Gilgal*

Regarding the translation of the section heading The Kings Defeated by Joshua, see comments at the previous section heading, verse
1 (The Kings Defeated by Moses).

12.7   Joshua and the people of Israel defeated all the
kings in the territory west of the Jordan, from Baalgad in the valley of Lebanon to Mount Halak in the
south near Edom. Joshua divided this land among the
tribes and gave it to them as a permanent possession.

The northern limit of the territory west of the Jordan was Baalgad; the southern limit was Mount Halak (see 11.17). The territory was
divided by Joshua among the nine and one-half western tribes (see chapters 14—19 for a detailed account).

It may be appropriate to begin a new sentence after west of the
Jordan: "They defeated the kings from the city of Baalgad in the
valley of Lebanon to Mount Halak in the south near the territory of
Edom."

Possession translates the same noun used in verse 6, and permanent
possession is more literally "possession according to their allotments"
(RSV). The meaning is that Joshua portioned out to each tribe their
share of the land. TEV renders the phrase "according to their allotments" by permanent, since this was the land which God had promised
would be theirs forever. However, it is quite likely that for many
readers divided...among, gave...to, and as a permanent possession may
be essentially equivalent in meaning. That is, one generally assumes
that something given is given with the intention of being the permanent
possession of the person to whom it is given. The sentence may then be
translated either "Joshua divided this land among the tribes" or "Joshua
gave each tribe its share of the land."

12.8 This portion included the hill country, the western
foothills, the Jordan Valley and its foothills, the
eastern slopes, and the dry country in the south.
This land had been the home of the Hittites, the
Amorites, the Canaanites, the Perizzites, the Hivites, and the Jebusites.

This portion included may be translated "The land that Joshua
divided among them included...."

For the TEV language of verse 8a see 10.40 and 11.16. One word
occurs here which is not used in the two other passages: the eastern
slopes (RSV "the wilderness"); as Bright says, this is "the desert to
the south and east, not sharply distinguishable from the Arabah and
the Negeb."

For the list of peoples mentioned in this verse, see 3.10.

This land had been the home of may be rendered "Before Joshua and the people of Israel took this land, the Hittites...and the Jebusites had lived there."

12.9-24   The people of Israel defeated the kings of the follow-
           ing cities: Jericho, Ai (near Bethel), 10 Jerusalem,
           Hebron, 11 Jarmuth, Lachish, 12 Eglon, Gezer, 13 Debir,
           Geder, 14 Hormah, Arad, 15 Libnah, Adullam, 16 Makkedah,
           Bethel, 17 Tappuah, Hepher, 18 Aphek, Lasharon, 19 Madon,
           Hazor, 20 Shimron Meron, Achshaph, 21 Taanach, Megiddo,
           22 Kedesh, Jokneam (in Carmel), 23 Dor (on the coast),
           Goiim (in Galilee*g*), 24 and Tirzah—thirty-one kings
           in all.

       gOne ancient translation Galilee; *Hebrew* Gilgal.

In this list of thirty-one kings, the kings of the following cities have already been named: Jericho (6.1-27; see note on 8.2; 10.1); Ai (8.10-29); Jerusalem, Hebron, Jarmuth, Lachish, and Eglon (10.22-27); Gezer (10.33); and Debir (10.38).
RSV reproduces the formal features of the Hebrew: from verses 9-23 the Hebrew lists two kings in each of the fifteen verses, giving the name of the king and then adding the numeral "one" after each name; in verse 24a the last king is named, followed also by the numeral "one." This gives a total of thirty-one kings.
TEV has simplified the form in an attempt to make the list easier to read. AT uses a tabular form:

```
 9the king of Jericho . . . . . . . . . . 1
   the king of Ai which is near Bethel . . 1
10the king of Jerusalem . . . . . . . . . 1
   the king of Hebron. . . . . . . . . . . 1
11the king of Jarmuth . . . . . . . . . . 1
   the king of Lachish . . . . . . . . . . 1
12the king of Eglon . . . . . . . . . . . 1
   the king of Gezer . . . . . . . . . . . 1
13the king of Debir . . . . . . . . . . . 1
   the king of Geder . . . . . . . . . . . 1
14the king of Hormah. . . . . . . . . . . 1
   the king of Arad. . . . . . . . . . . . 1
15the king of Libnah. . . . . . . . . . . 1
   the king of Adullam . . . . . . . . . . 1
16the king of Makkedah. . . . . . . . . . 1
   the king of Bethel. . . . . . . . . . . 1
17the king of Tappuah . . . . . . . . . . 1
   the king of Hepher. . . . . . . . . . . 1
18the king of Aphek . . . . . . . . . . . 1
   the king of Aphek in Sharon . . . . . . 1
19the king of Madon . . . . . . . . . . . 1
   the king of Hazor . . . . . . . . . . . 1
20the king of Shimron . . . . . . . . . . 1
   the king of Achshaph. . . . . . . . . . 1
```

²¹the king of Taanach 1
the king of Megiddo 1
²²the king of Kedesh. 1
the king of Jokneam in Carmel 1
the king of Dor in the uplands of
²³Dor 1
the king of the peoples of Galilee. . 1
²⁴the king of Tirzah. 1

———

A total of   31
kings

If the form of TEV is preferred over the tabular form of AT, then verse numbers "9-24" may be indicated at verse 9, so as to avoid the awkwardness of having verse numbers precede so many of the names in the text.

In such a list as this the precise location of each city is not important, since there is no movement from one place to the next. The cities in verses 9-16a (Jericho to Makkedah) are in the south: the cities in verses 16b-24 are in the central and northern part of the country. Commentators point out that no campaigns in the central part of the country (in the territories of Ephraim and Manasseh) have been described.

There are several textual problems in this list.[42] In verse 23a the Hebrew for "Naphath-dor" (see RSV) is taken by TEV to mean (see 11.2) "the Dor on the coast" (NEB has "Dor in the district of Dor"; JB "Dor on the hillsides of Dor"; TOB "Dor on the crest of Dor").

In verse 23b the Masoretic text has "Gilgal." The Septuagint has "Galilee" (so AT, RSV, TEV, BJ, JB), supported by HOTTP, which judges that the reading "Gilgal" represents either a misunderstanding of the historical situation by a later scribe, or a scribal error. NAB, TOB prefer the Masoretic text. Goiim represents the transliteration of a Hebrew word which as a common noun means "nations, peoples, Gentiles": so AT, BJ. NAB translates the Masoretic text by "the foreign king at Gilgal." Gray suggests a scribal mistake for "Harosheth-of-the-Gentiles" (see Judges 4.2), which was in Galilee.

Chapter 13

The Land Still to Be Taken

1 Joshua was now very old. The LORD said to him, "You are very old, but there is still much land to be taken: 2 all the territory of Philistia and Geshur, 3 as well as all the territory of the Avvim to the south. (The land from the stream Shihor, at the Egyptian border, as far north as the border of Ekron was considered Canaanite; the kings of the Philistines lived at Gaza, Ashdod, Ashkelon, Gath, and Ekron.) 4 There is still all the Canaanite country, and Mearah (which belonged to the Sidonians), as far as Aphek, at the Amorite border; 5 the land of the Gebalites; all of Lebanon to the east, from Baalgad, which is south of Mount Hermon, to Hamath Pass. 6 This includes all the territory of the Sidonians, who live in the hill country between the Lebanon Mountains and Misrephoth Maim. I will drive all these peoples out as the people of Israel advance. You must divide the land among the Israelites, just as I have commanded you to do. 7 Now then, divide this land among the other nine tribes and half of the tribe of Manasseh, for them to possess as their own."

1 Now Joshua was old and advanced in years; and the LORD said to him, "You are old and advanced in years, and there remains yet very much land to be possessed. 2 This is the land that yet remains: all the regions of the Philistines, and all those of the Geshurites 3 (from the Shihor, which is east of Egypt, northward to the boundary of Ekron, it is reckoned as Canaanite; there are five rulers of the Philistines, those of Gaza, Ashdod, Ashkelon, Gath, and Ekron), and those of the Avvim, 4 in the south, all the land of the Canaanites, and Mearah which belongs to the Sidonians, to Aphek, to the boundary of the Amorites, 5 and the land of the Gebalites, and all Lebanon, toward the sunrising, from Baal-gad below Mount Hermon to the entrance of Hamath, 6 all the inhabitants of the hill country from Lebanon to Misrephoth-maim, even all the Sidonians. I will myself drive them out from before the people of Israel; only allot the land to Israel for an inheritance, as I have commanded you. 7 Now therefore divide this land for an inheritance to the nine tribes and half the tribe of Manasseh."

This second part of the book, describing the division of the land among the tribes, occupies chapters 13-21, and falls naturally into four sections: (1) the land east of the Jordan (13.1-33); (2) the land west of the Jordan (14.1—19.51); (3) the cities of refuge (20.1-9); and (4) the cities of the Levites (21.1-45).

In this introductory section the Lord tells Joshua what yet remains to be conquered in Canaan, the land west of the Jordan. The Lord assures Joshua of his help and commands him to divide the territory among the nine and one-half western tribes.

The section heading, The Land Still to Be Taken, may be translated "The LORD commands Joshua to take the rest of the land." Or, on the basis of verse 7, "The LORD commands Joshua to take the rest of the land and divide it among the other tribes of Israel."

13.1   Joshua was now very old. The LORD said to him, "You are very old, but there is still much land to be taken:

Joshua was now very old: it is impossible to state precisely how many years had elapsed since the death of Moses. Notice in Exodus 33.11 that Joshua is referred to as a youth; in Joshua 11.18 the campaigns in Canaan are said to have taken a long time; and in 24.29 it is reported that Joshua was 110 years old when he died.

Very old translates the Hebraic idiom "old and gone forward in days," which signifies a considerable time lapse. In order to indicate more accurately the temporal relation between this and the previous events, Joshua was now very old may be translated "Many years had gone by, and Joshua was now an old man."

Some transitional marker may be necessary to connect The LORD said to him with the previous statement. For example, "One day the LORD said to him."

In place of You are very old, it may be more effective if the Lord says "You do not have much longer to live," which seems to be the point in focus. That is, Joshua does not have much longer to live, but there is still much land to be taken. This second clause may be shifted to an active clause: "And there is still much land that you have not taken (or, conquered)."

13.2-3   all the territory of Philistia and Geshur, 3 as well as all the territory of the Avvim to the south. (The land from the stream Shihor, at the Egyptian border, as far north as the border of Ekron was considered Canaanite; the kings of the Philistines lived at Gaza, Ashdod, Ashkelon, Gath, and Ekron.)

Verses 2-3 give part of the land yet to be conquered. At the end of verse 3 some information is given which TEV takes as not explicitly part of the yet unconquered territory. That is why TEV puts this within parentheses. Notice also that the first words of verse 4 (RSV "in the south") go with the Avvim of verse 3; so TEV has placed all this before the parenthetical material in verse 3.

Philistia was west of Canaan, along the Mediterranean coast; Geshur, according to I Samuel 27.8, was southeast of the Philistine city of Gaza.

(This Geshur is not to be confused with the Geshur east of the Jordan in 12.5 and 13.11.) The Avvim in the south seem also to have lived in the region around Gaza (see Deut 2.23).

The stream Shihor is located by the biblical writer at the Egyptian border, to the southeast (perhaps the same as "the stream on the border of Egypt" in 15.4,47). Ekron was one of the five Philistine cities along the Mediterranean coast. The word translated kings is used only of the Philistine rulers.

As already indicated, there is considerable confusion regarding the part of verse 3 placed in parentheses by TEV. Although the TEV interpretation follows sound scholarly opinion, it is still quite possible that the regions mentioned in the TEV parenthetical statement were considered by the author to be portions of the yet unconquered territories. If this is the case, the following restructuring may be useful as a guideline:

You have yet to conquer all the territory of the Philistines with their five cities of Gaza, Ashdod, Ashkelon, Gath, and Ekron. You also must conquer the territory of the Geshurites east of Egypt and the territory of the Avvim in the south. And you have not yet conquered the land from the stream Shihor, at the Egyptian border, as far north as the city of Ekron.

Following this cue, verse 4 may be rendered, "You have as yet to conquer the entire territory of the Canaanites, from the city of Mearah, which belongs to Sidon, to the city of Aphek, at the Amorite border."

13.4-5   There is still all the Canaanite country, and Mearah (which belonged to the Sidonians), as far as Aphek, at the Amorite border; 5 the land of the Gebalites; all of Lebanon to the east, from Baalgad, which is south of Mount Hermon, to Hamath Pass.

Verses 4-6 describe territory in the north. Mearah is located north of Sidon, the important Phoenician city on the Mediterranean coast, north of Palestine. Aphek here is not the same as in 12.18; perhaps it lay east of Gebal (the land of the Gebalites, verse 5), which is known also as Byblos, north of Beirut (in Lebanon). Baalgad: see 11.17. Hamath Pass was regarded as the northern limit of Israel, in the valley between the two ranges of the Lebanon Mountains. Misrephoth Maim (see 11.8) was the southern boundary of the Sidonians, as the Lebanon Mountains were the northern boundary.[43]

A proposed restructuring for verse 4 is given in conjunction with the comments at 13.2-3.

In order to aid the reader's comprehension, one may want to begin a new sentence at verse 5, or even divide it into two complete sentences: "You still have not conquered the land of the Gebalites. You have not taken the territory of Lebanon to the east, from the city of Baalgad, which is south of Mount Hermon, to Hamath Pass." Or, "You have still not taken the territory that belongs to the city of Gebal. And you have not conquered all the territory of Lebanon from the city of Baalgad at the foot of Mount Hermon to Hamath Pass."

13.6   This includes all the territory of the Sidonians,
who live in the hill country between the Lebanon
Mountains and Misrephoth Maim. I will drive all
these peoples out as the people of Israel advance.
You must divide the land among the Israelites,
just as I have commanded you to do.

The Lord promises Joshua that he, the Lord, will give victory
to the Israelites, and he commands Joshua to divide the land among
the Israelites, that is, among the nine tribes and the half-tribe of
West Manasseh, which settled west of the Jordan.

This includes serves merely as a transitional marker in the restructuring of TEV; one could also translate "The territory which you
still have to conquer includes." RSV maintains the form of the Hebrew
by continuing the sentence begun at verse 2 through the end of this
verse. In each language, attention should be given to what must be
done in order to divide the lengthy sentence into units that are more
easily managed by the reader.

As the people of Israel advance may be translated either "as the
people of Israel move into these territories" or "...spread out into
these territories."

13.7   Now then, divide this land among the other nine
tribes and half of the tribe of Manasseh, for
them to possess as their own."

The Hebrew particle translated Now then may serve either as a
temporal marker or else as a transitional to a new thought, as in TEV.
In either case the implication is that Joshua must now divide the land,
at least in principle, among the other nine tribes and half of the
tribe of Manasseh.

For them to possess as their own translates the Hebrew "for an
inheritance" (RSV; see 1.6).[44]

TEV   13.8-14   RSV

The Division of the Territory East of the Jordan

TEV	RSV
8 The tribes of Reuben and Gad and the other half of the tribe of Manasseh had already received the land that Moses, the LORD's servant, had given them; it was on the east side of the Jordan River. 9 Their territory extended to Aroer (on the edge of the Arnon Valley) and the city in the middle of that valley and included all of the plateau from Medeba to Dibon. 10 It went as far as the border of Ammon and	8 With the other half of the tribe of Manasseh[g] the Reubenites and the Gadites received their inheritance, which Moses gave them, beyond the Jordan eastward, as Moses the servant of the LORD gave them: 9 from Aroer, which is on the edge of the valley of the Arnon, and the city that is in the middle of the valley, and all the tableland of Medeba as far as Dibon; 10 and all the cities of Sihon king of the Amorites, who

included all the cities that had
been ruled by the Amorite king
Sihon, who had ruled at Heshbon.
11 It included Gilead, the regions
of Geshur and Maacah, all of Mount
Hermon, and all of Bashan as far
as Salecah. 12 It included the
kingdom of Og, the last of the
Rephaim, who had ruled at Ashtaroth and Edrei. Moses had defeated
these people and driven them out.
13 However, the Israelites did not
drive out the people of Geshur and
Maacah; they still live in Israel.
14 Moses had given no land to
the tribe of Levi. As the LORD had
told Moses, they were to receive
as their possession a share of the
sacrifices burned on the altar to
the LORD God of Israel.

reigned in Heshbon, as far as the
boundary of the Ammonites; 11 and
Gilead, and the region of the
Geshurites and Ma-acathites, and
all Mount Hermon, and all Bashan
to Salecah; 12 all the kingdom
of Og in Bashan, who reigned in
Ashtaroth and in Edre-i (he alone
was left of the remnant of the
Rephaim); these Moses had defeated and driven out. 13 Yet the
people of Israel did not drive out
the Geshurites or the Ma-acathites;
but Geshur and Maacath dwell in
the midst of Israel to this day.
14 To the tribe of Levi alone
Moses gave no inheritance; the
offerings by fire to the LORD God
of Israel are their inheritance,
as he said to him.

*g*Cn: Heb *With it*

Verses 8-33 describe the extension of the area east of the Jordan conquered by the Israelites under the leadership of Moses, and give the limits for each of the three territories that Moses assigned to the tribes of Reuben, Gad, and East Manasseh. Twice (verses 14,33) the statement is made that no territory was assigned to the tribe of Levi. Within this larger unit, verses 8-14 describe what had already happened years before when Moses was still alive and the Israelites were on the east side of the Jordan River.

The section heading, The Division of the Territory East of the Jordan, may be given as a complete sentence: "Moses divides the terri-tory among the Israelite tribes east of the Jordan." Or, spelled out in more detail, "This is the land that Moses had given the tribes of Reuben and Gad and the other half of the tribe of Manasseh on the east side of the Jordan River."

13.8   The tribes of Reuben and Gad and the other half
           of the tribe of Manasseh had already received the
           land that Moses, the LORD's servant, had given them;
           it was on the east side of the Jordan River.

Verse 8 in Hebrew begins: "with it (that is, presumably, "half the tribe of Manasseh" at the end of verse 7) the Reubenites and the Gadites received their inheritance." In verse 7, however, the half-tribe of Manasseh is West Manasseh; and verse 8 deals with the other half of the tribe, that is, East Manasseh. Some adjustment of the He-brew text, such as that adopted by RSV, NEB, NAB, BJ, JB, seems neces-sary; TEV has taken the Hebrew "with it" to mean the other half of Manasseh (that is, the eastern half), and this is also the judgment of HOTTP.

[181]

13.8

The division of the land east of the Jordan among the two and one-half eastern tribes is given in Numbers 32.1-42 and Deuteronomy 3.12-17. This verse may be restructured as follows:

> Moses, the LORD's servant, had already assigned land to the tribes of Reuben and Gad and the other half of the tribe of Manasseh. Their land was on the east side of the Jordan River, and they had already taken control of it.

13.9-10   Their territory extended to Aroer (on the edge of the Arnon Valley) and the city in the middle of that valley and included all of the plateau from Medeba to Dibon. 10 It went as far as the border of Ammon and included all the cities that had been ruled by the Amorite king Sihon, who had ruled at Heshbon.

For the geographical data in verses 9-10, see comments on 12.2. Medeba is about 12 kilometers south of Heshbon, and Dibon is approximately another 22 kilometers further south. Ammon was the land east of the territory conquered by the Israelites.

In the translation of these two verses it may be useful to include some information regarding the geographical directions. For example:

> The territory of these tribes reached as far southeast as the city of Aroer on the edge of the Arnon Valley. It also included the city in the middle of the Arnon Valley, as well as all of the plateau from the town of Dibon in the south up to the town of Medeba. 10 Their territory went as far east as the border of Ammon. It also included all the cities that King Sihon, the Amorite king, had ruled over from the city of Heshbon.

13.11-12   It included Gilead, the regions of Geshur and Maacah, all of Mount Hermon, and all of Bashan as far as Salecah. 12 It included the kingdom of Og, the last of the Rephaim, who had ruled at Ashtaroth and Edrei. Moses had defeated these people and driven them out.

For all the geographical data in verses 11-12, and for a proposed restructuring in terms of the points on the compass, see the comments at 12.4-5.

13.13   However, the Israelites did not drive out the people of Geshur and Maacah; they still live in Israel.

Verse 13 points out that the people of Geshur and Maacah had not been driven out of their territories; and at the time of the writing of the account they were still living in Israel. Apparently this verse comes as an afterthought, to correct a false impression which the reader is likely to receive from verse 11. It is then possible to join the last part of verse 12 to verse 13 as follows:

Moses and the people of Israel had defeated all these people.
And they had driven all of them out of their territory, 13 except the people of Geshur and Maacah, who still live among the
people of Israel today.

13.14   Moses had given no land to the tribe of Levi.
As the LORD had told Moses, they were to receive
as their possession a share of the sacrifices burned
on the altar to the LORD God of Israel.

Verse 14 points out why the tribe of Levi was not assigned a territory of their own. Their "inheritance" (RSV) was a share of the sacrifices which the Israelites offered to the Lord.45
As the LORD had told Moses represents the clause which comes last
in the Hebrew text (see RSV "as he said to him"). It is quite possible
that the translation will be clear enough without including either "to
him" or had told Moses. For example: "The LORD had said that their
possession would be a share of the sacrifices that the people burned
on the altar to him." Or direct discourse may be introduced: "The LORD
had said, 'The tribe of Levi will receive as their possession a share
of the sacrifices that the people burn to me.'"

TEV   13.15-23   RSV

The Territory Assigned to Reuben

15 Moses had given a part of the land to the families of the tribe of Reuben as their posses-sion. 16 Their territory extended to Aroer (on the edge of the Arnon Valley) and the city in the middle of that valley and included all the plateau around Medeba. 17 It included Heshbon and all the cities on the plateau: Dibon, Bamoth Baal, Beth Baalmeon, 18 Jahaz, Kedemoth, Mephaath, 19 Kiriathaim, Sibmah, Zereth Shahar on the hill in the valley, 20 Bethpeor, the slopes of Mount Pisgah, and Beth Jeshimoth. 21 It included all the cities of the plateau and the whole kingdom of the Amorite king Sihon, who had ruled at Heshbon. Moses defeated him, as well as the rulers of Mid-ian: Evi, Rekem, Zur, Hur, and Reba. All of them had ruled the land for King Sihon. 22 Among those whom the people of Israel

15 And Moses gave an inherit-ance to the tribe of the Reuben-ites according to their families. 16 So their territory was from Aroer, which is on the edge of the valley of the Arnon, and the city that is in the middle of the valley, and all the tableland by Medeba; 17 with Heshbon, and all its cities that are in the table-land; Dibon, and Bamoth-baal, and Bethbaal-meon, 18 and Jahaz and Kedemoth, and Mepha-ath, 19 and Kiriathaim, and Sibmah, and Zer-eth-shahar on the hill of the valley, 20 and Bethpeor, and the slopes of Pisgah, and Beth-jesh-imoth, 21 that is, all the cities of the tableland, and all the kingdom of Sihon king of the Amo-rites, who reigned in Heshbon, whom Moses defeated with the leaders of Midian, Evi and Rekem and Zur and Hur and Reba, the

killed was the fortuneteller Balaam son of Beor. 23 The Jordan was the western border of the tribe of Reuben. These were the cities and towns given to the families of the tribe of Reuben as their possession.

princes of Sihon, who dwelt in the land. 22 Balaam also, the son of Beor, the soothsayer, the people of Israel killed with the sword among the rest of their slain. 23 And the border of the people of Reuben was the Jordan as a boundary. This was the inheritance of the Reubenites, according to their families with their cities and villages.

Reuben was the southernmost of the tribes on the east side of the Jordan River, and its territory included the land formerly ruled by King Sihon. The section heading, The Territory Assigned to Reuben, may be formulated as a statement: "This is the territory which Moses assigned to the tribe of Reuben" or "...which the LORD told Moses to assign to the tribe of Reuben."

13.15   Moses had given a part of the land to the
             families of the tribe of Reuben as their possession.

The expression the families of the tribe of Reuben is probably better rendered "the clans of the tribe of Reuben," the word translated "clan" being the next classification for a large group within a "tribe." Usually several related "families" were members of a single "clan." Whereas many languages will have a readily understood word meaning "clan," the distinction between tribe, clan, and family may not exist in a number of languages. English does have the word "clan," but it is a rarely used term, and for that reason, TEV prefers the better known "family," although the distinction may not be as precise.

13.16   Their territory extended to Aroer (on the edge of
             the Arnon Valley) and the city in the middle of
             that valley and included all the plateau around
             Medeba.

For the geographical data in verse 16, see comments on 12.2; for Medeba see 13.9.
It may be helpful to divide this verse into two or more sentences, and at the same time to identify the place-names by their geographical relationships.

13.17-20   It included Heshbon and all the cities on the
             plateau: Dibon, Bamoth Baal, Beth Baalmeon,
             18 Jahaz, Kedemoth, Mephaath, 19 Kiriathaim,
             Sibmah, Zereth Shahar on the hill in the valley,
             20 Bethpeor, the slopes of Mount Pisgah, and
             Beth Jeshimoth.

[184]

Heshbon (verse 17) was the capital city of King Sihon (see 12.2). Of all the cities on the plateau (verses 17-20), the following have already appeared: Dibon (13.9) and Beth Jeshimoth (12.3), Jahaz, Kedemoth, and Mephaath (verse 18) appear also in 21.36-37; and Beth-peor (verse 20) may be the same as Peor in 22.17.

Verses 17-20 (actually 17-23) form a unit and may be handled in several ways. For example, the arrangement of TEV may be followed, or it may be appropriate to print the names of the cities in list form, one below the other. Or, on the basis of on the plateau (verse 17) and of the plateau (verse 21), one may translate "Their territory reached as far as the city of Heshbon. In this region lay the cities of Dibon, Bamoth, Baal...18...19...20...21 and the other cities of the plateau." This restructuring would take in the text down through It included all the cities of the plateau of verse 21. Following that, a new sentence would begin, as will be indicated in the comments at verse 21.

13.21   It included all the cities of the plateau and the
         whole kingdom of the Amorite king Sihon, who had
         ruled at Heshbon. Moses defeated him, as well as
         the rulers of Midian: Evi, Rekem, Zur, Hur, and Reba.
         All of them had ruled the land for King Sihon.

For the defeat of Sihon see Numbers 21.21-26. Midian was the territory east of the Gulf of Aqaba, south of Edom. The rulers of Midian were subject to King Sihon (RSV "the princes of Sihon"; compare NEB "the vassals of Sihon").

It is not easy to put the contents of this verse into a very readable arrangement. If the proposed restructuring of verses 17-21a is adopted, then the form of TEV may be followed from 21b onward: "It also included the whole kingdom...." Or a slightly different pattern may be used:

         It also included all of the territory ruled over from the
         city of Heshbon by King Sihon, the Amorite king. Five tribal
         leaders by the names of Evi, Rekem, Zur, Hur, and Reba had
         ruled part of this land for King Sihon. But Moses defeated
         King Sihon and all of these other leaders, and he took their
         territory.

13.22   Among those whom the people of Israel killed was
         the fortuneteller Balaam son of Beor.

Among those whom of TEV translates "also" (RSV) of the Hebrew text. One may render "Together with these" or "In addition."

The noun fortuneteller is made from a Hebrew verb which means "practice divination," something that was generally done by consulting lots which had been cast.

For the fortuneteller Balaam, see Numbers chapters 22—24; his death (and that of the leaders of Midian) is reported also in Numbers 31.8.

The identifying noun phrase <u>son of Beor</u> makes restructuring into English somewhat awkward. Without this phrase one could translate "In addition the people of Israel also killed Balaam the fortuneteller." In some languages <u>son of Beor</u> may be rendered following Balaam without this problem, since that is the formal way of indicating a person's name, as, for example, "Ismael bin (son of) Hussain." But for English readers "Balaam son of Beor the fortuneteller" would cause the reader (particularly the person who hears the scripture read) to understand Beor as the fortuneteller. If "son of Beor" is retained in the text, the verse may be translated as two sentences: "In addition the people of Israel killed Balaam the fortuneteller. He was the son of Beor."

<u>13.23</u>   The Jordan was the western border of the tribe
of Reuben. These were the cities and towns given
to the families of the tribe of Reuben as their
possession.

<u>The western border of the tribe of Reuben</u> was <u>the Jordan River</u> and, of course, the Dead Sea. For <u>families</u> see comments on verse 15. Although the first sentence of this verse is simple in TEV, it may also be translated, "The tribe of Reuben had the Jordan River as its western border." The Hebrew text does not include the adjective 'western," though it is redundant in other ways (see RSV "And the border of the people of Reuben was the Jordan as a boundary").
The Hebrew noun translated <u>towns</u> (RSV "villages") refers to a permanent settlement that is without walls. <u>Cities and towns</u> would probably have reference to the walled cities and the outlying towns or farms, and so the sentence may be rendered, "All these cities with their villages were given to the families of the tribe of Reuben. These cities and villages were to belong to them forever."

| TEV | 13.24-28 | RSV |

The Territory Assigned to Gad

24 Moses had also given a part of the land to the families of the tribe of Gad as their possession. 25 Their territory included Jazer and all the cities of Gilead, half the land of Ammon as far as Aroer, which is east of Rabbah; 26 their land extended from Heshbon to Ramath Mizpeh and Betonim, from Mahanaim to the border of Lodebar. 27 In the Jordan Valley it included Beth Haram, Bethnimrah, Sukkoth, and Zaphon, the rest of the kingdom of King Sihon of Heshbon. Their western

24 And Moses gave an inheritance also to the tribe of the Gadites, according to their families. 25 Their territory was Jazer, and all the cities of Gilead, and half the land of the Ammonites, to Aroer, which is east of Rabbah, 26 and from Heshbon to Ramath-mizpeh and Betonim, and from Mahanaim to the territory of Debir,[h] 27 and in the valley Beth-haram, Beth-nimrah, Succoth, and Zaphon, the rest of the kingdom of Sihon king of Heshbon, having the Jordan as a boundary,

border was the Jordan River as far
north as Lake Galilee. 28 These
were the cities and towns given
to the families of the tribe of
Gad as their possession.

to the lower end of the Sea of
Chinnereth, eastward beyond the
Jordan. 28 This is the inheritance
of the Gadites according to their
families, with their cities and
villages.

[h]Gk Syr Vg: Heb *Lidebir*

The section heading, <u>The Territory Assigned to Gad</u>, may be translated similarly to the section heading at verse 15.

<u>13.24</u>   Moses had also given a part of the land to the
         families of the tribe of Gad as their possession.

The territory of Gad lay between that of Reuben to the south, and
that of East Manasseh to the north. In order to indicate this geographical relationship, the verse may be translated, "The territory which
Moses had given to the families of the tribe of Gad lay immediately to
the north of that which he had given to the tribe of Reuben," or "...
immediately to the south of that which he had given to the tribe of
East Manasseh," or else "...between that of East Manasseh to the north
and Reuben to the south."

<u>13.25</u>   Their territory included Jazer and all the cities
         of Gilead, half the land of Ammon as far as Aroer,
         which is east of Rabbah;

The locations of some of the cities mentioned in verses 25-27 have
not been identified; others have been identified and are to be found on
modern biblical maps, such as the maps in the RSV Oxford Study Edition
and the NEB Oxford Study Edition.
    The <u>Aroer</u> mentioned in this verse (also in Judges 11.33) is not
the same as the Aroer in the territory of Reuben (verse 16); the text
locates it to the east.[46] <u>Rabbah</u> is the shortened form of the name
Rabbah-Ammon, today Amman, the capital of Jordan.
    The translation of this verse may require: (1) that <u>Jazar</u>, <u>Aroer</u>,
and <u>Rabbah</u> be identified as cities, and (2) that the sentence be
divided into two or more parts. For example, "Their territory included
the city of Jazar and all the cities in the region of Gilead. It also
included the land of Ammon as far as the city of Aroer, which is east
of the city of Rabbah."

<u>13.26</u>   their land extended from Heshbon to Ramath Mizpeh
         and Betonim, from Mahanaim to the border of Lodebar.

<u>Lodebar</u> does not represent the actual form of the Masoretic text,
which seems to mean "to Debir" (so RSV "to the territory of Debir";
see also AT, TOB). NEB, NAB, BJ, JB are like TEV;[47] TEV has no footnote,
since the consonants of the Hebrew text are retained, but supplied with
different vowels.

13.26

It would perhaps be advisable to make verse 26 into a complete sentence, and also to identify Heshbon, Ramath Mizpeh, Betonim, and Mahanaim as cities or towns and Lodebar merely as a place, since scholarly opinion differs regarding exactly what it is.

13.27   In the Jordan Valley it included Beth Haram,
        Bethnimrah, Sukkoth, and Zaphon, the rest of
        the kingdom of King Sihon of Heshbon. Their
        western border was the Jordan River as far
        north as Lake Galilee.

To avoid confusion, the pronoun it may need to be translated "their territory." Moreover, Beth Haram, Bethnimrah, Sukkoth, and Zaphon may need to be identified as cities. It is possible also to translate verses 26-27 as a unit:

Their land included the rest of the territory that had belonged to King Sihon of the Amorites. It extended north from the city of Heshbon and took in the cities of Ramath Mizpeh and Betonim. It continued as far as the city of Mahanaim and over to the borders of Lodebar. In addition, the tribe of Gad received the land along the eastern side of the Jordan River as far north as the southern end of Lake Galilee. This included the cities of Beth Haram, Bethnimrah, Sukkoth, and Zaphon, which were in the Jordan Valley.

13.28   These were the cities and towns given to the
        families of the tribe of Gad as their possession.

For families, see verse 15. For the translation of this verse, see comments at verse 23, where the last sentence is of the same construction.

TEV	13.29-33	RSV

The Territory Assigned
to East Manasseh

29 Moses had given a part of the land to the families of half the tribe of Manasseh as their possession. 30 Their territory extended to Mahanaim and included all of Bashan—the whole kingdom of Og, the king of Bashan, as well as all sixty of the villages of Jair in Bashan. 31 It included half of Gilead, as well as Ashtaroth and Edrei, the capital cities of Og's kingdom in Bashan. All this was

29 And Moses gave an inheritance to the half-tribe of Manasseh; it was allotted to the half-tribe of the Manassites according to their families. 30 Their region extended from Mahanaim, through all Bashan, the whole kingdom of Og king of Bashan, and all the towns of Jair, which are in Bashan, sixty cities, 31 and half Gilead, and Ashtaroth, and Edre-i, the cities of the kingdom

[188]

given to half the families descended from Machir son of Manasseh.

32 This is how Moses divided
the land east of Jericho and the
Jordan when he was in the plains
of Moab. 33 But Moses did not
assign any land to the tribe of
Levi. He told them that their
possession was to be a share of
the offerings to the LORD God of
Israel.

of Og in Bashan; these were allotted to the people of Machir the
son of Manasseh for the half of
the Machirites according to their
families.

32 These are the inheritances
which Moses distributed in the
plains of Moab, beyond the Jordan
east of Jericho. 33 But to the
tribe of Levi Moses gave no inheritance; the LORD God of Israel
is their inheritance, as he said
to them.

After describing the territory assigned to East Manasseh (verses
29-31), north of that assigned to Gad, the writer concludes the story
of the division of the land east of the Jordan with a statement of why
the tribe of Levi received no territory (verses 32-33).

For the translation of the section heading, The Territory Assigned
to East Manasseh, see comments at the section heading preceding verse
15.

13.29   Moses had given a part of the land to the
             families of half the tribe of Manasseh as their
             possession.

The Hebrew of this verse is not natural: "And Moses gave to half
the tribe of Manasseh and it was to half the tribe of the descendants
of Manasseh, according to their clans." It is possible to translate
verses 29-30 so that they fit together more closely than is indicated
by TEV. This would require the continuing into verse 30 of a sentence
begun in this verse. For a model of how this may be done, see the
comments at verse 30.

13.30   Their territory extended to Mahanaim and included
             all of Bashan—the whole kingdom of Og, the king
             of Bashan, as well as all sixty of the villages
             of Jair in Bashan.

Mahanaim is at the southern border of East Manasseh, where its
territory touched that of Gad (verse 26). For Og, the king of Bashan
see 12.4-5 (also 9.10).

In Numbers 32.41 Jair is identified as "the son of Manasseh"
(RSV; see other references to him in Deut 3.14; 1 Kgs 4.13); TEV has
taken the Hebrew word generally rendered "son" to mean "descendant"
and not "son," because in the lists of the descendants of Manasseh,
the only son named is Machir (see Gen 50.23; Num 26.29; Josh 17.1).

Verses 29-30 may be translated,
        29 Moses had given to the families of the half tribe
    of Manasseh 30 the land which extended north from the city

of Mahanaim. This included all of Bashan, together with the
sixty villages that Jair had once conquered in that region.
King Og of Bashan had once ruled over all of this territory.

13.31   It included half of Gilead, as well as Ashtaroth
                and Edrei, the capital cities of Og's kingdom in
                Bashan. All this was given to half the families
                descended from Machir son of Manasseh.

One of the clans of the tribe of Manasseh was that of Machir son
of Manasseh; and this territory east of the Jordan went to half of the
clans descended from Machir. For other references to the clan of Machir,
see Numbers 32.39-40; Deuteronomy 3.15.
    As a comparison between TEV and RSV will indicate, the Hebrew text
is somewhat redundant. But it is possible to be even more economical
than TEV: "To this half-tribe of Mansseh, which descended from Manasseh's son Machir, Moses gave half of Gilead, together with the cities
of Ashtaroth and Edrei, where king Og had once ruled."

13.32-33   This is how Moses divided the land east of Jericho
               and the Jordan when he was in the plains of Moab.
               33 But Moses did not assign any land to the tribe
               of Levi. He told them that their possession was to
               be a share of the offerings to the LORD God of Israel.

Verse 32 is a summary statement of the division of the land east
of the Jordan, and verse 33 states again the reason why the tribe of
Levi was assigned no territory (see verse 14). The Hebrew text says
only "The LORD the God of Israel he (is) their inheritance," which
TEV has taken to mean that they were to receive a share of the offerings made to the Lord.
    This is how Moses divided the land is more literally "These are
the inheritances which Moses distributed" (RSV). The entire verse may
be rendered, "Moses divided among the people of Israel all the territory of Moab in the Jordan Valley east of Jericho."
    It is to be noticed that in the concluding words of verse 33, the
Hebrew says "as he said to them"; the subject could be Moses (so TEV,
He told them) or the Lord.
    A portion of verse 33 may be turned into direct discourse: "But
Moses did not assign any land to the tribe of Levi. Instead he told
them, 'Your possession is to be a share of the offerings which the
people of Israel give to the LORD God.'" Or "...he said, 'In place of
land the tribe of Levi will have as their possession a share of the
offerings which the people of Israel make to the LORD God.'"

Chapter 14

The Division of the Territory West of the Jordan

1 What follows is an account of how the land of Canaan west of the Jordan was divided among the people of Israel. Eleazar the priest, Joshua son of Nun, and the leaders of the families of the Israelite tribes divided it among the population. 2 As the LORD had commanded Moses, the territories of the nine and one-half tribes west of the Jordan were determined by drawing lots.*h* 3-4 Moses had already assigned the land east of the Jordan to the other two and one-half tribes. (The descendants of Joseph were divided into two tribes: Manasseh and Ephraim.) However, Moses gave the Levites no portion of the territory. Instead, they received cities to live in, with fields for their cattle and flocks. 5 The people of Israel divided the land as the LORD had commanded Moses.

1 And these are the inheritances which the people of Israel received in the land of Canaan, which Eleazar the priest, and Joshua the son of Nun, and the heads of the fathers' houses of the tribes of the people of Israel distributed to them. 2 Their inheritance was by lot, as the LORD had commanded Moses for the nine and one-half tribes. 3 For Moses had given an inheritance to the two and one-half tribes beyond the Jordan; but to the Levites he gave no inheritance among them. 4 For the people of Joseph were two tribes, Manasseh and Ephraim; and no portion was given to the Levites in the land, but only cities to dwell in, with their pasture lands for their cattle and their substance. 5 The people of Israel did as the LORD commanded Moses; they allotted the land.

*h*DRAWING LOTS: *This was usually done by using specially marked stones to determine God's will.*

In 14.1—19.51 the story is told of how the territory west of the Jordan River was divided among the other nine and one-half tribes.

These introductory verses inform the reader how the twelve tribes, descended from the twelve sons of Jacob, are accounted for: Levi was not given any territory (verses 3b,4b; see also 13.14,33), which would reduce the number of tribes with land to eleven. But the descendants of Joseph were divided into two tribes, named for his two sons Manasseh and Ephraim, which made the total number of landed tribes twelve (verse 4).

This information also serves to emphasize the preeminent role of Moses (verses 2,5). Although the importance of Moses is stressed in this section, still it stands as a contrast to chapter 13, where he was the one who divided the territory east of the Jordan. The territory west of the Jordan is divided among the remaining tribes by Eleazar the priest and Joshua. Therefore the section heading, The Division of the Territory West of the Jordan, may be translated "Eleazar and Joshua divide the territory west of the Jordan among the other tribes of Israel." Or, since Joshua is more in focus than Eleazar, "Joshua divides the territory west of the Jordan River."

14.1   What follows is an account of how the land of Canaan west of the Jordan was divided among the people of Israel. Eleazar the priest, Joshua son of Nun, and the leaders of the families of the Israelite tribes divided it among the population.

West of the Jordan is introduced by TEV in order to clarify for the reader the location of this territory in the land of Canaan. Eleazar the priest was the son and successor of Aaron (see Deut 10.6); together with Joshua and the leaders of the families of the Israelite tribes, he assigned the territories to the nine and one-half western tribes. (See Num 34.16-29, which names Eleazar and Joshua, and a representative from each tribe.)

The passive was divided may necessitate considerable restructuring in order to indicate who divided the land among the people of Israel. In identifying the persons who did the distributing, it really seems unnecessary to qualify Joshua as son of Nun, since he is the only Joshua with whom the readers are familiar. On the other hand, to specify Eleazar as the priest is helpful, since most readers are not as familiar with him. The entire first verse may be translated, "Eleazar the priest, Joshua, and the leaders of the families of the Israelite tribes divided the land of Canaan west of the Jordan River among the people of Israel. And this is how it was done."

14.2   As the LORD had commanded Moses, the territories of the nine and one-half tribes west of the Jordan were determined by drawing lots.*h*

      *h*DRAWING LOTS: *This was usually done by using specially marked stones to determine God's will.*

The method used to determine God's will was by drawing lots, that is, using the Urim and Thummim; this explains the role of Eleazar in the division of the land, for it was the priest who drew the lots. If this information cannot be clearly expressed in the text, then the translation should carry a footnote such as one finds in TEV. By drawing lots of TEV is a cultural equivalent; but the decision was most likely determined by throwing a stone or stones (Urim and Thummim), rather than by drawing or pulling them out. TEV uses drawing lots, since this is known and understood by readers of English, whereas "by throwing stones" or "by rolling stones" may easily be misunderstood. Some languages will doubtless have specific terms which may be used.

The shift to direct discourse and the removal of the passive (were determined) may result in an easier translation:

They did it this way because the LORD had commanded Moses, "Divide the territory west of the Jordan River among the other nine and one-half tribes of Israel. Let each tribe draw lots to see what territory it will receive."

In place of "each tribe," one may say "someone from each tribe."

14.3-4   Moses had already assigned the land east of the Jordan to the other two and one-half tribes. (The descendants of Joseph were divided into two tribes: Manasseh and Ephraim.) However, Moses gave the Levites no portion of the territory. Instead, they received cities to live in, with fields for their cattle and flocks.

In verses 3-4 the Hebrew states twice that no territory was assigned to the tribe of Levi (see 3b,4b, RSV): they received cities and also fields for their cattle and flocks (see chapter 21).

The repetition of the Hebrew accounts for the reason that TEV places verses 3-4 together. But the statement about the descendants of Joseph (placed in parentheses by TEV) interrupts the flow of the narrative, and for many readers the inclusion of parentheses is difficult. It may be to the benefit of the reader if the first half of 3-4 is translated,

The descendants of Joseph were divided into two tribes, the tribe of Manasseh and the tribe of Ephraim. And Moses had already assigned the land east of the Jordan to the tribe of Reuben, to half of the tribe of Manasseh, and to the tribe of Gad.

The word translated flocks (RSV "substance") refers to movable personal property. If the interpretation of TEV is followed, then some languages will need to combine cattle and flocks as "herds."

14.5   The people of Israel divided the land as the LORD had commanded Moses.

This verse may be arranged to reflect chronological sequence: "The LORD had commanded Moses to cause the people of Israel to divide the land, and so the people obeyed the LORD's command." Or, if direct discourse is preferable: "The LORD had commanded Moses, 'Let the people of Israel divide the land.' So they divided the land, as the LORD had commanded." Or "...So the people obeyed the LORD's command and divided the land."

Hebron Is Given to Caleb

TEV	RSV
6 One day some people from the tribe of Judah came to Joshua at Gilgal. One of them, Caleb son of Jephunneh the Kenizzite, said to him, "You know what the LORD said in Kadesh Barnea about you and me to Moses, the man of God. 7 I was forty years old when the LORD's servant Moses sent me from Kadesh Barnea to spy out this land. I brought an honest report back to him. 8 The men who went with me, however, made our people afraid. But I faithfully obeyed the LORD my God. 9 Because I did, Moses promised me that my children and I would certainly receive as our possession the land which I walked over. 10 But now, look. It has been forty-five years since the LORD said that to Moses. That was when Israel was going through the desert, and the LORD, as he promised, has kept me alive ever since. Look at me! I am eighty-five years old 11 and am just as strong today as I was when Moses sent me out. I am still strong enough for war or for anything else. 12 Now then, give me the hill country that the LORD promised me on that day when my men and I reported. We told you that the race of giants called the Anakim were there in large walled cities. Maybe the LORD will be with me, and I will drive them out, just as the LORD said."	6 Then the people of Judah came to Joshua at Gilgal; and Caleb the son of Jephunneh the Kenizzite said to him, "You know what the LORD said to Moses the man of God in Kadesh-barnea concerning you and me. 7 I was forty years old when Moses the servant of the LORD sent me from Kadesh-barnea to spy out the land; and I brought him word again as it was in my heart. 8 But my brethren who went up with me made the heart of the people melt; yet I wholly followed the LORD my God. 9 And Moses swore on that day, saying, 'Surely the land on which your foot has trodden shall be an inheritance for you and your children for ever, because you have wholly followed the LORD my God.' 10 And now, behold, the LORD has kept me alive, as he said, these forty-five years since the time that the LORD spoke this word to Moses, while Israel walked in the wilderness; and now, lo, I am this day eighty-five years old. 11 I am still as strong to this day as I was in the day that Moses sent me; my strength now is as my strength was then, for war, and for going and coming. 12 So now give me this hill country of which the LORD spoke on that day; for you heard on that day how the Anakim were there, with great fortified cities: it may be that the LORD will be with me, and I shall drive them out as the LORD said."
13 Joshua blessed Caleb son of Jephunneh and gave him the city of Hebron as his possession. 14 Hebron still belongs to the descendants of Caleb son of Jephunneh the Kenizzite, because he faithfully obeyed the LORD, the God of Israel. 15 Before this, Hebron was called the city of Arba. (Arba had been the greatest of the Anakim.)	13 Then Joshua blessed him; and he gave Hebron to Caleb the son of Jephunneh for an inheritance. 14 So Hebron became the inheritance of Caleb the son of Jephunneh the Kenizzite to this day, because he wholly followed the LORD, the God of Israel. 15 Now
There was now peace in the land.	

> the name of Hebron formerly was
> Kiriath-arba;^{i} this Arba was the
> greatest man among the Anakim.
> And the land had rest from war.
>
> ^{i}That is *The city of Arba*

Caleb and Joshua were two of the twelve men who had been sent by Moses to explore the land of Canaan, and they were the only ones who maintained that the Israelites, because of the Lord's help, could successfully invade the land. The other ten men were frightened at the strength of the fortified cities and the size of the inhabitants of the land. For this reason, Caleb and Joshua were the only two of the twelve who lived to enter the land of Canaan (see Num 13.1—14.38).

The section heading, Hebron Is Given to Caleb, may be translated "Joshua gives (or, assigns) the city of Hebron to Caleb."

14.6   One day some people from the tribe of Judah
        came to Joshua at Gilgal. One of them, Caleb son
        of Jephunneh the Kenizzite, said to him, "You know
        what the LORD said in Kadesh Barnea about you and
        me to Moses, the man of God.

One day is introduced by TEV in an attempt to make a natural transition. It is possible also to introduce a more specific indicator of time such as "Before Joshua divided the land among the remaining tribes of Israel..." or "Before Joshua divided the land on the west side of the Jordan River among the other tribes...."

The Israelites are still camped at Gilgal (see 10.43), east of Jericho (that is, on the west side of the Jordan River; see 4.19). Some of the members of the tribe of Judah come to Joshua there; among them is Caleb. In Numbers 13.6; 34.19 he is said to be a member of the tribe of Judah, and that is why TEV here (and in 15.13) specifically identifies him as belonging to that tribe.[48]

Some people from the tribe of Judah is literally "the people of Judah" (RSV). It is possible either that all the people of the tribe approached Joshua or else that only a representative group from the tribe came to him. Quite frequently Hebrew will use "the people" to mean no more than "some of the people," just as "all of the people" often means either "most of the people" or "many of the people."

The relation between people and places in this verse may cause some difficulties for the reader. A hurried reading (or even a careful analysis) of the verse in TEV may suggest that the people of Judah had traveled from some distance to reach Joshua at the city of Gilgal. The actual situation, however, is that the people of Israel are already in their camp at Gilgal. While there, some of the people from the tribe of Judah approached Joshua about this matter. In order to make all of this clear, the first part of the verse may be rendered, "While the people of Israel were still camped at Gilgal, some men from the tribe of Judah...."

14.6

   One of them, Caleb son of Jephunneh the Kenizzite, said to him
may become clearer if structured otherwise: "One of the men was Caleb.
He was a son of Jephunneh from the Kenizzite clan. Caleb said to
Joshua...." Since he is the only Caleb mentioned in the book, it is
legitimate to drop **son of Jephunneh** and translate "One of the men was
Caleb from the Kenizzite clan...."
   Depending upon the restructuring followed for the earlier part of
the verse, **said to him** may need to be rendered, "said to Joshua."
   Caleb recalls to Joshua what the Lord had said about himself and
Joshua after the two of them had returned from exploring the land
(Num 14.30). Joshua and Caleb brought back an encouraging report, and
so the Lord promised that Caleb would have some of the land (Num 14.24).
So Caleb now claims the Lord's promise.
   Caleb's opening words to Joshua may be somewhat simplified: "Moses
spoke in behalf of the LORD, and you know what he said about you and
me when we were still in the town of Kadesh Barnea."

14.7   I was forty years old when the LORD's servant Moses
         sent me from Kadesh Barnea to spy out this land. I
         brought an honest report back to him.

   I was forty years old when may be translated as a complete statement: "At that time I was forty years old." If this is done, then the
remainder of the verse may be rendered as one sentence: "The Lord's
servant..., and I brought an honest report back to him." Or, if a restructuring similar to TEV is maintained, the last sentence of this
verse may be connected with the first sentence of verse 8 in order to
underscore the contrast: "I brought an honest report back to him, 8 but
the men...."
   To spy out translates a different verb from that used at 2.2,3,
but the meaning is essentially the same, and the translational problems
are identical.
   An honest report translates the Hebrew "word according to my
heart" (TOB "according to my conscience"; NAB "a conscientious report").
But it may be necessary to translate this noun structure as a verb
phrase: "And I told the truth (about what we had seen)" or "And I told
the people what we really had seen." The account emphasizes Caleb's
faithfulness in obeying the Lord (verses 8,14).
   Verses 7,10 give the most precise statement in the record of the
time that elapsed between the events at Kadesh Barnea and the completion
of the invasion of Canaan: a total of forty-five years, which would,
presumably, mean forty years' wandering in the wilderness (verse 10)
plus five years for the conquest.

14.8   The men who went with me, however, made our people
         afraid. But I faithfully obeyed the LORD my God.

   Made our people afraid is literally "made the heart of the people
melt" (RSV). The idiom is the same as that used of the Israelites at
2.11.

[196]

Faithfully obeyed is translated "wholly followed" by RSV; in such a context it seems that "completely relied on" or "trusted fully" is more satisfactory than either TEV or RSV.

14.9   Because I did, Moses promised me that my children
        and I would certainly receive as our possession
        the land which I walked over.

In Hebrew the clause which begins that my children is in direct discourse, as RSV indicates. In many languages the use of direct discourse will be more acceptable than the form of TEV: 'Moses promised me, 'You fully trusted the LORD, and so he will give you the land which you have walked over. It will belong to you and your family forever.'''

14.10-11 But now, look. It has been forty-five years since
          the LORD said that to Moses. That was when Israel
          was going through the desert, and the LORD, as he
          promised, has kept me alive ever since. Look at me!
          I am eighty-five years old 11 and am just as strong
          today as I was when Moses sent me out. I am still
          strong enough for war or for anything else.

But now, look translates the Hebrew "And now, behold" (RSV), which serves as an attention getter. In some languages this expression will be best left implicit.
It has been forty-five years since the LORD said that to Moses may be abbreviated as "Since that time forty-five years have gone by" or "That was forty-five years ago." By a slight rearrangement of TEV clauses, one may translate "That was forty-five years ago, and the LORD kept me alive all the time that our people traveled through the desert, just as he promised. Look at me! I am eighty-five years old...."
And am just as strong today as I was when Moses sent me out translates a Hebrew parallelism: "I am still as strong today as I was in the day that Moses sent me out; as my strength was then, so also my strength is now." TEV avoids the redundancy, though for some languages the repetition may make the affirmation stronger. Also, in TEV this represents a continuation of a sentence begun at the end of verse 10. In order to simplify this structure for English readers, one may translate "and I am" in place of and am. For other languages it may be more acceptable to begin a new sentence at the beginning of the verse.
Or for anything else represents "and for going and coming" (RSV). In Hebrew "to go and come" is an idiomatic expression indicating daily activity. The force of this expression may be included implicitly by the use of "even" if one translates either "I am strong enough (even) for war" or "and I am still strong enough (even) to fight in war."

14.12   Now then, give me the hill country that the LORD
         promised me on that day when my men and I reported.
         We told you then that the race of giants called the

[197]

> Anakim were there in large walled cities. Maybe
> the LORD will be with me, and I will drive them
> out, just as the LORD said."

Now then translates "And now" of the Hebrew text, a frequently
used transitional.

It is important that the imperative give me not sound rude or
overbearing. If there is a choice between a polite and a harsh form,
the polite form should be used. The context requires a firm request,
not a harsh demand.

On that day when my men and I reported represents "on that day"
of the Hebrew text. TEV my men and I may be represented by "my fellow
spies and I." But it is quite possible that for many readers this information will be clearly implicit without inclusion in the translation.
The first sentence of this verse may then be translated, "Now then, it
is only right that you give me the hill country that the LORD promised
me."

We told you then translates "for you heard on that day," which is
in reality a passive structure. The second person subject of the Hebrew
may be retained and the clause translated "And you have known since
that time."

For the Anakim see 11.21-22, where they are specifically connected
with Hebron; and for Hebron, in the highlands of Judah, see 10.36. If
We told you then is translated "And you have known since that time,"
then were there may need to be translated "lived there."

Large walled cities describes the cities according to both their
size and defensive capabilities (RSV "great fortified cities").

Will be with me may be rendered either "will stand beside me" or
"will help me."

Will drive them out translates a Hebrew verb which means both
(1) drive someone out from his property, and (2) take possession of
the property for one's self.

14.13   Joshua blessed Caleb son of Jephunneh and gave
          him the city of Hebron as his possession.

Joshua blessed Caleb may be translated either "Joshua asked the
LORD's blessings upon Caleb" or "Joshua asked the LORD to bless Caleb."
Direct discourse is possible: "Joshua prayed, 'LORD, bless Caleb.'"

It is certainly not necessary to identify Caleb as son of Jephunneh
(especially if this was done in verse 6); its inclusion will prove awkward for many readers, and its omission does not really delete from the
text.

14.14   Hebron still belongs to the descendants of Caleb son
          of Jephunneh the Kenizzite, because he faithfully
          obeyed the LORD, the God of Israel.

Still belongs refers to the time of the writing of the account.

Even if <u>son of Jephunneh</u> is felt to be obligatory in verse 13, certainly <u>son of Jephunneh the Kenizzite</u> should be deleted from this verse.

The verse may be inverted to reflect chronological order, "Because Caleb fully trusted in the LORD, the God of Israel, the city of Hebron still belongs to his descendants." Some languages may require explicit mention of the Lord's giving the city to Caleb: "Caleb trusted fully in the LORD, and so the LORD gave him the city of Hebron. His descendants still live there."

<u>14.15</u>   Before this, Hebron was called the city of Arba.
            (Arba had been the greatest of the Anakim.)
            There was now peace in the land.

<u>Before this</u> translates "Now...formerly" (RSV) of the Hebrew text. Further definition may be necessary; for example, "Before the city of Hebron belonged to Caleb, it was called..." or "Before Caleb captured the city of Hebron...."

<u>The city of Arba</u> is a translation of the Hebrew *Kiriath Arba* (which RSV transliterates). In 15.13 Arba is said to have been the father of Anak (for whom the Anakim were named). The first sentence of this verse may then be translated, "Before the city of Hebron belonged to Caleb, its name was Arba City." The parenthetical statement would then say "A man named Arba had been the greatest of the Anakim." It may also be advisable to remove the parentheses markers (round brackets), except for rather sophisticated readers.

<u>There was now peace in the land</u> translates "And the land had rest from war" (RSV). Many languages will have idiomatic expressions which will be quite satisfactory for the rendering of this statement.

Chapter 15

The Territory Assigned to Judah

1 The families of the tribe of Judah received a part of the land described as follows:

The land reached south to the southernmost point of the wilderness of Zin, at the border of Edom. 2 This southern border ran from the south end of the Dead Sea, 3 went southward from the Akrabbim Pass and on to Zin. It ran south of Kadesh Barnea, past Hezron and up to the Addar, turned toward Karka, 4 went on to Azmon, and followed the stream on the border of Egypt to the Mediterranean Sea, where the border ended. That was the southern border of Judah.

5 The eastern border was the Dead Sea, all the way up to the inlet where the Jordan empties into it.

The northern border began there, 6 extended up to Beth Hoglah, and went north of the ridge overlooking the Jordan Valley. Then it went up to the Stone of Bohan (Bohan was a son of Reuben), 7 from Trouble Valley up to Debir, and then turned north toward Gilgal, which faces Adummin Pass on the south side of the valley. It then went on to the springs of Enshemesh, out to Enrogel, 8 and up through Hinnom Valley on the south side of the hill where the Jebusite city of Jerusalem was located. The border then proceeded up to the top of the hill on the west side of Hinnom Valley, at the

1 The lot for the tribe of the people of Judah according to their families reached southward to the boundary of Edom, to the wilderness of Zin at the farthest south. 2 And their south boundary ran from the end of the Salt Sea, from the bay that faces southward; 3 it goes out southward of the ascent of Akrabbim, passes along to Zin, and goes up south of Kadesh-barnea, along by Hezron, up to Addar, turns about to Karka, 4 passes along to Azmon, goes out by the Brook of Egypt, and comes to its end at the sea. This shall be your south boundary. 5 And the east boundary is the Salt Sea, to the mouth of the Jordan. And the boundary on the north side runs from the bay of the sea at the mouth of the Jordan; 6 and the boundary goes up to Beth-hoglah, and passes along north of Beth-arabah; and the boundary goes up to the stone of Bohan the son of Reuben; 7 and the boundary goes up to Debir from the Valley of Achor, and so northward, turning toward Gilgal, which is opposite the ascent of Adummin, which is on the south side of the valley; and the boundary passes along to the waters of En-shemesh, and ends at Enrogel; 8 then the boundary goes up by the valley of the son of Hinnom at the southern shoulder of the Jebusite (that is Jerusalem);

northern end of Rephaim Valley.
9 From there it went to the Springs
of Mephtoah and out to the cities
near Mount Ephron. There it turned
toward Baalah (or Kiriath Jearim),
10 where it circled west of Baalah
toward the hill country of Edom,
went on the north side of Mount
Jearim (or Chesalon), down to Beth
Shemesh, and on past Timnah. 11 The
border then went out to the hill
north of Ekron, turned toward
Shikkeron, past Mount Baalah, and
on to Jamnia. It ended at the
Mediterranean Sea, 12 which formed
the western border.

Within these borders lived
the people of the families of
Judah.

and the boundary goes up to the
top of the mountain that lies
over against the valley of Hinnom,
on the west, at the northern end
of the valley of Rephaim; 9 then
the boundary extends from the top
of the mountain to the spring of
the Waters of Mephtoah, and from
there to the cities of Mount
Ephron; then the boundary bends
round to Baalah (that is, Kiriath-
jearim); 10 and the boundary cir-
cles west of Baalah to Mount Seir,
passes along to the northern
shoulder of Mount Jearim (that is,
Chesalon), and goes down to Beth-
shemesh, and passes along by
Timnah; 11 the boundary goes out
to the shoulder of the hill north
of Ekron, then the boundary bends
round to Shikkeron, and passes
along to Mount Baalah, and goes
out to Jabneel; then the boundary
comes to an end at the sea. 12 And
the west boundary was the Great
Sea with its coast-line. This is
the boundary round about the people of Judah according to their
families.

This chapter gives the limits of the territory assigned to the
tribe of Judah (verses 1-12), reports Caleb's conquest of the cities
of Hebron and Debir in the territory of Judah (verses 13-19), and names
the cities within Judah's territory (verses 20-63). Judah's territory
lay in the southern part of the land; only Simeon was farther south,
but its precise boundaries were never well defined.

The section heading, The Territory Assigned to Judah, is a type
of passive structure in which the agent is not specified. At least two
restructurings are possible so that the heading becomes a complete
sentence: "This is the territory which was given to the tribe of Judah"
and "This is the territory which Joshua assigned to the tribe of Judah."

15.1   The families of the tribe of Judah received a
         part of the land described as follows:
         The land reached south to the southernmost point
         of the wilderness of Zin, at the border of Edom.

In tracing the southern border of Judah, TEV tries to make the
geographical data easier to understand by using modern names (Dead Sea
in verse 2 for "Salt Sea"; Mediterranean Sea in verse 4, not "the sea";
compare RSV) and by indicating, as much as possible, the directions the

border took, from the southern end of the Dead Sea, on the east, as far
south as the frontier with Egypt, and ending at the Mediterranean Sea,
on the west. All the place-names in verses 1-4 can be located on biblical maps; such maps will help the translator indicate directions in
the translated text.

The word families would more accurately be expressed as "clans,"
but for many English speakers the word "clan" is not very familiar.
Many other languages, however, will have a word equivalent to "clan"
which is in current and widespread usage. However, there is another
option which the translator may follow: the phrase the families of the
tribe of Judah represents an attempt on the part of the Hebrew author
to include everyone who was a member of the tribe. The same idea may
be expressed either "The people of the tribe of Judah" or "The tribe
of Judah." The focus is not upon the distribution of land to each of
the individual clans within the tribe, but rather upon the borders
marking the edge of the land which the whole tribe received. Moreover,
the phrase a part of may make the statement somewhat confusing to the
reader, since the biblical writer apparently assumes that all the territory within the region described was assigned to the tribe of Judah.
Therefore verse 1 may be translated, "The tribe of Judah received the
land which reached south to the southernmost point of the wilderness
of Zin, which was the northern border of Edom." Or, to allow for a
different interpretation of the text, the second half of the verse may
be translated, "In the south their territory bordered on the wilderness
of Zin, which belonged to Edom."

15.2-4   This southern border ran from the south end of the
           Dead Sea, 3 went southward from the Akrabbim Pass
           and on to Zin. It ran south of Kadesh Barnea, past
           Hezron and up to Addar, turned toward Karka, 4 went
           on to Azmon, and followed the stream on the border
           of Egypt to the Mediterranean Sea, where the border
           ended. That was the southern border of Judah.

Inasmuch as verses 2-4 give the details of the southern border of
Judah, it may be useful to introduce this information by some formula
such as "Specifically, this southern border ran...."

It may also be helpful to identify Zin (verse 3) as the wilderness
of Zin, and Kadesh Barnea, Hezron, Addar, Karka, and Azmon as cities.
Furthermore, in place of went southward (verse 3) it would be more
nearly accurate to render "went in a southwesterly direction."

In restructuring, it may be wise at some point to break the
lengthy sentence which runs from the last half of verse 2 to the first
part of verse 4. For example: "4 went on to the city of Azmon. From
there it followed the stream on the border of Egypt in a northwesterly
direction to the Mediterranean Sea."

In Hebrew That was the southern border of Judah is in direct discourse, and it states "This shall be your southern border" (see RSV).
This statement is addressed either to the people of the tribe of Judah
or to the Israelites as a whole; HOTTP recommends the second interpretation, which is not followed by TEV.

Since the southern borders of Judah and the Israelite nation are
the same, it is possible to combine both interpretations: "That was the
southern border of Judah and also of all the tribes of Israel." Or, on
the assumption that it is implicitly the southern border of Judah, one
may translate "That was at the same time the southern border of all the
tribes of Israel."

15.5   The eastern border was the Dead Sea, all the way
             up to the inlet where the Jordan empties into it.
             The northern border began there,

Verses 5-12 give the eastern border, which was the Dead Sea
(verse 5a); the northern border (verses 5b-11); and the western border,
which was the Mediterranean Sea (verses 11b-12a).

At this point it may be useful to repeat that the eastern border
referred to is that of the tribe of Judah: "The eastern border of the
tribe of Judah was the Dead Sea. This eastern border extended as far
north as the place where the Jordan River empties into the Dead Sea."
Or the sentence may be restructured in a slightly different manner:
"The Dead Sea formed the eastern border for the tribe of Judah."

The northern border began there, though representing the Hebrew
"And the boundary on the north side runs from" (RSV), may be somewhat
misleading. That is, although Beth Hoglah (verse 6) is north of the
Dead Sea, it is also the point from which the account moves generally
in a westwardly direction. There is no way that a reader can be expected to grasp the account fully without looking at a map, but it will
be helpful in translation if it is noted that the description of the
northern border moves from east (the mouth of the Jordan River) toward
the Mediterranean Sea in the west.

15.6   extended up to Beth Hoglah, and went north of the
             ridge overlooking the Jordan Valley. Then it went
             up to the Stone of Bohan (Bohan was a son of Reuben),

The translator should notice the places where TEV differs from
the literal Hebrew (as represented by RSV): "North of Beth-Arabah"
(RSV) is in TEV north of the ridge overlooking the Jordan Valley, which
is interpreted as the same location given as the southern border of
the tribe of Benjamin in 18.18 (see the text there); "the Arabah" in
this context is the Jordan Valley.

The last part of verse 5 and the beginning of verse 6 may be
translated,

             From here the border extended in a northerly direction
             6 to Beth Hoglah, and it proceeded north of the ridge over-
             looking the Jordan Valley. From there it went up to the Stone
             of Bohan, which was named after Bohan, a son of Reuben.

Nothing precisely is known about the Stone of Bohan; here Bohan is
merely identified as a son of Reuben. It should be remembered that the
territory of the tribe of Reuben was on the east side of the Jordan
River.

15.7   from Trouble Valley up to Debir, and then turned north
       toward Gilgal, which faces Adummim Pass on the south
       side of the valley. It then went on to the springs of
       Enshemesh, out to Enrogel,

Trouble Valley (RSV "Valley of Achor") translates the name, as in
7.24-26.
       Gilgal is not the place northeast of Jericho (4.19), the first
camping place of the Israelites upon entering Canaan. In 18.17 it is
given the spelling Geliloth, and some think this is preferable also
for the present verse. It should further be noted that Debir is not
the same one as in 10.38-39; the location of this Debir is unknown.

15.8   and up through Hinnom Valley on the south side of
       the hill where the Jebusite city of Jerusalem was
       located. The border then proceeded up to the top of
       the hill on the west side of Hinnom Valley, at the
       northern end of Rephaim Valley.

Hinnom Valley (RSV "valley of the son of Hinnom") is the name of
the valley south of Jerusalem.
       The Jebusite city of Jerusalem is translated "the Jebusites (that
is, Jerusalem)" by RSV. It appears as though this parenthetical statement, together with the two in verses 9 and 10, were explanations added
by a later scribe to make sure that the readers would understand what
was meant. TEV is able to avoid the interruption of a parenthetical
statement in this verse, though parentheses are included by TEV in
verses 9 and 10.

15.9   From there it went to the Springs of Mephtoah and
       out to the cities near Mount Ephron. There it turned
       toward Baalah (or Kiriath Jearim).

The last part of this verse may be rendered, "There it (the border) turned toward the city of Baalah, which today is called Kiriath
Jearim...."

15.10 where it circled west of Baalah toward the hill
       country of Edom, went on the north side of Mount
       Jearim (or Chesalon), down to Beth Shemesh, and
       on past Timnah.

If the model of TEV is being followed, then some attention should
be given to the advisability of beginning a new sentence somewhere in
this verse. In fact, it is possible that verse 10 may well be broken
into two or more sentences. The hill country of Edom, as elsewhere in
TEV, translates "Mount Seir" (RSV).
       The parenthetical statement (or Chesalon) may be handled similarly
to that of verse 9. Both Beth Shemesh and Timnah are cities, and it
would be helpful to identify them as such in translation.

15.11   The border then went out to the hill north of
Ekron, turned toward Shikkeron, past Mount
Baalah, and on to Jamnia. It ended at the
Mediterranean Sea,

Ekron, Shikkeron, and Jamnia should be identified as cities. In
place of "Jabneel" (RSV), TEV uses the more current name, Jamnia.

15.12   which formed the western border.
      Within these borders lived the people of the
families of Judah.

The people of the families of Judah may be shortened to "the people of Judah." The sentence may either be inverted ("The people of
Judah lived within these borders") or considerably restructured ("This
was the territory that belonged to the tribe of Judah").

	TEV	15.13-19	RSV

Caleb Conquers Hebron and Debir

13 As the LORD commanded Joshua, part of the territory of Judah was given to Caleb son of Jephunneh, from the tribe of Judah. He received Hebron, the city belonging to Arba, father of Anak. 14 Caleb drove the descendants of Anak out of the city—the clans of Sheshai, Ahiman, and Talmai. 15 From there he went to attack the people living in Debir. (This city used to be called Kiriath Sepher.) 16 Caleb said, "I will give my daughter Achsah in marriage to the man who succeeds in capturing Kiriath Sepher." 17 Othniel, the son of Caleb's brother Kenaz, captured the city, so Caleb gave him his daughter Achsah in marriage. 18 On the wedding day Othniel urged her[i] to ask her father for a field. She got down from her donkey, and Caleb asked her what she wanted. 19 She answered, "I want some water holes. The land you have given me is in the dry country." So Caleb gave her the uppper and

13 According to the commandment of the LORD to Joshua, he gave to Caleb the son of Jephunneh a portion among the people of Judah, Kiriath-arba, that is, Hebron (Arba was the father of Anak). 14 And Caleb drove out from there the three sons of Anak, Sheshai and Ahiman and Talmai, the descendants of Anak. 15 And he went up from there against the inhabitants of Debir; now the name of Debir formerly was Kiriath-sepher. 16 And Caleb said, "Whoever smites Kiriath-sepher, and takes it, to him will I give Achsah my daughter as wife." 17 And Othni-el the son of Kenaz, the brother of Caleb, took it; and he gave him Achsah his daughter as wife. 18 When she came to him, she urged him to ask her father for a field; and she alighted from her ass, and Caleb said to her, "What do you wish?" 19 She said to him, "Give me a present; since you have set me in the land of the Negeb, give

lower springs.

iProbable text (see Jg 1.14)
Othniel urged her; Hebrew she
urged Othniel.

me also springs of water." And
Caleb gave her the upper springs
and the lower springs.

This section refers back to 14.6-15, which tells how Joshua gave
Caleb the city of Hebron, in the highlands of Judah. In 10.36-37 it is
reported that Joshua had conquered and completely destroyed Hebron,
killing all its citizens as well as the people in the nearby towns.
The city of Debir, some 20 kilometers southwest of Hebron, is conquered
by Othniel, verse 17; in 10.38-39 it is reported that Joshua had taken
the city and killed all its inhabitants.

Although the section entitled Caleb Conquers Hebron and Debir
encompasses only seven verses, its content touches on several subjects.
For that reason a section heading is somewhat difficult to formulate.
Following the model of TEV, one may translate "Caleb conquers the cities
of Hebron and Debir"; otherwise, it may be expanded to say "Caleb conquers the cities of Hebron and Debir and gives his daughter in marriage."

15.13   As the LORD commanded Joshua, part of the ter-
         ritory of Judah was given to Caleb son of Jephunneh,
         from the tribe of Judah. He received Hebron, the
         city belonging to Arba, father of Anak.

For Caleb...from the tribe of Judah, see comments at 14.6. Here
again it may be unnecessary to include the identification son of Jephunneh in the text. This information was important for the Hebrew writer,
but it is the sort of detail which need not be repeated as frequently
in other languages as in Hebrew; where it becomes burdensome for the
reader, consideration should be given to omitting it.

Here the Hebrew says only that Caleb was given a share "among the
descendants of Judah," which seems to imply that he was not one of
them. The Hebrew name Kiriath Arba means "city of Arba," who is identified as the father of Anak. Here Anak stands for the name of a man
(as RSV, TEV take it to be) or else means "the Anakim," that is, the
race of giants called Anakim (see 14.12,15).

This verse may be restructured so that the Lord's command appears
in direct discourse:

         The LORD had commanded Joshua, "Give part of the terri-
         tory to Caleb from the tribe of Judah." So Joshua gave him
         the city of Hebron. Before this, the city had belonged to
         Arba, father of Anak.

If the noun Anak means "the Anakim," then it is allowable to
translate "...Joshua gave him the city of Hebron, which had been
founded by Arba, the ancestor of the Anakim."

15.14   Caleb drove the descendants of Anak out of the city—
         the clans of Sheshai, Ahiman, and Talmai.

Caleb drove...out of Hebron Anak's descendants, that is, the clans of Sheshai, Ahiman, and Talmai. It is clear that these three proper names do not refer to individuals, as RSV makes it appear, but to clans who are named after their ancestors (see Num 13.22; Judges 1.10,20).

Although TEV avoided the use of the word clan at 15.1, it is now used as a translation of the Hebrew word "son," which here has the extended meaning of clan. Translators are not always consistent! The verse may be restructured, "The clans of Sheshai, Ahiman, and Talmai lived in the city of Hebron. They were descendants of Anak, and Caleb drove them all out of the city." It may be important to indicate not only that he drove them out of the city, but also that he took it over for himself: "The clans of Sheshai, Ahiman, and Talmai, the descendants of Anak, lived in the city of Hebron at that time. Caleb drove them all out of the city, and took it over for himself."

15.15   From there he went to attack the people living in
          Debir. (This city used to be called Kiriath Sepher.)

For Debir see 10.38-39.
The people living in Debir is almost a word-for-word repetition of the Hebrew text; see RSV "the inhabitants of Debir." The sentence may be formulated to say "From there he went to attack the city of Debir, which used to be called Kiriath Sepher."

15.16-17 Caleb said, "I will give my daughter Achsah in
          marriage to the man who succeeds in capturing
          Kiriath Sepher." 17 Othniel, the son of Caleb's
          brother Kenaz, captured the city, so Caleb gave
          him his daughter Achsah in marriage.

The account that follows (verses 16-19) is paralleled in Judges 1.11-15. The passage in Judges specifies that Kenaz, the father of Othniel, was the younger brother of Caleb.

In verse 16 it may be better to invert the order of Caleb's promise so that it follows chronological sequence: "Whoever succeeds in capturing Kiriath Sepher can marry my daughter Achsah." Or, since Caleb would have been addressing his men, the text may be translated, "If any one of my men is able to capture the city of Kiriath Sepher, I will let him marry my daughter Achsah."

Verse 17 of TEV is already arranged in proper sequence. However, for some languages it may seem unnecessary to mention the name of Caleb's daughter again this soon. TEV does so to avoid the possible misunderstanding that his daughter refers back to Othniel. By the inclusion of the proper name Achsah the text is immediately clear.

15.18   On the wedding day Othniel urged her^i to ask her
          father for a field. She got down from her donkey,
          and Caleb asked her what she wanted.

ᶦProbable text (see Jg 1.14) Othniel urged her;
Hebrew she urged Othniel.

On the wedding day translates the Hebrew "and when she came" (see
NAB "On the day of her marriage to Othniel"). The Hebrew text then says
"and she urged him." Since in the following verse it is she who speaks
to her father, TEV has here followed one manuscript of the Septuagint
(and the Septuagint and Latin Vulgate of Judges 1.14) where the text
is "he urged her," which seems preferable (so NEB, BJ, JB, Zür).[49]
Soggin objects that the Hebrew verb is always used in a bad sense, to
seduce someone to do something bad; he feels that it is inappropriate
here, and that it was not in the original text. He believes the text
must have had "she decided."

Given the complexities of the verse, it is advisable to follow
the model of a translation which attempts to make some sense of the
text. On the basis of TEV one may translate "On the wedding day Othniel
said to her, 'Ask your father for a field.'" Or "...'Ask your father
to give you (or, us) a field.'"

She got down translates a Hebrew verb which occurs only here, in
the parallel passage Judges 1.14, and in Judges 4.21. In Judges 4.21
it means "to beat," "to drive" (the peg). Here and in the parallel
passage Koehler-Baumgartner says "clap one's hands (to attract attention)." The meaning "to dismount" is more or less a guess, but it
fits the context, and most translations adopt it.[50]

In translation it is frequently necessary to spell out the events
in more detail: "She got down from her donkey and went to Caleb. He
asked her, 'What do you want?'" Or, if Caleb is assumed to have approached her: "She got down from her donkey. Caleb then came to her
and asked her, 'What would you like for a wedding present?'"

15.19   She answered, "I want some water holes. The land
         you have given me is in the dry country." So Caleb
         gave her the upper and lower springs.

In reply to Caleb's question, Achsah says "I want a blessing" (see
RSV)—the word "blessing" here meaning 'present, gift." It is possible
to translate so that the girl's answer to her father more adequately
expresses the original cultural setting: "She answered, 'Give me your
blessing as I leave your home. And as a sign of this blessing, give
me a gift. I want some water holes....'" Or "She answered, '...a gift.
You have already given me some land, but it is in the dry country. So
now I want you go give me some water holes.'"

"The land of the Negeb" (RSV) is the dry country in the south. In
response to her request, Caleb gave her the upper and lower springs.
Although the locations of the upper and lower springs are not further
defined, it is quite likely that the geographical point of reference
is the city of Hebron. Therefore, if it is necessary in the receptor
language to be specific: "the upper and lower springs near the city
of Hebron."

The Cities of Judah

20 This is the land that the families of the tribe of Judah received as their possession. 21 The cities farthest south that belonged to them, those that were near the border of Edom, were Kabzeel, Eder, Jagur, 22 Kinah, Dimonah, Adadah, 23 Kedesh, Hazor, Ithnan, 24 Ziph, Telem, Bealoth, 25 Hazor Hadattah, Kerioth Hezron (or Hazor), 26 Amam, Shema, Moladah, 27 Hazar Gaddah, Heshmon, Bethpelet, 28 Hazar Shual, Beersheba, Biziothiah, 29 Baalah, Iim, Ezem, 30 Eltolad, Chesil, Hormah, 31 Ziklag, Madmannah, Sansannah, 32 Lebaoth, Shilhim, Ain, and Rimmon: twenty-nine cities in all, along with the towns around them.

33 The cities in the foothills were Eshtaol, Zorah, Ashnah, 34 Zanoah, Engannim, Tappuah, Enam, 35 Jarmuth, Adullam, Socoh, Azekah, 36 Shaaraim, Adithaim, Gederah, and Gederothaim: fourteen cities, along with the towns around them.

37 There were also Zenan, Hadashah, Migdalgad, 38 Dilean, Mizpah, Joktheel, 39 Lachish, Bozkath, Eglon, 40 Cabbon, Lahmam, Chitlish, 41 Gederoth, Bethdagon, Naamah, and Makkedah: sixteen cities, along with the towns around them.

42 There were also Libnah, Ether, Ashan, 43 Iphtah, Ashnah, Nezib, 44 Keilah, Achzib, and Mareshah: nine cities, along with the towns around them.

45 There was Ekron with its towns and villages, 46 and all the cities and towns near Ashdod, from Ekron to the Mediterranean Sea.

47 There were Ashdod and Gaza, with their towns and villages, reaching to the stream on the border of Egypt and the coast of the

This is the inheritance of the tribe of the people of Judah according to their families. 21 The cities belonging to the tribe of the people of Judah in the extreme South, toward the boundary of Edom, were Kabzeel, Eder, Jagur, 22 Kinah, Dimonah, Adadah, 23 Kedesh, Hazor, Ithnan, 24 Ziph, Telem, Bealoth, 25 Hazor-hadattah, Keri-oth-hezron (that is, Hazor), 26 Amam, Shema, Moladah, 27 Hazargaddah, Heshmon, Beth-pelet, 28 Hazar-shual, Beer-sheba, Biziothiah, 29 Baalah, Iim, Ezem, 30 Eltolad, Chesil, Hormah, 31 Ziklag, Madmannah, Sansannah, 32 Lebaoth, Shilhim, Ain, and Rimmon: in all, twenty-nine cities, with their villages.

33 And in the lowland, Eshtaol, Zorah, Ashnah, 34 Zanoah, En-gannim, Tappuah, Enam, 35 Jarmuth, Adullam, Socoh, Azekah, 36 Shaaraim, Adithaim, Gederah, Gederothaim: fourteen cities with their villages.

37 Zenan, Hadashah, Migdal-gad, 38 Dilean, Mizpeh, Joktheel, 39 Lachish, Bozkath, Eglon, 40 Cabbon, Lahmam, Chitlish, 41 Gederoth, Beth-dagon, Naamah, and Makkedah: sixteen cities with their villages.

42 Libnah, Ether, Ashan, 43 Iphtah, Ashnah, Nezib, 44 Keilah, Achzib, and Mareshah: nine cities with their villages.

45 Ekron, with its towns and its villages; 46 from Ekron to the sea, all that were by the side of Ashdod, with their villages.

47 Ashdod, its towns and its villages; Gaza, its towns and its villages; to the Brook of Egypt, and the Great Sea with

Mediterranean Sea.

48 In the hill country there were Shamir, Jattir, Socoh, 49 Dannah, Kiriath Sepher (or Debir), 50 Anab, Eshtemoa, Anim, 51 Goshen, Holon, and Giloh: eleven cities, along with the towns around them.

52 There were Arab, Dumah, Eshan, 53 Janim, Beth Tappuah, Aphekah, 54 Humtah, Hebron, and Zior: nine cities, along with the towns around them.

55 There were Maon, Carmel, Ziph, Juttah, 56 Jezreel, Jokdeam, Zanoah, 57 Kain, Gibeah, and Timnah: ten cities, along with the towns around them.

58 There were Halhul, Bethzur, Gedor, 59 Maarath, Bethanoth, and Eltekon: six cities, along with the towns around them.

60 There were Kiriath Baal (or Kiriath Jearim) and Rabbah: two cities, along with the towns around them.

61 In the desert there were Beth Arabah, Middin, Secacah, 62 Nibshan, Salt City, and Engedi: six cities, along with the towns around them.

63 But the people of Judah were not able to drive out the Jebusites, who lived in Jerusalem. The Jebusites still live there with the people of Judah.

its coast-line.

48 And in the hill country, Shamir, Jattir, Socoh, 49 Dannah, Kiriath-sannah (that is, Debir), 50 Anab, Eshtemoh, Anim, 51 Goshen, Holon, and Giloh: eleven cities with their villages.

52 Arab, Dumah, Eshan, 53 Janim, Beth-tappuah, Aphekah, 54 Humtah, Kiriath-arba (that is, Hebron), and Zior: nine cities with their villages.

55 Maon, Carmel, Ziph, Juttah, 56 Jezreel, Jokde-am, Zanoah, 57 Kain, Gibeah, and Timnah: ten cities with their villages.

58 Halhul, Beth-zur, Gedor, 59 Maarath, Beth-anoth, and Eltekon: six cities with their villages.

60 Kiriath-baal (that is, Kiriath-jearim), and Rabbah: two cities with their villages.

61 In the wilderness, Beth-arabah, Middin, Secacah, 62 Nibshan, the City of Salt, and Engedi: six cities with their villages.

63 But the Jebusites, the inhabitants of Jerusalem, the people of Judah could not drive out; so the Jebusites dwell with the people of Judah at Jerusalem to this day.

The cities in this list are grouped into eleven different districts. The Septuagint adds another district after verse 59, which HOTTP believes to represent a more original text. The actual number of the cities named and the totals given do not always match, but the text must be faithfully translated regardless of the outcome.

The section heading, The Cities of Judah, may be translated "This is a list of the cities that Joshua gave to the tribe of Judah." It may also be rendered, "These are the cities which the tribe of Judah received as its possession."

15.20-32   This is the land that the families of the tribe of Judah received as their possession. 21 The cities farthest south that belonged to them, those that were near the border of Edom, were Kabzeel, Eder, Jagur, 22 Kinah, Dimonah, Adadah, 23 Kedesh, Hazor, Ithnan,

24 Ziph, Telem, Bealoth, 25 Hazor Hadattah, Kerioth
Hezron (or Hazor), 26 Amam, Shema, Moladah, 27 Hazar
Gaddah, Heshmon, Bethpelet, 28 Hazar Shual, Beersheba,
Biziothiah, 29 Baalah, Iim, Ezem, 30 Eltolad, Chesil,
Hormah, 31 Ziklag, Madmannah, Sansannah, 32 Lebaoth,
Shilhim, Ain, and Rimmon: twenty-nine cities in all,
along with the towns around them.

THE FIRST DISTRICT: cities in the extreme south.
Since these cities are grouped into districts by the writer, it
may be helpful to arrange the text in such a way as to indicate this
fact. For example:
21 The cities of the first district were located in the
extreme south near the border of Edom. These were the cities
of....
33 The cities of the second district were located in the
foothills....
37 The cities of the third district were Zenan....
Or another form may be:
(1) 21-32 The cities farthest south that belonged to
them were near the border of Edom. These were the cities
of....
(2) 33-36 Their cities in the foothills were....
(3) 37-41 There were also the cities of Zenan....
Where the total is indicated at the end of the grouping, this information may be shifted to the beginning and the verses numbered together. For example, "48-51 In the hill country there were eleven
cities, along with the towns around them. These cities were: Shamir,
Jattir...." Or, "48-51 The cities of the sixth district were located
in the hill country. There were eleven of them, along with the towns
around them. These cities were: Shamir, Jattir...."
The verse numbers may even be placed at the end of each section:
(5) There was the city of Ekron with all its towns and
villages that reached as far as the Mediterranean Sea. There
were also the cities of Ashdod and Gaza. Their towns and villages reached to the stream on the border of Egypt and the
coast on the Mediterranean Sea. (45-47)
The TEV spelling is identical with that of RSV. The text, as understood by RSV, TEV, and others, names thirty-six cities in all;[51] the
total in verse 32 is given as twenty-nine cities in all (besides the
neighboring towns). Cities were generally fortified settlements, and
towns open settlements, no more than a few houses or sheepfolds (see
Gray).

15.33-36   The cities in the foothills were Eshtaol, Zorah,
Ashnah, 34 Zanoah, Engannim, Tappuah, Enam, 35 Jarmuth,
Adullam, Socoh, Azekah, 36 Shaaraim, Adithaim, Gederah,
and Gederothaim: fourteen cities, along with the towns
around them.

THE SECOND DISTRICT: cities in the foothills.
Here fifteen cities are named; the total (verse 36b) is given as
fourteen cities.[52]

<u>15.37-41</u>   There were also Zenan, Hadashah, Migdalgad,
           38 Dilean, Mizpah, Joktheel, 39 Lachish, Bozkath,
           Eglon, 40 Cabbon, Lahmam, Chitlish, 41 Gederoth,
           Bethdagon, Naamah, and Makkedah: sixteen cities,
           along with the towns around them.

THIRD DISTRICT: cities also in the foothills.
The number of cities named agrees with the total given in verse
41: sixteen cities.

<u>15.42-44</u>   There were also Libnah, Ether, Ashan, 43 Iphtah,
           Ashnah, Nezib, 44 Keilah, Achzib, and Mareshah: nine
           cities, along with the towns around them.

FOURTH DISTRICT: cities in the central part of the foothills,
between districts two and three.
It is to be noticed that <u>Ether</u> and <u>Ashan</u> (verse 42) are assigned
to Simeon in 19.7.

<u>15.45-47</u>   There was Ekron with its towns and villages,
           46 and all the cities and towns near Ashdod, from
           Ekron to the Mediterranean Sea.
               47 There were Ashdod and Gaza, with their towns
           and villages, reaching to the stream on the border
           of Egypt and the coast of the Mediterranean Sea.

FIFTH DISTRICT: cities in the Philistine coastal area.
<u>Ashdod</u> was about 22 kilometers west of <u>Ekron</u>; <u>Gaza</u> was about 68
kilometers southwest of Ashdod. The other two Philistine cities, Ashkelon and Gath, are not included.

<u>15.48-51</u>   In the hill country there were Shamir, Jattir,
           Socoh, 49 Dannah, Kiriath Sepher (or Debir), 50 Anab,
           Eshtemoa, Anim, 51 Goshen, Holon, and Giloh: eleven
           cities, along with the towns around them.

SIXTH DISTRICT: cities in the highlands.
In verse 49 TEV has <u>Kiriath Sepher</u> instead of Hebrew *Kiriath-
Sannah* (see RSV), in keeping with its principle of using the better
known form of a name when a person or place is called by two or more
different names (see 15.15-16; Judges 1.11-12). The same applies in
verse 50 to <u>Eshtemoa</u> (see Josh 21.14; 1 Sam 20.28; 1 Chr 6.57) instead
of the Hebrew *Eshtemoh*, which occurs only here.
In verse 51 Goshen is to be understood as the capital city of the
region of Goshen (see 10.41).

15.52-54   There were Arab, Dumah, Eshan, 53 Janim, Beth
            Tappuah, Aphekah, 54 Humtah, Hebron, and Zior; nine
            cities, along with the towns around them.

SEVENTH DISTRICT: cities also in the highlands.
The Hebrew in verse 54 gives the old name of Hebron, namely *Kiriath
Arba* (see RSV); in light of verse 13 this information has become re-
dundant and so is omitted by TEV.

15.55-57   There were Maon, Carmel, Ziph, Juttah, 56 Jez-
            reel, Jokdeam, Zanoah, 57 Kain, Gibeah, and Timnah:
            ten cities, along with the towns around them.

EIGHTH DISTRICT: cities also in the highlands, southeast of Hebron.

15.58-59   There were Halhul, Bethzur, Gedor, 59 Maarath,
            Bethanoth, and Eltekon: six cities, along with the
            towns around them.

NINTH DISTRICT: cities in the highlands, north of Hebron.
The Septuagint adds another district at the end of verse 50, as
follows: "Tekoa, Ephrath (that is, Bethlehem), Peor, Etam, Culon, Tatam,
Shoresh, Cerem, Gallim, Bether, and Manach: eleven cities, along with
the towns around them." HOTTP ("A" decision) believes that the Septuagint preserves the original text here, and recommends that this material be included, NEB, NAB, BJ, and JB include it. In light of the
firm decision of HOTTP (also Gray, Soggin, Smith) and the inclusion
of this material by the translations cited, a translator will be justified in including it.

15.60   There were Kiriath Baal (or Kiriath Jearim)
            and Rabbah: two cities, along with the towns
            around them.

TENTH (ELEVENTH) DISTRICT: only two cities are listed. Kiriath
Jearim is known (see 9.17), but Rabbah has not been definitely identified. The district seems to lie near the northern border of Judah,
where it touches the border of Benjamin.

15.61-62   In the desert there were Beth Arabah, Middin,
            Secacah, 62 Nibshan, Salt City, and Engedi: six
            cities, along with the towns around them.

ELEVENTH (TWELFTH) DISTRICT: cities in the arid region of the
eastern slopes, which reached down to the Jordan Valley. Engedi was
about halfway down the length of the Dead Sea, on its west bank.

[213]

15.63   But the people of Judah were not able to drive
              out the Jebusites, who lived in Jerusalem. The Jeb-
              usites still live there with the people of Judah.

     This final verse explains why some Jebusites, descendants of the
original inhabitants of Jerusalem, were still living in the city at
the time of the writing of the account. This verse makes it appear that
Jerusalem was to have been assigned to Judah, whereas it was assigned
to Benjamin (see 18.28; Judges 1.21).
     Who lived in Jerusalem may be misunderstood by the reader, for
whom it could imply that the people of Judah were able to drive out
other Jebusites, who did not live in Jerusalem. One may translate "But
the people of Judah were not able to drive the Jebusites out of Jerusalem. Therefore they still live there with them in the city today."

Chapter 16

The Territory Assigned to Ephraim and West Manasseh

1 The southern boundary of the land assigned to the descendants of Joseph started from the Jordan near Jericho, at a point east of the springs of Jericho, and went into the desert. It went from Jericho up into the hill country as far as Bethel. 2 From Bethel it went to Luz, passing on to Ataroth Addar, where the Archites lived. 3 It then went west to the area of the Japhletites, as far as the area of Lower Beth Horon. It went on from there to Gezer and ended at the Mediterranean Sea.

4 The descendants of Joseph, the tribes of Ephraim and West Manasseh, received this land as their possession.

1 The allotment of the descendants of Joseph went from the Jordan by Jericho, east of the waters of Jericho, into the wilderness, going up from Jericho into the hill country to Bethel; 2 then going from Bethel to Luz, it passes along to Ataroth, the territory of the Archites; 3 then it goes down westward to the territory of the Japhletites, as far as the territory of Lower Beth-horon, then to Gezer, and it ends at the sea.

4 The people of Joseph, Manasseh and Ephraim, received their inheritance.

Chapters 16 and 17 describe the territory on the west side of the Jordan given to the descendants of Joseph's two sons, Manasseh and Ephraim. The tribe of Ephraim's territory was immediately north of Benjamin, and West Manasseh was north of Ephraim.

The section heading, <u>The Territory Assigned to Ephraim and West Manasseh</u>, may be restructured in a manner similar to that suggested for the previous section heading (<u>The Cities of Judah</u>, 15.20). See also the comments at 15.1 (<u>The Territory Assigned to Judah</u>).

<u>16.1</u>   The southern boundary of the land assigned to the descendants of Joseph started from the Jordan near Jericho, at a point east of the springs of Jericho, and went into the desert. It went from Jericho up into the hill country as far as Bethel.

Verses 1-4 describe the southern boundary of Ephraim; since it bordered on the territory of the tribe of Benjamin, the geographical

[215]

information here is similar to that given for the northern boundary of
Benjamin (18.12-14a).

TEV retains some of the redundancy and ambiguity of the Hebrew
text. For example, went into the desert is left dangling at the end of
the sentence in TEV, and it is impossible to determine from TEV the
geographical relationship between the desert and Jericho. It may be
possible to restructure for clarity and fewer words, and at the same
time to indicate the general westerly movement of the border line.
For example,

> The southern boundary of the land assigned to the descend-
> ants of Joseph started east of the springs of Jericho near the
> Jordan River. It then moved past Jericho in a northwesterly
> direction through the desert and into the hill country as far
> as Bethel.

16.2-3   From Bethel it went to Luz, passing on to Ataroth
          Addar, where the Archites lived. 3 It then went west
          to the area of the Japhletites, as far as the area
          of Lower Beth Horon. It went on from there to Gezer
          and ended at the Mediterranean Sea.

It is strange that the text here speaks of Bethel and Luz as two
different places (verse 2), whereas in other texts Luz is said to be
the earlier name of Bethel (see 18.13; Judges 1.23; Gen 28.19; 35.6).
Consequently, Bright says the text here cannot be right, and he proposes changes; but most translations retain the form of the Hebrew text.

In verse 2 TEV has Ataroth Addar, as in 16.5; 18.13, so as to
distinguish it from the other Ataroth (verse 7); Hebrew has only "Ataroth" here (see RSV).

Nothing definite is known of the tribal groups the Archites (see
2 Sam 15.32) or the Japhletites.

For Lower Beth Horon see 10.10, and for Gezer see 10.33.

Verses 2-3 should not pose too many difficulties, since TEV is
rather easy to understand. Two minor alterations may be made: (1) the
place names may need to be marked specifically as cities; and (2) one
of the occurrences of it (once in verse 2 and twice in verse 3) may
need to be marked specifically as "the southern boundary of the land."
Moreover, it may be advisable to keep the readers aware that the directions are toward the west.

16.4   The descendants of Joseph, the tribes of Ephraim
          and West Manasseh, received this land as their posses-
          sion.

Unless a reader is experienced with commas, he may not realize
that The descendants of Joseph and the tribes of Ephraim and West Manasseh are one and the same. To clarify, one possibility would be "The
tribes of Ephraim and Manasseh received this land as their possession.
These tribes were the descendants of Joseph."

Ephraim

5 This was the territory of the Ephraimite families: their border ran from Ataroth Addar eastward to Upper Beth Horon, 6 and from there to the Mediterranean Sea. Michmethath was on their north. East of there the border bent toward Taanath Shiloh and went past it on the east to Janoah. 7 Then it went down from Janoah to Ataroth and Naarah, reaching Jericho and ending at the Jordan. 8 The border went west from Tappuah to the stream Kanah and ended at the Mediterranean Sea. This was the land given to the families of the tribe of Ephraim as their possession, 9 along with some towns and villages that were within the borders of Manasseh, but given to the Ephraimites. 10 But they did not drive out the Canaanites who lived in Gezer, so the Canaanites have lived among the Ephraimites to this day, but they have been forced to work as slaves.

5 The territory of the Ephraimites by their families was as follows: the boundary of their inheritance on the east was Ataroth-addar as far as Upper Beth-horon, 6 and the boundary goes thence to the sea; on the north is Michmethath; then on the east the boundary turns round toward Taanath-shiloh, and passes along beyond it on the east to Jan-oah, 7 then it goes down from Jan-oah to Ataroth and to Naarah, and touches Jericho, ending at the Jordan. 8 From Tappuah the boundary goes westward to the brook Kanah, and ends at the sea. Such is the inheritance of the tribe of the Ephraimites by their families, 9 together with the towns which were set apart for the Ephraimites within the inheritance of the Manassites, all those towns with their villages. 10 However they did not drive out the Canaanites that dwelt in Gezer; so the Canaanites have dwelt in the midst of Ephraim to this day but have become slaves to do forced labor.

The tribe of Ephraim was located between Benjamin and Dan on the south and southwest, and West Manasseh on the north. The section heading Ephraim may be translated, "This is the territory that Joshua assigned to the tribe of Ephraim."

<u>16.5</u>   This was the territory of the Ephraimite families: their border ran from Ataroth Addar eastward to Upper Beth Horon,

A difficulty arises in the text of TEV, which speaks of the line running eastward from Ataroth Addar to Upper Beth Horon, whereas Upper Beth Horon was west of Ataroth Addar. It is better to follow RSV "the boundary...on the east" (similarly NEB "their eastern boundary").

In translation it will be helpful not only to follow the interpretation of RSV, but also to identify the line from Ataroth Addar to Upper Beth Horon as their southern border: "Their southern border ran from a point east of the city of Ataroth Addar to Upper Beth Horon."

16.6-9   and from there to the Mediterranean Sea. Michmethath
was on their north. East of there the border bent
toward Taanath Shiloh and went past it on the east
to Janoah. 7 Then it went down from Janoah to Ataroth
and Naarah, reaching Jericho and ending at the Jordan.
8 The border went west from Tappuah to the stream
Kanah and ended at the Mediterranean Sea. This was
the land given to the families of the tribe of
Ephraim as their possession, 9 along with some
towns and villages that were within the borders of
Manasseh, but given to the Ephraimites.

The northernmost city, Michmethath, is in 17.7 said to be east of
Shechem; and Taanath Shiloh is located by Bright east of Michmethath.
Janoah, Ataroth (not the same as Ataroth Addar), Naarah, and Jericho
describe the eastern boundary, from north to south.

Tappuah and the stream Kanah are to be found in biblical maps.
Kanah runs into the Mediterranean about 6 kilometers north of Jaffa.

Verse 9 specifies that some towns and villages, which are not
identified, and which were inside West Manasseh's territory, were alloted to Ephraim (see 17.8-9).

If verses 6-9 are combined, a more logical arrangement results:

6-9 and from there to the Mediterranean Sea. Their northern
border began at the city of Taanath Shiloh and went westward
to the city of Michmethath and then followed the stream Kanah
to the Mediterranean Sea. From Michmethath the eastern border
went south through the cities of Taanath Shiloh, Janoah,
Ataroth, Naarah, and finally to the Jordan River at a point
near Jericho. This territory, together with its cities and
villages, lay within the territory of the tribe of Manasseh.
But Joshua gave it to the tribe of Ephraim as its possession.

This represents a slightly different interpretation of the text than
that of TEV in verses 8b-9, but it does appear to represent more accurately the meaning of the Hebrew. To the families of the tribe of
Ephraim (verse 8) has been shortened to "to the tribe of Ephraim." But
"at the city of Tannath Shiloh" may need further identification
to indicate the movement of description from the Mediterranean Sea
of the previous sentence: "...Taanath Shiloh on the edge of the Jordan
Valley."

16.10   But they did not drive out the Canaanites who lived
in Gezer, so the Canaanites have lived among the
Ephraimites to this day, but they have been forced
to work as slaves.

Verse 10 takes notice of the fact that the original inhabitants
of Gezer were not driven out of their city, but that their descendants
were still living there as slaves at the time of the writing of the
account.

But they did not drive out the Canaanites who lived in Gezer may
be translated, "But the people of Ephraim did not drive the Canaanites
out of the city of Gezer," by which who lived in is clearly implicit.

So the Canaanites have lived among the Ephraimites to this day
may be translated, "That is why the Canaanites still live among the
people of Ephraim."

The Hebrew expression translated forced to work as slaves implies
the lowest form of compulsory labor, that is, complete enslavement.
The expression is used also at Genesis 49.15.

Chapter 17

West Manasseh

1 A part of the land west of the Jordan was assigned to some of the families descended from Joseph's older son Manasseh. Machir, the father of Gilead, was Manasseh's oldest son and a military hero, so Gilead and Bashan, east of the Jordan, were assigned to him. 2 Land west of the Jordan was assigned to the rest of the families of Manasseh: Abiezer, Helek, Asriel, Shechem, Hepher, and Shemida. These were male descendants of Manasseh son of Joseph, and they were heads of families. 3 Zelophehad, son of Hepher, son of Gilead, son of Machir, son of Manasseh, did not have any sons, but only daughters. Their names were Mahlah, Noah, Hoglah, Milcah, and Tirzah. 4 They went to Eleazar the priest and to Joshua son of Nun and to the leaders, and said, "The LORD commanded Moses to give us, as well as our male relatives, a part of the land to possess." So, as the LORD had commanded, they were given land along with their male relatives. 5 This is why Manasseh received ten shares in addition to Gilead and Bashan on the east side of the Jordan, 6 since his female descendants as well as his male descendants were assigned land. The land of Gilead was assigned to the rest of the descendants of Manasseh.

7 The territory of Manasseh reached from Asher to Michmethath,

1 Then allotment was made to the tribe of Manasseh, for he was the first-born of Joseph. To Machir the first-born of Manasseh, the father of Gilead, were alloted Gilead and Bashan, because he was a man of war. 2 And allotments were made to the rest of the tribe of Manasseh, by their families, Abi-ezer, Helek, Asri-el, Shechem, Hepher, and Shemida; these were the male descendants of Manasseh the son of Joseph, by their families.

3 Now Zelophehad the son of Hepher, son of Gilead, son of Machir, son of Manasseh, had no sons, but only daughters; and these are the names of his daughters: Mahlah, Noah, Hoglah, Milcah, and Tirzah. 4 They came befor Eleazar the priest and Joshua the son of Nun and the leaders, and said, "The LORD commanded Moses to give us an inheritance along with our brethren." So according to the commandment of the LORD he gave them an inheritance among the brethren of their father. 5 Thus there fell to Manasseh ten portions, besides the land of Gilead and Bashan, which is on the other side of the Jordan; 6 because the daughters of Manasseh received an inheritance along with his sons. The land of Gilead was allotted to the rest of the Manassites.

7 The territory of Manasseh reached from Asher to Mich-methath,

east of Shechem. The border then
went south to include the people
of Entappuah. 8 The land around
Tappuah belonged to Manasseh, but
the town of Tappuah, on the border,
belonged to the descendants of
Ephraim. 9 The border then went
down to the stream Kanah. The
cities south of the stream belonged to Ephraim, even though
they were in the territory of
Manasseh. The border of Manasseh
proceeded along the north side of
the stream and ended at the Mediterranean Sea. 10 Ephraim was to
the south, and Manasseh was to the
north, with the Mediterranean Sea
as their western border. Asher was
to the northwest, and Issachar to
the northeast. 11 Within the territories of Issachar and Asher,
Manasseh possessed Beth Shan and
Ibleam, along with their surrounding towns, as well as Dor (the one
on the coast),ʲ Endor, Taanach,
Megiddo, and their surrounding
towns. 12 The people of Manasseh,
however, were not able to drive
out the people living in those
cities, so the Canaanites continued
to live there. 13 Even when the
Israelites became stronger, they
did not drive out all the Canaanites, but they did force them to
work for them.

ʲ*Probable text* Dor (the one on the
  coast); *Hebrew unclear*.

which is east of Shechem; then the
boundary goes along southward to
the .inhabitants of En-tappuah.
8 The land of Tappuah belonged to
Manasseh, but the town of Tappuah
on the boundary of Manasseh belonged to the sons of Ephraim.
9 Then the boundary went down to
the brook Kanah. The cities here,
to the south of the brook, among
the cities of Manasseh, belong to
Ephraim. Then the boundary of
Manasseh goes on the north side
of the brook and ends at the sea;
10 the land to the south being
Ephraim's and that to the north
being Manasseh's, with the sea
forming its boundary; on the north
Asher is reached, and on the east
Issachar. 11 Also in Issachar and
in Asher Manasseh had Beth-shean
and its villages, and Ibleam and
its villages, and the inhabitants
of Dor and its villages, and the
inhabitants of En-dor and its
villages, and the inhabitants of
Taanach and its villages, and the
inhabitants of Megiddo and its
villages; the third is Naphath.ʲ
12 Yet the sons of Manasseh could
not take possession of those
cities; but the Canaanites persisted in dwelling in that land.
13 But when the people of Israel
grew strong, they put the Canaanites to forced labor, and did not
utterly drive them out.

ʲHeb obscure

The information in this section is considerably easier to understand, and the translations do not differ so widely from one another.
The section heading West Manasseh may be translated in the same manner
suggested for the section heading at 16.5.

17.1   A part of the land west of the Jordan was
        assigned to some of the families descended from
        Joseph's older son Manasseh. Machir, the father
        of Gilead, was Manasseh's oldest son and a mili-
        tary hero, so Gilead and Bashan, east of the
        Jordan, were assigned to him.

[221]

Verses 1-6 explain why some of the descendants of Manasseh were given land on the east side of the Jordan (East Manasseh) while the rest were given land on the west side of the Jordan (West Manasseh).

A part of the land west of the Jordan was assigned to is more literally "Then allotment was made to" (RSV). That is, the Hebrew text does not define as precisely as TEV the location of the land assigned to the tribe of Manasseh. The meaning may be either what is represented in TEV, or else the reference could be to the entire apportionment of land given the tribe of Manasseh. The alternative interpretation appears more likely, inasmuch as Gilead and Bashan, territories east of the Jordan, are mentioned in this verse. Following this interpretation one may translate "Joshua assigned the largest portion of land to the tribe of Manasseh, which was descended from Joseph's older son Manasseh." Or "...Manasseh. These were the descendants of Manasseh, who was Joseph's older son."

Manasseh's oldest son Machir was assigned Gilead and Bashan, east of the Jordan (see 13.29-31). This second sentence of TEV is difficult because it has two appositional modifiers (the father of Gilead and east of the Jordan), and the two subjects (Machir and Gilead and Bashan) are separated by the modifiers from their verbs (was and were assigned). If the sentence is broken into smaller units and restructured, it should become more readable:

Machir was Manasseh's oldest son, and he himself had a son named Gilead. Machir was a military hero, and Joshua had earlier assigned to him the territories of Gilead and Bashan, which were east of the Jordan River.

A military hero may be translated "a famous soldier" or "a brave soldier." It is quite possible also that and a military hero, so Gilead and Bashan...were assigned to him may mean, "He was a great soldier and had conquered the territories of Gilead and Bashan."

<u>17.2</u>   Land west of the Jordan was assigned to the rest
        of the families of Manasseh: Abiezer, Helek, Asriel,
        Shechem, Hepher, and Shemida. These were male de-
        scendants of Manasseh son of Joseph, and they were
        heads of families.

Territory west of the Jordan was assigned to other descendants of Machir.

This verse may be rendered so as to avoid the use of the passive, and at the same time to contrast the present distribution of land west of the Jordan with the past distribution of land east of the Jordan. For example,

Now Joshua assigned the land west of the Jordan River to the rest of the tribe of Manasseh. The male descendants of Manasseh were Abiezer, Helek, Asriel, Shechem, Hepher, and Shemida. All of these men were heads of families (or, clans), and each of their families (clans) received territory west of the Jordan River.

17.3   Zelophehad, son of Hepher, son of Gilead, son of
     Machir, son of Manasseh, did not have any sons,
     but only daughters. Their names were Mahlah, Noah,
     Hoglah, Milcah, and Tirzah.

    Zelophehad, the greatgrandson of Machir, had five daughters but
had no sons. The account of the daughters' encounter with Moses is given
in Numbers 27.1-7. So, in accordance with the Lord's decision, Joshua
commanded that they be given land on the west side of the Jordan, together with the other male descendants of Manasseh. The total on the
west side was ten shares: the five sisters received five shares, representing the one share belonging by rights to their grandfather Hepher
(Zelophehad appears to have been the only son of Hepher; see Num 26.33);
the other five shares went to the clans of Abiezer, Helek, Asriel,
Shechem, and Shemida (verse 2). (All six mentioned in verse 2 are said
in Num 26.29-32 to be descended from Gilead, son of Machir.)
    Zelophehad, son of Hepher, son of Gilead, son of Machir, son of
Manasseh may present problems to the reader. By the time the last name
in the list is mentioned, the reader is likely to have forgotten the
name of the person who did not have any sons. Since it is known from
verse 1 that Gilead is the grandson of Manasseh through his father
Machir, one may translate "Manasseh's grandson Gilead had a son named
Hepher. Hepher had a son named Zelophehad, who did not have any sons.
But he did have five daughters, and their names were...."

17.4   They went to Eleazar the priest and to Joshua son of
     Nun and to the leaders, and said, "The LORD commanded
     Moses to give us, as well as our male relatives, a
     part of the land to possess." So, as the LORD had com-
     manded, they were given land along with their male
     relatives.

    For the role of Eleazar, Joshua, and the leaders of the tribes in
dividing the land, see 14.1. Because of the overwhelming number of
names in this section, it would seem advisable to omit son of Nun as
an identifier of Joshua. This was the biblical writer's way of distin-
guishing this Joshua from other Joshuas—something totally unnecessary
for today's readers, for whom there is only one biblical Joshua.
    It is possible to place Moses' command in direct discourse:
The LORD told Moses, "Zelophehad does not have any sons. So
give each of his daughters a share of the land." Joshua
obeyed the LORD's command. He gave land to Zelophehad's
daughters at the same time that he gave land to their male
relatives.

17.5-6   This is why Manasseh received ten shares in addition
     to Gilead and Bashan on the east side of the Jordan,
     6 since his female descendants as well as his male
     descendants were assigned land. The land of Gilead
     was assigned to the rest of the descendants of Ma-
     nasseh.

The information ends (verse 6b) with the redundant note that the land of Gilead, on the east side of the Jordan was assigned to the rest of the descendants of Manasseh.

For the sake of avoiding unnecessary words, it is possible to place verses 5-6 together:

Joshua assigned land to Manasseh's male descendants and to his female descendants. That is why the tribe of Manasseh received ten shares of land on the west side of the Jordan River in addition to the territories of Gilead and Bashan on the east side.

17.7   The territory of Manasseh reached from Asher to Michmethath, east of Shechem. The border then went south to include the people of Entappuah.

Verse 7 gives the northwestern limit, the tribe of Asher; the southern limit was the city of Michmethath (see 16.6). At the end of the verse, TEV translates the Hebrew text with its later traditional vowels as the people of Entappuah (also RSV). By a change of vowels in the Hebrew text, HOTTP understands it to mean "to Jashib-en-Tappuah"; BJ, JB have "to Yashib at the spring of Tappuah"; NEB "Jashub by En-tappuah." Whatever the precise meaning of the Hebrew phrase, the place is on the border with Ephraim (see 16.8).

The translation of this verse may be managed so as to indicate that reference is to the northern and southern borders of West Manasseh:

In the northwest the territory of West Manasseh bordered on the territory of the tribe of Asher. The southern border ran from the city of Michmethath east of the city of Shechem and then south to the region where the people of Entappuah live.

To represent the alternative interpretation, one may translate "From the city of Shechem south to the city of Jashub (or, Jashib) near the spring of Tappuah."

17.8   The land around Tappuah belonged to Manasseh, but the town of Tappuah, on the border, belonged to the descendants of Ephraim.

Verse 8 points out that Tappuah itself was assigned to Ephraim, while the land around it belonged to West Manasseh.

In TEV the city of Tappuah is mentioned as though it were a place already known by the reader (old information). To avoid this, the verse may be translated,

On the border between the territory of Manasseh and the territory of Ephraim was the city of Tappuah. The city itself belonged to the tribe of Ephraim, but the land around it belonged to the tribe of Manasseh.

17.9-10   The border then went down to the stream Kanah. The
           cities south of the stream belonged to Ephraim, even
           though they were in the territory of Manasseh. The
           border of Manasseh proceeded along the north side
           of the stream and ended at the Mediterranean Sea.
           10 Ephraim was to the south, and Manasseh was to
           the north, with the Mediterranean Sea as their
           western border. Asher was to the northwest, and
           Issachar to the northeast.

Verses 9-10a further define the relation between the two neighboring tribes; verse 10b locates West Manasseh in relation to the tribe
of Asher and the tribe of Issachar.
     It may be more effective to translate verses 9-10 as a unit:
From there the southern border followed the stream Kanah westward to the Mediterranean Sea. The main territory of Manasseh
was located north of the Kanah stream, but south of it were
some cities that belonged to the tribe of Ephraim, even though
they were in the territory of Manasseh. In the northwest Manasseh bordered on the tribe of Asher, and in the northeast it
bordered on the tribe of Issachar.

17.11   Within the territories of Issachar and Asher, Manasseh
           possessed Beth Shan and Ibleam, along with their sur-
           rounding towns, as well as Dor (the one on the coast),^{j}
           Endor, Taanach, Megiddo, and their surrounding towns.

           ^{j}*Probable text* Dor (the one on the coast); *Hebrew*
           unclear.

     The Hebrew of this verse is difficult to understand; after listing
in succession the cities of Beth Shan, Ibleam, Dor, Endor, Taanach, and
Megiddo, the verse ends with two words which mean "three (is) Naphath";
by a change of vowels the Hebrew text can be made to read "the third
(is) Naphath" (RSV). TEV, following 12.33 (see also 11.2), takes the
words to be a later note: "the third city named (that is, Dor) is the
one on the coast" (similarly HOTTP).
     It is possible to combine and shorten along with their surrounding
towns...and their surrounding towns. Moreover, since Issachar and Asher
were mentioned by name at the end of the previous verse, they may be
referred to with pronouns: "Within these two territories there were
several cities together with their surrounding towns that belonged to
Manasseh: Beth Shan, Ibleam, Dor (the one on the coast), Endor, Taanach,
and Megiddo." Or, in order to avoid the use of a colon, a second sentence may be introduced: "...Manasseh. These cities were...."

17.12-13   The people of Manasseh, however, were not able to
           drive out the people living in those cities, so
           the Canaanites continued to live there. 13 Even
           when the Israelites became stronger, they did

[225]

not drive out all the Canaanites, but they did force
them to work for them.

Verses 12-13 indicate that the same thing happened in those cities
that happened elsewhere (see 15.63; 16.10): the Israelites were unable
to drive out the native Canaanites from those places and reduced them
to a slave class. In verse 12 it should be made clear that the people
living in those cities and the Canaanites are the same people. To ac-
complish this it may be necessary to translate "...were not able to
drive out the Canaanites who lived in those cities, so the Canaanites...."

In Hebrew the verb did not drive out (RSV "did not utterly drive
...out") is emphatic, and so the verse may be translated, "Later the
Israelites became stronger, and they forced the Canaanites to work for
them. But they still did not drive all the Canaanites out of the land."

TEV	17.14-18	RSV

Ephraim and West Manasseh
Request More Land

14 The descendants of Joseph
said to Joshua, "Why have you
given us only one part of the land
to possess as our own? There are
very many of us because the LORD
has blessed us."

15 Joshua answered, "If there
are so many of you and the hill
country of Ephraim is too small
for you, then go into the forests
and clear ground for yourselves in
the land of the Perizzites and the
Rephaim."

16 They replied, "The hill
country is not big enough for us,
but the Canaanites in the plains
have iron chariots, both those
who live in Beth Shan and its surrounding towns and those who live
in Jezreel Valley."

17 Joshua said to the tribes
of Ephraim and West Manasseh,
"There are indeed many of you,
and you are very powerful. You
shall have more than one share.
18 The hill country will be yours.
Even though it is a forest, you
will clear it and take possession
of it from one end to the other.
As for the Canaanites, you will

14 And the tribe of Joseph
spoke to Joshua, saying, "Why have
you given me but one lot and one
portion as an inheritance, although I am a numerous people,
since hitherto the LORD has
blessed me?" 15 And Joshua said
to them, "If you are a numerous
people, go up to the forest, and
there clear ground for yourselves
in the land of the Perizzites and
the Rephaim, since the hill country
of Ephraim is too narrow for you."
16 The tribe of Joseph said, "The
hill country is not enough for us;
yet all the Canaanites who dwell
in the plain have chariots of
iron, both those in Beth-shean
and its villages and those in the
Valley of Jezreel." 17 Then Joshua
said to the house of Joseph, to
Ephraim and Manasseh, "You are a
numerous people, and have great
power; you shall not have one lot
only, 18 but the hill country
shall be yours, for though it is
a forest, you shall clear it and
possess it to its farthest borders;
for you shall drive out the Canaanites, though they have chariots

```
drive them out, even though they          of iron, and though
do have iron chariots and are a           strong."
strong people."
```

A numerous and energetic people, the tribes of Ephraim and West
Manasseh request more land in which to expand, and Joshua gives them
the right to possess additional territory for themselves. Although the
section heading in TEV is given as a complete statement, it may be useful in other languages to indicate the person from whom the request
was made: "The tribes of Ephraim and West Manasseh ask Joshua to give
them more land."

In this section Joseph appears as a single tribe (verses 14,16,
17—RSV); in verse 17 it seems that a later scribe added an explanation:
"the house of Joseph (that is, Ephraim and Manasseh)." Perhaps there was
a period when Joseph was considered a single tribe. Commentators point
out that there are two narratives here: the first one is verses 14-15,
the second one verses 16-18 (see RSV).

17.14   The descendants of Joseph said to Joshua, "Why
               have you given us only one part of the land to possess
               as our own? There are very many of us because the LORD
               has blessed us."

As a comparison of TEV and RSV will indicate, there are at least
two major differences between TEV and the form of the Hebrew text: (1)
In Hebrew the first person pronoun is singular, while TEV uses the
plural form us; and (2) only one part of the land translates two synonymous expressions in Hebrew, "one lot and one portion" (RSV). The text
may be even further reduced by deleting to possess as our own, since
this will be automatically assumed in the request.

Two other adjustments to the text would be (1) to indicate by
some temporal marker the time at which the request was made, and (2) to
translate the question as a statement. The relationship in time to the
preceding events may be shown by using either "One day" or "When Joshua
was dividing out the land among the tribes." The rest of the verse may
then be translated, "...the descendants of Joseph came to Joshua. They
said, 'The LORD has blessed us with many people, but you have given us
only one part of the land.'" In order to make explicit the intention of
their remarks, one may add "We ought to have more land."

17.15   Joshua answered, "If there are so many of you
               and the hill country of Ephraim is too small for you,
               then go into the forests and clear ground for your-
               selves in the land of the Perizzites and the Rephaim."

It is not clear where the forests in the land of the Perizzites
and the Rephaim are to be located. The Rephaim are the race of giants
(see 12.4), usually located east of the Jordan, but also west of the
river (see 15.8 Rephaim Valley near Jerusalem).

Since the geographical references are unknown, it will be impossible to indicate in translation the directions in which Joshua told the people to move. It is possible, however, to divide his answer into more than one sentence:

"It may be true that the hill country of Ephraim is too small for the large number of people in your tribes. Then go into the forests which belong to the Perizzites and the Rephaim, and clear ground for yourselves there."

17.16   They replied, "The hill country is not big enough for us, but the Canaanites in the plains have iron chariots, both those who live in Beth Shan and its surrounding towns and those who live in Jezreel Valley."

Beth Shan is on the eastern border of West Manasseh, not far from the Jordan River; Jezreel Valley runs east and west, north of Beth Shan.

For people who lived in the plains, the iron plated chariots were formidable weapons (see chariots in 11.4). At this time the Israelites had nothing to compare with them, and so they had to stay in the hill country.

In place of They replied, it may be useful to translate "The descendants of Joseph replied." It should be made clear that the descendants of Joseph in verse 14, They of this verse, and the tribes of Ephraim and West Manasseh of verse 17 are the same people. This may be achieved by translating "The tribes of Ephraim and West Manasseh, which were the descendants of Joseph, replied...." Here again the lengthy sentence of TEV may be divided into smaller units:

"There is not enough room for us in the hill country, but the Canaanites live in the plains and the valleys. And all of them have war chariots made of iron. Those who live in the city of Beth Shan and its surrounding towns, and those who live in Jezreel Valley, all have war chariots."

17.17-18   Joshua said to the tribes of Ephraim and West Manasseh, "There are indeed many of you, and you are very powerful. You shall have more than one share. 18 The hill country will be yours. Even though it is a forest, you will clear it and take possession of it from one end to the other. As for the Canaanites, you will drive them out, even though they do have iron chariots and are a strong people."

Joshua encourages the people of Ephraim and West Manasseh, telling them that they will be able to defeat the Canaanites, despite their superior armament.

In Hebrew There are indeed many of you is joined to you are very powerful by the conjuction and, as TEV indicates. However, it is quite possible that the function of and in such a structure is to indicate that the clause which follows expresses either a cause or a result. In other words, Joshua says that the strength of the tribes of Ephraim and

West Manasseh lies in the large numer of people in their tribes. So one may translate "There are indeed many people in your tribes, and for that reason you are very powerful."

You shall have more than one share. 18 The hill country will be yours may be translated, "I will give you more than one share. 18 I will give you the hill country as well."

In order to avoid the Even though construction, the second sentence of verse 18 may be translated, "This land is a forest, but you will (be able to) take possession of it and clear it from one end to the other." In this proposed restructuring it should be noticed that the verbs clear and take possession of are given in reverse order so as to indicate logical sequence.

As for the Canaanites, you will drive them out is a difficult structure which may be simplified: "You will drive out all the Canaanites, even though they do have iron chariots and are a strong people." Or the two clauses may be reversed: "The Canaanites do indeed have iron chariots and they are a strong people. But you will (be able to) drive them out of their land."

Chapter 18

The Division of the Rest of the Land

1 After they had conquered the land, the entire community of Israel assembled at Shiloh and set up the Tent of the LORD's presence. 2 There were still seven tribes of the people of Israel who had not yet been assigned their share of the land. 3 So Joshua said to the people of Israel, "How long are you going to wait before you go in and take the land that the LORD, the God of your ancestors, has given you? 4 Let me have three men from each tribe. I will send them out over the whole country to map out the territory that they would like to have as their possession. Then they are to come back to me. 5 The land will be divided among them in seven parts; Judah will stay in its territory in the south, and Joseph in its territory in the north. 6 Write down a description of these seven divisions and bring it to me. Then I will draw lots^k to consult the LORD our God for you. 7 The Levites, however, will not receive a share of the land with the rest of you, because their share is to serve as the LORD's priests. And of course, the tribes of Gad, Reuben, and East Manasseh have already received their land east of the Jordan, which Moses, the LORD's servant gave to them."

8 The men went on their way to map out the land after Joshua had given them these instructions:

1 Then the whole congregation of the people of Israel assembled at Shiloh, and set up the tent of meeting there; the land lay subdued before them. 2 There remained among the people of Israel seven tribes whose inheritance had not yet been apportioned. 3 So Joshua said to the people of Israel, "How long will you be slack to go in and take possession of the land, which the LORD, the God of your fathers, has given you? 4 Provide three men from each tribe, and I will send them out that they may set out and go up and down the land, writing a description of it with a view to their inheritances, and then come to me. 5 They shall divide it into seven portions, Judah continuing in his territory on the south, and the house of Joseph in their territory on the north. 6 And you shall describe the land in seven divisions and bring the description here to me; and I will cast lots for you here before the LORD our God. 7 The Levites have no portion among you, for the priesthood of the LORD is their heritage; and Gad and Reuben and half the tribe of Manasseh have received their inheritance beyond the Jordan eastward, which Moses the servant of the LORD gave them."

8 So the men started on their way; and Joshua charged those who went to write the description of

"Go all over the land and map it out, and come back to me. And then here in Shiloh I will consult the LORD for you by drawing lots." 9 So the men went all over the land and set down in writing how they divided it into seven parts, making a list of the towns. Then they went back to Joshua in the camp at Shiloh. 10 Joshua drew lots to consult the LORD for them, and assigned each of the remaining tribes of Israel a certain part of the land.

the land, saying, "Go up and down and write a description of the land, and come again to me; and I will cast lots for you here before the LORD in Shiloh." 9 So the men went and passed up and down in the land and set down in a book a description of it by towns in seven divisions; then they came to Joshua in the camp at Shiloh, 10 and Joshua cast lots for them in Shiloh before the LORD; and there Joshua apportioned the land to the people of Israel, to each his portion.

*k*DRAW LOTS: *See 14.2.*

Chapters 18 and 19 describe the territories west of the Jordan assigned to the remaining seven tribes: Benjamin, Simeon, Zebulun, Issachar, Asher, Naphtali, and Dan.

The Israelites now make Shiloh their central sanctuary, the place where the Tent of the Lord's presence is located. The conclusion of the whole section (19.51) emphasizes the role of the priest Eleazar, Joshua, and the tribal leaders in the distribution of the land among the seven tribes.

The section heading, The Division of the Rest of the Land, may be translated as a sentence: "Joshua divides the rest of the land." Or "Joshua assigns land to the other tribes."

18.1-2   After they had conquered the land, the entire community of Israel assembled at Shiloh and set up the Tent of the LORD's presence. 2 There were still seven tribes of the people of Israel who had not yet been assigned their share of the land.

After they had conquered the land (RSV "the land lay subdued be-fore them") comes at the end of verse 1 in Hebrew. TEV places it first for purposes of chronological sequence. The pronoun they refers to the entire community of Israel in the second clause of TEV, but a more natural arrangement would be achieved by changing the order: "After the people of Israel had conquered the land, all of them...."

Shiloh, in the highlands of Ephraim, was 32 kilometers north of Jerusalem. The name has not recently been mentioned in the text, and translation in some languages may require "the city of Shiloh."

Even though it is true that the entire community of Israel assem-bled at Shiloh, it is obvious that not all of them set up the Tent of the LORD's presence. Therefore a new subject may need to be introduced: "...assembled at Shiloh. There the priests and their helpers set up the Tent of the LORD's presence."

This is the first time that the Tent of the LORD's presence has been mentioned in the book. But the Covenant Box implies also the

[231]

presence of the Tent (see 3.3; 8.33). For the description of the Tent, see Exodus 26. The Tent of the LORD's presence may be translated "The Tent where the LORD met the people of Israel" or "The Tent where the people of Israel worshiped the LORD."

The passive structure had not yet been assigned (verse 2) may be translated, "to whom Joshua had not yet assigned."

18.3   So Joshua said to the people of Israel, "How long
        are you going to wait before you go in and take
        the land that the LORD, the God of your ancestors,
        has given you?

Joshua's question implies that the Israelites have not shown the determination needed to claim the territory that the Lord had already given them.

The Hebrew verb translated to wait means "be inactive" (NEB "neglect"; AT "put off"; JB "How much more time will you waste before..."). Since Joshua's question does not expect an answer, it may be represented as a statement: "Do not wait any longer before you go in...."

18.4-6   Let me have three men from each tribe. I will send
          them out over the whole country to map out the
          territory that they would like to have as their
          possession. Then they are to come back to me. 5 The
          land will be divided among them in seven parts; Judah
          will stay in its territory in the south, and Joseph
          in its territory in the north. 6 Write down a descrip-
          tion of these seven divisions and bring it to me. Then
          I will draw lots^k to consult the LORD our God for you.

^{k}DRAW LOTS: *See 14.2.*

Joshua proposes that three men from each tribe go out and survey the land, determine the boundaries for each of the seven tribes, and return with their findings to Joshua, who will then draw lots to determine the Lord's will in the matter (see 14.2). The men probably are only of the seven tribes involved, and not of all nine and one-half tribes west of the Jordan.

These three verses form a sense unit and so may be placed together and arranged in logical order. TEV has already deleted some of the redundancy (compare RSV), but it is possible to omit even more. A pattern for translating may be:
      The tribe of Judah already has its territory in the south,
      and the descendants of Joseph have their territory in the
      north. So let each of the seven remaining tribes select
      three men and send them to me. I will send them out to
      write down a description of the entire territory that they
      would like to receive. They will divide the territory into
      seven parts and bring the information to me. Then I will
      draw lots to determine which section the LORD wants each
      tribe to receive.

18.7   The Levites, however, will not receive a share of
        the land with the rest of you, because their share
        is to serve as the LORD's priests. And of course,
        the tribes of Gad, Reuben, and East Manasseh have
        already received their land east of the Jordan,
        which Moses, the LORD's servant, gave to them."

Verse 7 repeats information that is given in 13.14,33, that the
Levites are not to receive any land (except for the forty-eight cities
distributed throughout the territories of the other tribes; 21.1-42);
their share is to serve as the LORD's priests. And the two and one-half
tribes east of the Jordan have already been assigned their territory.
    Will not receive may be translated with Joshua as subject: "How-
ever, I will not assign a share of the land to the Levites...." Similarly, have already received may be translated, "Moses, the LORD's
servant, has already assigned land to Gad, Reuben, and East Manasseh."
    Because their share is to serve as the LORD's priests translates
the Hebrew clause "for the priesthood of the LORD is their heritage"
(RSV). This clause equates the noun phrases "the priesthood of the
LORD" and "their heritage." The use of these noun phrases makes a con-
venient balance (as in TEV's share of the land and their share), but
many languages will prefer to use a verb construction similar to TEV's
to serve as....

18.8-9   The men went on their way to map out the land
        after Joshua had given them these instructions: "Go
        all over the land and map it out, and come back to
        me. And then here in Shiloh I will consult the LORD
        for you by drawing lots." 9 So the men went all over
        the land and set down in writing how they divided it
        into seven parts, making a list of the towns. Then
        they went back to Joshua in the camp at Shiloh.

The twenty-one representatives of the seven tribes carry out
Joshua's instructions, which are repeated (verse 8b).
    In verses 8-9 there is a great deal of repetition (see RSV), some
of which is carried over into TEV. For example, The men went on their
way to map out the land (8a) is essentially repeated in the first
sentence of verse 9 (So the men went all over the land...a list of
the towns). If these two verses are rendered as a unit, considerable
space may be saved. For example,
        Joshua told the men who had been selected, "Go through
        all the land and write down its description. Then bring the
        description back here to me, so that I can ask the LORD how
        to divide the land among your tribes." The men went through
        all the land and described it in seven sections. They also
        made a list of the towns in each section. Then they returned
        to Joshua in Shiloh.

18.10   Joshua drew lots to consult the LORD for them,
and assigned each of the remaining tribes of
Israel a certain part of the land.

Their mission completed, the representatives from the seven tribes
return to Joshua at Shiloh, and he assigns each of the seven tribes a
part of the territory, as determined by the drawing of lots. Here Joshua
acts alone; at the end of the process (19.51) the writer includes the
priest Eleazar and the tribal leaders in the action.

To consult the LORD for them may be translated "to find out how
the LORD wanted the land divided" or "to find out from the LORD how to
divide the land."

And assigned each of the remaining tribes of Israel a certain part
of the land may be translated as a separate sentence: "Then he assigned
a certain part of the land to each of the remaining tribes of Israel."

TEV   18.11-28   RSV

The Territory Assigned to
    Benjamin

11 The territory belonging to the families of the tribe of Benjamin was the first to be assigned. Their land lay between the tribes of Judah and Joseph. 12 On the north their border began at the Jordan and then went up the slope north of Jericho and westward through the hill country as far as the desert of Bethaven. 13 The border then went to the slope on the south side of Luz (also called Bethel), then down to Ataroth Addar, on the mountain south of Lower Beth Horon. 14 The border then went in another direction, turning south from the western side of this mountain and going to Kiriath Baal (or Kiriath Jearim), which belongs to the tribe of Judah. This was the western border. 15 The southern border started on the edge of Kiriath Jearim and went*l* to the Springs of Nephtoah. 16 It then went down to the foot of the mountain that overlooks Hinnom Valley, at the north end of Rephaim Valley. It then went south through Hinnom Valley, south of the Jebusite

11 The lot of the tribe of Benjamin according to its families came up, and the territory allotted to it fell between the tribe of Judah and the tribe of Joseph. 12 On the north side their boundary began at the Jordan; then the boundary goes up to the shoulder north of Jericho, then up through the hill country westward; and it ends at the wilderness of Bethaven. 13 From there the boundary passes along southward in the direction of Luz, to the shoulder of Luz (the same is Bethel), then the boundary goes down to Atarothaddar, upon the mountain that lies south of Lower Beth-horon. 14 Then the boundary goes in another direction, turning on the western side southward from the mountain that lies to the south, opposite Beth-horon, and it ends at Kiriath-baal (that is, Kiriath-jearim), a city belonging to the tribe of Judah. This forms the western side. 15 And the southern side begins at the outskirts of Kiriath-jearim; and the boundary goes from there to Ephron,*k* to the

[234]

ridge, toward Enrogel. 17 It then turned north to Enshemesh and then on to Geliloth, opposite Adummim Pass. The border then went down to the Stone of Bohan (Bohan was a son of Reuben) 18 and passed north of the ridge overlooking the Jordan Valley. It then went down into the valley, 19 passing north of the ridge of Beth Hoglah, and ended at the northern inlet on the Dead Sea, where the Jordan River empties into it. This was the southern border. 20 The Jordan was the eastern border. These were the borders of the land which the families of the tribe of Benjamin received as their possession.

21 The cities belonging to the families of the tribe of Benjamin were Jericho, Beth Hoglah, Emek Keziz, 22 Beth Arabah, Zemaraim, Bethel, 23 Avvim, Parah, Ophrah, 24 Chepharammoni, Ophni, and Geba: twelve cities, along with the towns around them. 25 There were also Gibeon, Ramah, Beeroth, 26 Mizpah, Chephirah, Mozah, 27 Rekem, Irpeel, Taralah, 28 Zela, Haeleph, Jebus (or Jerusalem), Gibeah, and Kiriath Jearim: fourteen cities, along with the towns around them. This is the land which the families of the tribe of Benjamin received as their possession.

*l*Probable text and went; Hebrew and went westward.

spring of the Waters of Nephtoah; 16 then the boundary goes down to the border of the mountain that overlooks the valley of the son of Hinnom, which is at the north end of the valley of Rephaim; and it then goes down the valley of Hinnom, south of the shoulder of the Jebusites, and downward to En-rogel; 17 then it bends in a northerly direction going on to En-shemesh, and thence goes to Geliloth, which is opposite the ascent of Adummim; then it goes down to the stone of Bohan the son of Reuben; 18 and passing on to the north of the shoulder of Beth-arabah*l* it goes down to the Arabah; 19 then the boundary passes on to the north of the shoulder of Beth-hoglah; and the boundary ends at the northern bay of the Salt Sea, at the south end of the Jordan; this is the southern border. 20 The Jordan forms its boundary on the eastern side. This is the inheritance of the tribe of Benjamin, according to its families, boundary by boundary round about.

21 Now the cities of the tribe of Benjamin according to their families were Jericho, Beth-hoglah, Emek-keziz, 22 Beth-arabah, Zemaraim, Bethel, 23 Avvim, Parah, Ophrah, 24 Chepharammoni, Ophni, Geba—twelve cities with their villages: 25 Gibeon, Ramah, Beeroth, 26 Mizpeh, Chephirah, Mozah, 27 Rekem, Irpeel, Taralah, 28 Zela, Ha-eleph, Jebus*m* (that is, Jerusalem), Gibe-ah*n* and Kiriath-jearim*o*—fourteen cities with their villages. This is the inheritance of the tribe of Benjamin according to its families.

*k*Cn See 15.9. Heb *westward*

*l*Gk: Heb *to the shoulder over against the Arabah*

*m*Gk Syr Vg: Heb *the Jebusite*

[235]

*n*Heb *Gibeath*

*o*Gk: Heb *Kiriath*

After describing the boundaries of the territory (verses 11-20), the text names the twenty-six cities in the territory (verses 21-28).
The section heading, The Territory Assigned to Benjamin, may be translated in the same way as The Territory Assigned to Reuben at 13.15. See also the section headings at 13.24,29; 15.1; 16.1.

18.11   The territory belonging to the families of the tribe of Benjamin was the first to be assigned. Their land lay between the tribes of Judah and Joseph.

The first to be assigned translates "The lot...came up" (RSV) of the Hebrew text. It is not necessary, of course, to maintain in translation the form by which the decision was reached, since the important factor is that the division of the land was accomplished according to the revealed will of God.
The territory belonging to the families of the tribe of Benjamin could suggest that this land was either already owned or previously owned by the tribe of Benjamin. To avoid this misunderstanding, the verse may be translated, "The first tribe that received territory from Joshua was the tribe of Benjamin. He assigned them land which lay between the tribes of Judah and Joseph."
Benjamin's territory was between the territory of Judah (on the south) and the territory of Ephraim (on the north). The "tribe of Joseph" is, of course, the two tribes of Ephraim and West Manasseh (see RSV 17.14,17). In order to indicate the geographical relationships and at the same time to define the meaning of the tribe of Joseph, the second sentence of this verse may be translated, "He assigned them land which lay between the tribe of Judah on the south and the tribes of Ephraim and West Manasseh on the north." It may also be translated, "...between the tribe of Judah on the south and the descendants of Joseph on the north."

18.12-13   On the north their border began at the Jordan and then went up the slope north of Jericho and westward through the hill country as far as the desert of Bethaven. 13 The border then went to the slope on the south side of Luz (also called Bethel), then down to Ataroth Addar, on the mountain south of Lower Beth Horon.

Verses 12-14 trace the northern boundary (where it touched the territory of Ephraim) from the Jordan River westward and then southward to Kiriath Jearim. For the places listed in verse 12, see 16.1-2; notice that in verse 13, unlike in 16.2, Luz and Bethel are different names for the same city; and in verse 12 Bethaven ("house of wickedness") may be a way of referring to Bethel itself (see comments and footnote on 7.2).

On the north their border began at the Jordan does indicate that
the northern border of Benjamin's territory is being described. Then
later in the verse the use of westward indicates that the description
is from east to the west. It is possible to be even more specific:
"Their northern border began in the east at the Jordan River...and
westward...."

To the reader who hears the text read, the desert of Bethaven may
sound like a proper name; to avoid this ambiguity it is better to translate "the desert near the city of Bethaven."

In verse 13 Luz, Ataroth Addar, and Lower Beth Horon may need to
be identified as cities.

18.14   The border then went in another direction, turning
         south from the western side of this mountain and
         going to Kiriath Baal (or Kiriath Jearim), which
         belongs to the tribe of Judah. This was the western
         border.

The border then went in another direction...Kiriath Jearim may be
translated, "The border then turned south from the western side of this
mountain and went to the city of Kiriath Baal, which is also called
Kiriath Jearim." The last clause of this sentence may then be translated as an independant sentence: "This city belongs to the tribe of
Judah."

18.15   The southern border started on the edge of Kiriath
         Jearim and went^l to the Springs of Nephtoah.

    ^lProbable text and went; Hebrew and went westward.

Verses 15-19 trace the southern boundary from Kiriath Jearim
eastward to the Dead Sea. The southern border was the northern border
of Judah (see 15.5b-10 for much of the same data describing the land).

After Kiriath Jearim, the Masoretic text has "and the boundary
westward and it went to the springs of the waters of Nephtoah." The
direction "westward" is wrong (see 15.9), and there are various ways
in which the matter has been handled. TEV, NEB, NAB omit; Soggin, BJ,
JB transliterate the Septuagint "towards Gasin"; RSV gets its solution
from 15.9 "to Ephron." HOTTP recommends a solution here which is similar to what it arrives at in 15.9, where instead of "to the cities of
Mount Ephron" it proposes "towards Iyyim (or, the ruins) of Mount
Ephron"; here it recommends "towards Iyyim (or, the ruins)."

Whatever alternative is followed as a solution to the textual
problem, a footnote will be required (as in TEV). Moreover, one may
wish to specify in the text the geographical movement: "and went eastward to...."

18.16   It then went down to the foot of the mountain that
         overlooks Hinnom Valley, at the north end of Rephaim
         Valley. It then went south through Hinnom Valley,
         south of the Jebusite ridge, toward Enrogel.

The Jebusite ridge (RSV "the shoulder of the Jebusites") refers to
the ridge south of Jerusalem. Enrogel is a spring of water at the
southeast corner of the city, just below Hinnom Valley.
    Since the name Jebusite is lesser known than Jerusalem, it may be
better in translation to use the more familiar name. Moreover, the two
references to Hinnom Valley may be drawn together so that a less cumbersome translation results:
    It then ran down to the foot of the mountain on the north side
    of Rephaim Valley, where Hinnom Valley begins. From there it
    went south through Hinnom Valley to the ridge south of Jeru-
    salem and then to Enrogel Spring.

18.17   It then turned north to Enshemesh and then on to
         Geliloth, opposite Adummim Pass. The border then
         went down to the Stone of Bohan (Bohan was a son
         of Reuben)

Enshemesh and Adummim Pass are mentioned at 15.7. Geliloth, mentioned only here in the Old Testament, is perhaps to be identified
with Gilgal. The Stone of Bohan is mentioned at 15.6.

18.18   and passed north of the ridge overlooking the
         Jordan Valley. It then went down into the val-
         ley,

The Hebrew of this verse is "and it passes to the ridge opposite
the Arabah to the north and goes down to the Arabah" (see RSV footnote).
TEV, NEB, TOB translate the Masoretic text, as does HOTTP; RSV follows
the Septuagint; BJ, JB, take the Hebrew noun translated ridge (RSV
"shoulder") as a place name, "Cheteph."

18.19   passing north of the ridge of Beth Hoglah, and
         ended at the northern inlet on the Dead Sea,
         where the Jordan River empties into it. This
         was the southern border.

Beth Hoglah was first mentioned at 15.6. In the translation of
this verse, it may be necessary to begin a new sentence after Beth
Hoglah: "The southern border then ended at the northern inlet on the
Dead Sea, where the Jordan River empties into it." Or "The southern
border then ended where the Jordan River empties into the Dead Sea."

18.20   The Jordan was the eastern border. These were the
         borders of the land which the families of the tribe
         of Benjamin received as their possession.

     The description of the limits of the territory ends with the east-
ern border, the Jordan River. In place of the families of the tribe of
Benjamin, one may translate "the tribe of Benjamin."

18.21-28   The cities belonging to the families of the tribe
         of Benjamin were Jericho, Beth Hoglah, Emek Keziz,
         22 Beth Arabah, Zemaraim, Bethel, 23 Avvim, Parah,
         Ophrah, 24 Chepharammoni, Ophni, and Geba: twelve
         cities, along with the towns around them. 25 There
         were also Gibeon, Ramah, Beeroth, 26 Mizpah, Che-
         phirah, Mozah, 27 Rekem, Irpeel, Taralah, 28 Zela,
         Haeleph, Jebus (or Jerusalem), Gibeah, and Kiriath
         Jearim: fourteen cities, along with the towns around
         them. This is the land which the families of the
         tribe of Benjamin received as their possession.

     Two lists of cities are given, presumably in two districts; the
first one names twelve cities in all, along with the towns around them
(verses 21-24); the second one, fourteen cities and the surrounding
towns (verses 25-28).
     It is possible to translate verses 21-24 as a unit and to do the
same with verses 25-28:
         21-24 There were twelve cities, along with the towns
     around them, which belonged to the tribe of Benjamin. These
     cities were: Jericho...and Geba.
         25-28 There were another fourteen cities, along with
     the towns around them, which also belonged to the tribe of
     Benjamin. These cities were: Gibeon...and Kiriath Jearim.
     This is the land which Joshua assigned to the tribes of
     Benjamin.

Chapter 19

The Territory Assigned to Simeon

1 The second assignment made was for the families of the tribe of Simeon. Its territory extended into the land assigned to the tribe of Judah. 2 It included Beersheba, Sheba, Moladah, 3 Hazar Shual, Balah, Ezem, 4 Eltolad, Bethul, Hormah, 5 Ziklag, Beth Marcaboth, Hazar Susah, 6 Beth Lebaoth, and Sharuhen: thirteen cities, along with the towns around them.

7 There were also Ain, Rimmon, Ether, and Ashan: four cities, along with the towns around them. 8 This included all the towns around these cities as far as Baalath Beer (or Ramah), in the south. This was the land which the families of the tribe of Simeon received as their possession. 9 Since Judah's assignment was larger than was needed, part of its territory was given to the tribe of Simeon.

1 The second lot came out for Simeon, for the tribe of Simeon, according to its families; and its inheritance was in the midst of the inheritance of the tribe of Judah. 2 And it had for its inheritance Beer-sheba, Sheba, Moladah, 3 Hazar-shual, Balah, Ezem, 4 Eltolad, Bethul, Hormah, 5 Ziklag, Beth-marcaboth, Hazar-susah, 6 Beth-lebaoth, and Sharu-hen—thirteen cities with their villages; 7 En-rimmon, Ether, and Ashan—four cities with their villages; 8 together with all the villages round about these cities as far as Baalath-beer, Ramah of the Negeb. This was the inheritance of the tribe of Simeon according to its families. 9 The inheritance of the tribe of Simeon formed part of the territory of Judah; because the portion of the tribe of Judah was too large for them, the tribe of Simeon obtained an inheritance in the midst of their inheritance.

The territory of the tribe of Simeon was the one farthest south, below the territory of Judah. Its boundaries are not given, only the vague statement that part of its territory extended into the territory of Judah (verses 1,9).

The section heading, <u>The Territory Assigned to Simeon</u>, may be translated in the same way as <u>The Territory Assigned to Reuben</u> (13.15).

<u>19.1-6</u>   The second assignment made was for the families of the tribe of Simeon. Its territory extended into the land assigned to the tribe of Judah. 2 It included

> Beersheba, Sheba, Moladah, 3 Hazar Shual, Balah,
> Ezem, 4 Eltolad, Bethul, Hormah, 5 Ziklag, Beth
> Marcaboth, Hazar Susah, 6 Beth Lebaoth, and
> Sharuhen: thirteen cities, along with the towns
> around them.

For the translation of the first sentence of this verse, see the proposed restructuring at 18.11. One may also translate "The second lot fell to the tribe of Simeon."

Its territory extended into the land assigned to the tribe of Judah is more literally "And its inheritance was in the midst of the inheritance of the tribe of Judah." This appears to be a more accurate representation of the text, especially in light of verse 9, which states that the tribe of Simeon was given a part of the territory within the land of Judah, because Judah had been given more land than it needed. Accordingly, one may translate "Its territory lay within the territory of the tribe of Judah."

In verse 2 the second name in Hebrew is Sheba. This, however, seems like an accidental repetition of the second part of the name of the preceding city, Beersheba, and makes a total of fourteen place-names, whereas verse 6 gives the total as thirteen. Consequently NEB (with a footnote that refers to the lack of this name in 1 Chr 4.18) omits Sheba; BJ, JB, NAB and HOTTP revise the Hebrew to "Shema" (see 15.26); TEV, RSV, TOB follow the Masoretic text. It seems best to follow the Masoretic text here.

19.7   There were also Ain, Rimmon, Ether, and Ashan:
        four cities, along with the towns around them.

In verse 7 TEV (also NEB, BJ, JB, TOB) has Ain and Rimmon, thus making a total of four cities; RSV, NAB take the Hebrew to mean only one place, "Enrimmon." HOTTP (as in a similar case in 15.32) also prefers the one name, "En-rimmon"; in additon, with one manuscript of the Septuagint (and the Hebrew text in 1 Chr 4.32), the Committee adds "Trachan," thus making a total of four.[53]

The verse may be restructured as follows: "The tribe of Simeon also received four other cities, along with the towns around them. These cities were Ain, Rimmon, Ether, and Ashan."

19.8-9   This included all the towns around these cities as
        far as Baalath Beer (or Ramah), in the south. This
        was the land which the families of the tribe of
        Simeon received as their possession. 9 Since Judah's
        assignment was larger than was needed, part of its
        territory was given to the tribe of Simeon.

Verse 8 may be somewhat abbreviated: "This territory included all the cities and towns as far south as the city of Baalath Beer, which is also known as Ramah." The second sentence of TEV is repetitious and need not be included.

Verse 9 may be translated, "Joshua had given the tribe of Judah more territory than they needed, so he gave part of its territory to the tribe of Simeon."

TEV	19.10-16	RSV

The Territory Assigned to Zebulun

10 The third assignment made was for the families of the tribe of Zebulun. The land which they received reached as far as Sarid. 11 From there the border went west to Mareal, touching Dabbesheth and the stream east of Jokneam. 12 On the other side of Sarid it went east to the border of Chisloth Tabor, then to Daberath and up to Japhia. 13 It continued east from there to Gath Hepher and Ethkazin, turning in the direction of Neah on the way to Rimmon. 14 On the north the border turned toward Hannathon, ending at Iphtahel Valley. 15 It included Kattath, Nahalal, Shimron, Idalah, and Bethlehem; twelve cities, along with the towns around them. 16 These cities and their towns were in the land which the families of the tribe of Zebulun received as their possession.

10 The third lot came up for the tribe of Zebulun, according to its families. And the territory of its inheritance reached as far as Sarid; 11 then its boundary goes up westward, and on to Mareal, and touches Dabbesheth, then the brook which is east of Jokne-am; 12 from Sarid it goes in the other direction eastward toward the sunrise to the boundary of Chisloth-tabor; thence it goes to Daberath, then up to Japhia; 13 from there it passes along on the east toward the sunrise to Gath-hepher, to Eth-kazin, and going on to Rimmon it bends toward Neah; 14 then on the north the boundary turns about to Hannathon, and it ends at the valley of Iphtahel; 15 and Kattath, Nahalal, Shimron, Idalah, and Bethlehem—twelve cities with their villages. 16 This is the inheritance of the tribe of Zebulun, according to its families—these cities with their villages.

Zebulun's territory lay north of West Manasseh and had common borders with Asher on the west, Naphtali on the east, and Issachar on the southeast.

It should be noticed that the border lists for the Galilean tribes (Zebulun, Issachar, Naphtali, and Asher) are much less precise than for the more important tribes in the south.

For a proposed restructuring of the section heading, see comments at 13.15.

19.10   The third assignment made was for the families of the tribe of Zebulun. The land which they received reached as far as Sarid.

Verses 10b-12 give the southern border, verse 13 the eastern border, and verse 14 the northern border. Bright says the area included "is roughly the western half of the southern Galilean hills."

For suggestions regarding the translation of 10a, see comments at 18.11. And 10b may be translated so as to indicate the geographical direction: "Joshua assigned them the land which reached as far southeast as the city of Sarid."

19.11-14   From there the border went west to Mareal, touching Dabbesheth and the stream east of Jokneam. 12 On the other side of Sarid it went east to the border of Chisloth Tabor, then to Daberath and up to Japhia. 13 It continued east from there to Gath Hepher and Ethkazin, turning in the direction of Neah on the way to Rimmon. 14 On the north the border turned toward Hannathon, ending at Iphtahel Valley.

In the translation of verses 11-14, TEV has fairly well marked out the directions of movement; however, attention should be given to the need for marking each of the place-names as a city.

In addition, the three participial phrases (touching, verse 11; turning, verse 13; ending, verse 14) as well as then to Daberath and up to Japhia (verse 12) may need drastic restructuring. That is, the participial phrases presuppose a subject ("the border"), while the "then" clause of verse 12 presupposes both subject ("the border") and verb ("went").

Finally, some languages may find it appropriate to divide the text into sentences at places other than where this is done in TEV.

In verse 13 Gath Hepher (5 kilometers northeast of Nazareth) is identified as the birthplace of the prophet Jonah (2 Kgs 14.25).

19.15-16   It included Kattath, Nahalal, Shimron, Idalah, and Bethlehem: twelve cities, along with the towns around them. 16 These cities and their towns were in the land which the families of the tribe of Zebulun received as their possession.

In verse 15 only five of the twelve cities are named; it should be noticed that Bethlehem here is not the more famous one south of Jerusalem; this Bethlehem was a town about 12 kilometers west of Nazareth.[54]

In verse 15, instead of Shimron of the Masoretic text, HOTTP prefers "Shimeon" (as in 11.1; 12.20); instead of Idalah, HOTTP (with some Hebrew manuscripts, the Syriac Old Testament, and the Latin Vulgate) prefers "Iralah" (also JB), or, as it spells it, "Jiralah."

Verse 15 may be translated, "It included twelve cities, along with the towns around them. Some of these twelve cities were Kattath... and Bethlehem."

Verse 16 may be translated similarly to 19.8b.

The Territory Assigned to Issachar

TEV	RSV
17 The fourth assignment made was for the families of the tribe of Issachar. 18 Its area included Jezreel, Chesulloth, Shunem, 19 Hapharaim, Shion, Anaharath, 20 Rabbith, Kishion, Ebez, 21 Remeth, Engannin, Enhaddah, and Beth-pazzez. 22 The border also touched Tabor, Shahazumah, and Beth She-mesh, ending at the Jordan. It in-cluded sixteen cities along with the towns around them. 23 These cities and their towns were in the land which the families of the tribe of Issachar received as their possession.	17 The fourth lot came out for Issachar, for the tribe of Issa-char, according to its families. 18 Its territory included Jezreel, Chesulloth, Shunem, 19 Haphara-im, Shion, Anaharath, 20 Rabbith, Kishion, Ebez, 21 Remeth, En-gan-nim, En-haddah, Beth-pazzez; 22 the boundary also touches Ta-bor, Shahazumah, and Beth-shemesh, and its boundary ends at the Jor-dan—sixteen cities with their villages. 23 This is the inherit-ance of the tribe of Issachar, according to its families—the cities with their villages.

Issachar had West Manasseh to the south and west; Zebulun to the northwest; Naphtali to the north; and the Jordan River to the east.

For the translation of the section heading, The Territory Assigned to Issachar, see comments at 13.15.

19.17   The fourth assignment made was for the families of the tribe of Issachar.

For the translation of this verse, see comments at 18.11.

19.18-23   Its area included Jezreel, Chesulloth, Shunem, 19 Hapharaim, Shion, Anaharath, 20 Rabbith, Kishion, Ebez, 21 Remeth, Engannim, Enhaddah, and Bethpazzez. 22 The border also touched Tabor, Shahazumah, and Beth Shemesh, ending at the Jordan. It included six-teen cities along with the towns around them. 23 These cities and their towns were in the land which the families of the tribe of Issachar received as their possession.

Rabbith (so TEV and RSV) translates the Masoretic text; HOTTP pre-fers the spelling "Daberath" (identifying it with the city of this name in 19.12; 21.28); also Soggin and BJ.

In the Masoretic text fifteen cities are named, but the total given in verse 22 is sixteen; Soggin adds in verse 19 (after Shion) "Reeroth," in accordance with one manuscript of the Septuagint. It seems best to stay with the Masoretic text here.

Verses 18-22, as they stand in TEV, present several problems. First, it is important to tell a city from a mountain. Tabor is a mountain; the other places, except for the Jordan, are cities. Second, the mention of sixteen cities in verse 22b may be taken as a reference to cities other than those listed above. Third, because of a fairly literal rendering of verses 22b-23, there is some unnecessary repetition. This problem of overlap may be resolved either by translating verses 18-23 as a unit, or by translating verses 18-21 in sequence, and then placing verses 22-23 together. These two alternatives may be represented as follows:

(1) Their territory included sixteen cities, along with the towns around them. These cities were Jezreel...Shahazumah, and Beth Shemesh. In the north their border ran east from Mount Tabor to the Jordan River. Joshua gave this entire region, including its cities and towns, to the tribe of Issachar.

Or it is possible to follow this same restructuring and list separately the towns of Shahazumah and Beth Shemesh:

Their territory included sixteen cities, along with the towns around them. Some of these cities were Jezreel... and Bethpazzez. In the north their border ran east from Mount Tabor to the Jordan River, including the cities of Shahazumah and Beth Shemesh....

(2) Their territory included the cities of Jezreel... 19 ... 20 ... 21 ... and Bethpazzez. 22-23 In the north their border ran east from Mount Tabor to the Jordan River, and it took in the cities of Shahazumah and Beth Shemesh. All this territory, including these sixteen cities and their towns, belonged to the tribe of Issachar.

TEV	19.24-31	RSV

The Territory Assigned to Asher

24 The fifth assignment made was for the families of the tribe of Asher. 25 Its area included Helkath, Hali, Beten, Achshaph. 26 Allam Melech, Amad, and Mishal. On the west it touched Carmel and Shihor Libnath. 27 As it turned east, the border went to Beth-dagon, touching Zebulun and Iphtahel Valley on the way north to Bethemek and Neiel. It continued north to Cabul, 28 Ebron, Rehob, Hammon, and Kanah, as far as Sidon. 29 The border then turned to Ramah, reaching the

24 The fifth lot came out for the tribe of Asher according to its families. 25 Its territory included Helkath, Hali, Beten, Achshaph, 26 Allammelech, Amad, and Mishal; on the west it touches Carmel and Shihor-libnath, 27 then it turns eastward, it goes to Beth-dagon, and touches Zebulun and the valley of Iphtahel northward to Beth-emek and Neiel; then it continues in the north to Cabul, 28 Ebron, Rehob, Hammon, Kanah, as far as Sidon the Great; 29 then the boundary turns to

fortified city of Tyre; then it turned to Hosah and ended at the Mediterranean Sea. It included Mahalab, Achzib, 30 Ummah, Aphek, and Rehob: twenty-two cities, along with the towns around them. 31 These cities and their towns were in the land which the families of the tribe of Asher received as their possession.

Ramah, reaching to the fortified city of Tyre; then the boundary turns to Hosah, and it ends at the sea; Mahalab,p Achzib, 30 Ummah, Aphek and Rehob—twenty-two cities with their villages. 31 This is the inheritance of the tribe of Asher according to its families—these cities with their villages.

pCn Compare Gk: Heb *Mehebel*

The territory of Asher was along the Mediterranean coast, north of Mount Carmel. The information given in the text is "a bewildering combination of incomplete boundary points and groups of settlements" (Gray).

For a translation of this section heading, The Territory Assigned to Asher, see comments at 13.15.

19.24   The fifth assignment made was for the families of the tribe of Asher.

For the translation of this verse, see comments at 18.11.

19.25-31   Its area included Helkath, Hali, Beten, Achshaph, 26 Allam Melech, Amad, and Mishal. On the west it touched Carmel and Shihor Libnath. 27 As it turned east, the border went to Bethdagon, touching Zebulun and Iphtahel Valley on the way north to Bethemek and Neiel. It continued north to Cabul, 28 Ebron, Rehob, Hammon, and Kanah, as far as Sidon. 29 The border then turned to Ramah, reaching the fortified city of Tyre; then it turned to Hosah and ended at the Mediterranean Sea. It included Mahalab, Achzib, 30 Ummah, Aphek, and Rehob: twenty-two cities, along with the towns around them. 31 These cities and their towns were in the land which the families of the tribe of Asher received as their possession.

RSV and TEV follow the Masoretic text spelling of the places cited. In verse 28, instead of Masoretic text Ebron, Soggin, citing 1 Chronicles 6.74, prefers "Abdon"; so NEB, NAB, BJ, JB, and HOTTP.

Sidon (RSV "Sidon the Great") in verse 28 and Tyre in verse 29 are the two important Phoenician cities on the Mediterranean.

In verse 29 the Masoretic text has "Mehebel" (which could be taken to mean "from Hebel"); the Septuagint favors Mahalab (so RSV, TEV and others); HOTTP prefers to spell it "Mahlab." It seems best to follow RSV and TEV spelling.

In verse 30, for Ummah of the Masoretic text, the Septuagint has "Acco" (see Judges 1.31), which is modern Acre; BJ, JB, NEB, and HOTTP prefer to follow the Septuagint. A translator should feel free to follow the Septuagint here.

Since some of the cities in verses 25-30 are mentioned in geographical relationship to other cities, the passage may be translated similarly to the first proposal for verses 18-23.

It is possible to translate verses 30-31 as a unit, and a proposal for doing so is given below. But first, it should be noted that TEV once again fails to identify the place-names as cities, and this causes confusion, since Zebulun (verse 27) represents a tribe, not a city. To help with this difficulty, verses 25 and 27 may be translated,

25 The southern border of its territory led westward from the city of Helkath to.... 27 The eastern border went north from the city of Helkath to the city of Bethdagon. It touched the territory of the tribe of Zebulun....

The last part of verse 29 and all of verses 30-31 may be translated, "It included Mahalab, Achzib, 30-31 Ummah, Aphek, and Rehob, a total of twenty-two cities, along with the towns around them. This entire region was given to the tribe of Asher."

TEV	19.32-39	RSV

The Territory Assigned to Naphtali

32 The sixth assignment made was for the families of the tribe of Naphtali. 33 Its border went from Heleph to the oak in Zaanannim, on to Adaminekeb and to Jamnia, as far as Lakkum, and ended at the Jordan. 34 There the border turned west to Aznoth Tabor, from there to Hukkok, touching Zebulun on the south, Asher on the west, and the Jordan[m] on the east. 35 The fortified cities were Ziddim, Zer, Hammath, Rakkath, Chinnereth, 36 Adamah, Ramah, Hazor, 37 Kedesh, Edrei, Enhazor, 38 Yiron, Migdalel, Horem, Bethanath, and Beth Shemesh: nineteen cities, along with the towns around them. 39 These cities and their towns were in the land which the families of the tribe of Naphtali received as their possession.

[m]*One ancient translation* the Jordan; *Hebrew* Judah at the Jordan.

32 The sixth lot came out for the tribe of Naphtali, for the tribe of Naphtali, according to its families. 33 And its boundary ran from Heleph, from the oak in Za-anannim, and Adami-nekeb, and Jabneel, as far as Lakkum; and it ended at the Jordan; 34 then the boundary turns westward to Aznoth-tabor, and goes from there to Hukkok, touching Zebulun at the south, and Asher on the west, and Judah on the east at the Jordan. 35 The fortified cities are Ziddim, Zer, Hammath, Rakkath, Chinnereth, 36 Adamah, Ramah, Hazor, 37 Kedesh, Edre-i, En-hazor, 38 Yiron, Migdal-el, Horem, Bethanath, and Beth-shemesh—nineteen cities with their villages. 39 This is the inheritance of the tribe of Naphtali according to its families—the cities with their villages.

Naphtali lay between Asher on the west and Lake Galilee on the east, where the border ran on northward to a point north of Lake Huleh. For translation of the section heading, The Territory Assigned to Naphtali, see comments at 13.15.

19.32   The sixth assignment made was for the families
           of the tribe of Naphtali.

For the translation of this verse, see comments at 18.11.

19.33   Its border went from Heleph to the oak in Zaanannim,
           on to Adaminekeb and to Jamnia, as far as Lakkum, and
           ended at the Jordan.

TEV has to the oak in Zaanannim, while most others have "from the oak" (which is what the Hebrew appears to mean; see RSV). As in 15.11, TEV has Jamnia (RSV "Jabneel").
     In the translation of this verse it may be useful to indicate that the border referred to is the northern border: "The northern border of its territory went from the town of Heleph to the oak near the town of Zaanannim...."

19.34   There the border turned west to Aznoth Tabor, from
           there to Hukkok, touching Zebulun on the south,
           Asher on the west, and the Jordan^m on the east.

     ^{m}One ancient translation the Jordan; Hebrew Judah
     at the Jordan.

And the Jordan on the east represents the Septuagint, which is preferred by TEV, NAB, BJ, JB. The Masoretic text has "and Judah of the Jordan on the east," followed by AT, RSV, TOB. HOTTP recommends the Masoretic text, but with the spelling "Jehudah," on the grounds that the noun here refers to neither the tribe nor the territory of Judah, but rather is a corrupted form which cannot be reconstructed. It may be better to follow the Masoretic text here.
     As in verse 33, it will be helpful here also to indicate which borders are referred to. Moreover, Zebulun and Asher should be marked specifically as tribal regions so as to distinguish them from the other places listed. As a model of what may be done:
           The southern border of Naphtali began at the Jordan River
           and went west to the city of Aznoth near Mount Tabor. There
           its border turned north and followed the eastern border of
           the tribe of Zebulun to the city of Hukkok. Its border then
           ran west along the entire northern border of Zebulun. The
           territory of the tribe of Asher was its western border, and
           the Jordan River was its eastern border.

[248]

<u>19.35-39</u> The fortified cities were Ziddim, Zer, Hammath,
Rakkath, Chinnereth, 36 Adamah, Ramah, Hazor,
37 Kedesh, Edrei, Enhazor, 38 Yiron, Migdalel,
Horem, Bethanath, and Beth Shemesh: nineteen
cities, along with the towns around them.
39 These cities and their towns were in the
land which the families of the tribe of Naphtali received as their possession.

For the translation of verses 35-39, the two alternatives suggested
for verses 18-23 will serve as a pattern.

| | TEV | 19.40-48 | RSV |

**The Territory Assigned to
Dan**

TEV	RSV
40 The seventh assignment made was for the families of the tribe of Dan. 41 Its area included Zorah, Eshtaol, Irshemesh, 42 Shaalbim, Aijalon, Ithlah, 43 Elon, Timnah, Ekron, 44 Elte-keh, Gibbethon, Baalath, 45 Jehud, Beneberak, Gathrimmon, 46 Mejarkon, and Rakkon, as well as the terri-tory around Joppa. 47 When the people of Dan lost their land, they went to Laish and attacked it. They captured it, killed its peo-ple, and claimed it for themselves. They settled there and changed the name of the city from Laish to Dan, naming it after their ancestor Dan. 48 These cities and their towns were in the land which the families of the tribe of Dan received as their possession.	40 The seventh lot came out for the tribe of Dan, according to its families. 41 And the territory of its inheritance included Zorah, Eshta-ol, Ir-shemesh, 42 Sha-alabbin, Aijalon, Ithlah, 43 Elon, Timnah, Ekron, 44 Eltekeh, Gib-bethon, Baalath, 45 Jehud, Bene-berak, Gathrimmon, 46 and Me-jarkon and Rakkon with the terri-tory over against Joppa. 47 When the territory of the Danites was lost to them, the Danites went up and fought against Leshem, and after capturing it and putting it to the sword they took posses-sion of it and settled in it, calling Leshem, Dan, after the name of Dan their ancestor. 48 This is the inheritance of the tribe of Dan, according to their families—these cities with their villages.

Although Dan was originally assigned territory in the southern
part of the country, its people were not able to maintain control over
the land, and so they migrated north. That is why Dan's assignment is
the last one given. For the translation of the section heading, <u>The
Territory Assigned to Dan</u>, see comments at 13.15.

<u>19.40</u>   The seventh assignment made was for the families
of the tribe of Dan.

19.40

For the translation of this verse, see comments at 18.11.

19.41-46　Its area included Zorah, Eshtaol, Irshemesh,
　　　　　42 Shaalbim, Aijalon, Ithlah, 43 Elon, Timnah,
　　　　　Ekron, 44 Eltekeh, Gibbethon, Baalath, 45 Jehud,
　　　　　Beneberak, Gathrimmon, 46 Mejarkon, and Rakkon,
　　　　　as well as the territory around Joppa.

In verse 41 Its area included may be more accurately rendered, "Its area included the cities of...."
Of the towns listed in the south, Zorah and Eshtaol appear in 15.33 (second district of Judah), and Ekron in 15.45 (fifth district of Judah).
In verse 42 TEV has Shaalbim (compare Judges 1.35; 1 Kgs 4.9) instead of RSV "Shaalabbin"; the TEV spelling follows some Hebrew manuscripts; RSV follows the spelling of the Masoretic text. It may be well to follow the Masoretic text here.
In verse 45 Jehud represents the Masoretic text; one form of the Septuagint has "Azor" (so BJ); for some unexplained reason HOTTP prefers "Jehud and Azor." It seems best to follow the Masoretic text here.

19.47-48　When the people of Dan lost their land, they went
　　　　　to Laish and attacked it. They captured it, killed
　　　　　its people, and claimed it for themselves. They
　　　　　settled there and changed the name of the city from
　　　　　Laish to Dan, naming it after their ancestor Dan.
　　　　　48 These cities and their towns were in the land
　　　　　which the families of the tribe of Dan received as
　　　　　their possession.

The tribe of Dan was unable to control this territory, so they migrated north all the way to the headwaters of the Jordan, on the east bank (see Judges 18); there they conquered Laish and changed the name to that of their ancestor, Dan.
When the people of Dan lost their land is literally "And the territory of the people of Dan went out from them." The temporal conjunction When may be translated either "Later" or "Sometime later," indicating an indefinite period of time. Lost their land implies an agent and may be translated "some enemies (or, some people) captured the territory that belonged to the tribe of Dan." Finally, Laish should perhaps be identified as a city.
Since the first part of verse 48 refers directly to the cities of verses 41-46, verses 47-48 may be placed together:
　　　All of these cities, along with their villages, belonged to
　　　the tribe of Dan. But later their enemies captured their land,
　　　and so the people of Dan went north to the city of Laish and
　　　attacked it. They captured the city, killed its people, and
　　　claimed it for themselves. Then they named the city after
　　　their ancestor Dan.

The Final Assignment of the Land

TEV	RSV
49 When the people of Israel finished dividing up the land, they gave Joshua son of Nun a part of the land as his own. 50 As the LORD had commanded, they gave him the city he asked for: Timnath Serah, in the hill country of Ephraim. He rebuilt the city and settled there. 51 Eleazar the priest, Joshua son of Nun, and the leaders of the families of the tribes of Israel assigned these parts of the land by drawing lots$n$ to consult the LORD at Shiloh, at the entrance of the Tent of the LORD's presence. In this way they finished dividing the land.	49 When they had tributing the several of the land as inheri᷉ ᷉ᷜᷓ people of Israel gave an inheritance among them to Joshua the son of Nun. 50 By command of the LORD they gave him the city which he asked, Timnath-serah in the hill country of Ephraim; and he rebuilt the city, and settled in it. 51 These are the inheritances which Eleazar the priest and Joshua the son of Nun and the heads of the fathers' houses of the tribes of the people of Israel distributed by lot at Shiloh before the LORD, at the door of the tent of meeting. So they finished dividing the land.

nDRAWING LOTS: See 14.2.

The account of the division of the territory ends with a note about the city assigned to Joshua, and a summary statement of the whole process. The section heading, The Final Assignment of the Land, may be translated, "This is the land which the people of Israel gave to Joshua."

19.49-51　　　When the people of Israel finished dividing up the land, they gave Joshua son of Nun a part of the land as his own. 50 As the LORD had commanded, they gave him the city he asked for: Timnath Serah, in the hill country of Ephraim. He rebuilt the city and settled there.

51 Eleazar the priest, Joshua son of Nun, and the leaders of the families of the tribes of Israel assigned these parts of the land by drawing lots$n$ to consult the LORD at Shiloh, at the entrance of the Tent of the LORD's presence. In this way they finished dividing the land.

nDRAWING LOTS: See 14.2.

In verse 49 the people of Israel...they reverses the Hebrew order, which has the pronoun "they" before the noun phrase "the people of Israel" (see RSV). If the pronoun "they" is a reference to the people of Israel, then the phrase the people of Israel would surely be equivalent to "the leaders of the families of the tribes of Israel" (verse 51). Given this interpretation, verses 49-51 may be placed together and translated as a unit (see below).

In verse 49 and again in verse 51 the identification son of Nun follows the name Joshua. Here again is a phrase which was important for the writer and his original readers, though it would seem unnecessary to reproduce it in translation, especially two times in such close sequence.

If the verse order is maintained, then a portion of verse 50 may be rendered as direct discourse: "The LORD had commanded the people of Israel, 'Give Joshua any city that he wants.' So they gave him the city of Timnath Serah, which was in the hill country of Ephraim." Or it may be obligatory to indicate explicitly Joshua's choice: "...Joshua wanted the city of Timnath Serah, which was in the hill country of Ephraim. So the people of Israel gave him that city."

Joshua was given the city of Timnath Serah, in the highlands of Ephraim, about 27 kilometers northwest of Jerusalem. It should be remembered that Joshua was a member of the tribe of Ephraim (Num 13.8).

The final verse emphasizes the role of the priest Eleazar and the tribal leaders, together with Joshua, in the division of the territory. The priest would use the Urim and Thummin in determining the Lord's will in the matter (see 14.2).

These parts of the land must be understood in relation to the division of the entire territory, not limited to the content of verses 49-51.

If the above proposal is accepted, and verses 49-51 are rendered as a unit, the following model for verse 51 may be followed:

All the people of Israel gathered in front of the Covenant Tent at Shiloh. They gathered there so that the priest Eleazar, Joshua, and the leaders of the tribes could divide all the land west of the Jordan River. They used lots to find out how the LORD wanted them to divide the land.

Chapter 20

The Cities of Refuge

1 Then the LORD told Joshua
2 to say to the people of Israel,
"Choose the cities of refuge that
I had Moses tell you about. 3 A
person who kills someone accidentally can go there and escape the
man who is looking for revenge.
4 He can run away to one of these
cities, go to the place of judgment at the entrance to the city,
and explain to the leaders what
happened. Then they will let him
into the city and give him a place
to live in, so that he can stay
there. 5 If the man looking for
revenge follows him there, the
people of the city must not hand
him over to him. They must protect
him because he killed the person
accidentally and not out of anger.
6 He may stay in the city until he
has received a public trial and
until the death of the man who is
then the High Priest. Then the man
may go back home to his own town,
from which he had run away."

7 So, on the west side of the
Jordan they set aside Kedesh in
Galilee, in the hill country of
Naphtali; Shechem, in the hill
country of Ephraim; and Hebron,
in the hill country of Judah.
8 East of the Jordan, on the desert
plateau east of Jericho, they chose
Bezer in the territory of Reuben;
Ramoth in Gilead, in the territory
of Gad; and Golan in Bashan, in the
territory of Manasseh. 9 These were
the cities of refuge chosen for all
the people of Israel and for any

1 Then the LORD said to Joshua,
2 "Say to the people of Israel,
'Appoint the cities of refuge, of
which I spoke to you through Moses,
3 that the manslayer who kills any
person without intent or unwittingly
may flee there; they shall be for
you a refuge from the avenger of
blood. 4 He shall flee to one of
these cities and shall stand at
the entrance of the gate of the
city, and explain his case to the
elders of that city; then they
shall take him into the city, and
give him a place, and he shall
remain with them. 5 And if the
avenger of blood pursues him,
they shall not give up the slayer
into his hand; because he killed
his neighbor unwittingly, having
had no enmity against him in
times past. 6 And he shall remain
in that city until he has stood
before the congregation for judgment, until the death of him who
is high priest at the time: then
the slayer may go again to his
own town and his own home, to the
town from which he fled.'"
7 So they set apart Kedesh in
Galilee in the hill country of
Naphtali, and Shechem in the hill
country of Ephraim, and Kiriath-
arba (that is, Hebron) in the hill
country of Judah. 8 And beyond
the Jordan east of Jericho, they
appointed Bezer in the wilderness
on the tableland, from the tribe
of Reuben, and Ramoth in Gilead,
from the tribe of Gad, and Golan

foreigner living among them. Anyone who killed a person accidentally could find protection there
from the man looking for revenge;
he could not be killed unless he
had first received a public trial.

in Bashan, from the tribe of
Manasseh. 9 These were the cities
designated for all the people of
Israel, and for the stranger so-
journing among them, that any one
who killed a person without intent
could flee there, so that he might
not die by the hand of the avenger
of blood, till he stood before the
congregation.

The need for cities of refuge arose from the fact that it was the
duty of the nearest relative of a man who had been killed to search
out and kill the killer. But when it was clearly not a murder (intentional killing) but manslaughter (accidental killing), then the killer
could seek asylum in one of the six cities of refuge, three on the west
side and three on the east side of the Jordan River.

The Cities of Refuge may be a difficult concept to express completely in a section heading. Even if it were rendered "Cities where a
person could run for safety," the reason for which the person needed
to run to these cities would still not be known. Therefore it seems
that the best thing to do in the section heading is to make a complete
sentence, giving a clue to the meaning, and then to depend upon the
content of the passage itself to give the full meaning. The section
heading may then be translated, "Joshua appoints cities where people
could run for safety" or "Joshua appoints cities where a person who
had accidentally killed another person could run for safety." This
second alternative does express the meaning fully.

20.1-2   Then the LORD told Joshua 2 to say to the
            people of Israel, "Choose the cities of refuge
            that I had Moses tell you about.

The instructions are clearly given, and there are no particular
textual or exegetical difficulties in these verses. The instructions
to Moses, referred to in verse 2, are given in Numbers 35.9-29; Deuteronomy 4.41-43; 19.1-13.

The translation of these verses, however, may be difficult in that
they assume several layers of discourse and describe two events that
are separated in time: the Lord speaks to Joshua; Joshua speaks to the
people of Israel; the Lord spoke to Moses; and Moses spoke to the people of Israel. Moreover, the events are not narrated in chronological
sequence; the event of the last clause in verse 2 (that I had Moses
tell you about) happened before that of verse 1 (Then the LORD told
Joshua). In addition to these problems, it may be necessary to use a
more specific transitional marker than the temporal conjunction Then
of TEV.

At least two solutions are possible, each of which has within
itself alternative possibilities. (1) Verses 1-2 may be translated
together: "After this, the LORD spoke to the people of Israel through
Joshua. He said, 'Now is the time to choose the cities of refuge that

I earlier spoke to Moses about.'" Or, if a causative form of the verb
is possible: "After this, the Lord caused Joshua to say to the people
of Israel...." (2) Verses 1-3 may be translated as a unit:

> When Moses was still alive, the LORD had said to him, "A
> person who accidentally kills someone will need a city where
> he can run for safety. Otherwise, the dead man's relatives
> will kill him." So now the LORD said to Joshua, "Tell the
> people of Israel to choose these cities."

Or it is possible to go directly from verse 3 to verse 4: "...to choose
these cities, where a man can run to the place of judgment at the entrance to the city and explain to the leaders what happened."

20.3   A person who kills someone accidentally can go there
          and escape the man who is looking for revenge.

Accidentally translates two synonymous expressions in Hebrew: RSV
"without intent or unwittingly"; NAB "accidental and unintended homi-
cide." This would include a case of pure accident or of killing someone
in a fight, where there had been no intent to kill. Some languages such
as Hebrew may prefer to retain two synonymous expressions, but many
languages will choose to use only one of the forms.

The man who is looking for revenge refers to the relative of the
dead man whose duty it was to kill the killer, and it may be helpful
to make this explicit. For example, "The relative of the dead man who
wants to kill him in revenge."

For a proposed restructuring of this verse, see comments on verses
1-2.

20.4   He can run away to one of these cities, go to the
          place of judgment at the entrance to the city, and
          explain to the leaders what happened. Then they
          will let him into the city and give him a place to
          live in, so that he can stay there.

The place of judgment was an open space inside the city, near the
main gate; here all judicial matters were dealt with.

Explain...what happened is more literally "explain his case" (RSV);
it is quite possible that the literal form is a more natural way of
expressing the meaning in some languages.

If the city leaders are convinced that the man is telling the
truth, then they allow him to live in the city, safe from the dead
man's avenging relative. The word translated leaders by TEV is literally "elders" (RSV), and it describes men who were respected because
their years have proven them to be persons of wisdom and understanding.
Similar expressions exist in a number of cultures.

20.5   If the man looking for revenge follows him there,
the people of the city must not hand him over to
him. They must protect him because he killed the
person accidentally and not out of anger.

The man looking for revenge translates the same phrase rendered
the man who is looking for revenge of verse 3. Depending upon the previous rendering of this expression, one may adopt the form of TEV or
translate "a relative of the dead man." If both aspects of the meaning,
a relative and one looking for revenge, are included in verse 3, it may
be necessary to use only one of them here.
    Him over to him must be translated so as not to confuse the pro-
nominal references: the meaning is "hand the man who ran to their city
for safety over to the man who came to kill him."
    In the second sentence of this verse, They must protect him may
need to be placed in final position: "He killed the person accidentally
and not out of anger, and so they must protect him."

20.6   He may stay in the city until he has received a
public trial and until the death of the man who
is then the High Priest. Then the man may go back
home to his own town, from which he had run away."

Two matters are joined which appear to be separate: (1) the ac-
cused will be given a public trial; if found guilty, he is to be turned
over to the avenging relative of the dead man (see Num 35.19); (2) if
found innocent, he remains in the city until the death of the ruling
High Priest (see Num 35.25,28). After the High Priest's death he is
allowed to go back home.
    Until he has received a public trial may need to be translated
more specifically as "until he has been proven innocent in a public
trial." Inasmuch as two separate matters are here spoken of (see above
comments), one may wish to begin a new sentence with the clause which
begins and until: "Then he must remain in the city until the man who
is High Priest at that time has died."
    Go back home translates "go again to his own town and his own
home" (RSV) of the Hebrew text. If both expressions are retained, they
may be inverted: "to his family and to his own home town." It may not
be necessary to render explicitly the clause from which he had run
away, since this information is clearly implicit.

20.7-8   So, on the west side of the Jordan they set
aside Kedesh in Galilee, in the hill country of
Naphtali; Shechem, in the hill country of Ephraim;
and Hebron, in the hill country of Judah. 8 East of
the Jordan, on the desert plateau east of Jericho,
they chose Bezer in the territory of Reuben; Ramoth
in Gilead, in the territory of Gad; and Golan in
Bashan, in the territory of Manasseh.

Six cities are chosen, three on each side of the Jordan. On the
west side (verse 7): Kedesh in the north, Shechem in the center, and
Hebron in the south; on the east side (verse 8): Bezer in the south,
Ramoth in the center, and Golan in the north. All six cities are listed
as levitical cities in chapter 21.

Verses 7-8 may be translated separately or they may be translated
as a unit. But whatever is done, the pronoun they in both verses needs
to be specified as "the people of Israel," since they were last referred to in verse 2. (1) If the verses are translated separately: "So
the people of Israel set apart (or, chose) three cities on the west
side of the Jordan River. These cities were...." (2) If placed together, verses 7-8 may be translated:

So the people of Israel set aside (or, chose) six cities,
three on the west side of the Jordan River and three on the
east side. The cities west of the Jordan River were: .... The
cities east of the Jordan River were: ....

20.9   These were the cities of refuge chosen for all
        the people of Israel and for any foreigner living
        among them. Anyone who killed a person accidentally
        could find protection there from the man looking
        for revenge; he could not be killed unless he had
        first received a public trial.

Chosen (RSV "designated") translates a word found only here in
the Hebrew Old Testament. This verse makes it clear that the rule applies to resident aliens as well as to Israelites; they also have the
right to flee to a city of refuge.

These were the cities of refuge chosen may seem unnecessarily repetitious. Moreover, could not be killed unless he had first received a
public trial is ambiguous in that it suggests that only a trial was
necessary, not the proof of guilt. This ambiguity may be cleared up
and the verse somewhat shortened:

Any Israelite and any foreigner living among them who had
accidentally killed someone could run to one of these cities
for protection. He could stay there until he had been tried
publicly. And then he could not be killed by the man who
wanted to kill him, unless he had been proven guilty.

Chapter 21

The Cities of the Levites

1 The leaders of the Levite families went to Eleazar the priest, Joshua son of Nun, and to the heads of the families of all the tribes of Israel. 2 There at Shiloh in the land of Canaan they said to them, "The LORD commanded through Moses that we were to be given cities to live in, as well as pasture land around them for our livestock." 3 So in accordance with the LORD's command the people of Israel gave the Levites certain cities and pasture lands out of their own territories.

4 The families of the Levite clan of Kohath were the first to be assigned cities. The families who were descended from Aaron the priest were assigned thirteen cities from the territories of Judah, Simeon, and Benjamin. 5 The rest of the clan of Kohath was assigned ten cities from the territories of Ephraim, Dan, and West Manasseh.

6 The clan of Gershon was assigned thirteen cities from the territories of Issachar, Asher, Naphtali, and East Manasseh.

7 The families of the clan of Merari were assigned twelve cities from the territories of Reuben, Gad, and Zebulun.

8 By drawing lots,^{o} the people of Israel assigned these cities and their pasture lands to the Levites, as the LORD had commanded through Moses.

1 Then the heads of the fathers' houses of the Levites came to Eleazar the priest and to Joshua the son of Nun and to the heads of the fathers' houses of the tribes of the people of Israel; 2 and they said to them at Shiloh in the land of Canaan, "The LORD commanded through Moses that we be given cities to dwell in along with their pasture lands for our cattle." 3 So by command of the LORD the people of Israel gave to the Levites the following cities and pasture lands out of their inheritance.

4 The lot came out for the families of the Kohathites. So those Levites who were descendants of Aaron the priest received by lot from the tribes of Judah, Simeon, and Benjamin, thirteen cities.

5 And the rest of the Kohathites received by lot from the families of the tribe of Ephraim, from the tribe of Dan and the half-tribe of Manasseh, ten cities.

6 The Gershonites received by lot from the families of the tribe of Issachar, from the tribe of Asher, from the tribe of Naphtali, and from the half-tribe of Manasseh in Bashan, thirteen cities.

7 The Merarites according to their families received from the tribe of Reuben, the tribe of Gad, and the tribe of Zebulun, twelve cities.

8 These cities and their pasture

lands the people of Israel gave
by lot to the Levites, as the
LORD had commanded through Moses.

A total of forty-eight cities distributed through all the tribes
were assigned to the Levites, who are classified according to the three
clans, Kohath, Gershon, and Merari, the three sons of Levi (see Exo
6.16).

The section heading, The Cities of the Levites, may be translated
"The people of Israel give cities to the Levites" (see verse 3). Or, on
the assumption that the assignment would actually have been made by
Eleazar the priest, Joshua, and the heads of the tribes of Israel, it
may be translated, "Eleazar the priest, Joshua, and the heads of the
tribes of Israel assign cities to the Levites" (see verse 1).

<u>21.1-2</u>   The leaders of the Levite families went to
          Eleazar the priest, Joshua son of Nun, and to the
          heads of the families of all the tribes of Israel.
          2 There at Shiloh in the land of Canaan they said
          to them, "The LORD commanded through Moses that we
          were to be given cities to live in, as well as
          pasture land around them for our livestock."

The same people who had been responsible for assigning the western
tribes their territory are responsible for assigning the cities to the
Levites: Eleazar, Joshua, and the tribal leaders (see 19.51). They use
the same process, that of drawing lots, and it is done in the same
place, Shiloh (see 18.1).

The reference to the instructions given to Moses is to be found in
Numbers 35.1-8, where it is specified that the Levites be assigned the
six cities of refuge plus forty-two other cities, a total of forty-eight.

By translating verses 1-2 as a unit, it is possible to remove some
of the repetition and reorder certain of the phrases:
          When the people of Israel were camped near the city of
          Shiloh in the land of Canaan, the leaders of the Levite fam-
          ilies went to Eleazar the priest, Joshua, and to the heads
          of the families of all of the tribes of Israel, and said....
Or the sentence may be divided into two sentences, with the indirect
discourse of TEV changed to direct discourse:
          The people of Israel were now camped near the city of
          Shiloh in the land of Canaan. While they were there, the
          leaders of the Levite families went to Eleazar the priest,
          Joshua, and to the heads of the families of all the tribes
          of Israel, and said, "The LORD said to Moses, 'Give the
          Levites cities to live in, and give them the pasture land
          around the cities for their livestock.'"
In some languages the shift to direct discourse for the Lord's words to
Moses may require a time marker or verb tense which indicates that this
event had happend some time ago.

21.3   So in accordance with the LORD's command the people
of Israel gave the Levites certain cities and pasture
lands out of their own territories.

So in accordance with the LORD's command the people of Israel
gave may be rendered in a slightly different form: "So the people of
Israel obeyed the LORD's command and gave."
Certain cities may be translated "some of their cities."

21.4-8   The families of the Levite clan of Kohath were
the first to be assigned cities. The families who
were descended from Aaron the priest were assigned
thirteen cities from the territories of Judah,
Simeon, and Benjamin. 5 The rest of the clan of
Kohath was assigned ten cities from the territories
of Ephraim, Dan, and West Manasseh.
6 The clan of Gershon was assigned thirteen
cities from the territories of Issachar, Asher,
Naphtali, and East Manasseh.
7 The families of the clan of Merari were
assigned twelve cities from the territories of
Reuben, Gad, and Zebulun.
8 By drawing lots,^o the people of Israel
assigned these cities and their pasture lands to
the Levites, as the LORD had commanded through
Moses.

^oDRAWING LOTS: See 14.2.

Verses 4-8 classify the Levites according to their clans, which
descended from Levi's three sons, Kohath, Gershon, and Merari. The
clans descended from Kohath are divided into two groups (verses 4-5),
one of which consists of the descendants of Aaron, grandson of Kohath
(Exo 6.18-20), the other one consisting of the other descendants of
Kohath. Although Gershon was the oldest son (Exo 6.16; Num 3.17),
Kohath is named first because of Aaron.
The Hebrew text mentions the use of the sacred lots in this initial classification of the levitical clans (see RSV verses 4,5,6;
strangely enough, it is not mentioned in verse 7). TEV has taken these
references to be anticipatory, that is, they actually refer to the
choosing of the cities as such, and so the matter is mentioned specifically in verse 8, where a summary statement is made of the assignment of the cities.
It is possible, however, either to follow the pattern of the Hebrew (see RSV), or else to introduce an initial summary statement. If
this second suggestion is followed, then verse 4 and the first part of
verse 5 may be restructured as follows:
Each clan received its cities by drawing lots. The descendants of Aaron from the tribe of Kohath received their
cities first. They were given thirteen cities from the territories of Judah, Simeon, and Benjamin. 5 Then the rest of
the clan of Kohath....

So as to arrange verse 8 in a somewhat more chronological sequence, it may be translated:
The LORD had commanded Moses to let the tribe of Levi draw lots to see what cities they would receive. So they drew lots, and the people of Israel gave them these cities together with the pasture lands around them.
A shift may also be made to direct discourse: "The LORD had commanded Moses, 'The tribe of Levi will draw lots, and they will receive the cities according to the lots that they draw.' So they drew lots....''

TEV   21.9-19   RSV

9 These are the names of the cities from the territories of Judah and Simeon which were given 10 to the descendants of Aaron who were of the clan of Kohath, which was descended from Levi. Their assignment was the first to be made. 11 They were given the city of Arba (Arba was Anak's father), now called Hebron, in the hill country of Judah, along with the pasture land surrounding it. 12 However, the fields of the city, as well as its towns, had already been given to Caleb son of Jephunneh as his possession.

13 In addition to Hebron (one of the cities of refuge), the following cities were assigned to the descendants of Aaron the priest: Libnah, 14 Jattir, Eshtemoa, 15 Holon, Debir, 16 Ain, Juttah, and Beth Shemesh, with their pasture lands; nine cities from the tribes of Judah and Simeon. 17 From the territory of Benjamin they were given four cities: Gibeon, Geba, 18 Anathoth, and Almon, with their pasture lands. 19 Thirteen cities in all, with their pasture lands, were given to the priests, the descendants of Aaron.

9 Out of the tribe of Judah and the tribe of Simeon they gave the following cities mentioned by name, 10 which went to the descendants of Aaron, one of the families of the Kohathites who belonged to the Levites; since the lot fell to them first. 11 They gave them Kiriath-arba (Arba being the father of Anak), that is Hebron, in the hill country of Judah, along with the pasture lands round about it. 12 But the fields of the city and its villages had been given to Caleb the son of Jephunneh as his possession.

13 And to the descendants of Aaron the priest they gave Hebron, the city of refuge for the slayer, with its pasture lands, Libnah with its pasture lands, 14 Jattir with its pasture lands, Eshtemoa with its pasture lands, 15 Holon with its pasture lands, Debir with its pasture lands, 16 Ain with its pasture lands, Juttah with its pasture lands, Beth-shemesh with its pasture lands—nine cities out of these two tribes; 17 then out of the tribe of Benjamin, Gibeon with its pasture lands, Geba with its pasture lands, 18 Anathoth with its pasture lands, and Almon with its pasture lands— four cities. 19 The cities of the descendants of Aaron, the priests, were in all thirteen cities with their pasture lands.

[261]

The first assignment was made to the descendants of Aaron. They are classified as priests (verse 19), while the other descendants of Levi are not.

21.9-10   These are the names of the cities from the territories of Judah and Simeon which were given 10 to the descendants of Aaron who were of the clan of Kohath, which was descended from Levi. Their assignment was the first to be made.

TEV in verse 10 seems to imply that there were (or could be) descendants of Aaron who were *not* members of the clan of Kohath; Instead of the present TEV text, it would be better to say "...to the members of the clan of Kohath who were the descendants of Aaron." It is not necessary to repeat the information that they were Levites, since this is very redundant in the context. Aaron was the grandson of Kohath, one of the three sons of Levi.

Verses 9-10 may then be translated as a unit: "The members (or, those members) of the clan of Kohath who were the descendants of Aaron received nine cities from the tribes of Judah and Simeon." For some languages it would also be acceptable to use a passive: "Nine cities from the tribes of Judah and Simeon were given to the members (or, those members) of the clan of Kohath who were the descendants of Aaron."

21.11-16   They were given the city of Arba (Arba was Anak's father), now called Hebron, in the hill country of Judah, along with the pasture land surrounding it. 12 However, the fields of the city, as well as its towns, had already been given to Caleb son of Jephunneh as his possession.
            13 In addition to Hebron (one of the cities of refuge), the following cities were assigned to the descendants of Aaron the priest: Libnah, 14 Jattir, Eshtemoa, 15 Holon, Debir, 16 Ain, Juttah, and Beth Shemesh, with their pasture lands: nine cities from the tribes of Judah and Simeon.

For "Kiriath-arba" (RSV), the old name of Hebron in verse 11, see 14.15; 15.13. In verses 11-12 the point is made that the city of Hebron itself was assigned to the Levites, while the fields of the city, as well as its towns, belonged to Caleb (see 14.13-14). It is difficult to distinguish precisely between the pasture land around Hebron, which belonged to the Levites (verse 11), and the fields of the city, which belonged to Caleb (verse 12); the fields of the city should perhaps be understood to mean "the open country near the city" (NEB; see NAB).

Verses 11-16 name nine cities from the territories of the tribes of Judah and Simeon.[55] Verse 13 calls attention to the fact that Hebron was a city of refuge (see 20.7).

If verses 9-10 are translated as a unit, then verses 11-16 may be dealt with similarly:

They received the city of Hebron, which was also a city of
refuge, and the cities of Libnah...and Beth Shemesh. The
city of Hebron lay in the hill country of Judah, and at
that time it was called the city of Arba, after Arba, the
father of Anak. The city and its pasture lands were given
to the descendants of Aaron, but its fields and towns had
already been given to Caleb.

Or, so as not to separate the initial mention of Hebron from the description of the city:

They received the city of Hebron, which was also a city of
refuge. It lay in the hill country of Judah, and at that
time it was called Arba City, after Arba, the father of
Anak. The fields and towns around it had already been given
to Caleb, but the city and its pasture lands were now given
to the descendants of Aaron. They also received the cities
of Libnah...and Beth Shemesh.

21.17-19 From the territory of Benjamin they were given four
cities: Gibeon, Geba, 18 Anathoth, and Almon, with
their pasture lands. 19 Thirteen cities in all, with
their pasture lands, were given to the priests, the
descendants of Aaron.

Verses 17-18 name four cities from the territory of Benjamin.
Verse 17 may be stated, "They were given four cities from the territory
of Benjamin. These cities were...."

Verse 19 may adequately be shortened: "This made a total of thirteen cities, together with their pasture lands." Or, if the full content of the verse is retained: "The priests, the descendants of Aaron,
were given thirteen cities in all, with their pasture lands."

| TEV | **21.20-26** | RSV |

20 The other families of the
Levite clan of Kohath were assigned
some cities from the territory of
Ephraim. 21 They were given four
cities: Shechem and its pasture
lands in the hill country of
Ephraim (one of the cities of refuge), Gezer, 22 Kibzaim, and Beth
Horon, with their pasture lands.
23 From the territory of Dan they
were given four cities: Eltekeh,
Gibbethon, 24 Aijalon, and Gath-
rimmon, with their pasture lands.
25 From the territory of West
Manasseh they were given two cities:
Taanach and Gathrimmon, with their
pasture lands. 26 These families

20 As to the rest of the
Kohathites belonging to the Kohathite families of the Levites,
the cities allotted to them were
out of the tribe of Ephraim. 21 To
them were given Shechem, the city
of refuge for the slayer, with its
pasture lands in the hill country
of Ephraim, Gezer with its pasture
lands, 22 Kibza-im with its pasture lands, Beth-horon with its
pasture lands—four cities; 23 and
out of the tribe of Dan, Elteke
with its pasture lands, Gibbethon
with its pasture lands, 24 Aijalon
with its pasture lands, Gath-
rimmon with its pasture lands—

of the clan of Kohath received ten cities in all, with their pasture lands.

four cities; 25 and out of the half-tribe of Manasseh, Taanach with its pasture lands, and Gath-rimmon with its pasture lands—two cities. 26 The cities of the families of the rest of the Ko-hathites were ten in all with their pasture lands.

Ten cities are assigned to the other Kohathite clans, those not descended from Aaron.

<u>21.20-22</u>　　The other families of the Levite clan of Kohath were assigned some cities from the territory of Ephraim. 21 They were given four cities; Shechem and its pasture lands in the hill country of Ephraim (one of the cities of refuge), Gezer, 22 Kibzaim, and Beth Horon, with their pasture lands.

Four cities are in the tribe of <u>Ephraim</u>, one of which, <u>Shechem</u>, was a city of refuge (see 20.7).

Since all four of the cities mentioned in verses 20-22 are in the territory of Ephraim, it is possible to translate the verses as a unit. Moreover, since the summary in verse 26 indicates that they also re-ceived the pasture land around the cities, it may not be necessary to mention that information at this time. One may then translate:

The rest of the clan of Levi was given four cities in the territory of Ephraim. The cities were Shechem in the hill country of Ephraim, Gezer, Kibzaim, and Beth Horon. Shechem was also one of the cities of refuge.

Or, "...One of these cities was Shechem. It was located in the hill country, and it was also one of the cities of refuge. The other three cities were...."

<u>21.23-25</u>　From the territory of Dan they were given four cities: Eltekeh, Gibbethon, 24 Aijalon, and Gathrimmon, with their pasture lands. 25 From the territory of West Manasseh they were given two cities: Taanach and Gathrimmon, with their pasture lands.

Four cities are in the tribe of <u>Dan</u>, that is, in the south, the area which the Danites eventually aban<u>d</u>oned, according to 19.40-48.

Two cities are in <u>West Manasseh</u>. <u>Gathrimmon</u> in verse 25 seems to be a scribal error (see in verse 2<u>4</u>, <u>Gathrimmon</u> in the territory of Dan). In 17.11 a city in West Manasseh named <u>Ibleam</u> is listed; and in 1 Chronicles 6.70 the two levitical cities are <u>Aner and Bileam</u>. In this passage JB has "Jibleam" (BJ "Yibleam"); NAB has <u>"Ibleam</u>." HOTTP recom-mends "Jibleam." If the translator abandons <u>Gathrimmon</u> here, the town could be called either "Jibleam" (so Soggin) or "Ib<u>leam"</u> (so Bright), as in 17.11.

[264]

It is surely unnecessary to repeat twice the phrase with their pasture lands (verses 24,25). The restructuring of verses 23-25 may follow the pattern suggested for verses 17-18.

21.26   These families of the clan of Kohath received ten cities in all, with their pasture lands.

If the phrase with their pasture lands is omitted in its various occurrences in the previous verses, then it should definitely be included here. This verse may be translated in a way similar to the model proposed for verse 19.

TEV

27 Another group of Levites, the clan of Gershon, received from the territory of East Manasseh two cities: Golan in Bashan (one of the cities of refuge) and Beesh-terah, with their pasture lands. 28 From the territory of Issachar they received four cities: Kishion, Daberath, 29 Jarmuth, and Engannim, with their pasture lands. 30 From the territory of Asher they received four cities: Mishal, Abdon, 31 Helkath, and Rehob, with their pasture lands. 32 From the territory of Naphtali they received three cities: Kedesh in Galilee, with its pasture lands (one of the cities of refuge), Hammoth Dor, and Kartan, with their pasture lands. 33 The various families of the clan of Gershon received a total of thirteen cities with their pasture lands.

21.27-33

RSV

27 And to the Gershonites, one of the families of the Le-vites, were given out of the half-tribe of Manasseh, Golan in Bashan with its pasture lands, the city of refuge for the slayer, and Be-eshterah with its pasture lands—two cities; 28 and out of the tribe of Issachar, Kishion with its pasture lands, Daberath with its pasture lands, 29 Jar-muth with its pasture lands, En-gannim with its pasture lands— four cities; 30 and out of the tribe of Asher, Mishal with its pasture lands, Abdon with its pasture lands, 31 Helkath with its pasture lands, and Rehob with its pasture lands—four cities; 32 and out of the tribe of Naph-tali, Kedesh in Galilee with its pasture lands, the city of refuge for the slayer, Hammoth-dor with its pasture lands, and Kartan with its pasture lands—three cities. 33 The cities of the sev-eral families of the Gershonites were in all thirteen cities with their pasture lands.

Thirteen cities are assigned to the clan of Gershon.
Two cities are in East Manasseh (verse 27), one of which, Golan, was a city of refuge (see 20.8)
Four cities are in Issachar (verses 28-29).
Four cities are in Asher (verses 30-31).
Three cities are in Naphtali (verse 32), one of which, Kedesh, was a city of refuge (see 20.7).

For the translation of these verses, the same format may be followed as for verses 20-26. In particular, verses 27-32 should be patterned after verses 20-25, while verse 33 should follow the pattern of verse 26. The restructuring should be similar, and the problem with the repetition of with their pasture lands also is the same.

TEV	21.34-40	RSV

TEV	RSV
34 The rest of the Levites, the clan of Merari, received from the territory of Zebulun four cities: Jokneam, Kartah, 35 Dimnah, and Nahalal, with their pasture lands. 36 From the territory of Reuben they received four cities: Bezer, Jahaz, 37 Kedemoth, and Mephaath, with their pasture lands. 38 From the tribe of Gad they received four cities: Ramoth in Gilead, with its pasture lands (one of the cities of refuge), Mahanaim, 39 Heshbon, and Jazer, with their pasture lands. 40 So the clan of Merari was assigned a total of twelve cities.	34 And to the rest of the Levites, the Merarite families, were given out of the tribe of Zebulun, Jokne-am with its pasture lands, Kartah with its pasture lands, 35 Dimnah with its pasture lands, Nahalal with its pasture lands—four cities; 36 and out of the tribe of Reuben, Bezer with its pasture lands, Jahaz with its pasture lands, 37 Kedemoth with its pasture lands, and Mepha-ath with its pasture lands—four cities; 38 and out of the tribe of Gad, Ramoth in Gilead with its pasture lands, the city of refuge for the slayer, Mahanaim with its pasture lands, 39 Heshbon with its pasture lands, Jazer with its pasture lands—four cities in all. 40 As for the cities of the several Merarite families, that is, the remainder of the families of the Levites, those allotted to them were in all twelve cities.

Twelve cities are assigned to the clan of Merari.
Four cities are in Zebulun (verses 34-35).[56]
Four cities are in Reuben (verses 36-37). The first part of verse 36 in the Masoretic text is "and from the tribe of Reuben, Bezer with its pasture lands" (see RSV). The Septuagint (see also 1 Chr 6.78) has "and *on the east side of the Jordan, opposite Jericho,* from the tribe of Reuben, *one of the cities of refuge,* Bezer *in the wilderness on the plateau,* with its pasture lands" (the passages in italics are not in the Masoretic text). HOTTP, rating its decision highly probable, takes this to be original and recommends its adoption (so Soggin; BJ, NEB, NAB, and JB include part of the Septuagint additional matter).
Four cities are in Gad (verses 38-39), one of which, Ramoth, was a city of refuge (see 20.9).
The translation of verses 34-39 should follow the pattern of verses 17-18, and the translation of verse 40 should follow that of verse 19. Although the phrase with their pasture lands is not found in verse 40, it may be introduced there by way of summary and omitted from its occurrences in the previous verses.

TEV	21.41-42	RSV

41-42 From the land that the people of Israel possessed, a total of forty-eight cities, with the pasture lands around them, was given to the Levites.

41 The cities of the Levites in the midst of the possession of the people of Israel were in all forty-eight cities with their pasture lands. 42 These cities had each its pasture lands round about it; so it was with all these cities.

These verses conclude the section. The Hebrew text is quite repetitious (see RSV); TEV has reduced the number of words without omitting any information, but one may also translate "The Levites received from the other tribes of Israel a total of forty-eight cities, with the pasture lands around them." Or "The other tribes of Israel gave to the tribe of Levi a total of forty-eight cities, with the pasture lands around them."

TEV	21.43-45	RSV

Israel Takes Possession of
the Land

43 So the LORD gave to Israel all the land that he had solemnly promised their ancestors he would give them. When they had taken possession of it, they settled down there. 44 The LORD gave them peace throughout the land, just as he had promised their ancestors. Not one of all their enemies had been able to stand against them, because the LORD gave the Israelites the victory over all their enemies. 45 The LORD kept every one of the promises that he had made to the people of Israel.

43 Thus the LORD gave to Israel all the land which he swore to give to their fathers; and having taken possession of it, they settled there. 44 And the LORD gave them rest on every side just as he had sworn to their fathers; not one of all their enemies had withstood them, for the LORD had given all their enemies into their hands. 45 Not one of all the good promises which the LORD had made to the house of Israel had failed; all came to pass.

This final statement brings to an end the story of the conquest of the land west of the Jordan and its division among the tribes. The material that comes after this (chapters 22-24) is in the nature of an appendix.

The section heading, Israel Takes Possession of the Land, should cause no basic translational difficulties; the sentence structure is simple, with subject, verb, and direct object. With a slightly different focus it may be rendered, "The LORD keeps his promise to the people of Israel."

21.43   So the LORD gave to Israel all the land that
         he had solemnly promised their ancestors he would
         give them. When they had taken possession of it,
         they settled down there.

This concluding statement recalls the promises the Lord made to
Joshua at the beginning of the book (1.5-6). That he had solemnly promised may be translated "that he had promised with an oath." If this
restructuring is followed, care should be taken that the word used for
"oath" does not have negative implications. The sentence may be inverted
to reflect proper historical sequence: "The LORD had promised the ancestors of the people of Israel that he would give them this land. Now
he had kept this promise." Or, using direct discourse, "Long ago the
LORD had promised the ancestors of the people of Israel, 'I will give
you this land.' So the LORD had now kept his promise."
     As a substitute for the clause indicating a previous event (When
they had taken possession of it), one may translate "They took possession of the land, and settled down there."

21.44   The LORD gave them peace throughout the land, just
         as he had promised their ancestors. Not one of all
         their enemies had been able to stand against them,
         because the LORD gave the Israelites the victory
         over all their enemies.

Gave them peace translates a Hebrew verb which in 1.13 TEV has
translated as your home and in 1.15 given safety. The word emphasizes
the peace and security Israel enjoyed in the land as a result of the
Lord's promise and action. The statement about the total defeat of all
their enemies is somewhat exaggerated, since in many places the Israelites were not able to drive out the Canaanites completely from their
cities, as the text itself has made clear.
     The contents of this verse may be arranged into what is almost a
chronological order:
         The LORD caused the people of Israel to defeat all their en-
         emies. Not one of their enemies could stand up against them.
         The LORD had promised the ancestors of the people of Israel
         that he would let them live in peace throughout the land. So
         the LORD kept this promise.
Or, making explicit the other aspect of the Lord's promise:
         The LORD had promised the ancestors of the people of Israel,
         "You will defeat all your enemies and live in peace through-
         out the land." So the LORD kept his promise. He caused the
         people of Israel to defeat all their enemies. Not one of
         their enemies could stand against them, and they lived in
         peace throughout the land.

21.45   The LORD kept every one of the promises that he
         had made to the people of Israel.

The emphasis, as throughout the narrative, is on the Lord; it was his power that enabled the Israelites to conquer Canaan. The Lord kept every one of the promises that he had made to his people. This verse may be phrased negatively: "The LORD had made many promises to the people of Israel, and he did not break even one of them."

Chapter 22

Joshua Sends the Eastern Tribes Home

1 Then Joshua called together the people of the tribes of Reuben, Gad, and East Manasseh. 2 He said to them, "You have done everything that Moses the LORD's servant ordered you to do, and you have obeyed all my commands. 3 All this time you have never once deserted your fellow Israelites. You have been careful to obey the commands of the LORD your God. 4 Now, as he promised, the LORD your God has given your fellow Israelites peace. So go back home to the land which you claimed for your own, the land on the east side of the Jordan, that Moses, the LORD's servant, gave you. 5 Make sure you obey the law that Moses commanded you: love the LORD your God, do his will, obey his commandments, be faithful to him, and serve him with all your heart and soul." 6-8 Joshua sent them home with his blessing and with these words: "You are going back home very rich, with a lot of livestock, silver, gold, bronze, iron, and many clothes. Share with your fellow tribesmen what you took from your enemies." Then they left for home.

Moses had given land east of the Jordan to one half of the tribe of Manasseh, but to the other half Joshua had given land west of the Jordan, along with the other tribes.

9 So the people of the tribes of Reuben, Gad, and East Manasseh

1 Then Joshua summoned the Reubenites, and the Gadites, and the half-tribe of Manasseh, 2 and said to them, "You have kept all that Moses the servant of the LORD commanded you, and have obeyed my voice in all that I have commanded you; 3 you have not forsaken your brethren these many days, down to this day, but have been careful to keep the charge of the LORD your God. 4 And now the LORD your God has given rest to your brethren, as he promised them; therefore turn and go to your home in the land where your possession lies, which Moses the servant of the LORD gave you on the other side of the Jordan. 5 Take good care to observe the commandment and the law which Moses the servant of the LORD commanded you, to love the LORD your God, and to walk in all his ways, and to keep his commandments, and to cleave to him, and to serve him with all your heart and with all your soul." 6 So Joshua blessed them, and sent them away; and they went to their homes.

7 Now to the one half of the tribe of Manasseh Moses had given a possession in Bashan; but to the other half Joshua had given a possession beside their brethren in the land west of the Jordan. And when Joshua sent them away to their homes and blessed them, 8 he said to them, "Go back to

went back home. They left the
rest of the people of Israel at
Shiloh in the land of Canaan and
started out for their own land,
the land of Gilead, which they had
taken as the LORD had commanded
them through Moses.

your homes with much wealth, and
with very many cattle, with silver,
gold, bronze, and iron, and with
much clothing; divide the spoil of
your enemies with your brethren."
9 So the Reubenites and the Gadites
and the half-tribe of Manasseh
returned home, parting from the
people of Israel at Shiloh, which
is in the land of Canaan, to go
to the land of Gilead, their own
land of which they had possessed
themselves by command of the LORD
through Moses.

Chapters 22-24 include the following: (1) the return home of the
two and one-half eastern tribes and the controversy about the altar by
the Jordan River (22.1-34); (2) Joshua's farewell address (23.1-16);
(3) the covenant at Shechem (24.1-26); and (4) the death and burial of
Joshua and of Eleazar (24.29-33).

Chapter 22 itself falls into two distinct sections: (1) the return
of the two and one-half tribes (verses 1-9) and (2) the altar by the
Jordan (verses 10-34). The first of these two sections tells that the
men of the two and one-half eastern tribes had kept their promise
(1.12-18) and had helped their fellow Israelites conquer the land west
of the Jordan. Now they are allowed to return to their home and families.

The section heading, Joshua Sends the Eastern Tribes Home, is a
simple and accurate representation of the material contained within
this section. However, in the translation of this section heading, one
should take care that the verb Sends is not taken to imply force on
Joshua's part. To avoid this, the heading may be rendered, "Joshua
allows the eastern tribes to go home." If a passive form is preferable,
"The eastern tribes are permitted to return to their homes."

22.1   Then Joshua called together the people of the
           tribes of Reuben, Gad, and East Manasseh.

Then is a literal rendering of the Hebrew text; one may translate
"After the tribes of Israel had conquered the land west of the Jordan
River."

Joshua calls together the men of the tribes of Reuben, Gad, and
East Manasseh and recalls how Moses had commanded them to help their
fellow Israelites conquer Canaan (Num 32.28-32; Deut 3.18-20). Although
the Hebrew text does not specify, it is better to assume that Joshua
called together only the men of the tribes, rather than all the people
(TEV), and one may want to make this specific in translation.

22.2   He said to them, "You have done everything that Moses
           the LORD's servant ordered you to do, and you have
           obeyed all my commands.

The men of these tribes had obeyed Moses' command and had also obeyed all of Joshua's orders, so now they are allowed to return home.

The LORD"'s servant may be translated as a verb phrase and the verse arranged in chronological sequence: "Moses served the LORD. He told you what to do, and you always obeyed him. I also gave you commands, and you obeyed all my commands." Or, in more detail, "Moses served the LORD, and he gave you commands in behalf of the LORD. You obeyed all his commands. Then after Moses died, I gave you commands in behalf of the LORD. You also obeyed all my commands."

22.3   All this time you have never once deserted your
          fellow Israelites. You have been careful to obey
          the commands of the LORD your God.

All this time (RSV "these many days") may refer to a period of several years. It is best translated by a phrase which refers to an indefinite but lengthy period of time.

You have never once deserted your fellow Israelites may be translated by a positive statement: "Whenever your fellow Israelites needed you, you always came to help them."

In order to bring verses 2 and 3 closer together as a sense unit, it may be advisable to invert the order of the two sentences in verse 3. By doing so, You have been careful to obey the commands of the LORD your God would serve to reinforce the content of verse 2. As the first sentence of the verse may be rendered positively, so this sentence may be rendered negatively. The verse may then be translated, "You have never disobeyed the commands of the LORD your God, and when your fellow Israelites needed you, you always came to help them."

22.4   Now, as he promised, the LORD your God has given
          your fellow Israelites peace. So go back home to
          the land which you claimed for your own, the land
          on the east side of the Jordan, that Moses, the
          LORD's servant, gave you.

The contents of the first sentence in this verse may be slightly reordered: "The LORD your God promised peace to your fellow Israelites. And now he has kept that promise." As pointed out in the earlier chapters in this book, it may be more natural to use "the LORD our God" in place of the LORD your God, which might imply that he is not the Lord of all the tribes.

Given your fellow Israelites peace may be too abstract; if so, it is possible to translate "caused your fellow Israelites to live in peace." For previous comments on the expression "give peace," see 21.44. Many languages will have appropriate idiomatic expressions.

The second sentence of this verse, So go back home...gave you, is rather lengthy and should perhaps be divided into several smaller units. But before suggesting how this may be done, attention should be called to several other aspects of this sentence. Go back home translates "turn and go" (RSV) of the Hebrew text, while the land which you claimed

<u>for your own</u> translates a noun phrase in Hebrew ("the land of your <u>possession</u>"), in which the root meaning of the noun "possession" is "land taken by force," the same meaning it obviously has here. Finally, it may not be advisable to repeat <u>the LORD's servant</u> so soon as an identifier of Moses. The entire sentence may then be translated, 'Moses gave you land on the east side of the Jordan River, and you have already claimed that land as your own. So you may now go back home to that land."

22.5   Make sure you obey the law that Moses commanded you:
        love the LORD your God, do his will, obey his command-
        ments, be faithful to him, and serve him with all your
        heart and soul."

Joshua instructs the men of the eastern tribes to be good and faithful Israelites, that is, devoted and dedicated to the Lord alone. <u>The law</u> translates what is in Hebrew two synonymous words: "the commandment and the law" (RSV). TEV has taken the five verbs that follow to express the contents of that commandment, not as additional commands.

<u>Make sure you obey</u> translates a Hebrew expression which emphasizes the absolute urgency of obedience. A negative form may be employed: "Make sure that you never forget."

<u>The law that Moses commanded you</u> makes a difficult construction in English, and this is probably the case for many other languages as well. Keeping to the exegesis of TEV, one may translate "everything that Moses commanded you to do."

Here, as in verses 2 and 4, Moses is identified as "the LORD's servant" (see RSV). TEV drops this descriptive phrase, since in TEV restructuring it occurs in both of the previous instances.

In the listing of things that the Israelites are to do, the writer once again uses much repetition of synonymous and almost synonymous expressions for the sake of emphasis. For example, <u>do his will, obey his commandments</u> is equivalent to "do what the LORD commands you to do" or "obey everything that the LORD commands you to do." <u>With all your heart and soul</u> translates a fixed formula in Hebrew, and refers to the whole person. It should be noted that in Hebrew the noun "heart" generally refers more to the activities of the mind than to the emotions, as the term implies in English. One may translate 'with all your heart and strength" or "in all that you think and feel."

Moses' commands may be formulated as direct discourse: "Be sure that you never forget what Moses urged you to do. He said, 'Love the LORD our God and obey all of his commands. Serve him faithfully with all of your heart and soul.'"

22.6-8   Joshua sent them home with his blessing and with
          these words: "You are going back home very rich,
          with a lot of livestock, silver, gold, bronze,
          iron, and many clothes. Share with your fellow
          tribesmen what you took from your enemies." Then
          they left for home.

[273]

> Moses had given land east of the Jordan to one
> half of the tribe of Manasseh, but to the other half
> Joshua had given land west of the Jordan, along with
> the other tribes.

TEV has rearranged verses 6-8 in a more orderly manner; for the
way in which the material appears in Hebrew, see RSV. Notice that verse
6a is repeated in the last part of verse 7, and verse 6b is taken up
again in verse 9a.

The information about how Moses had assigned territory east of the
Jordan to one half of Manasseh and land west of the Jordan was assigned
by Joshua to the other half is quite redundant in the context of the
whole book. As it stands in the text, the command in verse 8 (see RSV)
appears to be directed to the men of East Manasseh alone (so Bright),
but it is reasonable to assume that it applies to the two other eastern
tribes as well (so TEV; see also NEB, NAB).

If the command is understood to be directed to the men of East
Manasseh alone, then it would seem advisable to retain the order of the
text essentially as it appears in the Hebrew. The last part of verse 7
would then be "Now as Joshua sent the men of East Manasseh home with
his blessing, 8 he said to them...." If the order of TEV is retained,
it may be helpful to translate with his blessing as part of the direct
quotation: "6-8 Before the men started home Joshua said to them, 'May
the LORD continue to bless your lives. You are going back....'" Or,
"6-8 ...'May the LORD (continue to) be with you....'"

The command to share with their fellow Israelites the loot taken
from enemies is in keeping with ancient Israelite practice (see Num
31.27; 1 Sam 30.21-25).

22.9   So the people of the tribes of Reuben, Gad, and
> East Manasseh went back home. They left the rest of
> the people of Israel at Shiloh in the land of Canaan
> and started out for their own land, the land of Gilead,
> which they had taken as the LORD had commanded them
> through Moses.

The two and one-half tribes start back, leaving their fellow
Israelites in Shiloh (see 18.1).

In TEV the movement homeward of the two and one-half eastern
tribes is described as went back home...started out for their own land.
This sequence may be a problem for some readers, since went back home
suggests arrival, while started out for their own land signifies the
beginning of their journey. Therefore it may be more satisfactory to
translate:

> So the tribes of Reuben, Gad, and East Manasseh left
> the rest of the people of Israel at Shiloh in the land of
> Canaan, and started back home. Their land lay east of the
> Jordan River. Long ago Moses had told them, "This is the
> land that the LORD wants you to take for your own."

Or:

> ...in the land of Canaan. They started back home to their
> land east of the Jordan River. Before Moses died, he had

told them, "The LORD wants you to take this land for your own."

TEV   22.10-20   RSV

The Altar by the Jordan

TEV	RSV

10 When the tribes of Reuben, Gad, and East Manasseh arrived at Geliloth, still on the west side[p] of the Jordan, they built a large, impressive altar there by the river. 11 The rest of the people of Israel were told, "Listen! The people of the tribes of Reuben, Gad, and East Manasseh have built an altar at Geliloth, on our side of the Jordan!" 12 When the people of Israel heard this, the whole community came together at Shiloh to go to war against the eastern tribes.

13 Then the people of Israel sent Phinehas, the son of Eleazar the priest, to the people of the tribes of Reuben, Gad, and East Manasseh in the land of Gilead. 14 Ten leading men went with Phinehas, one from each of the western tribes and each one the head of a family among the clans. 15 They came to the land of Gilead, to the people of Reuben, Gad, and East Manasseh, 16 and speaking for the whole community of the LORD, they said to them, "Why have you done this evil thing against the God of Israel? You have rebelled against the LORD by building this altar for yourselves! You are no longer following him! 17 Remember our sin at Peor, when the LORD punished his own people with an epidemic? We are still suffering because of that. Wasn't that sin enough? 18 Are you going to refuse to follow him now? If you rebel against the LORD today, he will be angry with everyone in Israel tomorrow. 19 Now then, if your land is not fit to worship in, come

10 And when they came to the region about the Jordan, that lies in the land of Canaan, the Reubenites and the Gadites and the half-tribe of Manasseh built there an altar by the Jordan, an altar of great size. 11 And the people of Israel heard say, "Behold, the Reubenites and the Gadites and the half-tribe of Manasseh have built an altar at the frontier of the land of Canaan, in the region about the Jordan, on the side that belongs to the people of Israel." 12 And when the people of Israel heard of it, the whole assembly of the people of Israel gathered at Shiloh, to make war against them.

13 Then the people of Israel sent to the Reubenites and the Gadites and the half-tribe of Manasseh, in the land of Gilead, Phinehas the son of Eleazar the priest, 14 and with him ten chiefs, one from each of the tribal families of Israel, every one of them the head of a family among the clans of Israel. 15 And they came to the Reubenites, the Gadites, and the half-tribe of Manasseh, in the land of Gilead, and they said to them, 16 "Thus says the whole congregation of the LORD, 'What is this treachery which you have committed against the God of Israel in turning away this day from following the LORD, by building yourselves an altar this day in rebellion against the LORD? 17 Have we not had enough of the sin at Peor from which even yet we have not cleansed ourselves, and for which there came a plague

over into the LORD's land, where his Tent is. Claim some land among us. But don't rebel against the LORD or make rebels out of us by building an altar in addition to the altar of the LORD our God. 20 Remember how Achan son of Zerah refused to obey the command about the things condemned to destruction; the whole community of Israel was punished for that. Achan was not the only one who died because of his sin."

p still on the west side; *or* on the east side.

upon the congregation of the LORD, 18 that you must turn away this day from following the LORD? And if you rebel against the LORD today he will be angry with the whole congregation of Israel tomorrow. 19 But now, if your land is unclean, pass over into the LORD's land where the LORD's tabernacle stands, and take for yourselves a possession among us; only do not rebel against the LORD, or make us as rebels by building yourselves an altar other than the altar of the LORD our God. 20 Did not Achan the son of Zerah break faith in the matter of the devoted things, and wrath fell upon all the congregation of Israel? And he did not perish alone for his iniquity.'"

There is some uncertainty over the location of the altar built near the Jordan by the two and one-half eastern tribes on their way home. In any case, the western tribes interpreted the action as an attempt to establish another sanctuary in competition with the central sanctuary in Canaan. A delegation from the western tribes is sent to the eastern tribes, who explain that the altar is meant to be a witness to the oneness of the people of Israel, all of whom worship the Lord, the one God of Israel. This settles the matter, and the delegation, satisfied, returns home.

The section heading, The Altar by the Jordan, may be translated as a complete sentence: "The altar by the Jordan causes trouble" or "...leads to conflict among the tribes of Israel." One may also translate "The tribes east of the Jordan River build an altar to the LORD."

22.10   When the tribes of Reuben, Gad, and East Manasseh arrived at Geliloth, still on the west side*p* of the Jordan, they built a large, impressive altar there by the river.

p still on the west side; *or* on the east side.

TEV Geliloth takes the Hebrew word to be a proper name (so Soggin; NEB, TOB); it can be taken as a common noun, "region" (so Gray, Bright; AT, RSV, NAB; see also 13.2, all the territory); BJ, JB take it to mean "circle of stones." It may be better to translate "region" or "territory" (see RSV).

Still on the west side translates the Hebrew "which is in the land of Canaan." It is also possible to convey this same meaning without specifically mentioning the west side: "On their way home, the tribes of Reuben, Gad, and East Manasseh came to the town of Geliloth near the Jordan River. So they built a large, impressive altar there, before crossing the river."

Since the altar is described as large and impressive, some scholars have suggested that it was not just a place of worship but also a fortress. But the question has not been definitely settled.

22.11   The rest of the people of Israel were told, "Listen!
         The people of the tribes of Reuben, Gad, and East
         Manasseh have built an altar at Geliloth, on our
         side of the Jordan!"

The rest of the people of Israel were told may require either a shift to an active construction or else an explicit mention of the person or persons who told them. The entire verse may also be translated as indirect discourse: "The rest of the people of Israel heard that the people of the tribe of Reuben, Gad, and East Manasseh had built an altar at Geliloth, on their side of the Jordan." Or, as an alternative solution to the question of who did the telling: "The rest of the people of Israel said to one another, 'Have you heard that the tribes of Reuben, Gad, and East Manasseh have built...?'"

On our side of the Jordan translates the Hebrew "on the side towards (or, facing) the people of Israel."[57] It is not certain which side of the Jordan is meant. Bright says the altar was on the east side, but adds "but the sense of the verses is against this (see verses 10,11,19)." The following take it to have been the west bank: Soggin, Smith, Gray; TEV, AT, RSV, BJ, TOB; the east bank: NEB, NAB. BJ translates verse 10 as west side, verse 11 as east side, and adds that verse 11 is a later addition to the text. TEV supplies a footnote with the alternative: "*or* on the east side." Certainly the whole incident makes better sense if the altar was on the west side, that is, in the land of Canaan, strictly speaking.

On our side of the Jordan may be more precisely indicated as "here on the western bank, on our side of the river." Or, if the alternative interpretation of the text is followed, "there on the eastern bank, directly across from our territory."

22.12   When the people of Israel heard this, the whole
         community came together at Shiloh to go to war
         against the eastern tribes.

On hearing the news, the western tribes assembled at Shiloh (compare 18.1) and prepared to go to war against the eastern tribes. In some languages it may be unnecessary to repeat When the people of Israel heard this. Also, the whole community would in fact be limited to the fighting men of the western tribes. One may then translate "So all the men of the western tribes came together at Shiloh to go to war against the eastern tribes."

22.13-14

<u>22.13-14</u>   Then the people of Israel sent Phinehas, the
          son of Eleazar the priest, to the people of the
          tribes of Reuben, Gad, and East Manasseh in the
          land of Gilead. 14 Ten leading men went with
          Phinehas, one from each of the western tribes and
          each one the head of a family among the clans.

    The western tribes (always identified as the people of Israel)
sent a delegation headed by <u>Phinehas, the son of Eleazar the priest</u>
(for Eleazar see 14.1), and <u>composed of one representative from each</u>
of the ten western tribes (Phinehas represented Levi).
    <u>Each one the head of a family among the clans</u> (verse 14) may be
taken to mean "Each one was a respected leader within his clan."
    It may be advisable to indicate at the beginning of verse 13 that
a delegation (that is, a group of representatives) is being sent. And
it is also important to translate so as to avoid the heavy appositional
comment, <u>one from each of the western tribes and each one the head of</u>
<u>a family among the clans</u>. The two verses may then be translated as a
unit:

          Then the (people of the) ten western tribes sent a dele-
          gation to (the people of) the tribes of Reuben, Gad, and East
          Manasseh in the land of Gilead. They sent Phinehas, son of
          Eleazar the priest, together with a leader from each of their
          tribes. These ten tribal leaders were also respected leaders
          within their own clans.
Or:
          ...They sent Phinehas, son of Eleazar the priest, together
          with a respected clan leader from each of their ten tribes.

<u>22.15-16</u>   They came to the land of Gilead, to the people of
          Reuben, Gad, and East Manasseh, 16 and speaking for
          the whole community of the LORD, they said to them,
          "Why have you done this evil thing against the God
          of Israel? You have rebelled against the LORD by
          building this altar for yourselves! You are no
          longer following him!

    In Gilead, on the east side of the Jordan, they addressed the two
and one-half eastern tribes (verse 15).
    The language in verse 16 stresses the strong reaction of the
western tribes; they consider what the eastern tribes have done to be
"treachery," "sacrilege," "rebellion," an act of desertion (<u>no longer</u>
<u>following</u> the Lord). It is not, they say, so much a sin against their
<u>fellow Israelites</u> as against <u>the God of Israel</u>.
    Verse 15 may be considerably reduced in length, if it is assumed
that the reader can recall two things from the previous two verses:
(1) These tribal representatives are going to the land of Gilead, and
(2) they are going there to speak to the people of Reuben, Gad, and
East Manasseh. But before making a proposal for restructuring verse 15,
at least three observations should be made concerning verse 16. First,
<u>speaking for the whole community of the LORD</u> actually refers only to

the western tribes and so may be included as part of their address to
the eastern tribes. Second, in Hebrew the quotation contained in this
verse is in the form of a single, lengthy question (compare RSV). TEV
slightly rearranges the sentence parts and restructures them as a
question followed by two exclamatory statements. Third, done this evil
thing and rebelled translate two separate verbs in Hebrew, but the verbs
are close enough in meaning to be considered synonyms.

On the basis of these observations, verse 16 may be translated,
Then they (or, Phinehas and the men with him) said, 'We speak
in behalf of all the LORD's people. 'Why did you rebel against
the LORD and build this altar for yourselves? Why did you quit
following the God of Israel and do such an evil thing?'"

22.17   Remember our sin at Peor, when the LORD punished his
         own people with an epidemic? We are still suffering
         because of that. Wasn't that sin enough?

They recall the enormous sin at Peor (see Num 25.1-9), as a result
of which twenty-four thousand Israelites were killed by an epidemic;
they were all still suffering because of that (RSV "even yet we have
not cleansed ourselves").

Remember our sin...Wasn't that sin enough? apparently translates
the Hebrew "Was that sin too little for us?" NEB translates "Was that
offense so slight...?" and RSV "Have we not had enough of the sin...?"
The intent of the Hebrew seems to be to suggest that the sin of building an altar to a god other than the Lord is worse than the sin which
the Israelites earlier committed at Peor.

Both the possessive pronoun our and the phrase his own people have
the same referent, though this is not clear in TEV. With somewhat more
clarity the verse may be translated, "Remember what a terrible sin we
(inclusive) committed against the LORD at Peor. The LORD punished us
with an epidemic, even though we are his own people. And we are still
suffering because of that sin." Instead of the positive Remember, a
negative "Do not forget" may also be used.

The inclusion of a footnote, explaining what happened at Peor, or
at least giving the scripture reference, or both, may be useful. The
precise extent of the note will depend upon the intended readers and
whether the edition is a complete Old Testament, or a volume of Old
Testament selections in which Numbers 25.1-9 may not be included.

Two further observations may be made regarding the verse: (1) The
word epidemic may be translated "a terrible disease that killed many
people." (2) If the form of TEV is maintained, the question Wasn't that
sin enough? should not lead the reader to conclude that it was not
enough.

22.18   Are you going to refuse to follow him now? If you
         rebel against the LORD today, he will be angry with
         everyone in Israel tomorrow.

The western delegation stresses the fact that everyone in Israel will suffer if the eastern tribes persist in their rebellion. Refuse to follow is more literally "turn from after," which is rendered "turn away ...from following" by RSV. The verb translated rebel is the same one used in verse 16. It is quite likely that the two verbs are here used synonymously, in keeping with the manner in which the author elsewhere piles up expressions for the sake of emphasis. For many languages it will be better to shift from the question form of the Hebrew to a prohibition: "Do not refuse to obey the LORD today. If you do, he will be angry with everyone in Israel tomorrow." Or an "if" clause may be substituted: "If you rebel against the LORD today, he will be angry with everyone in Israel tomorrow."

22.19   Now then, if your land is not fit to worship in, come over into the LORD's land, where his Tent is. Claim some land among us. But don't rebel against the LORD or make rebels out of us by building an altar in addition to the altar of the LORD our God.

Now then (RSV "But now") indicates a logical transition in the argument. It is not to be confused with a marker of time sequence.

They propose to their fellow Israelites to come live among them, on the west side, if their land is not fit to worship in (RSV "is unclean"). This may imply that the rebellion at Peor, on the east side, had defiled the whole area, making it ceremonially unfit for proper worship of the Lord. Or it may imply that it was the location of the Tent of the Lord's presence which made the western region a fit place ("pure, clean") for the worship of the Lord.

The clause if your land is not fit to worship in does not necessarily imply that this is the opinion of the tribal representatives from the western tribes. The meaning may also be "If you think your land is not fit to worship in."

For the Lord's Tent in Shiloh, see 18.1. Where his Tent is may be expressed as either "where his dwelling place is" or "where he has chosen to live."

For some languages, Claim some land among us will require an indication of movement on the part of the eastern tribes: "Cross over to our territory and find a place where you can settle down."

Don't...make rebels out of us (RSV "make us as rebels") translates the Hebrew consonants with different vowels from those used in the Masoretic text, which has "don't rebel against us" (KJV, TOB). The majority of translations and commentators prefer the sense given by RSV, TEV, but HOTTP favors the Masoretic text, apparently on the grounds that it suits the context better.

Make rebels out of us may be translated "cause us to be rebels." Perhaps the idea may better be expressed: "But don't rebel against the Lord and make us guilty together with you." The translation should make it clear, as RSV and TEV do not, that us is inclusive, that is, it includes both the speakers and the listeners.

By building an altar is a difficult construction for many readers. In its place it may be preferable to introduce a new sentence with a prohibition: "But don't rebel against the LORD and make us guilty of your sins. Do not build an altar...."

22.20   Remember how Achan son of Zerah refused to obey
          the command about the things condemned to destruc-
          tion; the whole community of Israel was punished
          for that. Achan was not the only one who died be-
          cause of his sin."

The western delegation recalls the sin of Achan (see 7.1-26), which brought punishment upon all the people and the death not only of Achan but of his whole family. If one man's sins had such terrible consequences, what would be the result of the sin of two and one-half tribes of the Lord's people? Notice again the concept of things condemned to destruction because they were given to the Lord; this was what Achan disregarded.

In Hebrew Remember how...punished for that is in the form of a rhetorical question (see RSV). Since the form of the question in Hebrew automatically implies a "yes" answer, TEV is able to translate it as an affirmative statement. Remember how is the positive equivalent of "Do not ever forget."

Most translations retain son of Zerah, but for many readers the retention of this phrase will lessen the impact of the narrative. The problem is that the author of the text may have known several persons by the name of Achan, while the readers of the translation know only one.

Refused to obey the command implies two events: (1) The Lord gives a command, and (2) Achan refuses to obey. In addition, things condemned to destruction also implies a command on behalf of the Lord, who told the people of Israel to destroy all the things that were devoted to him. On the basis of these observations, verse 20 may be translated as follows:

          "...Do not forget what happened to Achan! The LORD told us,
          'Destroy everything in the city of Jericho.' But Achan did
          not obey the LORD's command, and so the LORD punished all
          of us. Achan died because of what he did, and many other
          Israelites also died because of Achan's sin."

Or a causative verb may be introduced in the last sentence: "...The LORD caused Achan to die because of what he did, and the LORD also caused many other Israelites to die because Achan did not obey him." A causal and noncausal combination is also possible: "...The LORD caused Achan to die because Achan did not obey him, and many other Israelites also died because of Achan."

21 The people of the tribes of Reuben, Gad, and East Manasseh answered the heads of the families of the western tribes: 22 "The Mighty One is God! He is the LORD! The Mighty One is God! He is the LORD! He knows why we did this, and we want you to know too! If we rebelled and did not keep faith with the LORD, do not let us live any longer! 23 If we disobeyed the LORD and built our own altar to burn sacrifices on or to use for grain offerings or fellowship offerings, let the LORD himself punish us. 24 No! We did it because we were afraid that in the future your descendants would say to ours, 'What do you have to do with the LORD, the God of Israel? 25 He made the Jordan a boundary between us and you people of Reuben and Gad. You have nothing to do with the LORD.' Then your descendants might make our descendants stop worshiping the LORD. 26 So we built an altar, not to burn sacrifices or make offerings, 27 but instead, as a sign for our people and yours, and for the generations after us, that we do indeed worship the LORD before his sacred Tent with our offerings to be burned and with sacrifices and fellowship offerings. This was to keep your descendants from saying that ours have nothing to do with the LORD. 28 It was our idea that, if this should ever happen, our descendants could say, 'Look! Our ancestors made an altar just like the LORD's altar. It was not for burning offerings or for sacrifice, but as a sign for our people and yours.' 29 We would certainly not rebel against the LORD or stop following him now by building an altar to burn offerings on or for grain offerings or sacrifices. We would not build any other altar

21 Then the Reubenites, the Gadites, and the half-tribe of Manasseh said in answer to the heads of the families of Israel, 22 "The Mighty One, God, the LORD! The Mighty One, God, the LORD! He knows; and let Israel itself know! If it was in rebellion or in breach of faith toward the LORD, spare us not today 23 for building an altar to turn away from following the LORD; or if we did so to offer burnt offerings or cereal offerings or peace offerings on it, may the LORD himself take vengeance. 24 Nay, but we did it from fear that in time to come your children might say to our children, 'What have you to do with the LORD, the God of Israel? 25 For the LORD has made the Jordan a boundary between us and you, you Reubenites and Gadites; you have no portion in the LORD.' So your children might make our children cease to worship the LORD. 26 Therefore we said, 'Let us now build an altar, not for burnt offering, nor for sacrifice, 27 but to be a witness between us and you, and between the generations after us, that we do perform the service of the LORD in his presence with our burnt offerings and sacrifices and peace offerings; lest your children say to our children in time to come, "You have no portion in the LORD."' 28 And we thought, If this should be said to us or to our descendants in time to come, we should say, 'Behold the copy of the altar of the LORD, which our fathers made, not for burnt offerings, nor for sacrifice, but to be a witness between us and you.' 29 Far be it from us that we should rebel against the LORD, and turn away this day from following the LORD by building an altar for burnt

than the altar of the LORD our God that stands in front of the Tent of his presence."	offering, cereal offering, or sacrifice, other than the altar of the LORD our God that stands before his tabernacle!"

It may be advisable to introduce a new section heading at this point: "The eastern and western tribes are reconciled" or "The eastern and western tribes resolve their difficulties." There is also the choice of a section heading with a different focus: "The eastern tribes explain the meaning of the altar."

22.21-22   The people of the tribes of Reuben, Gad, and East Manasseh answered the heads of the families of the western tribes: 22 "The Mighty One is God! He is the LORD! The Mighty One is God! He is the LORD! He knows why we did this, and we want you to know too! If we rebelled and did not keep faith with the LORD, do not let us live any longer!

The answer of the eastern tribes, the people of Reuben, Gad, and East Manasseh, is a vigorous denial of the charge that they intended apostasy or rebellion (22.21-29). In verse 22 three names for God are used: The Mighty One (el), God (elohim), the LORD (Yahweh). KJV, AT, NEB, NAB, BJ, JB take el elohim to be a superlative, "the God of gods." The eastern tribes call on their fellow Israelites (verse 22) and on the Lord (verse 23) to punish them if they intended rebellion. It was not for the purpose of offering sacrifices to the Lord that they had built the altar: the altar was to be a witness (verse 34) to the fact that they, the eastern tribes, worshiped the same God as the western tribes.

The heads of the families of the western tribes (verse 21) may be translated "the men (or, representatives) whom the western tribes had sent to them" or "the men who had been sent by the western tribes."

It seems that the forceful mention of the names of God at the beginning of verse 22, followed by the statement He knows, is actually an appeal to God as a witness to what they have done. This seems better than the understanding that the people of the two and one-half tribes merely shouted out the name of God, which is the impression which one receives from the reading of TEV. This first part of the verse may then be translated, "We appeal to the LORD, the Almighty God, as our witness. He knows why we did this, and we want you to know too!"

In the clause If we rebelled, it may be necessary to indicate against whom the rebellion was made: "If we rebelled against the LORD." The Hebrew verb translated rebelled is the same one used in verse 16. The verb did not keep faith with appears in that verse as "done this evil thing against." As previously indicated, the two verbs carry essentially the same meaning; used together they underscore the intensity of the sin. Did not keep faith with may be translated "broke our covenant with."

Do not let us live any longer may be translated "then you may kill us" or "...put us to death."

[283]

22.23   If we disobeyed the LORD and built our own altar
to burn sacrifices on or to use for grain offerings
or fellowship offerings, let the LORD himself punish
us.

Verse 23 lists the three main kinds of sacrifices: (1) burnt offerings, in which the whole animal was burned on the altar; (2) offerings
of various kinds of cereals and grains; and (3) <u>fellowship offerings</u>
(see 8.31). In verse 27, the second word of the three used there, <u>sacri-
fices</u>, is a general term for all kinds of offerings on the altar.
    The evident intention of listing these three types of sacrifice is
to be comprehensive; therefore they may be combined into something like
"any kind of sacrifices."
    Verses 22-23 may be placed together in such a way as to avoid some
of the overlap, and at the same time to make a more logical presentation:
    "We appeal to the LORD, the Almighty God, as our witness. He
knows why we did this, and we want all of Israel to know it
too! If we built this altar in order to rebel against the
LORD or to break our covenant with him, then may the LORD
himself turn us over to you so that you can kill us today.
We did not build this altar with the intention of burning
any kind of sacrifices on it...."

22.24   No! We did it because we were afraid that in the
future your descendants would say to ours, 'What
do you have to do with the LORD, the God of Israel?

In verses 24-28, as the RSV punctuation shows, there are several
levels of direct discourse included in the direct address of the eastern tribes. TEV has transformed some of it into indirect discourse so
as to have only two levels of direct discourse. The translator must
make sure that in all instances it is clear to the reader who the
speakers are and to whom they are speaking: the eastern tribes speaking to the delegation from the western tribes; the descendants of the
western tribes speaking to the descendants of the eastern tribes; and
the descendants of the eastern tribes replying to the descendants of
the western tribes.
    <u>No! We did it because we were afraid</u> is more literally "If we did
not do it from fear." The function of the negative is to indicate the
contrast between the assumption of the previous verse and its denial
in the statement to follow. In many languages it will be more forceful
not to use the negative form. For example, if the proposed restructuring of verses 22-23 is followed, it would seem better to omit the nega-
tion and proceed directly into verse 24.
    <u>What do you have to do with the LORD, the God of Israel?</u> is a
rhetorical question which may be phrased as a statement: "You have
nothing to do with the LORD, the God of Israel!"

22.25   He made the Jordan a boundary between us and you
    people of Reuben and Gad. You have nothing to do
    with the LORD.' Then your descendants might make
    our descendants stop worshiping the LORD.

It is to be noticed that in verse 25 (see also verses 32,33,34)
only the two tribes of Reuben and Gad are mentioned. This observation
leaves the translator with two options: either (1) to translate similarly
to TEV and mention explicitly the two tribes (between us and you people
of Reuben and Gad) or (2) to translate without explicit mention of the
tribes ("between us and you").

22.26   So we built an altar, not to burn sacrifices or
    make offerings,

This verse may be translated as a complete sentence, expressing
a strong denial: "We did build an altar, but we did not build it to
use for burning sacrifices or making offerings."

22.27   but instead, as a sign for our people and yours,
    and for the generations after us, that we do indeed
    worship the LORD before his sacred Tent with our
    offerings to be burned and with sacrifices and fellow-
    ship offerings. This was to keep your descendants from
    saying that ours have nothing to do with the LORD.

If verse 26 is rendered as a complete statement, then it will
probably be necessary to repeat the subject and verb at the beginning
of this verse: "We built it as a sign...."
    Sign (RSV "witness") states the purpose of the altar built by the
eastern tribes: it was to be evidence, proof, of the loyalty of the
eastern tribes to the Lord and their determination to offer sacrifices
only at the central place of worship (which, in the context of the
story, is Shiloh). The noun sign may be more effectively rendered as
a verb: "we built this altar to show to our people and your people...."
    All the offerings would be made before his sacred Tent (RSV "in
his presence").
    In order to divide verse 27 into smaller units, it may be advis-
able to begin a new sentence after before his sacred Tent. The sentence
may read: "We bring our offerings to be burned, our sacrifices, and our
fellowship offerings there before his sacred Tent." Or, in order to
combine and shorten: "We bring all our offerings there before his sacred
Tent."
    This was to keep...to do with the LORD may be translated, "Your
descendants must never tell our descendants that they do not belong to
the LORD." Direct discourse may also be employed: "Your descendants
must never tell our descendants, 'You do not belong to the LORD's
people.'"

22.28 It was our idea that, if this should ever happen,
our descendants could say, 'Look! Our ancestors
made an altar just like the LORD's altar. It was
not for burning offerings or for sacrifice, but
as a sign for our people and yours.'

It was our idea that is introduced by TEV to help make a smooth
transition from the previous verse. The same effect may be gained by
translating, "We built this altar so that...."

If this should ever happen may be translated "if your descendants
should ever say this to our descendants."

Verse 28 specifies that the altar built near the Jordan was just
like the LORD's altar—but it was not meant to compete with the one
legitimate altar of the Lord at Shiloh.

It was not for burning offerings or for sacrifice may be translated, "They did not build it to burn offerings or sacrifice."

But as a sign for our people and yours may be clearer if rendered,
"but they built it to show that we also belong to the LORD."

22.29 We would certainly not rebel against the LORD or
stop following him now by building an altar to burn
offerings on or for grain offerings or sacrifices.
We would not build any other altar than the altar
of the LORD our God that stands in front of the Tent
of his presence."

For the sake of persons who hear the scripture read, it will be
important to give some attention to the change of speakers introduced
in this verse: at the end of verse 28 the ancestors of these people are
speaking, whereas in verse 29 the people themselves speak again.

Rebel against the LORD and stop following him each convey the same
meaning, and the three terms, offerings, grain offerings, and sacrifices,
are comprehensive for all offerings made to the Lord. Therefore the
verse may be considerably reduced: "We would certainly not rebel against
the LORD and build another altar on which to offer sacrifices to the
LORD." Or, to differentiate between offerings and sacrifices: "...on
which to present offerings or make sacrifices to the LORD."

We would not build any other altar than the altar of may be confusing to the reader. The meaning may be expressed: "We would not build
an altar to compete with the altar" or "...to take the place of the
altar."

TEV	22.30-34	RSV

30 Phinehas the priest and the ten leading men of the commu-nity who were with him, the heads of families of the western tribes, heard what the people of the tribes of Reuben, Gad, and East Manasseh	30 When Phinehas the priest and the chiefs of the congrega-tion, the heads of the families of Israel who were with him, heard the words that the Reuben-ites and the Gadites and the

had to say, and they were satisfied. 31 Phinehas, the son of Eleazar the priest, said to them, "Now
we know that the LORD is with us.
You have not rebelled against him,
and so you have saved the people
of Israel from the LORD's punishment."

32 Then Phinehas and the leaders left the people of Reuben and
Gad in the land of Gilead and went
back to Canaan, to the people of
Israel, and reported to them.
33 The Israelites were satisfied
and praised God. They no longer
talked about going to war to devastate the land where the people of
Reuben and Gad had settled.

34 The people of Reuben and
Gad said, "This altar is a witness
to all of us that the LORD is God."
And so they named it "Witness."

Manassites spoke, it pleased them
well. 31 And Phinehas the son of
Eleazar the priest said to the
Reubenites and the Gadites and
the Manassites, "Today we know
that the LORD is in the midst of
us, because you have not committed
this treachery against the LORD;
now you have saved the people of
Israel from the hand of the LORD."

32 Then Phinehas the son of
Eleazar the priest, and the chiefs,
returned from the Reubenites and
the Gadites in the land of Gilead
to the land of Canaan, to the
people of Israel, and brought
back word to them. 33 And the report pleased the people of Israel;
and the people of Israel blessed
God and spoke no more of making
war against them, to destroy the
land where the Reubenites and the
Gadites were settled. 34 The Reubenites and the Gadites called
the altar Witness; "For," said
they, "it is a witness between
us that the LORD is God."

The explanation given by the two and one-half eastern tribes satisfied the delegation from the western tribes; no rebellion was intended,
all the Israelites worship the one Lord, and so he will not punish the
people of Israel (verses 30-31).

22.30-31   Phinehas the priest and the ten leading men of
             the community who were with him, the heads of fam-
             ilies of the western tribes, heard what the people
             of the tribes of Reuben, Gad, and East Manasseh had
             to say, and they were satisfied. 31 Phinehas, the
             son of Eleazar the priest, said to them, "Now we
             know that the LORD is with us. You have not rebelled
             against him, and so you have saved the people of
             Israel from the LORD's punishment."

The ten leading men of the community who were with him, the heads
of families of the western tribes may be narrowed down to either "the
ten leaders who had come with him from the western tribes" or "the ten
leaders from the western tribes."

In the clause heard what the people...had to say, the verb heard
must be translated so as to indicate intentional hearing rather than
accidental hearing: "listened to the explanation given by the men from
the tribes of...."

[287]

As verse 30 indicates, Phinehas himself is a priest, even though
he may also be referred to as the son of Eleazar the priest (verse 31).
Again, this was information of some significance to the original readers, though it is not necessary for it to be carried over into the discourse of other languages. One may translate "30 Phinehas the priest
.... 31 Phinehas said to them...."

Now we know that the LORD is with us must be translated with inclusive first personal pronouns for we and us, if such a distinction
exists in the receptor language. For languages which do not have the
inclusive and exclusive forms, it may be rendered: "Now we all know
that the LORD is with our people (or, nation)."

It is possible to rearrange the reply of Phinehas: "You did not
rebel against the LORD. So now we know that the LORD is with us, and
he will not have to punish our people."

22.32 Then Phinehas and the leaders left the people
of Reuben and Gad in the land of Gilead and went
back to Canaan, to the people of Israel, and reported to them.

Went back to, depending upon the perspective of the receptor language, may also be rendered "returned to." Since the act of leaving is
implied in went back to, the verse may be shortened: "Then Phinehas
and the ten leaders of the western tribes returned to the land of Canaan
and told the people of Israel everything," or "...and told the people
of Israel everything that had happened." In all probability the place
in Canaan to which they returned was the city of Shiloh, though this
should not be indicated in translation, since there is no basis for it
in the text.

22.33 The Israelites were satisfied and praised God. They
no longer talked about going to war to devastate the
land where the people of Reuben and Gad had settled.

The people of the western tribes were satisfied; they praised God
(RSV "blessed God") and gave up all ideas of going to war against the
eastern tribes.

In place of beginning this verse with The Israelites were satisfied, some languages will require a link with the preceding events:
"When the Israelites heard what Phinehas and the ten men told them,
they were satisfied." It is also possible to translate "The Israelites
were satisfied with what Phinehas the priest and their ten leaders reported to them."

And praised God may take the form of direct discourse: "and they
said, 'Let us praise God.'" If the word "praise" requires the reason
for praise, one may be supplied: "And they said, 'Let us praise God
for what has happened.'" In this context the verb "praise" is equivalent to "give thanks to."

They no longer talked about...had settled may also need to be
formulated as direct discourse: "They no longer said, 'Let's make war
against the people of Reuben and Gad and destroy their land.'"

22.34   The people of Reuben and Gad said, "This altar
          is a witness to all of us that the LORD is God." And
          so they named it "Witness."

A witness to all of us is literally "a witness between us" (RSV).
The meaning is "between the eastern tribes and the western tribes," not
between the tribes of Reuben and Gad; the translation of TEV is intended to avoid ambiguity. The noun witness may be transformed into a
verb: "(This altar is) to remind all of us...."
     The Masoretic text has "and the people of Reuben and of Gad named
the altar, for it is a witness between us that the LORD is God." The
name of the altar is missing, but a few Hebrew manuscripts and the
Syriac add the noun "witness" as a name for the altar, and so Witness
is the name given in RSV, TEV, NEB. BJ, JB use ellipses, without a
name. NAB has "gave the altar its name." TOB translates "the Reubenites
and the Gadites named the altar: 'It is a witness between us that the
LORD is God.'" HOTTP prefers the Masoretic text on the grounds that the
inclusion of the name represents a scribal attempt to ease the difficulty of the Hebrew text.
     If the Masoretic text is followed, then the following restructur-
ing is allowable: "The people of Reuben and Gad then gave the altar a
name. They explained, 'This altar stands here to show all of us that
the LORD is our God.'" It is, of course, obvious that the possessive
pronoun "our" would have to be inclusive, referring to all the tribes
of Israel.

Chapter 23

Joshua's Farewell Address

1 Much later the LORD gave Israel security from their enemies around them. By that time Joshua was very old, 2 so he called all Israel, the elders, leaders, judges, and officers of the people, and said, "I am very old now. 3 You have seen everything that the LORD your God has done to all these nations because of you. The LORD your God has been fighting for you. 4 I have assigned as the possession of your tribes the land of the nations that are still left, as well as of all the nations that I have already conquered, from the Jordan River in the east to the Mediterranean Sea in the west. 5 The LORD your God will make them retreat from you, and he will drive them away as you advance. You shall have their land, as the LORD your God has promised you. 6 So be careful to obey and do everything that is written in the book of the Law of Moses. Do not neglect any part of it, 7 and then you will not associate with these peoples left among you or speak the names of their gods or use those names in taking vows or worship those gods or bow down to them. 8 Instead, be faithful to the LORD, as you have been till now. 9 The LORD has driven great and powerful nations out as you advanced, and no one has ever been able to stand against you. 10 Any one of you can make a thousand men run away, because the LORD your God is fighting

1 A long time afterward, when the LORD had given rest to Israel from all their enemies round about, and Joshua was old and well advanced in years, 2 Joshua summoned all Israel, their elders and heads, their judges and officers, and said to them, "I am now old and well advanced in years; 3 and you have seen all that the LORD your God has done to all these nations for your sake, for it is the LORD your God who has fought for you. 4 Behold, I have allotted to you as an inheritance for your tribes those nations that remain, along with all the nations that I have already cut off, from the Jordan to the Great Sea in the west. 5 The LORD your God will push them back before you, and drive them out of your sight; and you shall possess their land, as the LORD your God promised you. 6 Therefore be very steadfast to keep and do all that is written in the book of the law of Moses, turning aside from it neither to the right hand nor to the left, 7 that you may not be mixed with these nations left here among you, or make mention of the names of their gods, or swear by them, or serve them, or bow down yourselves to them, 8 but cleave to the LORD your God as you have done to this day. 9 For the LORD has driven out before you great and strong nations; and as for you, no man has been able to withstand you to this day. 10 One

for you, just as he promised. 11 Be careful, then, to love the LORD your God. 12 If you are disloyal and join with the nations that are still left among you and intermarry with them, 13 you may be sure that the LORD your God will no longer drive these nations out as you advance. Rather, they will be as dangerous for you as a trap or a pit and as painful as a whip on your back or thorns in your eyes. And this will last until none of you are left in this good land which the LORD your God has given you.

14 "Now my time has come to die. Every one of you knows in his heart and soul that the LORD your God has given you all the good things that he promised. Every promise he made has been kept; not one has failed. 15 But just as he kept every promise that he made to you, so he will carry out every threat. 16 If you do not keep the covenant which the LORD your God commanded you to keep and if you serve and worship other gods, then in his anger he will punish you, and soon none of you will be left in this good land that he has given you."

man of you puts to flight a thousand, since it is the LORD your God who fights for you, as he promised you. 11 Take good heed to yourselves, therefore, to love the LORD your God. 12 For if you turn back, and join the remnant of these nations left here among you, and make marriages with them, so that you marry their women and they yours, 13 know assuredly that the LORD your God will not continue to drive out these nations before you; but they shall be a snare and a trap for you, a scourge on your sides, and thorns in your eyes, till you perish from off this good land which the LORD your God has given you.

14 "And now I am about to go the way of all the earth, and you know in your hearts and souls, all of you, that not one thing has failed of all the good things which the LORD your God promised concerning you; all have come to pass for you, not one of them has failed. 15 But just as all the good things which the LORD your God promised concerning you have been fulfilled for you, so the LORD will bring upon you all the evil things, until he have destroyed you from off this good land which the LORD your God has given you, 16 if you transgress the covenant of the LORD your God, which he commanded you, and go and serve other gods and bow down to them. Then the anger of the LORD will be kindled against you, and you shall perish quickly from off the good land which he has given to you."

In his address, Joshua briefly reviews what the Lord has done and will do for his people (verses 1-5). Then he exhorts them to be faithful to the Lord alone, else they will soon all be exterminated (verses 6-13). He finishes with another strong exhortation, followed by warning of severe consequences if they abandon the Lord and worship other gods (verses 14-16). Some scholars see this address in chapter 23 as a parallel of the address in chapter 24, which it was intended to replace. As the text now stands, chapter 23 adds practically nothing to the complete account.

[291]

23.1-16

The section heading, Joshua's Farewell Address, may be translated either "Joshua delivers his farewell address to the people of Israel" or "Joshua addresses the people of Israel for the last time." The verb "addresses" is chosen in place of "speaks to," since the reference is to a public speech. In the selection of a verb, one should take care not to imply that Joshua had no further conversations with any of the people.

23.1   Much later the LORD gave Israel security from
        their enemies around them. By that time Joshua was
        very old,

The text does not say where Joshua addressed the people. Presumably it was at Shiloh (see 22.9,12), the last place mentioned. But this takes place much later, after the Lord had given the Israelites security from all their enemies (see 21.44). Much later the LORD gave may be translated either "It had been a long time since the LORD had given" or "Many years had passed since the LORD gave."

Gave...security translates the Hebrew verb rendered "had given rest" by RSV. It is the same verb used in 1.13,15. See comments there.

By that time Joshua was very old may be translated "In the meanwhile Joshua had become very old" or "...a very old man." It may be best to make this statement into a complete sentence, since otherwise verse 2 becomes very lengthy.

Joshua was now very old, either 110 years old (24.29) or near that (see 13.1); the Hebrew expression is "an old man advanced in days" (see RSV).

23.2   so he called all Israel, the elders, leaders, judges,
        and officers of the people, and said, "I am very old
        now.

Joshua calls together the Israelites, including all their leaders—elders, leaders, judges, and officers (see 1.10; 8.33)—and addresses them. He reminds them of how the Lord has defeated all the nations in Canaan as he fought for his people (see 10.14,42; also 23.10). If elders, leaders, judges, and officers are taken in apposition to all Israel, then the meaning is that Joshua called together these people as representatives of all Israel. Accordingly the text may be translated, "So Joshua called together the representatives from all the tribes of Israel. He called together their elders, leaders, judges, and officers. Then he said...."

I am very old now translates the Hebrew idiom "I am old, having gone forward in days." RSV translates "I am now old and well advanced in years." It is legitimate also to translate "I am now very old and do not have much longer to live."

23.3   You have seen everything that the LORD your God
         has done to all these nations because of you. The
         LORD your God has been fighting for you.

It may help to arrange the contents of this verse somewhat more
chronologically: "The LORD your God has fought against your enemies
for you, and you have seen everything that he has done." This restructuring would also have the advantage of deleting one occurrence of the
rather heavy phrase the LORD your God. In order to avoid the misunderstanding that the Lord is not also Joshua's God, the phrase may better
be rendered "the LORD our God." Along these same lines, attention should
be given to the need for rendering because of you...for you by inclusive
first personal pronouns: "because of us...for us."

23.4   I have assigned as the possession of your tribes
         the land of the nations that are still left, as
         well as of all the nations that I have already
         conquered, from the Jordan River in the east to
         the Mediterranean Sea in the west.

Joshua tells the people that there are still nations to be conquered, whose land the Lord will give to Israel, as well as nations
Joshua has already defeated. The syntax of the Hebrew text is not normal, but most translations and commentators assume the meaning is that
given by RSV and TEV. For the idea of "inheritance" (RSV), see 1.6.
    In the translation of this verse it may be helpful to rearrange
the sentence parts so that from the Jordan River in the east to the
Mediterranean Sea in the west is identified at the beginning of the
verse as the totality of the land that has been assigned. For example:
    I have assigned to your tribes all of the land from the Jordan
    River in the east to the Mediterranean Sea in the west. I have
    given you the land of all the nations that we have already con-
    quered, and also the land of those nations that we have not yet
    conquered.
Since Joshua is the subject of the verb have already conquered, it may
be translated either "which you conquered under my leadership" or "which
I led you to conquer."

23.5   The LORD your God will make them retreat from you,
         and he will drive them away as you advance. You
         shall have their land, as the LORD your God has
         promised you.

Joshua refers in particular to the nations still to be defeated.
The Lord will defeat them, as he has promised.
    The referent of the pronoun them is not altogether clear in the
phrase will make them retreat from you. Attention also needs to be
given to at least two other matters: (1) A chronological arrangement
of the verse can be achieved by placing as the LORD your God has promised you first, and (2) it may be necessary to substitute direct

[293]

discourse for as the LORD...promised. In addition, there remains the problem of the LORD your God which appears twice in TEV. Here again the meaning should be expressed as "the LORD our God." For a model of what may be done:

> The LORD our God promised us, 'I will cause your enemies to retreat from you. I will drive them away as you advance, and you shall take their land.' The LORD our God will keep this promise. He will drive away those nations that are still in the land.

23.6   **So be careful to obey and do everything that is written in the book of the Law of Moses. Do not neglect any part of it,**

In verses 6-13 Joshua urges the people to remain faithful to the Lord by careful obedience to all the commands in the Law (verse 6), by absolute rejection of the Canaanite gods (verse 7), and by not intermarrying with the Canaanites (verse 12). He warns them of the consequences if they fail to heed his instructions (verse 13).

Be careful to obey and do is more literally "be very strong (or, courageous) to keep and do." The use of the two verb forms "keep and do" (RSV) represents once again the use of two synonyms to strengthen the thought. The same idea may be expressed as "obey completely." A negative expression may also be used: "not to neglect in any way" or "never to depart in any way from."

That is written in may be changed to an active: "that you read in." The entire clause that is written in the book of the Law of Moses may be translated "that Moses wrote in the book of the Law."

For the book of the Law of Moses, see 1.7.

Do not neglect any part of it translates the Hebrew idiom "not turning aside to the right or to the left." It means complete, total obedience and may be translated positively as "obey every part of it."

A greater effect may be achieved by breaking the sentence at the end of this verse. Otherwise, in combination with verse 7, it produces a very lengthy sentence. If a new sentence is begun at verse 7, then it may take the form of an imperative, similar to Do not neglect any part of it of this verse.

23.7   **and then you will not associate with these peoples left among you or speak the names of their gods or use those names in taking vows or worship those gods or bow down to them.**

Associate (RSV "be mixed with") translates the Hebrew "go into," which refers specifically to intermarriage (see verse 12). The danger in marrying Canaanites was that the Israelites would be led to worship their gods (see Bright).

In this verse, four different Hebrew verbs are used with reference to the worship of pagan gods: "to speak their names," "to swear,"[58] "to serve," and "to bow down." The first verb in this series of four ("to speak their names") may be taken as a reference to prayer. "To swear" by the name of a god means to use that god's name in making promises. The last two verbs in the series carry essentially the same meaning and refer to the act of worship. One may then translate "Do not worship their gods. Do not pray to them, or use their names when you take an oath."

23.8 Instead, be faithful to the LORD, as you have been till now.

Be faithful to translates a verb meaning "join to," "stay with"; NEB "hold fast to"; JB "be loyal to." The two clauses be faithful to the LORD, as you have been till now may be inverted so as to reflect proper historical sequence: "You have always been faithful to the LORD, so continue to be faithful to him."

23.9-10 The LORD has driven great and powerful nations out as you advanced, and no one has ever been able to stand against you. 10 Any one of you can make a thousand men run away, because the LORD your God is fighting for you, just as he promised.

In verses 9-10 Joshua reminds the Israelites of the reason why they have so easily defeated their enemies: it was because the Lord was fighting for them, so that one Israelite could defeat a thousand of the enemy (see similar language in Deut 32.30).
As you advanced of verse 9 may be placed first in the clause in order to make the sequence of events chronological: "You went against great and powerful nations, but the LORD drove them away."
In Hebrew no one is literally "no man" (RSV) and may be translated "not one of your enemies." However, it may be understood collectively as "not one of these nations."
Several translational adjustments may be necessary in verse 10. The LORD your God may need to be rendered "the LORD our God," and the Lord's promise may need to be placed in direct discourse near the beginning of the verse: "The LORD our God promised, 'I will fight for you.' That is why one of you can defeat a thousand men."

23.11 Be careful, then, to love the LORD your God.

Be careful translates the Hebrew verb rendered obey by TEV in verse 6. The root meaning of the verb is "guard" or "keep." Be careful, then, to love represents the Hebrew idiom "And guard exceedingly your souls to love." The Hebrew word "soul" is here the equivalent of "oneself," which is the basis for RSV "Take good heed to yourselves." In the context the expression "to guard oneself" seems to mean "to keep your life safe" (see Deut 4.15; Jer 17.27). Thus "to guard yourself carefully to love the LORD" is a way of saying "to keep your lives safe you must be sure to love the LORD." Finally, to love the LORD your God must surely have the meaning "to love only the LORD your God." The verse may then be expressed, "Above all else, love the LORD your God. Your very lives depend upon it."

23.12 **If you are disloyal and join with the nations that are still left among you and intermarry with them,**

If you are disloyal translates an intensive verb construction in Hebrew; "if you turn back" (RSV).
Join with the nations is ambiguous and conveys little if any meaning to the reader. **Join with** translates the same verb rendered **be faithful to** in verse 8, and the reference is to adopting the policies of the nations among whom the Israelites live, particularly that of intermarriage. By transforming the "if" clause to an imperative and the verb **disloyal** to a negative form, the following results: "Be faithful to the LORD. Do not mix with the nations that are left in the land, and do not intermarry with them." Or, the clauses of the second sentence may be inverted for what may be an arrangement that leads to a climax: "...Do not intermarry with any of the nations that are left in the land, and do not even associate with them." Or yet another possibility: "...Do not be friendly with any of the nations left in the land. And, above all else, do not intermarry with them."

23.13 **you may be sure that the LORD your God will no longer drive these nations out as you advance. Rather, they will be as dangerous for you as a trap or a pit and as painful as a whip on your back or thorns in your eyes. And this will last until none of you are left in this good land which the LORD your God has given you.**

You may be sure translates another intensive verb structure in Hebrew: "know assuredly" (RSV). If the proposed restructuring of verse 12 is followed, then it may be necessary to begin verse 13 "If you do, you may be sure that...."
The warning against mixed marriages with the Canaanites is more specifically stated and the consequences vividly portrayed by the use of four metaphors: **a trap** and **a pit** (that is, for catching animals) are figures of temptations and dangers. The second one, **a pit**, may mean specifically the lure, the bait, that draws the animal or bird into the trap. **A whip on your back** and **thorns in your eyes** (see similar language in Num 33.55) are figures of troubles and difficulties.[59] A **whip on your back** is a shortened form of "when someone beats you on the back with a whip," and **thorns in your eyes** means "when you accidentally stick thorns in your eyes."
The consequences of disloyalty described in the last sentence will be disastrous: the Israelites will not continue to possess the land but will eventually die out completely. **And this will last** may need to be rendered, "These terrible things will continue to happen to you...."

23.14   "Now my time has come to die. Every one of you
knows in his heart and soul that the LORD your
God has given you all the good things that he
promised. Every promise he made has been kept;
not one has failed.

Joshua ends his exhortation with a final warning (verses 14-16).
He prefaces it by saying that he hasn't long to live ("I am about to
go the way of all the earth," RSV; see similar language in 1 Kgs 2.2),
which adds weight to his instruction. He reminds them that the Lord
has kept all his promises (verse 14); in the same way, if they disobey
him, he will carry out all his threats (verse 15).

Now my time has come to die may also be rendered, "I do not have
much longer to live." Many languages, such as the Hebrew, will have
idiomatic expressions; however, as always, care must be taken to assure
that the idioms are of the proper language level.

Every one of you is an attempt on the part of TEV to represent the
plural form of "you" in the Hebrew text.

In his heart and soul is literally "in all your hearts and in all
your souls." RSV attempts both to retain the idiom and to indicate the
plural form by rendering "in your hearts and souls, all of you." For a
Hebrew writer the expression "heart and soul" is no less and no more
than a means of indicating the totality of a person's being. The same
effect may be achieved by dropping the idiom and shifting to an imperative: "Never forget that the LORD our God has given us all the good
things that he promised." A positive form may be preferable: "Always
remember that...."

Every promise he made has been kept may be difficult to render in
a number of languages, because promise refers to an event rather than
an object. It is also conceivable that a reader may have difficulty
with the passive has been kept. To resolve these two problems, one may
shift to an active and translate "The LORD has done everything that he
promised to do."

The additional affirmation not one has failed may not have the
effect of further stressing the Lord's faithfulness, as it would have
done for the Hebrew readers. Rather than speaking of the Lord's faithfulness in both a positive and negative fashion, it may be more effective to choose one or the other.

23.15   But just as he kept every promise that he made
to you, so he will carry out every threat.

Kept every promise that he made to you may be translated "did
every good thing for you that he said he would." Carry out every threat
may be rendered "do every evil thing to you that he said he would." Or,
so as not to assume that the Lord said he would do evil things without
reason, "...that he said he would do, if you did not obey him."

The end of verse 15 in Hebrew is practically the same as the end
of verse 16 and of verse 13 (see RSV). TEV has not represented it,
taking it to be redundant here. Using TEV language, the end of verse 15
could be translated, "...so he will carry out every threat and will

remove you completely from this good land which he has given you." This "removal" is not exile but destruction, death.

23.16   If you do not keep the covenant which the LORD
         your God commanded you to keep and if you serve
         and worship other gods, then in his anger he will
         punish you, and soon none of you will be left in
         this good land that he has given you."

The occurrence of two "if" clauses (If you do not...if you serve ...) in a single sentence tends to make comprehension difficult. Moreover, the verbs serve and worship are synonyms, and the phrase in his anger means "he will become angry." This verse may then be translated,
    The LORD our God made a covenant with you, and he expects you
    to be faithful to it. If you turn from him, and worship other
    gods, he will become angry with you and punish you. Soon none
    of you will be left in this good land that he has given you.
    The end of verse 16 is identical with the end of verse 13; here the adverb "quickly" (TEV soon) is added. In this verse the covenant is specifically mentioned; it is the sum and substance of the commandments in verses 6-11 (Bright).
    Although the last parts of verses 15 and 16 are essentially the same as the end of verse 13, one may feel uneasy about leaving out the last part of verse 15. On the other hand, the omission of this information from verse 15 may make its appearances in verses 13 and 16 more effective. One solution would be to number verses 15-16 as a unit, placing in the text only the ending of verse 16.

Chapter 24

Joshua Speaks to the People at Shechem

1 Joshua gathered all the tribes of Israel together at Shechem. He called the elders, the leaders, the judges, and the officers of Israel, and they came into the presence of God. 2 Joshua said to all the people, "This is what the LORD, the God of Israel, has to say: 'Long ago your ancestors lived on the other side of the Euphrates River and worshiped other gods. One of those ancestors was Terah, the father of Abraham and Nahor. 3 Then I took Abraham, your ancestor, from the land across the Euphrates and led him through the whole land of Canaan. I gave him many descendants. I gave him Isaac, 4 and to Isaac I gave Jacob and Esau. I gave Esau the hill country of Edom as his possession, but your ancestor Jacob and his children went down to Egypt. 5 Later I sent Moses and Aaron, and I brought great trouble on Egypt. But I led you out; 6 I brought your ancestors out of Egypt, and the Egyptians pursued them with chariots and cavalry. But when your ancestors got to the Red Sea 7 they cried out to me for help, and I put darkness between them and the Egyptians. I made the sea come rolling over the Egyptians and drown them. You know what I did to Egypt.

"'You lived in the desert a long time. 8 Then I brought you

1 Then Joshua gathered all the tribes of Israel to Shechem, and summoned the elders, the heads, the judges, and the officers of Israel; and they presented themselves before God. 2 And Joshua said to all the people, "Thus says the LORD, the God of Israel, 'Your fathers lived of old beyond the Euphrates, Terah, the father of Abraham and of Nahor; and they served other gods. 3 Then I took your father Abraham from beyond the River and led him through all the land of Canaan, and made his offspring many. I gave him Isaac; 4 and to Isaac I gave Jacob and Esau. And I gave Esau the hill country of Seir to possess, but Jacob and his children went down to Egypt. 5 And I sent Moses and Aaron, and I plagued Egypt with what I did in the midst of it; and afterwards I brought you out. 6 Then I brought your fathers out of Egypt, and you came to the sea; and the Egyptians pursued your fathers with chariots and horsemen to the Red Sea. 7 And when they cried to the LORD, he put darkness between you and the Egyptians, and made the sea come upon them and cover them; and your eyes saw what I did to Egypt; and you lived in the wilderness a long time. 8 Then I brought you to the land of the Amorites, who lived on the other side of the Jordan; they fought with you, and I gave them into

to the land of the Amorites, who
lived on the east side of the
Jordan. They fought you, but I
gave you victory over them. You
took their land, and I destroyed
them as you advanced. 9 Then the
king of Moab, Balak son of Zippor,
fought against you. He sent word
to Balaam son of Beor and asked
him to put a curse on you. 10 But
I would not listen to Balaam, so
he blessed you, and in this way I
rescued you from Balak. 11 You
crossed the Jordan and came to
Jericho. The men of Jericho fought
you, as did the Amorites, the Perizzites, the Canaanites, the Hittites, the Girgashites, the Hivites, and the Jebusites. But I
gave you victory over them all.
12 As you advanced, I threw them
into panic in order to drive out
the two Amorite kings. Your swords
and bows had nothing to do with
it. 13 I gave you a land that you
had never worked and cities that
you had not built. Now you are
living there and eating grapes
from vines that you did not plant,
and olives from trees that you did
not plant.'

your hand, and you took possession
of their land, and I destroyed
them before you. 9 Then Balak the
son of Zippor, king of Moab, arose
and fought against Israel; and he
sent and invited Balaam the son of
Beor to curse you, 10 but I would
not listen to Balaam; therefore
he blessed you; so I delivered
you out of his hand. 11 And you
went over the Jordan and came to
Jericho, and the men of Jericho
fought against you, and also the
Amorites, the Perizzites, the
Canaanites, the Hittites, the
Girgashites, the Hivites, and the
Jebusites; and I gave them into
your hand. 12 And I sent the hornet before you, which drove them
out before you, the two kings of
the Amorites; it was not by your
sword or by your bow. 13 I gave
you a land on which you had not
labored, and cities which you had
not built, and you dwell therein;
you eat the fruit of vineyards
and oliveyards which you did not
plant.'

At Shechem, some 50 kilometers north of Jerusalem, Joshua calls
together all the people and draws up a covenant for them. In many ways
it recalls the covenant made at Mount Sinai with the Israelites who
left Egypt.

The section heading, Joshua Speaks to the People at Shechem, focuses upon the fact of Joshua's speaking to the people. The emphasis may
be placed instead upon the content of Joshua's speech: "Joshua reminds
the people of Israel of what the LORD has done for them." Or the section heading might note that this is Joshua's final address to the people: "Joshua makes his farewell address to the people of Israel" or
"Joshua speaks to the people of Israel for the last time." See comments
at the section heading at 23.1.

Joshua begins by recalling the history of the people, starting with
Abraham's departure from Mesopotamia and going all the way to the conquest of Canaan (verses 2-13). Next he exhorts them to pledge their
loyalty to the Lord, to which they respond wholeheartedly (verses 15-24).
Joshua draws up the covenant and dedicates a large stone as a perpetual
witness to the people's promise (verses 25-27). After concluding his
farewell address, Joshua lets the people return to their own part of
the land (verse 28).

24.1 Joshua gathered all the tribes of Israel together at Shechem. He called the elders, the leaders, the judges, and the officers of Israel, and they came into the presence of God.

Joshua summons all the Israelites, with all the elders, the leaders, the judges, and the officers (see 23.2), and they come to him at Shechem (see 8.30), gathering around the sanctuary or the Covenant Box (which is what is meant by the presence of God).

At initial glance the text seems simple enough, but it does cause some confusion because of the number of events listed: (1) Joshua gathered all the tribes of Israel, (2) he called the elders and others, and (3) they came into the presence of God. Then event (4) is catalogued in verse 2: Joshua said to all the people. It is possible, of course, that the writer has used more than one source in the telling of the story. But the translator is concerned with how the text is to be understood as it stands now. Since the elders, the leaders, the judges, and the officers are representative of all the people of Israel, it is possible to join the text together as follows:

Joshua told all the tribes of Israel to come together at the city of Shechem. When they got there, he called the elders, the leaders, the judges, and the officers to come and stand before the LORD's Tent (or, the Covenant Box). 2 Then Joshua said to all the people....

24.2 Joshua said to all the people, "This is what the LORD, the God of Israel, has to say: 'Long ago your ancestors lived on the other side of the Euphrates River and worshiped other gods. One of those ancestors was Terah, the father of Abraham and Nahor.

This is what the LORD, the God of Israel, has to say may be rendered, "The LORD, the God of Israel, says to you."

On the other side of the Euphrates River (Hebrew "on the other side of the river") means "on the east bank of the Euphrates River," that is Mesopotamia (see the account in Gen 11.27—12.9). The point is made that Terah, the father of Abraham and Nahor, was not a worshiper of the Lord.

Other gods may be translated "foreign gods" or "the gods of the people in that land." It may also be expressed "gods other than me, the LORD."

One of those ancestors was Terah sounds a bit odd, as though Joshua was informing the Israelites of an ancestor they did not know they had. It may sound more natural to translate "This went on until the time of Terah." Or "This was true, even of your ancestor Terah."

24.3 Then I took Abraham, your ancestor, from the land across the Euphrates and led him through the whole land of Canaan. I gave him many descendants. I gave him Isaac,

From the land across the Euphrates may be translated "from that
land," since "on the other side of the Euphrates River" is expressly
mentioned in the previous verse.

I gave him many descendants. I gave him Isaac may be inverted to
reflect chronological order: "I gave him his son Isaac, and through
Isaac I gave him many descendants."

24.4   and to Isaac I gave Jacob and Esau. I gave Esau
the hill country of Edom as his possession, but
your ancestor Jacob and his children went down
to Egypt.

And to Isaac I gave Jacob and Esau may be rendered as a complete
sentence: "I gave Isaac two sons, Jacob and Esau."

Esau and his descendants are given the hill country of Edom (RSV
"Seir"), southwest of the Dead Sea.

TEV has added your ancestor (before Jacob) to distinguish him from
Esau, who was not their ancestor; but this does not seem necessary.

24.5   Later I sent Moses and Aaron, and I brought great
trouble on Egypt. But I led you out;

In verses 5-7a it is to be noticed how the text alternates between
"your ancestors" and "you" (plural) as participants in the events of the
exodus and the deliverance at the Sea of Reeds (see RSV). This is especially noticeable in verse 7. Some scholars may believe that the use of
different sources accounts for these variations. But this may be also
the author's way of reminding the people of his day that they are personally related to the great redemptive event that the Lord accomplished
for their ancestors in Egypt.

At the beginning of verse 5, TEV has introduced Later in order to
provide some sense of the lapse of time; Hebrew has simply "And I sent
Moses..." (RSV).

One may wish to introduce the persons to whom the Lord sent Moses
and Aaron: "Later I sent Moses and Aaron to your ancestors in Egypt."

And I brought great trouble on Egypt translates a Hebrew text which
has some repetition: "and I plagued Egypt with what I did in the midst
of it" (RSV). Although the land of Egypt suffered under the plagues
which the Lord sent, the people of Egypt are really the ones in focus.
Therefore the clause may be translated, "and brought great trouble on
the people of Egypt."

The great trouble refers to the plagues.

But I led you out may require the complete form, "But I led you
out of Egypt," or even "...safely out of Egypt."

24.6   I brought your ancestors out of Egypt, and the
Egyptians pursued them with chariots and cavalry.
But when your ancestors got to the Red Sea

The Hebrew text speaks twice of the body of water to which the Israelites came (see RSV "the sea" and "the Red Sea"); TEV has eliminated the repetition, as a matter of style. For Red Sea see 2.10.

But I led you out (verse 5) and I brought your ancestors out (verse 6) say basically the same thing, since in the narration of events the writer freely shifts from "you" to "your ancestors." Verses 5-6 may then be translated as a unit:

Later I sent Moses and Aaron to help your ancestors, and I brought great trouble on the people of Egypt. I led your ancestors out of Egypt and to the Red Sea. When the Egyptian army pursued them with war chariots and men on horses....

24.7a   they cried out to me for help, and I put darkness between them and the Egyptians. I made the sea come rolling over the Egyptians and drown them. You know what I did to Egypt.

And I put darkness between them and the Egyptians may need to be rendered as a separate statement. Moreover, some languages will experience difficulty with the abstract noun darkness. The clause may be restructured to say "so I put a dark cloud between them and the Egyptians."

I made the sea come rolling over the Egyptians and drown them leaves implicit an event which is not mentioned in the text. That is, according to the Exodus account the Lord first caused the sea to open up so that the Israelites could cross over on dry land. It was only when the Egyptians attempted to do the same thing that the sea came rolling over them. For readers not familiar with this event, a footnote referring to the exodus account may be useful. However, it may even be better to resolve this difficulty in the text: "I opened up the sea so that your ancestors could pass through safely. But when the Egyptians attempted to follow them, I caused the sea to roll over them and drown them." This will remove the impression that the sea overflowed its banks and engulfed the Egyptians.

You know what I did to Egypt is literally "And your eyes saw what I did to Egypt" (RSV). In the biblical account, however, Joshua and Caleb were the only adults who had left Egypt and had lived to enter the Promised Land; all the other adults had perished during the forty years in the wilderness. So TEV has You know, which seems more suitable.

24.7b-8   "'You lived in the desert a long time. 8 Then I brought you to the land of the Amorites, who lived on the east side of the Jordan. They fought you, but I gave you victory over them. You took their land, and I destroyed them as you advanced.

In verses 7b-10 Joshua recounts the events on the east side of the Jordan. A long time is literally "many days" and may also be rendered "many years."

The Amorites is a general term for all the peoples of the region, and not simply for one tribe; so the comma indicating a nonrestrictive relative clause after Amorites in TEV is wrong.

As you advanced is literally "from your faces" (RSV "before you"). The meaning may well be "for you" or "so that you could (take their land)." You took their land, and I destroyed them as you advanced may then be translated, "I fought for you and destroyed them, so that you could take their land for yourselves."

24.9-10   Then the king of Moab, Balak son of Zippor, fought
            against you. He sent word to Balaam son of Beor
            and asked him to put a curse on you. 10 But I would
            not listen to Balaam, so he blessed you, and in this
            way I rescued you from Balak.

For the account of Balak and Balaam, see Numbers 22.1—24.25. The king of Moab, Balak son of Zippor may be translated as "King Balak of Moab" or "Balak, king of Moab," without the modifier son of Zippor. As with so many of these "son of..." modifiers, so here also it gives information which was important for the Hebrew writer and his readers, but not for present-day readers, and it adds awkwardness to the text.

In verse 9 fought does not agree with the accounts in Numbers 22.6, 11; Deuteronomy 2.9; Judges 11.25, which specify that Balak, in fact, did not go to battle against the Israelites. So some commentators and translations propose "prepared to fight" as the meaning of the verb. It is also possible to use the verb in a more general sense of "stood up against" or "opposed." Some translations use the idiomatic "stood in your way" or "placed himself in your way." It may be better to translate "opposed."

Balaam son of Beor may be rendered, "Balaam" (see above comments on "son of Zippor").

Asked him to put a curse on you may be translated as direct discourse: "asked him, 'Put a curse on the people of Israel.'" The problem, however, is that this would make a third layer of discourse, a quotation within a quotation within a quotation, which is difficult for many readers. A simpler solution would be to translate the two verb structures sent word and asked by a single verb: "He sent for the prophet Balaam to put a curse on you" or "He sent for the prophet Balaam to come and place a curse on you."

But I would not listen to Balaam (so also RSV) represents a literal rendering of the Hebrew text. The meaning may be expressed "But I would not allow Balaam to place a curse on you."

So he blessed you may be expressed more fully, "Against his will, he blessed you." It may also be translated, "Instead I caused him to pronounce a blessing on you."

24.11   You crossed the Jordan and came to Jericho. The men
           of Jericho fought you, as did the Amorites, the Periz-
           zites, the Canaanites, the Hittites, the Girgashites,
           the Hivites, and the Jebusites. But I gave you victory
           over them all.

Verses 11-13 describe the invasion of Canaan, beginning with the battle for Jericho (chapter 6). For the seven peoples listed in this verse, see comments on 3.10.60 The phrase the men of Jericho represents the Hebrew "the lords (or, owners) of Jericho"; JB "those who held Jericho"; and TOB "the owners (or, masters) of Jericho." It also seems adequate to translate "The fighting men from Jericho" or "The soldiers from Jericho."

But I gave you victory over them all may more effectively be introduced earlier in the verse: "The people of Jericho fought you, but I caused you to defeat them. Then the Amorites...and the Jebusites fought against you. But I caused you to defeat all of them."

24.12   As you advanced, I threw them into panic in order
         to drive out the two Amorite kings. Your swords
         and bows had nothing to do with it.

As you advanced again represents the Hebrew "from your faces" (RSV "before you"). It will not be necessary to express this in translation, if this meaning is clearly enough understood apart from an explicit statement of it.

Panic translates a Hebrew word which some have understood to mean "hornet" (see RSV), used figuratively. As Soggin explains, it "is not the 'wasp' or 'hornet'...but 'dismay,' a typical consequence of divine intervention in the course of holy war" (see 2.11; and see the use of the word in Exo 23.28; Deut 7.20). I threw them into panic may be translated either "I caused them to panic" or "I caused them to fear and tremble." It is highly probable that an acceptable idiomatic expression of the proper level may be found in many languages.

The two Amorite kings are Sihon king of Heshbon and Og king of Bashan (see 2.26—3.11), whose territory was on the east side of the Jordan, not on the west side, in Canaan proper. This phrase seems misplaced (see Bright), and NAB shifts it back to verse 8, where it is more fitting; but there is no manuscript evidence to support this.

The last part of verse 12 and verse 13 emphasize again that the victories won by the Israelites were not the result of their skill and valor as fighters, but were due to the Lord's power. Your swords and bows had nothing to do with it may be translated without naming the specific weapons: "Your weapons and strength had nothing to do with it." It is possible also to translate by both a positive and negative statement: "I defeated them for you. It was not your own strength and weapons that did it."

24.13   I gave you a land that you had never worked and
         cities that you had not built. Now you are living
         there and eating grapes from vines that you did
         not plant, and olives from trees that you did not
         plant.'

The first sentence of this verse may be inverted: "You did not plant any crops in that land, and you did not build any of its cities.

But I gave it all to you." Or, in order to maintain a strong focus upon the Lord as the one who provided these things for the people of Israel: "I was the one who gave you their land and their cities. You did not have to plant any crops or build any cities."

It is possible to divide the second sentence of this verse into two sentences: "You are now living in this land that I gave you. You are eating grapes from vines that you did not plant, and olives from trees that you did not plant." That you did not plant may also be translated "that other people planted" or "that were planted by the people who lived there before you."

<table>
<tr><td>TEV</td><td>24.14-28</td><td>RSV</td></tr>
</table>

TEV	RSV
14 "Now then," Joshua continued, "honor the LORD and serve him sincerely and faithfully. Get rid of the gods which your ancestors used to worship in Mesopotamia and in Egypt, and serve only the LORD. 15 If you are not willing to serve him, decide today whom you will serve, the gods your ancestors worshiped in Mesopotamia or the gods of the Amorites, in whose land you are now living. As for my family and me, we will serve the LORD."	14 "Now therefore fear the LORD, and serve him in sincerity and in faithfulness; put away the gods which your fathers served beyond the River, and in Egypt, and serve the LORD. 15 And if you be unwilling to serve the LORD, choose this day whom you will serve, whether the gods your fathers served in the region beyond the River, or the gods of the Amorites in whose land you dwell; but as for me and my house, we will serve the LORD."
16 The people replied, "We would never leave the LORD to serve other gods! 17 The LORD our God brought our fathers and us out of slavery in Egypt, and we saw the miracles that he performed. He kept us safe wherever we went among all the nations through which we passed. 18 As we advanced into this land, the LORD drove out all the Amorites who lived here. So we also will serve the LORD; he is our God."	16 Then the people answered, "Far be it from us that we should forsake the LORD, to serve other gods; 17 for it is the LORD our God who brought us and our fathers up from the land of Egypt, out of the house of bondage, and who did those great signs in our sight, and preserved us in all the way that we went, and among all the peoples through whom we passed; 18 and the LORD drove out before us all the peoples, the Amorites who lived in the land; therefore we also will serve the LORD, for he is our God."
19 Joshua said to the people, "But you may not be able to serve the LORD. He is a holy God and will not forgive your sins. He will tolerate no rivals, 20 and if you leave him to serve foreign gods, he will turn against you and punish you. He will destroy you, even though he was good to you before."	19 But Joshua said to the people, "You cannot serve the LORD; for he is a holy God; he is a jealous God; he will not forgive your transgressions or your sins. 20 If you forsake the LORD and serve foreign gods, then he will turn and do you harm, and consume
21 The people said to Joshua,	

"No! We *will* serve the LORD."

22 Joshua told them, "You are your own witnesses to the fact that you have chosen to serve the LORD."

"Yes," they said, "we are witnesses."

23 "Then get rid of those foreign gods that you have," he demanded, "and pledge your loyalty to the LORD, the God of Israel."

24 The people then said to Joshua, "We will serve the LORD our God. We will obey his commands."

25 So Joshua made a covenant for^q the people that day, and there at Shechem he gave them laws and rules to follow. 26 Joshua wrote these commands in the book of the Law of God. Then he took a large stone and set it up under the oak tree in the LORD's sanctuary. 27 He said to all the people, "This stone will be our witness. It has heard all the words that the LORD has spoken to us. So it will be a witness against you, to keep you from rebelling against your God." 28 Then Joshua sent the people away, and everyone returned to his own part of the land.

you, after having done you good." 21 And the people said to Joshua, "Nay; but we will serve the LORD." 22 Then Joshua said to the people, "You are witnesses against yourselves that you have chosen the LORD, to serve him." And they said, "We are witnesses." 23 He said, "Then put away the foreign gods which are among you, and incline your heart to the LORD, the God of Israel." 24 And the people said to Joshua, "The LORD our God we will serve, and his voice we will obey." 25 So Joshua made a covenant with the people that day, and made statutes and ordinances for them at Shechem. 26 And Joshua wrote these words in the book of the law of God; and he took a great stone, and set it up there under the oak in the sanctuary of the LORD. 27 And Joshua said to all the people, "Behold, this stone shall be a witness against us; for it has heard all the words of the LORD which he spoke to us; therefore it shall be a witness against you, lest you deal falsely with your God." 28 So Joshua sent the people away, every man to his inheritance.

^{q}for; *or* with.

Having finished delivering the Lord's message (verses 2-13), Joshua himself now challenges the Israelites (verses 14-15), exhorting them to rid themselves of the gods their ancestors worshiped in Mesopotamia (see verse 2) and in Egypt. And if they were unwilling to worship the Lord, then they should make a definite choice between the gods of the people in whose land they were now livng and the gods their ancestors worshiped in Mesopotamia. These pagan gods would be represented by idols and ornaments of various kinds. By his own affirmation of loyalty to the Lord, Joshua hopes to evoke a similar pledge from his fellow Israelites.

Since a definite shift in the narrative does take place at this point, it may be wise to introduce a new section heading. For example, "Joshua calls on the people of Israel to make a decision" or "Joshua tells the people of Israel to decide between the Lord and the other gods."

"Now then," Joshua continued, "honor the LORD and
serve him sincerely and faithfully. Get rid of the gods
which your ancestors used to worship in Mesopotamia and
in Egypt, and serve only the LORD.

TEV introduces Joshua continued in order to indicate that Joshua
is no longer quoting the Lord's message to them. It is for stylistic
reasons alone that the first part of Joshua's address (Now then) is
placed before Joshua continued, which may as easily have been placed
first in this verse.

Honor translates a Hebrew verb which has traditionally been rendered "fear" (RSV) by the majority of English translations. Here the
focus of the verb is upon placing the Lord above all other gods. Serve,
in its two occurrences in this verse, may mean either "obey" or "worship."

The adverbs sincerely and faithfully may be translated as either
a verb or a verb plus adjective construction: "be true and faithful."

Get rid of the gods refers to the literal, physical removal of
these gods from the premises. Reference would be to the idols and other
items used in the worship of these gods. Even at this time in their
history, the people of Israel evidently still carried idols or other
objects which enabled them to worship and pray to these deities.

<u>24.15</u>   If you are not willing to serve him, decide today
whom you will serve, the gods your ancestors worshiped in Mesopotamia or the gods of the Amorites,
in whose land you are now living. As for my family
and me, we will serve the LORD."

The lengthy "if" clause at the beginning of this verse may cause
considerable difficulty for the reader, and it may be advisable to
break it into several shorter units. For example:
     If you are not willing to obey the LORD, then decide today
     what god you will obey. You will have to choose between the
     gods which your ancestors worshiped in Mesopotamia and the
     gods which the Amorites worship in the land where you are
     now living.

As for my family and me is literally "as for me and my house" (RSV).
The word "house" would include not only Joshua's immediate family and
all relatives who lived with him, but his slaves and servants as well.
One may translate "But my family and I have decided to obey the LORD."
Or, since this is a patriarchal society, "I have decided to obey the
LORD, and everyone in my family and all my slaves will also obey the
LORD," or "I will obey the LORD, and I will require my family and all
my slaves to obey the LORD."

<u>24.16</u>   The people replied, "We would never leave the
LORD to serve other gods!

The people respond enthusiastically to Joshua's challenge and
declare that they also will worship only the Lord (verse 16). They
recognize that it was the Lord who delivered them from slavery in
Egypt and brought them safely into Canaan: he is their God and they
will worship him (verses 17-18).

We would never translates the Hebrew idiom "Far be it from us"
(RSV). For languages where a rhetorical question is effective, one may
want to translate "How could we ever...?" One may even want to translate by two brief affirmations: "We would never be unfaithful to the
LORD! We would never serve other gods!"

24.17　　The LORD our God brought our fathers and us out
　　　　of slavery in Egypt, and we saw the miracles that
　　　　he performed. He kept us safe wherever we went
　　　　among all the nations through which we passed.

Brought...out of slavery translates the Hebrew idiom "brought...out
of the house of bondage" (RSV). The noun phrase slavery in Egypt may be
expanded into a clause using a verb phrase: "out of Egypt where we were
slaves" or "...where the Egyptians forced us to be their slaves."

Our fathers and us and and we saw represent a literal rendering of
the Hebrew text. Using "us" and "we" is the usual way by which the biblical writers identify their own generation as participating in the
exodus from Egypt. But for readers whose linguistic and cultural understanding is different, this may seem inaccurate, especially if the miracles referred to were those done in the course of bringing the people
out of Egypt. One may prefer to translate "The LORD our God brought our
fathers out of Egypt where they were slaves, and we know about the miracles that he performed there."

Wherever we went among all the nations through which we passed is
somewhat complicated. The reference is to the journeys that the Israelites made on their way to the land of Canaan, and the sentence may be
translated, "On our way here we traveled through the territory of many
nations, but the LORD always kept us safe."

24.18　　As we advanced into this land, the LORD drove out all
　　　　the Amorites who lived here. So we also will serve the
　　　　LORD; he is our God."

As we advanced once again translates "before our faces" of the
Hebrew text. The meaning may be expressed "As we went from one place
to the next" or "As we went from one part of the land to another." The
first sentence may be translated, "The Amorites lived in the land at
that time, but the LORD drove them all out for us."

For greater effectiveness, he is our God may be translated "he
alone is our God."

24.19　　Joshua said to the people, "But you may not be
　　　　able to serve the LORD. He is a holy God and will not
　　　　forgive your sins. He will tolerate no rivals,

Joshua's answer (verses 19-20) is that they must recognize the seriousness of their promise. They probably will not be able to keep it, which means that they will be punished for their idolatry. But you may not be able to serve the LORD may be translated either "But do not think that it is easy to serve the LORD" or "Do not be so quick to say, 'We will serve the LORD.'" One may also translate "It is not easy to serve the LORD."

Joshua reminds the people of Israel that the Lord is holy and that he will tolerate no rivals (RSV "is a jealous God"). The first adjective holy stresses his essential being, the quality which characterizes God and separates him from sinful humanity. He is a holy God may be translated, "No other god is like the LORD," "No other god can compare with the LORD," or "The LORD is different from all other gods."

The second adjective "jealous" is well represented by TEV, He will tolerate no rivals (see Exo 20.5; Deut 4.24; 5.9). It represents the unwillingness of the Lord to share with any other god the exclusive claim that he has on his people, and so it may be translated "he demands (or, requires) absolute obedience."

Will not forgive your sins represents "will not forgive your transgressions or your sins" (RSV), in which TEV combines the two nouns "transgressions" and "sins." Furthermore, as a comparison of RSV and TEV will reveal, TEV places the clause at a place other than where it is found in the Hebrew text. This is done in TEV so that He will tolerate no rivals may be joined with and if you leave him... of verse 20. However, it seems more probable that will not forgive your sins should be joined with either (a) He will tolerate no rivals or (b) with both He will tolerate no rivals and He is a holy God. In context, "will not forgive your sins" then means that God will not forgive the sin of unfaithfulness to him. Upon the assumption that this analysis of the text is correct, the following translation results: "The LORD is a holy God who demands absolute obedience. He will not forgive you if you are unfaithful to him." Or "The LORD is different from all other gods. He demands that you worship only him. If you worship other gods, he will not forgive you." Either of these proposed restructurings will also have the advantage of leading nicely into verse 20: "If you leave him to worship foreign gods...."

24.20   and if you leave him to serve foreign gods, he will
         turn against you and punish you. He will destroy
         you, even though he was good to you before."

It may be best to begin a new sentence with this verse. If you leave him to serve foreign gods may be translated, "If you quit worshiping the LORD and start worshiping other gods" or "...the gods which other people worship." This "if" clause may also take the form of an imperative: "Do not quit worshiping him and begin to worship other gods."

Even though he was good to you before, appearing as it does at the end of the verse, may be a slight stumbling block to the reader. It is possible to rearrange the entire verse so that this clause comes in its proper chronological place: "The LORD has always been good to you, but you must never quit worshiping him and start worshiping other gods. Then he will turn against you and punish you until he has completely destroyed you." Or "...other gods. If you do, he will turn against you. He will punish you until you are completely destroyed."

24.21-22   The people said to Joshua, "No! We *will* serve the LORD."
         22 Joshua told them, "You are your own witnesses to the fact that you have chosen to serve the LORD."
         "Yes," they said, "we are witnesses."

The No! with which the people answer Joshua is a denial of the possibility that they will reject the Lord and serve foreign gods. For many readers the response No will indicate denial or rejection of Joshua's advice. It may be better to translate No! as "What you have said is true" or "That is indeed true!"

The verb *will* is placed in italics by TEV for the sake of emphasis. Such a device is of no advantage for the person who must depend upon hearing the Scripture read.

So Joshua puts them under solemn oath, You are your own witnesses, and they voluntarily affirm the fact. To the fact that makes a somewhat awkward structure in English. In the present context its function is to indicate that the speaker, Joshua, is quoting indirectly what the other speakers, the people, have said. Accordingly one may shift to direct discourse: "You are your own witnesses. You said, 'We have chosen to serve the LORD!'"

Yes...we are witnesses may also be translated "That is true" or "What you have said is true."

24.23-24   "Then get rid of those foreign gods that you have," he demanded, "and pledge your loyalty to the LORD, the God of Israel."
         24 The people then said to Joshua, "We will serve the LORD our God. We will obey his commands."

Joshua commands the people to get rid of their idols and to pledge their loyalty to the Lord (Hebrew "bend, or turn, your hearts to"; see RSV). The people promise they will worship only the Lord and obey his commands.

As indicated at verse 14, get rid of implies the physical destruction of objects used in the worship of foreign gods. Joshua's command may be rendered, "Destroy all the idols that you have." The sentence may also be inverted: "Some of you still have idols of foreign gods with you. Destroy all of them and pledge your loyalty to the LORD, the God of Israel." Indirect discourse may be more acceptable: "...and say, 'We will be faithful to the LORD, the God of Israel.'" Or, if the God of Israel is a difficult phrase: "...and say, 'We will be faithful to the LORD. He is the God whom the people of Israel must worship.'"

Obey his commands translates the Hebrew "obey his voice" (see RSV). It may be more natural to translate the response of the people as a single sentence: "We will worship the LORD our God and obey his commands." Two sentences may be retained, but in a different form: "The LORD is our God. We will worship only him and obey all his commands."

24.25   So Joshua made a covenant for^q the people that
             day, and there at Shechem he gave them laws and rules
             to follow.

             ^qfor; *or* with.

The Hebrew expression translated for the people (BJ, JB) may also mean "with the people" (AT, RSV, NEB, NAB, TOB). It appears that Joshua is here portrayed as a representative of the Lord, and that the covenant he draws up is not between himself and the people but between the people and the Lord (so Gray, Soggin). If the interpretation of TEV is followed, one may translate "On that day when the people were gathered at Shechem, Joshua made a covenant between them and the LORD." Or "On that day at Shechem, Joshua stood as the representative of the people and made a covenant with the LORD." The noun "representative" may be transformed into a verb: "On that day at Shechem, Joshua represented the people of Israel and made a covenant between them and the LORD."
   Like the covenant at Mount Sinai, this one also included laws and rules for the Israelites to obey. The two nouns laws and rules are best understood as comprehensive terms describing the regulations contained within the covenant. In some languages one term will be satisfactory. There are some places in the Old Testament (in Deuteronomy, for example) where the biblical writer uses as many as five terms for law, which TEV generally translates as only two terms. The reasons for this are: (1) There are no terms in English (or in any other language) which overlap precisely with the Hebrew terms; (2) the Hebrew writers enjoyed accumulating synonyms for the sake of emphasis, which is not always done in English. He gave them laws and rules to follow may be translated, "This covenant contained laws which the people were to obey."

24.26   Joshua wrote these commands in the book of the Law
             of God. Then he took a large stone and set it up
             under the oak tree in the LORD's sanctuary.

These commands refers back to laws and rules of verse 25, and in translation it may be best to use the same phraseology in both places. Both phrases are summary terms of the regulations contained in the covenant.
   It is impossible to identify the book of the Law of God with any book or part of a book now in the Old Testament. Soggin says that the Hebrew noun usually translated "book" means here "written document of a treaty"; according to him the identification of the Law was added later, when the original sense of the Hebrew word was forgotten. So he

translates "And Joshua wrote these words in the document of God."
Soggin may well be right, but the translator cannot omit the noun Law
from the text. The book of the Law of God may be translated "the book
which contained (or, listed) God's Laws for his people."

Then he took a large stone and set it up may be translated "Then
he set up a large stone." The text obviously means that Joshua was the
one responsible for having this done, and so one may translate "Joshua
commanded some of his men to set up a large stone...." Or, so as not
to mention a third party, "Joshua caused a large stone to be set up."

Under the oak tree in the LORD's sanctuary leaves the impression
that a large oak tree was growing in the Lord's sanctuary. It would be
better to translate "under the large oak tree beside the LORD's sanctuary." In verse 25 the geographical reference "at Shechem" may be difficult to include with ease within the text. If that is the case, then
it may be deleted from verse 25 and included here: "in the LORD's sanctuary at Shechem."

The oak tree is probably a sacred tree at the shrine; reference is
made to it in Genesis 12.6; 35.4; Judges 9.6 (in this last passage a
different Hebrew phrase is used, the oak of the pillar).

24.27   He said to all the people, "This stone will be our
           witness. It has heard all the words that the LORD
           has spoken to us. So it will be a witness against
           you, to keep you from rebelling against your God."

The large stone which Joshua placed under the tree was to serve
as a witness against the Israelites, to remind them of their promise.
In graphic language, Joshua says that the stone has heard all the words
that the LORD has spoken to us.

This stone will be our witness is literally "Behold, this stone
will be a witness against us" (RSV). TEV deletes "against us" since it
is included in the form against you later in this verse. The effect of
"behold" (used here for emphasis, see RSV) may be achieved if this part
of the verse is translated, "Take a close look at this stone! It has
heard everything that the LORD has said to us." In this way the noun
witness can be avoided, since in some languages the choice of the term
will imply either an accusing witness or a defending witness, but not
both. If a choice must be made, the context favors the meaning of an
accusing witness.

Rebelling translates a Hebrew verb which may mean "deal falsely
with" (see RSV), "deceive" (TOB); "deny" (NAB, JB), "renounce" (NEB).
This last sentence of the verse may also be rendered in such a manner
as to avoid the use of the noun "witness." For example, "It is here to
remind you not to rebel against our God."

24.28   Then Joshua sent the people away, and everyone
           returned to his own part of the land.

The ceremony concluded, Joshua dismissed the people and they all
went back home. For a literal rendering of this verse, see RSV. In

order to make the second clause easier to understand, TEV supplies the verb returned. In some languages the use of a plural following people may be more appropriate than everyone...his of TEV: "...the people away, and all of them returned to their own part of the land."

| | TEV | 24.29-33 | RSV |

Joshua and Eleazar Die

29 After that, the LORD's servant Joshua son of Nun died at the age of a hundred and ten. 30 They buried him on his own land at Timnath Serah in the hill country of Ephraim north of Mount Gaash.

31 As long as Joshua lived, the people of Israel served the LORD, and after his death they continued to do so as long as those leaders were alive who had seen for themselves everything that the LORD had done for Israel.

32 The body of Joseph, which the people of Israel had brought from Egypt, was buried at Shechem, in the piece of land that Jacob had bought from the sons of Hamor, the father of Shechem, for a hundred pieces of silver. This land was inherited by Joseph's descendants.

33 Eleazar son of Aaron died and was buried at Gibeah, the town in the hill country of Ephraim which had been given to his son Phinehas.

29 After these things Joshua the son of Nun, the servant of the LORD, died, being a hundred and ten years old. 30 And they buried him in his own inheritance at Timnath-serah, which is in the hill country of Ephraim, north of the mountain of Gaash.

31 And Israel served the LORD all the days of Joshua, and all the days of the elders, who outlived Joshua and had known all the work which the LORD did for Israel.

32 The bones of Joseph which the people of Israel brought up from Egypt were buried at Shechem, in the portion of ground which Jacob bought from the sons of Hamor the father of Shechem for a hundred pieces of money;*q* it became an inheritance of the descendants of Joseph.

33 And Eleazar the son of Aaron died; and they buried him at Gibe-ah, the town of Phinehas his son, which had been given him in the hill country of Ephraim.

*q*Heb *qesitah*

The section heading, Joshua and Eleazar Die, may suggest that they died at the same time. The central human figure of this section, as of the entire book, is Joshua. Therefore, to avoid confusion, it may be enough to render the section heading "Joshua dies."

The book concludes with the death and burial of Joshua (verses 29-31), the burial of Joseph's body (verse 32), and the death and burial of the priest Eleazar (verse 33).

24.29   After that, the LORD's servant Joshua son of Nun died at the age of a hundred and ten.

After that represents a Hebrew construction which may mean either "After these things" (RSV) or "After these words." A literal rendering, as the rendering of TEV, gives the wrong meaning that as soon as Joshua finished speaking to the people, he fell over dead. After that may be translated "Some time later."

The inclusion of the full identification, the LORD's servant...son of Nun, may seem rather heavy in some languages. The LORD's servant must definitely be included, and at this point in the narrative son of Nun adds a fullness to the text which some will consider important. To include all of this information in a form that is natural, it may be necessary to translate by two sentences: "Some time later Joshua son of Nun died at the age of a hundred and ten. He had served the LORD while he lived." Or, "Some time later, the LORD's servant Joshua son of Nun died. He was a hundred and ten years old at the time."

24.30   They buried him on his own land at Timnath Serah
         in the hill country of Ephraim north of Mount
         Gaash.

The impersonal structure They buried him is the equivalent of a passive "He was buried." It may be translated, "The people of Israel buried him."

For Joshua's property, see 19.49-50; see also Judges 2.9, where the variant Timnath Heres (see RSV) is used.61 Mount Gaash is not mentioned elsewhere in the Bible.

24.31   As long as Joshua lived, the people of Israel
         served the LORD, and after his death they continued
         to do so as long as those leaders were alive who
         had seen for themselves everything that the LORD
         had done for Israel.

Joshua's greatness as a leader is emphasized. After his death the Israelites continued to be faithful—but only as long as those leaders (RSV "the elders") who had seen the Lord's great actions were still alive (see the parallel statement in Judges 2.7 and the discouraging epilogue in 2.10).

In order to make this verse more readable, it may be divided into smaller units:

         After Joshua died, the people of Israel remained faithful
         to the LORD for a while. Their leaders had seen everything that
         the LORD had done for Israel. So the people remained faithful
         to the LORD as long as those leaders were alive.

TEV states explicitly that the people of Israel were faithful to the Lord as long as Joshua lived. In this proposed restructuring the people's faithfulness during Joshua's lifetime is left implicit, though it is clearly assumed through the use of the verb "remained faithful" (twice): "After Joshua died, the people of Israel remained faithful.... So the people remained faithful...."

Everything includes all the great miracles wrought by the Lord in bringing his people out of Egypt and leading them to the Promised Land.

24.32   The body of Joseph, which the people of Israel
         had brought from Egypt, was buried at Shechem, in
         the piece of land that Jacob had bought from the sons
         of Hamor, the father of Shechem, for a hundred pieces
         of silver. This land was inherited by Joseph's descend-
         ants.

Finally the body of Joseph (Hebrew "bones of Joseph") is given permanent burial (see Gen 50.25-26; Exo 13.19). For the purchase of the field of Jacob, see Genesis 33.18-20. The sons of Hamor should probably be "the descendants of Hamor," as in Genesis 33.19. It is not known exactly how much the hundred pieces of silver would be worth in modern currency.

Which the people of Israel had brought from Egypt is chronologically prior to The body of Joseph...was buried at Shechem. Moreover, the piece of land that Jacob had bought comes first in the historical sequence of events. It is possible (1) to translate so that all three events fall in chronological sequence or (2) to place only the first two in chronological sequence with the mention of the purchase of the field as a flashback, as TEV has done. If all three events are placed in chronological sequence, the following will serve as a pattern:

     Many years ago the Israelites' ancestor Jacob had bought
     a piece of land from the sons of Hamor, the father of Shechem.
     He had paid them a hundred pieces of silver for this land.
     When the people of Israel left Egypt, they brought the body
     of their ancestor Joseph with them. They had carried it with
     them all this while, and now they buried it in that piece of
     land that Jacob had bought at Shechem.

The last part of the verse in the Masoretic text is "they were (or, became) for the sons (or, descendants) of Joseph an inheritance." Most translations (AT, RSV, TEV, JB, BJ, NAB) understand that the piece of land is being referred to; but NEB, TOB, and HOTTP take the plural to refer to "the bones of Joseph" (NEB "and they passed into the patrimony of the house of Joseph"). This seems strange but appears to be what the Masoretic text says. The singular "it was (or, became)" should be considered a textual change, based on the Syriac and Vulgate texts.

If the exegesis of TEV is maintained, This land was inherited by Joseph's descendants may be translated, "Joseph's descendants received this land as their own." If the alternative interpretation is accepted, "Joseph's descendants received these bones as their possession."

24.33   Eleazar son of Aaron died and was buried at
         Gibeah, the town in the hill country of Ephraim
         which had been given to his son Phinehas.

Nothing definite is known of the location of Gibeah. Instead of being a proper name, the Hebrew word could be the common noun "hill" (so KJV, TOB, NEB, NAB). For Phinehas see 22.13-14.

Was buried at Gibeah may be shifted to an active verb phrase with the subject expressly indicated: "When Eleazar son of Aaron died, the people of Israel buried him at the town of Gibeah. This town was in the hill country of Ephraim, and it belonged to his son Phinehas." Or, following the other interpretation, "When Eleazar son of Aaron died, the people of Israel buried his body in one of the hills in the hill country of Ephraim. This hill belonged to Eleazar's son Phinehas."

Notes

1. Joshua first appears when Moses sends twelve men, one from each of the tribes, from the wilderness of Paran, where the Israelites are camped (Num 12.16), to explore the land of Canaan (Num 13.1—14.10); of the twelve, only Joshua (from the tribe of Ephraim) and Caleb (from the tribe of Judah) believe that the Israelites can defeat the Canaanites; the others are afraid and are killed by the Lord for their cowardice (Num 14.36-38). Later Joshua is chosen as Moses' successor (Num 27.12-3; Deut 31.1-8). The name Joshua means "Yah (a shortened form of Yahweh) saves" or "May Yah save." In Num 13.16 we are told that Moses had changed his name from Hoshea to Joshua; the two names mean the same. The Greek form of Joshua is *Iesous*, translated "Jesus" in English.

2. The Hebrew text is not normal; in the phrase translated "the ark of the covenant" (RSV) the word for "the covenant" is not in the form normally used (the Hebrew seems to be "the ark, the covenant of the Lord..."), and so some (Soggin; NEB, JB) introduce the name Yahweh (as in verse 17), "the ark of the covenant of the LORD, the Lord of all the earth." HOTTP prefers the Masoretic text, saying that it means "the ark of the covenant, (i.e. that) of the lord of all the earth."

3. In verse 16 one form of the Masoretic text and some Hebrew manuscripts have "at Adam"; another form of the Masoretic text and the versions have "from Adam." In terms of translation the difference in meaning is not significant; what is meant is that no water flowed downstream from Adam, since the flow was stopped there.

4. Commentators point out that there are substantiated reports of one occasion (in December 1267) when a landslide of the walls of the Jordan (which are of soft limestone) blocked the flow of the river for 16 hours; on another occasion (July 11, 1927) an earthquake interrupted the flow of the water for 21 1/2 hours.

5. It should be noted that in the Masoretic text *hakin* in verse 3 is to be parsed as the hiphil infinitive of the verb *k-w-n* "to stand"; Soggin calls it "a curious form" and says it makes no sense here; but there are other explanations. NEB treats it as having the same meaning as *haken* in 3.17, "stood firmly."

6. The Masoretic text has "you will fear"; but by a change in vowels the Hebrew becomes "they (that is, the Gentiles) will fear"; so Gray, Bright; RV NEB BJ.

7. RSV "again" translates the Hebrew *weshub* "and turn, repeat"; the Septuagint has "and seated" (*wesheb*), which NEB prefers. This seems rather unlikely.

8. Commentators point out that the Israelites did have metal (bronze) tools and implements, and that the prescribed use of stone (flint) and not of metal reflects the antiquity of the ritual of circumcision; it had to be done in the ancient manner.

9. This may indicate, as some commentators believe, that originally this theophany was described as taking place inside Jericho, after the fall of the city.

10. Instead of the Masoretic text *lo'* "no," some Hebrew manuscripts, Septuagint, and Syriac have *lō* "to him," which NEB prefers.

11. Soggin suggests that it may be an emphatic, "Indeed!" and that it applies to the first part of Joshua's question; but this isn't of much help.

12. A translator of the Hebrew text detects the various doublets, repetitions, and additions which are preserved in the final form of the text, and he/she is forced to decide whether or not to smooth out the text or to translate it as it is, warts and all.

13. The Masoretic text of verse 18 has the verb *haram* "to dedicate to destruction" (RSV "lest when you have devoted them"); Septuagint translates the Hebrew verb *hamad* "to desire, covet," which is preferred by Bright and Gray and is followed by AT NEB NAB BJ JB, and also by HOTTP on the basis of what it calls Factor 12, "other scribal errors." This is certainly an easier text; but as Soggin says, "the correction is useful but not essential." RSV TEV TOB translate the Masoretic text.

14. Recent excavations date the destruction of the walls of Jericho to a long time before the Israelite invasion of Canaan; see commentaries, especially Soggin.

15. Bethaven (literally "house of evil/wickedness") often appears as an insulting nickname for Bethel itself (which means "house of God"; see Hos 4.15; 5.8; Amos 5.5b). So some scholars consider "near Bethaven" an editorial gloss. Others, however, take it to be a variant spelling of "Bethon."

16. In light of the number of Israelites killed—36—some scholars believe that instead of 3,000 men, only some 300 men were sent; but the Hebrew text has "about three *alaphim*" (plural of *eleph*). Many believe that *eleph* does not mean 1,000 but indicates a much smaller number; as yet, however, there is no scholarly consensus on the matter.

17. It is rather strange that in the Hebrew text in verse 13 "in the midst of you...you cannot stand...your enemies...you take" (RSV) the second personal pronoun is singular; only at the end of the verse "from among you" (RSV) is the pronoun plural. This is either a stylistic variation or else reflects the use of more than one source of the tradition.

18. It should be noticed that in verse 17b the Masoretic text says "he brought forward the clan of Zerah, man by man, and Zabdi was selected." Instead of "man by man" some Hebrew manuscripts (and Syriac and Vulgate) have, as expected, "family by family," since the next verse speaks of the family of Zabdi being brought forward. RSV follows the Masoretic text; TEV AT BJ JB NEB NAB TOB prefer the variant reading. HOTTP prefers the Masoretic text (a "C" decision), justifying its decision by Factor 5 ("Assimilation to parallel passages") and Factor 4 ("Simplification of the text [easier reading]").

19. Soggin, who translates "praise," says that "the confession of praise seems to have been necessary in order that no one should believe that the method employed was arbitrary." This does rather strain one's credulity.

Notes

20. In verse 23 <u>laid them down</u> translates the Hebrew verb *yatsaq*, which means "pour out"; Syriac and Septuagint seem to suggest the Hebrew verb *yatsag* "place, put."

21. It should be noticed that in verse 24 the silver, the cloak, and the gold bar are among the objects taken to Trouble Valley to be destroyed; but 6.19 specifies that all silver and gold was to be placed in the Lord's treasury (see also 6.24). The Septuagint omits "the silver, the cloak, the bar of gold," which may have been added to the original Hebrew text; see Bright.

22. The Masoretic text is literally "and all Israel stoned (verb *ragam*) him with stones, and they burned them with fire, and they stoned (verb *tsaqal*) them with stones." HOTTP says that *ragam* means "throw stones at," "stone," and that *tsaqal* means "heap stones upon." This distinction can hardly be maintained. The verb *tsaqal* occurs twenty times in the Old Testament; twice (Isa 5.2; 62.10) it means "to clear of stones," as the context makes perfectly clear; in all seventeen other instances (besides the present passage) it means "to throw stones at" in order to kill someone; see K-B, BDB, Holladay. The verb *ragam* occurs fifteen times in the Old Testament; in every place it also means "to throw stones at" in order to kill someone. It is most unlikely that in this one passage, Joshua 7.25, *tsaqal* means something different from the other places in which it is used. In all instances which describe stones being piled on a dead body, other expressions are used (as in the following verse). HOTTP also says that "him" (singular) in "stoned him" refers to Achan and his family, whereas the "them" in the second "and they stoned them" refers to the objects which Achan had stolen and to his own property. This may be so, but it is difficult to see on what basis HOTTP decides that "him" refers to Achan and his family. Therefore many scholars believe that the text combines two different traditions.

23. There is a textual problem in verse 6; TEV has omitted, translationally, the end of the verse "and we will flee from them" (see RSV); NEB BJ JB, following the Septuagint, omit. HOTTP labels this a "D" decision, which means that it is impossible to decide which is the correct reading.

24. The Hebrew for "the people" is *haam*; some scholars believe this should be emended to *haemeq* "the valley," as in verse 13. So NAB.

25. The Septuagint "Horites" (*ton Chorraion*) may perhaps represent the Hebrew for "Hurrians," an important non-Semitic people about whom quite a bit is known.

26. The Masoretic text begins verse 14 "and the men took of their provisions," which seems to mean, as TEV has it, <u>The men of Israel accepted some food from them.</u> But the Septuagint has "the leaders" (the same word used in verse 15b), which NEB BJ JB NAB prefer. HOTTP AT RSV TEV translate the Masoretic text.

27. The Hebrew phrase is unusual in this material, and some scholars believe it seems to indicate a different, later, writer.

28. It should be noticed that HOTTP says that the two periods of <u>three days</u> in verses 16 and 17 refer to the same three days, not to six days, and proposes a translation that will reflect this understanding of the text. On the face of it, this sounds correct, but it must be said that the Hebrew text as it now stands does not read as though the two three-day periods are just one three-day period.

29. This terminology appears in the Canaanite Keret text of the 14th century B.C. as designation of the village pursuits of women. Smith believes it implies "that the Gibeonites are to disband their army and depend on Israel for their defense." In any case, they are reduced to a servile status.

30. Instead of "for the house of my God," the Septuagint has "for me and my God," which Soggin understands as indicating a desire "to avoid the anachronism of the mention of the Jerusalem temple."

31. The Hebrew *adoni-tsedeq* means "my lord (is) Zedek"; the Hebrew word *tsedeq* itself (as a common noun) means "righteousness." See Melchizedek, king of Salem (Jerusalem), in Gen 14.18; his name is "my king (is) Zedek" (see Heb 7.1-2). The name "Zedek" appears to be, then, the name of one of the Amorite gods.

32. TEV translates the Masoretic text, which has the plural "they were afraid"; RSV NEB have the singular "he was afraid"; HOTTP prefers the Masoretic text plural, saying it is used in an impersonal sense, "there was a (great) fear"; so NAB BJ JB TOB.

33. Beth Horon was really two towns: Upper Beth Horon, about 8 kilometers northwest of Gibeon; the pass about 3 kilometers long, led to lower Beth Horon, about 210 meters lower down.

34. It is impossible to tell where NEB got its interpretation, "not a man of the Israelites suffered so much as a scratch on his tongue"—which seems an odd place to be wounded.

35. The Hebrew is rather clumsy at the end of verse 39: "as he did to Hebron so he did to Debir and its king and as he did to Libnah and its king." The final "and as he did to Libnah and its king" is omitted by one Hebrew manuscript and by the Septuagint.

36. The Masoretic text is *madon*; the Septuagint *marron* (and the Syriac, more or less) represents the Hebrew *maron*. The name of the place where the battle took place is Merom Brook (verse 5; RSV "waters of Merom"); Merom itself is identified as a city some 12 kilometers southwest of Hazor, and its location is certain. On the basis of historical and archaeological evidence, some scholars prefer to read Merom (and not Madon) here and in 12.19-20 (see below). (It should be noticed that Merom in the Masoretic text, verses 5,7, is spelled *merom* not *maron*.) HOTTP, citing Factors 12 (accidental change) and 9 (deliberate change), prefers to read here *maron* or *merom* (decision "D"), and recommends translating "Maron." BJ has "Merom" here; the other translations (AT RSV NAB NEB JB TOB TEV Zur) have Madon.

37. Instead of the Masoretic text *shimeron*, the Septuagint has *Sumoon*, which represents the Hebrew *shimeon*, which HOTTP prefers (decision "D"), recommending translating "Shimeon" (here and also in 12.20 and 19.15).

38. Some think that "Chinneroth" here means not Lake Galilee but the town of Chinnereth, on the northwest coast of the lake (see Bright, Gray, Smith).

39. In the New Oxford Bible maps the city of Dor is located on the coast, south of Mt. Carmel; and Naphath-Dor (as in 12.23; 1 Kgs 4.11) is identified as a region inland from the city.

40. The Hebrew *miteman* in verse 3 is translated by most "from the south" or "southward"; NEB, however, takes it to be a place name, "from Teman," a city in Edom, about halfway between the Gulf of Aqaba and the Dead Sea.

[321]

41. The Hebrew text begins verse 4 "and the boundary (or, territory) of Og"; the Septuagint has "and Og." HOTTP places the verse division not before "and the territory" (as does the Masoretic text) but after, thus including "and the territory" in verse 3, and beginning verse 4 with "Og." It translates the end of verse 3 "under the slopes of Pisgah and its (neighboring) territory." TOB retains the division of the Masoretic text and translates the beginning of verse 4 "Then the territory of Og...." BJ has the same text and footnote as RSV.

42. In verse 18 the Masoretic text lists two kings: of Aphek and of Lasharon. HOTTP emends the text by deleting the first numeral "one" and taking *lasharon* to mean "of Sharon," and translates "the king of Aphek-in-Sharon, one" (so Gray). Thus verse 18, following HOTTP, lists only one king. BJ translates "the king in Sharon" (not of Sharon).

In verse 19 HOTTP recommends deleting "king of Madon: one."

In verse 20, instead of two kings in the Masoretic text, of Shimron Meron and of Achshaph, HOTTP conjectures three kings: of Shimeon, of Meron, and of Achshaph.

There is some support from the Septuagint in some of these textual items; but it should be noted that the Septuagint lists only twenty-nine kings in all. HOTTP comes up with thirty (and not thirty-one) kings in all. It does not seem necessary to follow HOTTP here.

43. It should be noticed that the Hebrew text in such places as 13.2-6 can be understood in different ways, so translations do not always agree.

44. The Septuagint has a considerably longer text in verse 7: "And now divide this land as an inheritance for the nine tribes and half the tribe of Manasseh; you shall give it from the Jordan River to the Mediterranean Sea on the west. The Mediterranean Sea will be its frontier." And then verse 8 follows: "And to the two tribes of Reuben and Gad and to half the tribe of Manasseh Moses had given (land) on the east side of the Jordan River." Soggin follows this text in verse 7 (also BJ JB); HOTTP follows the Septuagint in verses 7 and 8 (see its notes on 13.7; 13.8, and the translation it proposes for the two verses). It must be said that the HOTTP conjectural restoration of the Hebrew text is not exactly what the Septuagint text is (at least the Septuagint in Rahlfs' edition). The Masoretic text may certainly be corrupt, as HOTTP says, and a translation may prefer to follow the Septuagint in verse 7.

45. The Masoretic text is "the offerings of fire (to Yahweh)"; but the Septuagint omits the Hebrew *ishey* "offerings of fire," reading, as in the Masoretic text verse 33, "Yahweh the God of Israel is their inheritance." The presence in verse 14 of the emphatic Hebrew pronoun "he" (*hu*) makes it very likely that the Septuagint reading is preferable (so AT JB BJ NEB NAB Zür). HOTTP prefers the Masoretic text.

46. Gray contends that the Hebrew phrase *al-peney* "opposite" does not mean "east" here but "west." NAB has "toward"; TOB BJ JB have "facing."

47. HOTTP says that this is surely the city of Lodebar (see 2 Sam 9.4,5; 17.27; Amos 6.13), and the committee voted "A" for this identification. But since Lodebar would here be a conjecture, HOTTP, following the Septuagint and the Tiberian vocalization of the Masoretic text, says the text should be represented in translation by "Lidebor."

48. It should be noticed, however, that neither in 14.6 nor in 15.13 does the Hebrew say that Caleb belonged to that tribe; rather it seems to imply that Caleb was not a Judahite, saying that he was a Kenizzite (also Num 33.12), a clan commentators suggest was not originally Israelite but was later incorporated into the tribe of Judah. The clan of Kenaz is usually identified as Edomite. It would seem preferable, therefore, both in 14.6 and in 15.13 not to specifically state, as TEV does, that Caleb belonged to the tribe of Judah.

49. HOTTP in both passages prefers to follow the Masoretic text "and she urged him."

50. NEB first edition was "As she sat on her ass, she broke wind"; the second edition has changed the second part to "she made a noise."

51. HOTTP proposes several changes: in verse 22 instead of Adadah they propose "Aradah"; in verse 23 instead of Hazor, Ithnan (two cities) they propose "Hazor of Ithnan" (one city)' in verse 28 instead of Beersheba, Biziothiah (two cities) they propose "Beersheba and its dependent villages" (one city, as in the Septuagint); in verse 32, instead of Ain, and Rimmon, HOTTP proposes "and En-Rimmon" (as in the Septuagint). The HOTTP list will have 33 cities in all.

52. The Septuagint, instead of and Gederothaim in verse 36, has "and its sheepfolds," thus making the total fourteen cities; but no current translation has this, and HOTTP does not favor it.

53. In 1 Chr 4.32 TEV RSV transliterate the Hebrew Tochen; if a translator follows HOTTP here in Josh 19.7, the form of the name should be the same as in 1 Chr.

54. Nazareth is not mentioned in the Old Testament, and it is uncertain whether it was located in the territory of Zebulun or of Naphtali.

55. In verse 16, instead of the Masoretic text Ain, HOTTP (and others), following some manuscripts of the Septuagint and 1 Chr 6.59, prefers "Ashan"; so NEB BJ JB NAB.

56. In verse 35, instead of the Masoretic text Dimnah, HOTTP prefers "Rimmonah" (as in 19.13); NEB BJ JB prefer "Rimmon."

57. RSV "frontier" in verse 11 translates the Hebrew el-mul, which in itself does not say whether it means the west bank or the east bank; the Septuagint has "the regions (of the land of Canaan)." TEV regards "the frontier of the land of Canaan" as redundant information which does not need to be represented in translation.

58. The Masoretic text has the hiphil (causative) form of the verb, "cause to swear" (so KJV); the Syriac, Targum and Vulgate have the qal form, "to swear," which is preferred by the other translations.

59. The Hebrew word translated whip occurs only here in the Old Testament; Gray and others prefer to change the Hebrew text to the plural of another word, similar in spelling, meaning "whip." BJ deems the Hebrew unintelligible and conjectures a word meaning "thorns"; HOTTP takes the Masoretic text to mean "whip."

60. NEB, without any textual justification, omits the list of seven peoples; it must be admitted that this list looks like a later addition (see Gray). HOTTP stays with the Masoretic text.

61. Gray says that the original name was "Timnath Heres," meaning "the portion of the Sun"; this was changed to "Timnath Serah" (a simple inversion of the consonants from ch-r-s to s-r-ch) in order to conceal the pagan implications of the original name.

Bibliography

BIBLE TEXTS AND VERSIONS CITED

Texts

Biblia Hebraica Stuttgartensia. 1977. K. Elliger and W. Rudolph, eds. Stuttgart: Deutsche Bibelstiftung.

Septuaginta (editio quarta). 1950. Alfred Rahlfs, ed. Stuttgart: Württembergische Bibelanstalt. (Cited as Septuagint.)

Versions

Die Bibel: Nach der Übersetzung Martin Luthers, Revidierter Text. 1975, 1978. Stuttgart: Deutsche Bibelstiftung. (Cited as Luther Rev.)

The Bible: A New Translation. 1922. Revised edition, 1935. James Moffatt. London, New York: Harper & Row. (Cited as Mft.)

La Bible de Jérusalem. 1973. Paris: Les Éditions du Cerf. (Cited as BJ.)

The Complete Bible: An American Translation. 1923. J.M. Powis Smith and Edgar J. Goodspeed. Chicago: University of Chicago Press. (Cited as AT.)

Good News Bible: The Bible in Today's English Version. 1976, 1979. New York: American Bible Society. (Cited as TEV.)

Die Heilige Schrift des Alten und des Neuen Testaments. 1935. Zürich. (Cited as Zür.)

The Holy Bible (King James Version). 1611. (Cited as KJV.)

The Holy Bible (Revised Standard Version). 1952, 1971, 1973. New York: Division of Christian Education of the National Council of the Churches of Christ in the United States of America. (Cited as RSV.)

The Jerusalem Bible. 1966. London: Darton, Longman & Todd. (Cited as JB.)

The Living Bible. 1971. Wheaton, Illinois: Tyndale House. (Cited as LB.)

The New American Bible. 1970. Paterson, New Jersey: St. Anthony Guild Press. (Cited as NAB.)

Bibliography

The New English Bible. 1961, 1970. London: Oxford University Press, and Cambridge University Press. (Cited as NEB.)

The Prophets: A new translation of the Holy Scriptures according to the Masoretic text. 1978. Philadelphia: The Jewish Publication Society of America. (Cited as NJV.)

Traduction Oecuménique de la Bible. 1977. Paris: Alliance Biblique Universelle/Les Éditions du Cerf. (Cited as TOB.)

GENERAL BIBLIOGRAPHY

Lexicons

Brown, Francis; S.R. Driver; and Charles A. Briggs. 1907. A Hebrew and English Lexicon of the Old Testament. London: Oxford University Press. (Cited as BDB.)

Holladay, William L. 1971. A Concise Hebrew & Aramaic Lexicon of the Old Testament. Grand Rapids: William B. Eerdmans.

Koehler, Ludwig, and Walter Baumgartner, eds. 1958. Lexicon in Veteris Testamenti Libros. Leiden: E.J. Brill.

Commentaries

Bright, John. 1953. The Book of Joshua (Interpreter's Bible, Vol. 2). New York: Abingdon Press.

Gray, John. 1967. Joshua, Judges, and Ruth (The Century Bible). London: Thomas Nelson & Sons.

Smith, Robert H. 1971. The Book of Joshua (The Interpreter's One-Volume Commentary on the Bible). New York: Abingdon Press.

Soggin, J. Alberto. 1972. Joshua (Old Testament Library). Philadelphia: Westminster Press. Translated by R.S. Wilson.

Other Works

Cowley, A.E. 1910. Gesenius' Hebrew Grammar: As Edited and Enlarged by the Late E. Kautzsch. Oxford: Clarendon Press.

Fauna and Flora of the Bible (Helps for Translators). 1972. Second edition, 1980. New York: United Bible Societies.

New English Bible with the Apocrypha: Oxford Study Edition. 1976. Samuel Sandmel et al., eds. New York: Oxford University Press.

The Oxford Annotated Bible with the Apocrypha: Revised Standard Version. 1962. Herbert G. May and Bruce M. Metzger, eds. New York: Oxford University Press.

Preliminary and Interim Report on the Hebrew Old Testament Text Project: Vol. 2, Historical Books. 1976. Stuttgart: United Bible Societies. (Cited as HOTTP.)

Glossary

This Glossary contains terms which are technical from an exegetical or a linguistic viewpoint. Other terms not defined here may be referred to in a Bible dictionary.

<u>abstract noun</u> is one which refers to a quality or characteristic, such as "beauty" or "darkness."

<u>active</u>. See <u>voice</u>.

<u>adjective</u> is a word which limits, describes, or qualifies a noun. In English, "red," "tall," "beautiful," and "important" are adjectives.

<u>adverb</u> is a word which limits, describes, or qualifies a verb, an adjective, or another adverb. In English, "quickly," "soon," "primarily," and "very" are adverbs.

<u>agent</u> is that which accomplishes the action in a sentence or clause, regardless of whether the grammatical construction is active or passive. In "John struck Bill" (active) and "Bill was struck by John" (passive), the agent in either case is John.

<u>ambiguity</u> is the quality of being <u>ambiguous</u> in meaning. See <u>ambiguous</u>.

<u>ambiguous</u> describes a word or phrase which in a specific context may have two or more different meanings. For example, "Bill did not leave because John came" could mean either (1) "the coming of John prevented Bill from leaving" or (2) "the coming of John was not the cause of Bill's leaving." It is often the case that what is ambiguous in written form is not ambiguous when actually spoken, since features of intonation and slight pauses usually make clear which of two or more meanings is intended. Furthermore, even in written discourse, the entire context normally serves to indicate which meaning is intended by the writer.

<u>anachronism</u> is an expression which is incorrectly used because it is historically or chronologically misplaced. For example, to refer to Jonah buying a ticket for his sea voyage would be an anachronism because it introduces a modern custom into an ancient setting.

<u>antecedent</u> describes a person or thing which precedes or exists prior to something or someone else. In grammar, an antecedent is the word, phrase, or clause to which a pronoun refers.

anticlimax (anticlimactic) is any part of a story, speech, or other form of discourse which is less important or less striking than expected, or is less important than the climax. See climax.

apposition (appositional) is the placing of two expressions together so that they both refer to the same object, event, or concept; for example, "my friend, Mr. Smith." The one expression is said to be the appositive of the other.

attributive is a term which limits or describes another term. In "The big man ran slowly," the adjective "big" is an attributive of "man." See adjective, adverb.

auxiliary is a word which combines closely with another word and which serves to specify certain important aspects of meaning. The term auxiliary is normally employed in referring to auxiliaries to verbs; for example, "shall," "will," "may," or "ought."

causative relates to events and indicates that someone or something caused something to happen, rather than that the person or thing did it directly. In "John ran the horse," the verb "ran" is a causative, since it was not John who ran, but rather it was John who caused the horse to run.

clause is a grammatical construction, normally consisting of a subject and a predicate. The main clause is that clause in a sentence which could stand alone as a complete sentence, but which has one or more dependent or subordinate clauses related to it. A subordinate clause is dependent on the main clause, but it does not form a complete sentence. For coordinate clause, see coordinate structure.

climax (climactic) is the point in a discourse, such as a story or speech, which is the most important, or the turning point, or the point of decision.

conjunctions are words which serve as connectors between words, phrases, clauses, and sentences. "And," "but," "if," and "because" are typical conjunctions in English.

consonants are symbols representing those speech sounds which are produced by obstructing, blocking, or restricting the free passage of air from the lungs through the mouth. They were originally the only spoken sounds recorded in the Hebrew system of writing; vowels were added later as marks associated with the consonants. See also vowels.

construction. See structure.

context is that which precedes and/or follows any part of a discourse. For example, the context of a word or phrase in Scripture would be the other words and phrases associated with it in the sentence, paragraph, section, and even the entire book in which it occurs. The context of a term often affects its meaning, so that a word does not mean exactly the same thing in one context that it does in another.

coordinate structure or coordinate construction is a phrase or clause joined to another phrase or clause, but not dependent on it. Coordinate structures are joined by such conjunctions as "and" or "but," as in "the man and the boys" or "he walked but she ran"; or they are paratactically related, as in "he walked; she ran."

culture (cultural) is the sum total of the beliefs, patterns of behavior, and sets of interpersonal relations of any group of people. A culture is passed on from one generation to another, but undergoes development or gradual change.

direct discourse. See discourse.

direct quotation. See discourse.

discourse is the connected and continuous communication of thought by means of language, whether spoken or written. The way in which the elements of a discourse are arranged is called discourse structure. Direct discourse (direct quotation) is the reproduction of the actual words of one person quoted and included in the discourse of another person; for example, "He declared 'I will have nothing to do with this man.' " Indirect discourse (indirect quotation) is the reporting of the words of one person within the discourse of another person, but in an altered grammatical form rather than as an exact quotation; for example, "He said he would have nothing to do with that man."

dynamic equivalence is a type of translation in which the message of the original text is so conveyed in the receptor language that the response of the receptors is (or, can be) essentially like that of the original receptors, or that the receptors can in large measure comprehend the response of the original receptors, if, as in certain instances, the differences between the two cultures are extremely great.

ellipsis (plural, ellipses) or elliptical expression refers to words or phrases normally omitted in a discourse when the sense is perfectly clear without them. In the following sentence, the words within brackets are elliptical: "If [it is] necessary [for me to do so], I will wait up all night."

emphasis (emphatic) is the special importance given to an element in a discourse, sometimes indicated by the choice of words or by position in the sentence. For example, in "Never will I eat pork again," "Never" is given emphasis by placing it at the beginning of the sentence.

exclusive first person plural excludes the person(s) addressed. That is, a peaker may use "we" to refer to himself and his companions, while specifically excluding the person(s) to whom he is speaking. See inclusive.

exegesis is the process of determining the meaning of a text (or the result of this process), normally in terms of "who said what to whom under what circumstances and with what intent." A correct exegesis is indispensable before a passage can be translated correctly.

explicit refers to information which is expressed in the words of a discourse. This is in contrast to implicit information. See implicit.

figure, figure of speech, or **figurative expression** involves the use of words in other than their literal or ordinary sense, in order to bring out some aspect of meaning by means of comparison or association. For example, "raindrops dancing on the street," or "his speech was like thunder." Metaphors and similes are figures of speech.

first person. See person.

flashback is a reference in a narrative to events prior to the time of the portion of the narrative under consideration.

focus is the center of attention in a discourse or in any part of a discourse.

future perfect is the tense which indicates that the event expressed by the verb will be completed before a specific future time or before another specific event will occur. For example, in "John will have returned before tomorrow," "will have returned" is in the future perfect tense. See also tense.

future. See tense.

general. See generic.

generic has reference to a general class or kind of objects, events, or abstracts; it is the opposite of specific. For example, the term "animal" is generic in relation to "dog," which is a specific kind of animal. However, "dog" is generic in relation to the more specific term "poodle."

Hebraism refers to Hebrew idioms and thought patterns that appear in the Greek writings of the New Testament. The Greek language belongs to quite another language family than that of Hebrew. However, in view of the Jewish ancestry and training of the writers of the New Testament, it is not surprising that such Hebraisms occur.

hendiadys is a figure in which a single complex idea is expressed by two words or structures, usually connected by a conjunction. For example, "weary and worn" may mean "very tired."

honorific is a form used to express respect or deference. In many languages such forms are obligatory in talking to or about royalty and persons of social distinction.

idiom or **idiomatic expression** is a combination of terms whose meanings cannot be understood by adding up the meanings of the parts. "To hang one's head," "to have a green thumb," and "behind the eightball" are American English idioms. Idioms almost always lose their meaning or convey a wrong meaning when translated literally from one language to another.

imperative refers to forms of a verb which indicate commands or requests. In "Go and do likewise," the verbs "Go" and "do" are imperatives. In most languages, imperatives are confined to the grammatical second person; but some languages have corresponding forms for the first and third persons. These are usually expressed in English by the use of "may" or "let"; for example, "May we not have to beg!" "Let them work harder!"

[332]

implicit (implied) refers to information that is not formally represented in a discourse, since it is assumed that it is already known to the receptor, or evident from the meaning of the words in question. For example, the phrase "the other son" carries with it the implicit information that there is a son in addition to the one mentioned. This is in contrast to explicit information, which is expressly stated in a discourse. See explicit.

imply. See implicit, implied.

inclusive first person plural includes both the speaker and the one(s) to whom that person is speaking. See exclusive.

indirect discourse. See discourse.

indirect quotation. See discourse.

infinitive is a verb form which indicates an action or state without specifying such factors as agent or time. It is in contrast to finite verb form, which distinguishes person, number, tense, mode, or aspect.

intensive refers to increased emphasis or force in any expression, as when "very" occurs in the phrase "very active," or "highly" in the phrase "highly competitive." The Hebrew language has a set of verb forms which indicate that the action of the verb is intensive.

Latin Vulgate. See Vulgate.

literal means the ordinary or primary meaning of a term or expression, in contrast with a figurative meaning. A literal translation is a word-for-word representation of the source language; such a translation is frequently unnatural or awkward in the receptor language.

main clause. See clause.

manuscripts are books, documents, or letters written by hand. Thousands of manuscript copies of various Old and New Testament books still exist, but none of the original manuscripts. See text.

markers (marking) are features of words or of a discourse which signal some special meaning or some particular structure. For example, words for speaking may mark the onset of direct discourse, a phrase such as "once upon a time" may mark the beginning of a fairy story, and certain features of parallelism are the dominant markers of poetry. The word "body" may require a marker to clarify whether a person, a group, or a corpse is meant.

Masoretic text is the form of the text of the Hebrew Old Testament established by Hebrew scholars around the eighth and ninth centuries A.D.

metaphor is likening one object, event, or state to another by speaking of it as if it were the other; for example, "flowers dancing in the breeze." Metaphors are the most commonly used figures of speech and are often so subtle that a speaker or writer is not conscious of the fact that he is using figurative langauge. See simile.

modifier is a grammatical term referring to a word or a phrase which is used to modify or affect the meaning of another part of the sentence, such as an adjective modifying a noun or an adverb modifying a verb.

noun is a word that names a person, place, thing, or idea, and often serves to specify a subject or topic of discourse.

noun phrase. See phrase.

object of a verb is the goal of an event or action specified by the verb. In "John hit the ball," the object of "hit" is "ball."

paragraph is a distinct segment of discourse dealing with a particular idea, and usually marked with an indentation on a new line.

parallel, parallelism, generally refers to some similarity in the content and/or form of a construction; for example, "The man was blind, and he could not see." The structures that correspond to each other in the two statements are said to be parallel.

parenthetical statement is a digression from the main theme of a discourse which interrupts that discourse. It is usually set off by marks of parenthesis ().

participle is a verbal adjective, that is, a word which retains some of the characteristics of a verb while functioning as an adjective. In "singing children" and "painted house," "singing" and "painted" are participles.

particle is a small word whose grammatical form does not change. In English the most common particles are prepositions and conjunctions.

passive. See voice.

perfect tense is a set of verb forms which indicate an action already completed when another action occurs. For example, in "John had finished his task when Bill came," "had finished" is in the perfect tense. See also tense.

person, as a grammatical term, refers to the speaker, the person spoken to, or the person or thing spoken about. First person is the person(s) speaking ("I," "me," "my," "we," "us," "our," "ours"). Second person is the person(s) or thing(s) spoken to ("thou," "thee," "thy," "thine," "ye," "you," "your," "yours"). Third person is the person(s) or thing(s) spoken about (such as "he," "she," "it," "his," "hers," "them," or "their"). The examples here given are all pronouns, but in many languages the verb forms have affixes which indicte first, second, or third person and also indicate whether they are singular or plural.

personal pronoun is one which indicates first, second, or third person. See person and pronoun.

phrase is a grammatical construction of two or more words, but less than a complete clause or a sentence. A phrase is usually given a name according to its function in a sentence, such as "noun phrase," "verb phrase," or "prepositional phrase."

play on words. See wordplay.

plural refers to the form of a word which indicates more than one. See singular.

possessive pronouns are pronouns such as "my," "our," "your," or "his," which indicate possession.

predicate is the part of a clause which contrasts with or supplements the subject. The subject is the topic of the clause, and the predicate is what is said about the subject. For example, in "The small boy ran swiftly," the subject is "The small boy," and the predicate is "ran swiftly." See subject.

preposition is a word (usually a particle) whose function is to indicate the relation of a noun or pronoun to another noun, pronoun, verb, or adjective. Some English prepositions are "for," "from," "in," "to," and "with."

pronominal refers to pronouns.

pronouns are words which are used in place of nouns, such as "he," "him," "his," "she," "we," "them," "who," "which," "this," or "these."

qualify is to limit the meaning of a term by means of another term. For example, in "old man," the term "old" qualifies the term "man."

receptor is the person(s) receiving a message. The receptor language is the language into which a translation is made. For example, in a translation from Hebrew into German, Hebrew is the source language and German is the receptor language.

redundant (redundancy) refers to anything which is entirely predictable from the context. For example, in "John, he did it," the pronoun "he" is redundant. A feature may be redundant and yet may be important to retain in certain languages, perhaps for stylistic or for grammatical reasons.

referent is the thing(s) or person(s) referred to by a pronoun, phrase, or clause.

reflexive has to do with verbs where the agent and goal are the same person. Sometimes the goal is explicit (as in "He dresses himself"); at other times it is implicit (as in "He dresses").

restructure. See structure.

rhetorical question is an expression which is put in the form of a question but which is not intended to ask for information. Rhetorical questions are usually employed for the sake of emphasis.

second person. See person.

sentence is a grammatical construction composed of one or more clauses and capable of standing alone.

Septuagint is a translation of the Hebrew Old Testament into Greek, made some two hundred years before Christ. It is often abbreviated as LXX.

simile (pronounced SIM-i-lee) is a <u>figure of speech</u> which describes one event or object by comparing it to another, using "like," "as," or some other word to mark or signal the comparison. For example, "She runs like a deer," "He is as straight as and arrow." Similes are less subtle than metaphors in that metaphors do not mark the comparison with words such as "like" or "as." See <u>metaphor</u>.

singular refers to the form of a word which indicates one thing or person in contrast to <u>plural</u>, which indicates more than one. See <u>plural</u>.

specific refers to the opposite of <u>general, generic</u>. See <u>generic</u>.

structure is the systematic arrangement of the elements of langauge, including the ways in which words combine into phrases, phrases into clauses, and clauses into sentences. Because this process may be compared to the building of a house or a bridge, such words as <u>structure</u> and <u>construction</u> are used in reference to it. To separate and rearrange the various components of a sentence or other unit of discourse in the translation process is to <u>restructure</u> it.

style is a particular or a characteristic manner in discourse. Each language has certain distinctive <u>stylistic</u> features which cannot be reproduced literally in another language. Within any language, certain groups of speakers may have their characteristic discourse styles, and among individual speakers and writers, each has his own style.

subject is one of the major divisions of a clause, the other being the predicate. Typically the subject is a noun phrase. It should not be confused with semantic <u>agent</u>. See <u>predicate</u>.

suffix is a letter or one or more syllables added to the end of a word, to modify the meaning in some manner. For example, "-s" suffixed to "tree" changes the word from singular to plural, "trees," while "-ing" suffixed to "sing" changes the verb to a participle, "singing."

synonyms are words which are different in form but similar in meaning, such as "boy" and "lad." Expressions which have essentially the same meaning are said to be <u>synonymous</u>. No two words are completely synonymous.

Syriac is the name of a Semitic language, a part of the Aramaic family, used in Western Asia, into which the Bible was translated at a very early date.

temporal refers to time. A <u>temporal marker</u> indicates time. See <u>markers</u>.

tense is usually a form of a verb which indicates time relative to a discourse or some event in a discourse. The most common forms of tense are past, present, and future. See also <u>perfect tense</u>.

text, <u>textual</u>, refers to the various Greek and Hebrew manuscripts of the Scriptures. <u>Textual evidence</u> is the cumulative evidence for a particular form of the text. <u>Textual problems</u> arise when it is difficult to reconcile or to account for <u>conflicting forms</u> of the same text in two or more manuscripts.

Textual variants are forms of the same passage that differ in one or more details in some manuscripts. See also manuscripts.

third person. See person.

transitionals are words or phrases which mark the connections between related events. Some typical transitionals are "next," "then," "later," "after this," "when he arrived."

translation is the reproduction in a receptor language of the closest natural equivalent of a message in the source language, first, in terms of meaning, and second, in terms of style.

transliterate is to represent in the receptor language the approximate sounds or letters of words occuring in the source language, rather than translating their meaning; for example, "Amen" from the Hebrew, or the title "Christ" from the Greek.

variant, textual. See text, textual.

verbs are a grammatical class of words which express existence, action, or occurrence, such as "be," "become," "run," or "think."

verbal has two meanings. (1) It may refer to expressions consisting of words, sometimes in distinction to forms of communication which do not employ words ("sign language," for example). (2) It may refer to word forms which are derived from verbs. For example, "coming" and "engaged" may be called verbals, and participles are called verbal adjectives.

versions are translations. The ancient, or early, versions are translations of the Bible, or of portions of the Bible, made in early times; for example, the Greek Septuagint, the ancient Syriac, or the Ethiopic versions.

voice in grammar is the relation of the action expressed by a verb to the participants in the action. In English and many other languages, the active voice indicates that the subject performs the action ("John hit the man"), while the passive voice indicates that the subject is being acted upon ("The man was hit").

vowels are symbols representing the sound of the vocal cords, produced by unobstructed air passing from the lungs through the mouth. They were not originally included in the Hebrew system of writing; they were added later as marks associated with the consonants. See also consonants.

Vulgate is the Latin version of the Bible translated and/or edited originally by Saint Jerome. It has been traditionally the official version of the Roman Catholic Church.

wordplay (play on words) in a discourse is the use of the similarity in the sounds of two words to produce a special effect.

Index

This index includes concepts, key words, and terms for which the Handbook contains a discussion useful for translators.

Printed in the United States of America

STRANGER THINGS

INTO THE FIRE

script
JODY HOUSER

pencils
RYAN KELLY

inks
LE BEAU UNDERWOOD

colors
TRIONA FARRELL

lettering
NATE PIEKOS OF BLAMBOT®

front cover art by
KYLE LAMBERT

chapter break art by
VIKTOR KALVACHEV

dark horse books

president and publisher
MIKE RICHARDSON

editor
SPENCER CUSHING

assistant editor
KONNER KNUDSEN

collection designer
PATRICK SATTERFIELD

digital art technician
ALLYSON HALLER

Special thanks to NETFLIX, SHANNON SCHRAM, ANASTACIA FERRY, and KYLE LAMBERT.

Advertising Sales: (503) 905-2315 | ComicShopLocator.com

SCHOLASTIC EDITION

STRANGER THINGS: INTO THE FIRE, July 2020. Published by Dark Horse Comics LLC, 10956 SE Main Street, Milwaukie, Oregon 97222. Stranger Things™ & © 2020 Netflix. All rights reserved. Dark Horse Comics® and the Dark Horse logo are trademarks of Dark Horse Comics LLC, registered in various categories and countries. All rights reserved. No portion of this publication may be reproduced or transmitted, in any form or by any means, without the express written permission of Dark Horse Comics LLC. Names, characters, places, and incidents featured in this publication either are the product of the author's imagination or are used fictitiously. Any resemblance to actual persons (living or dead), events, institutions, or locales, without satiric intent, is coincidental.

This volume collects issues #1 through #4 of the Dark Horse comic-book series
Stranger Things: Into the Fire.

Published by Dark Horse Books
A division of Dark Horse Comics LLC
10956 SE Main Street
Milwaukie, OR 97222

DarkHorse.com | Netflix.com

Scholastic Edition: July 2020

ISBN: 978-1-50672-301-3

1 3 5 7 9 10 8 6 4 2
Printed in Canada

NEIL HANKERSON executive vice president • TOM WEDDLE chief financial officer • RANDY STRADLEY vice president of publishing • NICK McWHORTER chief business development officer • DALE LaFOUNTAIN chief Information officer • MATT PARKINSON Vice President of Marketing • VANESSA TODD-HOLMES vice president of production and scheduling • MARK BERNARDI vice president of book trade and digital sales • KEN LIZZI general counsel • DAVE MARSHALL editor in chief • DAVEY ESTRADA editorial director • CHRIS WARNER senior books editor • CARY GRAZZINI director of specialty projects • LIA RIBACCHI art director • MATT DRYER director of digital art and prepress • MICHAEL GOMBOS senior director of licensed publications • KARI YADRO director of custom programs • KARI TORSON director of international licensing • SEAN BRICE director of trade sales

BOSTON, 1985.

"I THINK IT'S *PERFECT*, MARCY."

I DON'T KNOW...

HERE, LET'S TRY THIS.

I KNOW YOU HAVEN'T BEEN AT SCHOOL *THAT* LONG.

BUT YOU *SHOULD* KNOW BETTER THAN TO QUESTION SARAH'S TASTE BY NOW.

WHY DO YOU THINK DAWN LOOKS SO GOOD? SHE WAS *HOPELESS* BEFORE WE WERE BEST FRIENDS.

I WASN'T *THAT* BAD, THANK YOU.

NO, YOU'RE RIGHT. IT'S PRETTY GREAT.

AND YOU *REALLY* NEED TO UP YOUR FASHION GAME IF YOU WANT JOSH TO NOTICE YOU.

I DON'T... WHAT?

YOU MIGHT BE A *LITTLE* LESS OBVIOUS IF YOU WEREN'T STARING AT HIM LIKE *ALL* THE TIME.

THE ONLY REASON HE HASN'T NOTICED IS HE'S *KIND* OF AN IDIOT.

HE'S NOT AN IDIOT.

I SAID "KIND OF."

WE CAN INTRODUCE YOU, IF YOU INTRODUCE US TO YOUR BROTHER.

UGH, DON'T BE GROSS, YOU GUYS. HE'S LIKE *TWENTY-FIVE.*

"I SPENT YEARS THINKING THE PEOPLE WHO RAN THE PROGRAM REALLY WANTED TO HELP US ALL.

"BUT THE WAY THEY PUSHED YOUR SISTER UNTIL SHE BROKE...IT WAS CLEAR THEY NEVER CARED ABOUT US AT ALL.

"IF THEY COULDN'T USE US, CONTROL US, THEY'D PREFER WE WERE DEAD."

WE WERE BOTH LUCKY TO ESCAPE WHEN WE DID.

SIX... FRANCINE, SHE *DIED* TO MAKE SURE IT HAPPENED.

AND IF THERE'S *ANY* CHANCE THAT ANY OF THE OTHER SUBJECTS EVENTUALLY GOT OUT...

WE NEED TO FIND THEM. HELP THEM IF WE CAN. WE'LL BE SAFER TOGETHER.

BUT WHEN WILL ALL THAT BE OVER?

WHEN WILL WE JUST GET TO BE, YOU KNOW. *NORMAL.*

WHEN WE FIND THE OTHERS.

OR...AT LEAST FIND OUT WHAT *HAPPENED* TO THEM.

AND IF WE NEVER DO?

BETTER THAT THEN NOT TRYING AT ALL, RIGHT?

IF THEY'RE OUT THERE WAITING FOR SOMEONE TO HELP THEM...

I KNOW I'M NOT GREAT AT ANY OF THIS.

BUT WE'RE THE CLOSEST THING TO FAMILY THE OTHER HAS.

YOU'RE NOT THE *WORST* FAKE BIG BROTHER EVER.

PROBABLY.

15

WHA...

WHERE ARE WE?

I'M AWAKE! I'M AWAKE!

HASTINGS GLEN. WE DROVE ALL NIGHT.

WELL, I DID.

I'M *ALMOST* SIXTEEN. I COULD HELP WITH THE DRIVING.

IT'S NOT LIKE WE DON'T LIE ABOUT ALL THE OTHER STUFF.

MAYBE LATER.

I'M GOING TO GO SEE WHAT INFO I CAN GET FROM THE LOCAL COPS.

GO JEDI MIND TRICK THE CRAP OUT OF THEM.

IT SAYS THE PERPETRATORS WERE WEARING HALLOWEEN MASKS?

SO NO ONE KNOWS IF THEY WERE ADULTS OR KIDS?

YOU REALLY THINK *KIDS* COULD JUST PLUG A GUY LIKE THAT?

IF THEY'RE PUSHED HARD ENOUGH? SURE.

HEY, LOIS, ANY CALLS FROM--

IS THAT A **CASE** FILE, KID?

OH! HE'S A REPORTER. HERE DOING A STORY FOR... FOR...

WHERE DID YOU SAY YOU WERE FROM?

MIAMI HERALD.

BUT I DIDN'T MEAN TO GET LOIS IN ANY TROUBLE.

HERE'S THE FILE. NO HARM, NO FOUL. RIGHT?

RIGHT.

YOU GOT A BIT OF A NOSEBLEED THERE, SON. YOU OKAY?

I'LL BE FINE.

"CHICAGO AND THIS... DO YOU THINK IT'S EIGHT?"

THEY HAD ME BE A PART OF HER TRIALS A FEW TIMES.

SHE WAS TRYING TO MAKE IT SEEM LIKE SHE WASN'T THERE.

JUST THE KIND OF THING THOSE CREEPS WOULD DO TO A KID.

PROBABLY WANTED HER TO BE SOME KIND OF ASSASSIN OR SOMETHING.

LIKE SHE'S DOING NOW.

WE DON'T KNOW WHAT HAPPENED AFTER WE LEFT. HOW BAD THINGS GOT.

HE MIGHT HAVE DESERVED IT.

CHICAGO SIX MONTHS AGO. AND NOW THIS.

IT SEEMS LIKE SHE'S KEEPING A LOWER PROFILE. STAYING ON THE MOVE.

SO HOW DO WE FIND HER?

WE ASK AROUND, OBVIOUSLY.

THAT'S THE ONE I SAW IN THE SECURITY FOOTAGE.

SHK-SHK

FREEZE, CREEPS.

THIS IS PRIVATE PROPERTY. *SCRAM.*

UNLESS YOU WANT TO BE FERTILIZER.

WE'RE JUST LOOKING FOR A FRIEND.

DO YOU THINK YOU COULD HELP US?

PRETTY PLEASE?

...NOT SURPRISED WORD GOT OUT ABOUT CHICAGO. IT WAS REAL--

WHAT THE HELL, AXEL?

THEY'RE JUST LOOKING FOR THEIR FRIEND.

EIGHT?

JUST... JUST STAY CALM...

24

I **KNOW** THAT. I THOUGHT YOU **WERE** HER.

I SAW **HER** A LOT MORE RECENTLY THAN YOU, AFTER ALL.

JUST HOW MANY OF THESE KIDS **ARE** THERE?

NOT A CLUE.

BUT THE ACCIDENT...SHE WAS DYING...

SIX. FRANCINE. SHE TOLD US NINE WASN'T GOING TO MAKE IT.

I DON'T KNOW WHAT TO TELL YOU...

...BUT THE LAST TIME I SAW YOUR SISTER, SHE WAS VERY MUCH ALIVE.

THE PRINCESS WAS ALWAYS AFRAID TO SLEEP. AFRAID SHE WOULD FADE AWAY INTO HER DREAMS.

HER DREAMS WERE COLDER THAN THE TOWER, WHITE WALLS AND SHARP NEEDLES.

IF THE TOWER WAS PUNISHMENT, IT WAS ALSO SAFETY. HERE, SHE HAD FRIENDS. A CHANCE.

SHE ONLY HOPED THAT THIS ONE WOULDN'T BURN LIKE THE TOWERS BEFORE IT...

"YOU KNOW PART OF THE STORY.

"THE PROGRAM THAT **PRETENDED** IT WAS HELPING US.

"THE DAY THAT WOMAN BROKE IN.

"TURNS OUT SHE WAS JANE-- ELEVEN'S MOTHER."

JANE!

"HOW A FEW OF YOU TRIED TO ESCAPE IN THE CHAOS.

"HOW YOU DIDN'T ALL MAKE IT.

"DID YOU EVEN THINK ABOUT THE ONES YOU LEFT BEHIND?"

OF COURSE WE DID! WHY DO YOU THINK WE'RE HERE?!

I'M GUESSING BECAUSE YOU WANT SOMETHING?

LOOK, CAN WE TALK ABOUT THIS IN PRIVATE?

WITHOUT STREETS OF FIRE WATCHING?

I HAVE A LOT MORE REASONS TO TRUST THEM OVER YOU.

PLEASE, EIGHT. I NEED TO KNOW ABOUT MY SISTER.

FIVE MINUTES.

AND THE NAME IS KALI.

32

33

SAW HER A FEW MONTHS BACK. SHE GOT OUT. TRACKED ME DOWN WITH HER POWERS.

"DIDN'T BOTHER TO STICK AROUND. HAS FRIENDS SOMEWHERE."

SEEMED LIKE SHE WAS DOING JUST FINE WITHOUT ANY OF US.

BUT FROM WHAT YOU SAID, JAMIE WASN'T.

DO YOU HAVE ANY IDEA WHAT COULD HAVE HAPPENED TO HER? ANYTHING THAT COULD HELP US FIND HER?

I MAY HAVE SOMETHING...

WHERE DID YOU GET THESE?

NONE OF YOUR BUSINESS.

A REPORTER NEVER REVEALS HER SOURCES!

WE AREN'T EXACTLY REPORTERS, DOTTIE.

HERE. THIS IS THE DOCTOR WHO WAS WORKING WITH NINE THE MOST, LAST TIME I SAW HER.

IF ANYONE KNOWS WHAT HAPPENED TO HER, IT WOULD PROBABLY BE HIM.

GOOD THING WE HADN'T GOTTEN TO THAT ONE, YET.

QUIET, AXEL.

"GOTTEN TO?"

THE PROGRAM HURT US. MY FRIENDS AND I HURT THEM RIGHT BACK.

ONLY WE MAKE SURE *THEY* CAN'T HURT ANYONE EVER AGAIN.

YOU'RE WELCOME TO JOIN US AFTER YOU FINISH LOOKING FOR YOUR SISTER.

NO... NO THANK YOU.

THANK YOU FOR THE NAME.

OPEN INVITATION.

I HAVE A NAME FOR YOU TO LOOK UP. DR. EDWARD J. MORRIS...

JAMIE...

1975.

JAMIE AND MARCY, IS IT?

I'M SO SORRY TO HEAR ABOUT YOUR FAMILY.

YOU CAN'T TAKE JAMIE AWAY!

AND WHY WOULD I BE TAKING JAMIE AWAY?

BECAUSE I MADE THE FIRE HAPPEN.

AND NOW THEY'RE ALL DEAD.

AND THAT'S NOT YOUR FAULT. WE HAD APPROACHED YOUR PARENTS ABOUT GETTING YOU HELP FOR YOUR...CONDITION.

IF THEY HADN'T IGNORED OUR WARNINGS, THIS WOULD NEVER HAVE HAPPENED.

MY NAME IS DR. BRENNER. I RUN A PROGRAM FOR SPECIAL CHILDREN JUST LIKE YOU.

WE'LL BE ABLE TO HELP YOU SO THAT NOTHING LIKE THIS EVER HAPPENS AGAIN.

BUT WHAT ABOUT MARCY?

SHE ISN'T LIKE ME. SHE'S NORMAL. CAN SHE STILL COME TOO?

OF COURSE, JAMIE.

41

THE PRINCESS WONDERED IF SHE WOULD EVER BE WARM AGAIN.

OF COURSE, THERE WAS ALWAYS THE OLD WAY.

THE *DANGEROUS* WAY.

BUT THAT MAGIC HAD A STEEP PRICE.

SHE'S COMPLAINING SHE'S COLD AGAIN. ASKED TO SEE YOU.

WELL, LET'S TAKE A LOOK...

AND SHE WASN'T SURE SHE WAS READY TO PAY IT AGAIN. NOT JUST YET.

UNDER THE TONGUE. THAT'S A GOOD GIRL.

OF COURSE, THE PRICE COULD ALWAYS BE PAID BY THOSE AROUND HER, THE PRINCESS KNEW.

EVERYTHING LOOKS NORMAL. I'LL SEE IF WE CAN RAISE THE TEMPERATURE IN HERE A BIT FOR YOU.

AND DESPITE THE KINDNESS OF HER FEATHERED AND FURRY FRIENDS...

YOU GET SOME REST NOW.

...THE DEAL WITH THAT PARTICULAR DEVIL WAS VERY TEMPTING INDEED.

C...COLD...

GOT IT. OKAY, THANKS A MILLION.

GOOD, YOU'RE UP.

I GOT AN ADDRESS AND DIRECTIONS TO OUR DR. MORRIS.

IF WE LEAVE SOON, WE SHOULD BE ABLE TO GET THERE BEFORE TONIGHT.

G... GOOD.

YOU OKAY, MARCY?

YEAH.

JUST A WEIRD DREAM, IS ALL.

YOU OKAY? READY TO DO THIS?

I... I THINK SO.

HEY, I'M HERE FOR YOU ALL THE WAY, OKAY?

YOU DON'T HAVE TO DO THIS ALONE.

I KNOW.

WHERE IS JAMIE?!

WHAT HAPPENED TO MY SISTER?!

MARCY, THIS ISN'T THE WAY TO--

YOU TRY TO USE YOUR POWERS ON ME, RICKY...

...I'LL SHOOT HIM RIGHT NOW.

WASN'T GOING TO. PROMISE.

BUT IF YOU KILL HIM, WE MAY NEVER FIND YOUR SISTER.

I DIDN'T SAY I WAS GOING TO *KILL* HIM.

JUST *SHOOT* HIM.

YOU DON'T...YOU DON'T HAVE TO SHOOT ME.

I'LL TELL YOU EVERYTHING I KNOW.

WILL YOU GIVE ME THE GUN, PLEASE?

"YOUR TWIN, NINE, WAS ONE OF THE MORE PROMISING CANDIDATES IN THE PROGRAM."

AT LEAST IN TERMS OF SHEER POWER POTENTIAL.

BUT SHE HAD THE SAME PROBLEM MOST OF THE CHILDREN HAD.

"CONTROL. OR LACK THEREOF.

"AND WHEN YOU'RE USING CHILDREN WITH POWERS TO CONTROL OTHER CHILDREN WITH POWERS...

"...WELL, YOU DON'T NEED TO BE A SCIENTIST TO FIGURE OUT THAT THAT'S AN UNTENABLE SCENARIO."

JUST AS NINE WAS PROVING HERSELF TO BE QUITE A PROBLEM, DR. BRENNER HAD A BREAKTHROUGH ELSEWHERE.

ONE THAT CONVINCED HIM THE OTHER PARTICIPANTS IN THE PROGRAM WERE... REDUNDANT.

WHAT DO YOU MEAN, REDUNDANT?

THE PRICK OF A SPINDLE. THE BITE OF AN APPLE.

ANYTHING TO TAKE AWAY THE DARKNESS OF THE WAKING WORLD.

TO RETURN TO THE BRIGHTNESS OF HER DREAMS. THE WARMTH OF HER FRIENDS.

BUT NO MATTER HOW TIGHTLY SHE SQUEEZED HER EYES SHUT, THERE WAS ONLY MORE DARKNESS TO BE SEEN.

AND OF COURSE, THE DARKNESS IS WHERE THE MONSTERS LURK.

MONSTERS MORE POWERFUL THAN ANY SPELL A PRINCESS MIGHT WEAVE.

NO!

BUT WHILE HER FRIENDS WERE LOST TO THE LIGHT, THE DARKNESS HELD MORE THAN JUST MONSTERS.

THERE WERE ALLIES TOO, ALSO LOOKING TO ESCAPE TO FAIRER LANDS.

"WHEN BRENNER ASKED ME TO TAKE CARE OF THE CHILDREN HE DEEMED 'LIABILITIES', IT WAS CLEAR WHAT HE MEANT.

"I HAVE NO ILLUSIONS ABOUT BEING A GOOD PERSON. I'M SURE MANY WOULD CALL ME A MONSTER.

"BUT EVEN MONSTERS HAVE LINES THEY WON'T CROSS.

"I WORKED PRIMARILY WITH NINE, YOUR SISTER, BY THAT POINT. BRENNER WANTED ME TO...

"...*DISPOSE* OF HER.

"HOWEVER, I HAD A WAY TO SAVE HER LIFE, AT THE VERY LEAST.

"A DOCTOR WHO OWED ME A FAVOR WAS ABLE TO PLACE HER IN THEIR FACILITY.

"COMPLETELY OFF THE BOOKS.

"THEY AGREED TO KEEP HER ON A STRICT DRUG REGIMEN, ONE I DESIGNED TO SUPPRESS HER ABILITIES.

"AND MORE IMPORTANTLY, THEY WERE WILLING TO DO SO WITHOUT ASKING ANY QUESTIONS."

SO LET ME GET THIS STRAIGHT...

...YOU JUST DUMPED HER ON SOMEONE ELSE? DECIDED SHE WASN'T YOUR PROBLEM ANYMORE?

I *SAVED* HER! IF IT WASN'T FOR ME, SHE'D BE *DEAD* RIGHT NOW!

AND THEN YOU WOULD HAVE BEEN TOO.

MARCY...

WHAT'S THE NAME OF THE FACILITY WHERE YOU LEFT HER?

I CAN GIVE YOU THE NAME AND ADDRESS IF YOU LIKE.

BUT IF YOU'RE THINKING OF BREAKING HER OUT, YOU'D BE MAKING A MISTAKE.

59

I'M-- LOOK--

THIS ALL JUST SUCKS, OKAY? *SO* MUCH.

BUT I KNOW YOU'RE TRYING TO MAKE IT SUCK LESS. AND SOMETIMES YOU DO.

I'M DOING THE BEST I CAN.

AND I KNOW THAT'S NOT ALWAYS ENOUGH.

BUT IF WE WORK TOGETHER, IT'S MORE LIKELY THAT IT WILL BE.

MIRRORS COULD ALSO LIE. SHE KNEW THAT TOO WELL.

BUT THIS TIME, SHE SOMEHOW KNEW THAT THE REFLECTION WASN'T THE LIE.

PERHAPS THE REFLECTION WAS THE **LIAR.**

BANG

BANG

THIS FACE IN THE MIRROR HAD WOUNDED HER, LONG AGO AND FAR AWAY. A DEEP AND VICIOUS BLOW.

BANG

THERE WAS AN OLD ANGER HERE. A BETRAYAL HALF-REMEMBERED.

THE FACE, SO MUCH LIKE HER OWN, WASN'T HERS AT ALL.

HOW COULD SHE HAVE FORGOTTEN?

THAT'S WHAT MAGIC DID. MAGIC AND TIME.

BUT THE PRINCESS HAD FINALLY REMEMBERED. REMEMBERED HOW MUCH IT HURT.

KRAK

REMEMBERED HOW MUCH PAIN THERE WAS TO PAY BACK.

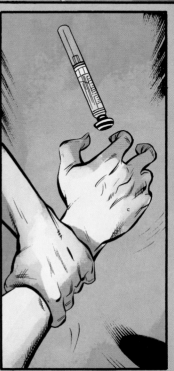

BUT MUCH LIKE PRINCESSES, MAGIC WAS HARD TO TRAP BEHIND A DOOR ONCE IT HAD BEEN SET FREE.

WAA-BWAA-BWAA

HEY! GET AWAY FROM THERE!

"I'M ALL SHE HAS."

SHE HAS ME TOO. YOU BOTH DO.

I JUST WORRY THAT WON'T BE--

WEEEOOO-WEEEOOO-WEEEOOO

WEEEOOO-WEEEOOO

WEEEOOO-WEE

ENGINE 597

THE PRINCESS FLED THROUGH THE WOODS, AS PRINCESSES OFTEN DO.

AND FIRE FOLLOWED IN HER FOOTSTEPS.

FOR SO LONG, FIRE HAD BEEN HER ONLY FRIEND. HER MAGIC. HER WEAPON.

HER TEMPTATION.

AND NOW THAT SHE HAD SET IT FREE, THE PRINCESS WASN'T SURE SHE IF IT WAS A MAGIC SHE COULD CONTROL...

"SEVERAL OF THE PATIENTS ARE STILL MISSING."

74

75

JAMIE?!

THE PRINCESS COULDN'T RUN FROM THE FIRE. SHE KNEW THAT NOW.

HER WILL. HER CURSE. HER WEAPON.

SO WHY RUN AT ALL?

FOR SO LONG, SHE HAD BEEN SCARED OF THE POWER INSIDE HER.

BUT IF SHE COULD TRULY WIELD IT...

...SHE WOULD NEVER NEED TO RUN AGAIN.

AND LOSS ISN'T SOMETHING THAT YOU SHATTER BEFORE IT SHATTERS YOU.

IT'S SOMETHING YOU PASS THROUGH...

...IN THE HOPE OF FINDING SOMETHING WORTHWHILE ON THE OTHER SIDE.

"WE HAVE A *LOT* OF CATCHING UP TO DO..."

MOTEL

I'M NOT SURE IF "ALL RIGHT" IS THE PHRASE I'D USE.

BUT WE GOT TO HER. SHE'S SAFE NOW.

THEN SHE HAS A CHANCE.

THAT'S ALL I EVER WANTED FOR HER. FOR ANY OF YOU.

A CHANCE FOR *WHAT*, EXACTLY?

BECAUSE I'M THINKING A NORMAL LIFE WAS NEVER REALLY IN THE CARDS.

A CHANCE TO...TO BE *HAPPY*.

OUTSIDE THE CONFINES OF A LABORATORY EXPERIMENT.

THE LAB YOU WORKED AT? THE LAB WHERE YOU WERE ONE OF THE MONSTERS?

THE LAB YOU DIDN'T DO A DAMN THING TO SHUT DOWN?

I COULD HAVE DONE MORE. I *KNOW* THAT.

BUT I WAS SCARED--

MORE SCARED THAN THE *CHILDREN?*

HOW ABOUT NOW? HOW SCARED ARE YOU NOW?

V-VERY...

GOOD.

I CAME TO GIVE THIS BACK TO YOU.

I'M SORRY. I--

YOU *KNOW* YOU'RE A MONSTER. YOU TOLD US AS MUCH.

YOU *HATE* YOURSELF *EVERY* SECOND OF *EVERY* DAY FOR WHAT YOU DID.

YOU KNOW *EXACTLY* WHAT YOU DESERVE.

THE GUN IS RIGHT THERE IN YOUR HAND.

YOU *KNOW* WHAT TO DO WITH IT.

Art by CHUNLO

HOWEVER, THERE ARE A FEW WHO KNOW THE TRUTH OF WHAT HAPPENED.

WHAT? PRETZELS ARE GREAT! YOU DON'T LIKE PRETZELS?

JUST... DON'T GIVE HER A REASON TO THROW YOU OUT, OKAY?

THE MONSTERS WHO LURKED IN THEIR MIDST. IN THE DARK.

AND THOUGH THEY MIGHT PRETEND...

...CAN THINGS EVER TRULY BE NORMAL FOR THEM AGAIN?

OH COME ON, YOUR MOM LOVES ME.

SHE TOLERATES YOU, AT LEAST.

I DON'T THINK SHE'S THRILLED WE'RE DATING.

BUT AT LEAST IT'S SOMETHING NORMAL. SOMETHING SHE UNDERSTANDS.

PLUS, I'M NOT LIVING IN YOUR BASEMENT.

NOT FUNNY.

MIKE IS STILL...

...HE'S REALLY UPSET ABOUT ELEVEN DISAPPEARING.

99

OH.

WELL, UH...WHAT DID YOU WANT TO KNOW?

THE PAPERS TALKED ABOUT WHEN HE CAME BACK FROM "THE DEAD."

BUT NOTHING AFTER THAT.

"AND WE HAVEN'T SEEN HIM SINCE THE NIGHT THEY PULLED HIM OUT OF...WHATEVER THAT WAS.

"DID HE GET OUT OF THE HOSPITAL?"

COULDN'T THEY JUST ASK JONATHAN ABOUT THIS STUFF?

YEAH. RIGHT BEFORE THANKSGIVING.

"WE WENT AND SAW HIM EVERY DAY IN THE HOSPITAL AFTER SCHOOL.

"BUT WE HAVEN'T BEEN BY HIS HOUSE YET. MRS. BYERS SAID HE NEEDED SOME TIME."

YEAH, IT WAS KIND OF...

WE MAY HAVE SET THE MONSTER ON FIRE IN THEIR HALLWAY.

WE SHOULD PROBABLY ASK IF THEY NEED ANY HELP FIXING THE PLACE UP...

LOOK, IT'S COOL THAT YOU GUYS ARE WORRIED ABOUT WILL...

...BUT IT SOUNDED LIKE THE DOCTORS THOUGHT HE'D BE OKAY.

WHAT YOU **NEED** IS A DISTRACTION.

WHAT DO YOU...YOU GUYS NORMALLY DO FOR FUN? PROBABLY NOT SPORTS, RIGHT?

WHY DON'T YOU RUN ONE OF YOUR GAMES?

THE LATEST ADVENTURE IS USUALLY ALL YOU AND YOUR FRIENDS CAN TALK ABOUT FOR LIKE A **WEEK** AFTER.

WHAT?

MAYBE...

SO... THEY **DO** PLAY SPORTS?

NO, IT'S A PEN AND PAPER THING. DUNGEONS AND DRAGONS.

IT'S THIS AMAZING GAME! IT'S LIKE...

HAVE YOU EVER READ LORD OF THE RINGS?

NOPE.

SO DUNGEONS AND DRAGONS IS THIS REALLY COOL FANTASY GAME.

YOU HAVE CLASSES LIKE FIGHTERS AND MAGIC-USERS. AND YOU CAN BE HUMANS OR DEMI-HUMANS.

THE PLAYERS ARE AN ADVENTURING PARTY. FIGHTING MONSTERS AND LOOKING FOR TREASURE AND STUFF.

THE LAST TIME WE PLAYED...

...WAS THE NIGHT WILL DISAPPEARED.

IT'S NOT YOUR FAULT, MIKE.

YOU GUYS HAVE BEEN PLAYING FOR *YEARS*.

"REMEMBER BACK WHEN I HELPED YOU MAKE THOSE COSTUMES?

"AND YOU HAD ME BE AN ELF FOR YOUR BIG STORY FINALE?"

I THINK HE'S GOING TO BE OKAY.

THANKS FOR HELPING.

WELL, IF YOU STILL HAVE THAT FANTASY ELF COSTUME...

YOU'RE SUCH AN IDIOT, STEVE HARRINGTON.

THE END

Dark Horse Direct Exclusive
Art by BELLA GRACE

Art by CLAIRE ROE

Art by EVAN CAGLE

Art by JONATHAN CASE

STRANGER THINGS

THE NOSTALGIA-IGNITING HIT NETFLIX ORIGINAL SERIES COMES TO COMICS!

VOLUME 1: THE OTHER SIDE
Jody Houser, Stefano Martino,
Keith Champagne, Lauren Affe
ISBN 978-1-50670-976-5
$17.99

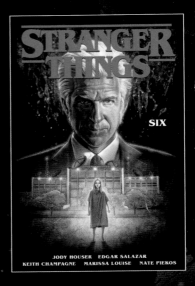

VOLUME 2: SIX
Jody Houser, Edgar Salazar,
Keith Champagne, Marissa Louise
ISBN 978-1-50671-232-1
$17.99

VOLUME 3: INTO THE FIRE
Jody Houser, Ryan Kelly,
Le Beau Underwood, Triona Farrell
ISBN 978-1-50671-308-3
$19.99

ZOMBIE BOYS
Greg Pak, Valeria Favoccia,
Dan Jackson
ISBN 978-1-50671-309-0
$10.99